ERICH FROMM'S CRITICAL THEORY

Also Available from Bloomsbury

Life Itself Is an Art: The Life and Work of Erich Fromm, Rainer Funk
Heine and Critical Theory, Willi Goetschel
Georg Lukács's Philosophy of Praxis: From Neo-Kantianism to Marxism,
Konstantinos Kavoulakos
Aesthetic Marx, ed. by Samir Gandesha and Johan F. Hartle

ERICH FROMM'S CRITICAL THEORY

Hope, Humanism, and the Future

Edited by
Kieran Durkin and Joan Braune

BLOOMSBURY ACADEMIC
LONDON • NEW YORK • OXFORD • NEW DELHI • SYDNEY

BLOOMSBURY ACADEMIC
Bloomsbury Publishing Plc
50 Bedford Square, London, WC1B 3DP, UK
1385 Broadway, New York, NY 10018, USA
29 Earlsfort Terrace, Dublin 2, Ireland

BLOOMSBURY, BLOOMSBURY ACADEMIC and the Diana logo are trademarks of
Bloomsbury Publishing Plc

First published in Great Britain 2020
This paperback edition published in 2021

Copyright © Kieran Durkin, Joan Braune, and Contributors, 2020

Kieran Durkin and Joan Braune have asserted their right under the Copyright,
Designs and Patents Act, 1988, to be identified as Editors of this work.

For legal purposes the Acknowledgments on p. vii constitute an extension
of this copyright page.

Cover design by Charlotte Daniels
Cover image: *Woman Shadows* by Jenny Speckels
(© Jewelee / Getty Images)

All rights reserved. No part of this publication may be reproduced or transmitted
in any form or by any means, electronic or mechanical, including photocopying,
recording, or any information storage or retrieval system, without prior permission
in writing from the publishers.

Bloomsbury Publishing Plc does not have any control over, or responsibility for, any third-
party websites referred to or in this book. All internet addresses given in this book were
correct at the time of going to press. The author and publisher regret any inconvenience
caused if addresses have changed or sites have ceased to exist, but can accept no
responsibility for any such changes.

A catalogue record for this book is available from the British Library.

A catalog record for this book is available from the Library of Congress.

ISBN: HB: 978-1-3500-8701-9
PB: 978-1-3502-7914-8
ePDF: 978-1-3500-8700-2
eBook: 978-1-3500-8703-3

Typeset by Deanta Global Publishing Services, Chennai, India

To find out more about our authors and books visit www.bloomsbury.com and sign up for
our newsletters.

CONTENTS

Acknowledgments   vii

INTRODUCTION: MAPPING FROMM'S CRITICAL THEORY   *Kieran Durkin*   1

Part I
RADICAL AND PROPHETIC HUMANISM

Chapter 1
ERICH FROMM AND THE ONTOLOGY OF SOCIAL
RELATIONS   *Michael J. Thompson*   23

Chapter 2
JEWISH MESSIANISM AND REVOLUTIONARY UTOPIAS IN CENTRAL
EUROPE: ERICH FROMM'S EARLY WRITINGS (1922–30)   *Michael Löwy*   43

Chapter 3
THE NECESSITY OF PROPHETIC HUMANISM IN PROGRESSIVE
SOCIAL CHANGE   *George Lundskow*   52

Part II
SOCIAL AND PSYCHOLOGICAL ASPECTS

Chapter 4
ERICH FROMM AND THE PROSPECTS FOR RENEWING CRITICAL
THEORY IN THE NEOLIBERAL ERA   *Roger Foster*   75

Chapter 5
FEMINISM, HUMANISM, AND ERICH FROMM   *Lynn S. Chancer*   96

Chapter 6
SOCIOPSYCHOANALYSIS AND RADICAL HUMANISM: A FROMM-
BOURDIEU SYNTHESIS   *Michael Maccoby and Neil McLaughlin*   108

Part III
AUTHORITARIANISM, FASCISM, AND THE CONTESTED FUTURE

Chapter 7
ANTI-AUTHORITARIAN MARXISM: ERICH FROMM, HILDE WEISS,
AND THE POLITICS OF RADICAL HUMANISM   *David Norman Smith*   131

Chapter 8
ESCAPE FROM REFLEXIVITY: FROMM AND GIDDENS ON
INDIVIDUALISM, ANXIETY, AND AUTHORITARIANISM *Charles Thorpe*   166

Chapter 9
SOCIAL CHARACTER, SOCIAL CHANGE, AND THE SOCIAL
FUTURE *Lauren Langman and George Lundskow*   194

CONCLUSION: WHY ANTI-FASCISM NEEDS ERICH FROMM'S
CRITICAL THEORY *Joan Braune*   216

List of Contributors   227
Index   230

ACKNOWLEDGMENTS

The editors would like to thank Berghahn Journals for permission to re-publish Michael Löwy's "Jewish Messianism and Revolutionary Utopias in Central Europe: Erich Fromm's Early Writings (1922–30)", which first appeared in European Judaism, Vol. 50, No. 1 (Spring 2017): 21–31.

This project has received funding from the European Union's Horizon 2020 research and innovation programme under the Marie Sklodowska-Curie grant agreement No 794656.

INTRODUCTION:
MAPPING FROMM'S CRITICAL THEORY

Kieran Durkin

The early part of the twenty-first century has borne witness to what can only be described as a Fromm renaissance. After decades of relative neglect—particularly in the English-speaking world—Fromm's writings are once again finding a deep resonance among scholars old and new, his ideas increasingly turned to in the quest to make sense of what is becoming an ever more fractured world. Since the turn of the century, a number of studies that place Fromm at their center have appeared in print.[1] This in itself is significant, but it is the *nature* of these studies that is particularly worth remarking on. What has been evident in these works is a determination to look anew at Fromm's writings: to rescue them from semi-obscurity and the assaults of his erstwhile critics, and to draw on the largely untapped potential that they have to speak to our present moment. In contradistinction to the majority of earlier writings on Fromm, these more recent writings evince a renewed focus on the *social and political aspects* of Fromm's thought, and, often implicitly, on articulating something of the uniqueness of the *form* of the critical theory that can be found within them. This is important, and it is so for a number of reasons.

Fromm and the Frankfurt Institute of Social Research

It is important, first of all, in terms of intellectual history—in relation to countering what is a powerful tendency in academic circles to reduce Fromm's contribution to intellectual life to what is considered to be the *pre*-history of Frankfurt School. In this picture, Fromm is represented as little more than a footnote—an incidental figure at the margins of critical theory during the nascent stage of its development, and therefore, more or less dispensable.[2] As a result of these more recent studies, it has become abundantly clear that Fromm was a central figure in the early period of Max Horkheimer's directorship of the Frankfurt *Institut für Sozialforschung*, playing a pivotal role in the development of the Institute's early research program and methodology.[3] During this period, Fromm worked intimately with Horkheimer, leading the pioneering study of the Weimar German working classes that prefigured *The Authoritarian Personality* and the development of authoritarian studies more generally. Second only to Horkheimer, it is not an exaggeration to suggest that during this period Fromm functioned as part of the central "collaborative pair" that formed the intellectual heart of the Institute.[4]

Fromm was particularly instrumental in the Institute's integration of psychoanalysis and sociology that was to characterize the early Institute studies. Having studied at the Berlin Psychoanalytical Institute prior to his association with Horkheimer, and being personally acquainted with Freida Reichmann, Siegfried Bernfeld, Karen Horney, Georg Groddeck, and Wilhelm Reich, Fromm brought with him a ready grasp of the practicalities involved in this interdisciplinary synthesis. Around the time he became associated with the Institute, Fromm also helped set up the Frankfurt Psychoanalytical Institute, alongside Karl Landauer, Heinrich Meng, and Freida Reichmann. At the inauguration of the Frankfurt Psychoanalytical Institute, Fromm gave a short paper on the relationship of psychoanalysis and sociology in which he outlined the potential psychoanalysis has to advance Marxian sociology.[5] In it, Fromm stressed the need to avoid the reduction of analysis from the sociological level to the psychological level, or vice versa, but also the need to be alive to situations where the issues at hand are *simultaneously* sociological and psychological, and where, therefore, analysis needs to be social-psychological in its entirety.

Publication of *Die Entwicklung des Christusdogmas, Eine Psychoanalytische Studie zur Sozialpsychologischen* in 1930 (it was published in English as *The Dogma of Christ* in 1963)—demonstrates the degree to which Fromm had advanced down this path. In this highly original work, Fromm undertakes a historical social-psychoanalytical analysis of early Christian communities, probing the motives conditioning the evolution of Christian dogma by relating the ideas conveyed in it relative to each stage of its development. Fromm was concerned to "show what influence social reality had in a specific situation upon a specific group of men [sic], and how emotional trends found expression in certain dogmas, in collective fantasies, and to show further what psychic change was brought about by a change in the social situation."[6] In particular, he wanted to enquire into how it could be that the psychic change found expression in new religious fantasies that could be said to have satisfied specific unconscious impulses. According to Fromm, Christianity arose as "a significant historical messianic-revolutionary movement," whose original adoptionist doctrine of man elevated to God spoke to unconscious wishes of the poor and oppressed classes.[7] As a new class state arose, in which nationalities were leveled and in which infinite dependencies were set up under the power of the emperor, Fromm notes that Christian dogma undergoes a corresponding change, morphing into a doctrine whereby love and grace are bestowed upon God the Father, a God who had undergone an anthropological conversion and literally *become* a "man." The psychic response that accompanies this shift, Fromm contends, is one from revolutionary passion and identification with God to one of submission in which displaced anger comes to be directed upon the self. Fromm is clear that his concern in the study is with the "character matrix"[8] that might be said to be common to a particular group of individuals, and that is not necessarily dominant in the character structure of each individual.

Two years later, in conjunction with his work on the German workers study, Fromm was responsible for two important papers that appeared in the *Zeitschrift for Socialforzung*, the Institute's journal.[9] In the first of these pieces, the discussion is explicitly focused on the capacity of psychoanalysis to investigate the role of the psychic apparatus in the overall functioning of the social process. Focusing on the *subjective factor*, Fromm stresses that psychoanalysis provides the potential to demonstrate, in a way that Marx and Engels could not, precisely *how* it is that the economic situation comes to be transformed into ideology via the human passions and drives. Through demonstration of how the content of ideologies are intimately connected to the wishes, instinctual drives, interests, and needs of groups and individuals (all of which expressed in the form of rationalizations), the dialectically materialist social psychology Fromm proposes proclaims to be able to offer an account of the *psychological basis* of the social structure—the active foundation upon which that structure rests, and a primary reason for its stability. Fromm develops upon this foundation in his second piece. Here, the focus is on the functionality of individual and collectivized character traits, and on the "social reward" they offer the individual in terms of adaptation to the demands of the social structure, suggesting also that such a focus provides a notable improvement upon the then prevailing understanding of the *spirit* of an epoch. Studies concerned with the spirit of a period, Fromm argues, mistakenly focus solely on ideology, rather than on "the sum total of character traits that are typical of human beings in this society" and that "can find expression in a wide variety of different and even opposing ideologies."[10] Instead of loosely speaking of the "spirit" of a given period, Fromm instead suggests that we think of the *dynamic function of character* as providing the psychic basis of that society and, thereby, as a productive force alongside the material base and ideological superstructure. In this connection, Fromm traces the social influence of society on character primarily to the family, which he describes as "the chief medium through which the child's psychic formation is oriented toward the surrounding society."[11] It is through the family and the wider educational process that the child's strivings are either suppressed or intensified, this suppression and intensification taking place generally in line with the wider economic, social, or class structure to which the family is related.[12]

Fromm's central role as part of institute life was apparent up until 1936, with the publication of *Studien über Autorität und Familie* (*Studies on Authority and the Family*).[13] Following the research program set out by Horkheimer in his inaugural address, *Studies on Authority and the Family* was primarily concerned with the transformation of the bourgeois character taking place in twentieth-century European capitalist societies. Fromm's contribution, "Sozialpsychologischer Teil" ("Social-Psychological Aspects"), appears in the theoretical first section of the volume, and is concerned with mapping out the social-psychological rise of authoritarianism in European capitalist societies. Fromm begins his account with a discussion of the decline of ego strength that he contends was brought about by changes in the dominant patriarchal family structure. The family, as the primary agent of socialization, had long been an important theoretical focal point for psychoanalysis. What Fromm argues here is that the routine suppression of emotional drives found within patriarchal family relations had actually intensified in the face of monopoly capitalism, but with a difference: as the influence of the family declined in proportion to the development of monopoly capital, feelings of powerlessness and inconsequentiality on behalf of large sections of the population lead to powerful psychological drives to connect with the dictates of a "superior power." Masochism—which is inseparable from sadism, and together forms an *authoritarian syndrome*—acts to fill the void.

Fromm's work here builds directly upon the empirical material collected as part of the Weimar study, the analysis of which was actively taking place at the same time as *Studies on Authority and the Family*. The interpretative basis of this study was the very same notion of *authoritarian-masochistic character*, this time operationalized in relation to the attitudinal responses of purportedly left-wing workers. Fromm and his team—including Hilde Weiss, who played a central role in the study[14]—were concerned with eliciting the deep emotional connections that lay behind ostensible political opinions. In pursuit of these underlying realities, they found that the majority of respondents, while outwardly associating with the left-wing slogans of their party, nevertheless demonstrated a much-reduced radicalism in response to other, seemingly unpolitical questions.[15] On the basis of these findings, Fromm and his team developed the notion of the "authoritarian attitude," which is marked by the affirmation, seeking out, and enjoyment of the subjugation of self and other under higher powers. The conceptual and empirical work carried out by Fromm in these early years of the Institute was clearly central to the development of the Institute's research program in these years. These newer studies into Fromm's thought have hewn out much of this history.

Toward a Distinct Form of Critical Theory

The newer studies on Fromm are important for a further reason, however. In addition to demonstrating the centrality of Fromm's involvement with the early Institute (and the prefiguration of later studies such as *The Authoritarian Personality*), these studies have also suggested at, and sought to laud, the *distinctiveness* of Fromm's thought considered relative to and beyond other Institute figures. They have engaged in greater detail with the central *differences* between Fromm and his Institute colleagues—differences which can be said to have played a role in Fromm's eventual split with Horkheimer and break from the Institute in general. Around the time that *Studies on Authority and the Family* was published, Fromm was engaged in a fundamental re-examination of Sigmund Freud's writings on psychoanalysis, which manifested in a lengthy, critical essay on Freud's system that Horkheimer declined to publish in the *Zeitschrift*.[16] In this essay, Fromm targets what he claims is the untenable sexual reductionism and bourgeois mechanism that frames Freud's whole schema: the theory of the Oedipus complex, Freud's account of the psychology of women, the role of the family, and the theory of drives (and libido theory) are all implicated. In its place,

Fromm proposes a far-reaching revision, which he sums up in a letter to Robert Lynd in the same year that the unpublished essay was submitted. In the letter, Fromm outlined what he now saw as the task of psychoanalytic theory: namely, the attempt "to understand the structures of character and instincts as a result of adaptation to the given social conditions and not as a product of the erogenous zones."[17] The resulting alternative position is described by Fromm as a "dialectical interpretation of psychic processes" in which "the psychic structure of man is regarded as the product of his activity and his manner of life and not as the reflex thrown up by his physical organization."[18]

The more recent studies on Fromm have acknowledged not only the fact of this revision but also its progressive character vis-à-vis the position adopted by Horkheimer, Adorno, and others.[19] This goes against the view that has prevailed for more than half a century, in which Fromm has been accused of "common sense psychology" and of "psychologiz[ing] culture and society,"[20] and of thereby harmonizing social antagonisms by positing a direct—and thus undialectical—connection between the institutional sphere and social experience. Fromm, in fact, has wrongly been included in the culturalist school of thought, alongside Harry Stack Sullivan and Karen Horney. This is a significant oversight given that, although Fromm readily admitted that Sullivan and Horney influenced the development of his thought, he repeatedly stressed that his position was more critical from the outset.[21]

Social contradictions were not ironed out by Fromm; they were very much there at the basis of his system, merely reconfigured in terms of existential-relational as opposed biological-libidinal terms.[22] The removal of libido as the driving force does not mean that depth (i.e., the unconscious) was surrendered; were this the case, it would not have been possible for Fromm to have spoken of the irrational pathogenic drives that develop as a response to the demands of different types of society.[23] As Rainer Funk has shown, the issue is one of relating our drive structure to the environment via adaptation, this adaptation taking place in various ways related to various characterological syndromes.[24]

In line with this, these studies have pointed to the fact that Fromm's dialectical revision of Freud—along with his parting from the Institute, and the Institute's realignment along more Benjaminian and Adornoian lines of inquiry—separates him from the stronger identification with Frankfurt School critical theory as canonically understood.[25] There are evident similarities of outlook that can be traced to similar geographical and biographical connections, of course, but also definite differences that need to be more fully understood.[26] Central to this is the willingness—evident in these newer studies on Fromm—to challenge the dualistic assumption that Fromm's earlier works as part of the Institute constitute the *entirety* of what can be said in a positive sense about his contribution to intellectual life. Although it is fair to point to the fact that after his split with the Institute Fromm's writings were increasingly pitched to the educated general public, insufficient attention, particularly in the social and political sciences, has been accorded to the serious *substance* of these later works. This is particularly important given the opprobrium that has often greeted Fromm's works during this period.

The hitherto accepted wisdom concerning Fromm in this period is that he undergoes a regression from critical theorist to "business-like revisionist" and "sermonistic social worker."²⁷ Implicated here is his revision of Freud, but also the very substance and tenor of his post-Institute works, which, as suggested, were notable by virtue of their attraction of a far wider audience that had been the case for Institute publications. *Escape from Freedom*, Fromm's first post-Institute work, appearing in 1941, made Fromm a noted figure in US intellectual culture, but it was also seen as exhibiting a worrying idealist tendency that threatened to pull him away from the stringent materialism practiced at the Institute. Particularly objected to was the apparent "existentialist" stress on *freedom* as a transhistorical category.²⁸ In defense of Fromm, it should be stressed that *Escape from Freedom* was explicitly framed around the general expression of newer social and political (and psychological) trends that had hitherto received insufficient analysis in the academic and wider community. In this work Fromm focuses on post–First World War democracy (and its process of diminishment) as the proximate culmination of a series of developments stretching back to the Italian Renaissance related to the successive abolition of forms of external domination (political, religious, and social) and, thereby, the increased freedom of the individual. What Fromm wanted to particularly focus on was the development of "new systems" (fascism, authoritarianism, and state capitalism) which denied "everything that had been won in centuries of struggle," and that functioned on the basis of sadomasochistic group conformity.²⁹

What should be clear is that the concerns that animate *Escape from Freedom* are *direct extensions* of the work Fromm was previously engaged in at the Institute, and that had erupted so violently in the wider world at the time. Importantly, this is not only representative of *Escape from Freedom*, *Man for Himself* and, later, *The Sane Society* develop some of the central themes of the Institute's work, even prefiguring the later critical theory concern with the critique of conformity, the culture industry, and so on. In his accounts of *automaton conformity*, the *marketing character*, and the *pathology of normalcy*, Fromm was staking out a ground that overlapped with that of his erstwhile colleagues. At the same time, these accounts are advanced in a framework that manifests a marked difference—one that centers particularly on the issue of *humanism*.

The explicit (and thematic) humanism that marks Fromm's post–Second World War writings, while not constituting a rupture in Fromm's thought,³⁰ does nevertheless represent a conscious decision to foreground this central aspect of his thinking. Explicit humanistic statements can be found in *Escape from Freedom* itself (which was written *during* the war), but it is certainly the case that they are even more clearly evident in *Man for Himself*. Here Fromm speaks in universalistic terms, talking explicitly of the "human condition," and of aspects of what can be considered our "nature" as human beings. Fromm is explicit here in pitting humanist and authoritarian ethics against one another— the former centered on the development of the human individual in itself and on self-legislated norms, the later on harsh and extraneously imposed norms that entail the submission of the human individual to higher powers. This is followed in *Psychoanalysis and Religion* by the application of the humanist/authoritarian distinction to the religious sphere, with humanist religions depicted as centering on individual and collective self-realization, and authoritarian religions depicted as centering around the individual and collective *surrender* to a power transcending the human.[31]

What is demonstrated here is Fromm's continued engagement with the issue of religion during this period.[32] The analytical preoccupation with the social-psychological effects of religion that characterized Fromm's early works—as we have seen earlier, and as can be seen in Löwy in this volume—is evident in *Escape from Freedom*, in which Fromm undertakes an analysis of the psychosocial effects of the doctrines of Luther and Calvin on their followers. What becomes increasingly clear in Fromm's post-Institute writings, however, is the extent to which the somewhat negative Freudian view of religion is transcended, and a new, *atheistic mysticism* takes hold. The change is first registered in *Man for Himself*, in his account of the *existential dichotomies* that he identifies as structuring human existence. This notion is further developed in *Psychoanalysis and Religion*, in which Fromm speaks of religion in general terms as "any system of thought and action shared by a group which gives the individual a frame of orientation and an object of devotion."[33] On this conception, every culture has religion in this broad sense: the question is not *whether* religion, but *which kind of religion*, and whether or not it furthers the development of the individual. The theme is continued in *The Sane Society*, where Fromm outlines a number of what he contends as universal existential human needs, which can be satisfied in better or worse ways for individual and collective human flourishing.

What we see in these works is an increasingly explicit drawing-out of the underlying evaluative and normative humanism that can be said to have animated Fromm's institute studies. In works such as the Weimar study, for instance, while the accent was clearly on the analytical, evaluative presuppositions are never far from the surface. While Fromm's central concern is with revealing social-psychological connections, there is nevertheless a clearly implicit evaluative schema found in his opposition of a radical as opposed to a reactionary attitude to authority.[34] The works of the post-Institute period are notable primarily because of their explicit stress on this normativity; but it is an error to suggest that critical and historical analysis fades from Fromm's writings. That this is so is apparent from a book such as *The Sane Society*, in which a normative social-psychological analysis that is historically contextualized and indexed to some of the main critical concerns of the day (such as affluent alienation) is advanced. The normative humanism Fromm advances here, while universal, is not a bland, abstract universalism, even if it is unashamed in affirming the pedagogical value of at least some abstraction. Fromm makes clear in *Man for Himself*, in relation to his philosophical anthropological discussion of "man":

> Man, however, does not exist "in general." While sharing the core of human qualities with all members of his species, he is always an individual, a unique entity, different from everybody else. He differs by his particular blending of

character, temperament, talents, dispositions, just as he differs at his fingertips. He can affirm his human potentialities only by realizing his individuality.[35]

This is not to say that Fromm's works are free of aspects of ethno- and androcentrism. It is certainly the case that his universalism does at times fail the test of precision, and there are definite silences on race and sexuality, as well as some clumsy statements on gender which are rightly critiqued today.[36] But Fromm is also at pains in many works from this period to engage "Eastern" as well as "Western" traditions, and he often repeats, as his motto, Terence's famous humanistic sentiment, "nothing human is alien to me." This openness to all human experience, however ethnocentric the framing may have been at times, was an absolutely central pillar to his humanist psychoanalytical approach that, in fact, sought to transcend the psychoanalytical encounter. Fromm's engagement with Eastern sources—particularly Buddhism—is not tantamount to a form of Orientalism on his part, although it does beg the question as to the existence of other world communities, and their contributions to knowledge.[37]

Fromm's works have also been criticized for their popular and supposedly idealist framing. While there are some justified concerns over idealism[38] and definite lapses into homily at points, it must be acknowledged that many of the pieces that are critiqued on these grounds were written as self-confessed activist contributions—interventions into the national and world debate framed and composed so as to stimulate action and discussion on the part of the wider population. In interventions such as *The Art of Loving, The Sane Society, Marx's Concept of Man, Let Man Prevail, Socialist Humanism, The Heart of Man*, and *The Revolution of Hope*, an explicit prophetic tone is to the fore, accompanied by the postulation of a series of alternatives framed around the respective paths of emancipation and regression. What emerges from Fromm's committed attempt to try to revivify the public sphere of his time toward a democratic form of socialism is the basis of a radical moral cosmopolitanism and revolutionary empathy that is indexed to a social and historical picture of human development and to practical change in the world. Fromm's is a particular kind of critical theory: one that takes praxis, and its organic connection to social transformation, seriously, as opposed to rendering it opaque, if not wholly sundered, as is characteristic of certain other forms of critical theory. Fromm's engagement does not elicit a "cult of subjectivity"[39] but clearly calls for individual development that leads out into structural changes as part of one and the same motion. There is, in fact, a strong case to be made in this connection for seeing Fromm as deviating productively from some of the more problematic aspects of Frankfurt School critical theory.[40]

The more Fromm's writings are built around this prophetic axis the more intimate the connection with the community to which he is speaking becomes, the more can it be characterized by a degree of self-referentiality. The directness and practical leaning adopted by Fromm in many works of this period has perhaps led to an underappreciation of the *understated complexity* of these works. It should be acknowledged that Fromm admits the foundational nature of much of what he writes during this period: there is repetition here also, and the works tend to lack the more encyclopedic quality of his works with the Institute, but they are full of fruitful even if not always fully developed postulations.[41] It is clear that Fromm's writings grapple with issues that have come into even sharper focus today: the rise of authoritarianism and other related issues, but also certain academic impasses, such as those that have followed the rise of structuralism, post-structuralism, and the various types of anti-humanism associated with these traditions. This is something that the more recent works on Fromm have brought to the fore, and something that the contributors in this volume seek to amplify and explore.

A Radical Humanist and Prophetic Critical Theory

The essence of Fromm's distinctive form of critical theory can be traced to its resolutely *humanist* character. Although what is meant by "humanist" today is not always clear, for Fromm humanism is the necessary grounding for a theory that wants to speak simultaneously to analytical-descriptive *and* normative categories (which it unites in the process), but also, and thereby, to categories capable of encouraging individual and collective praxis in the world at large. Fromm's humanism was not incidental to his thought but, rather, the central defining feature that unites all its various elements. In practical terms, and at its most basic, humanism for Fromm is *radical*. It is radical, in its most literal sense, in that it *goes to the root* (i.e., to the heart of what makes us human). In contradistinction to the hegemonic anti-humanism that proliferates in certain spheres of the academy, Fromm's critical theory operates with a provisional philosophical anthropology, positing human life as circumscribed by a series of "existential needs" and questions that need to be met and answered: needs for fulfillment, meaning, connection.[42] It is radical also because it is concerned with furthering *human emancipation* from alienating political, social, and economic relations.

This aspect of Fromm's humanism ought not to be seen as evidence of naiveté on his part but, rather, a grappling with the question of what it means to be human that meaningfully expands our analytical and normative conceptions of the individual and social life. As opposed to some theories that also bear that name "emancipatory," Fromm's critical theory, by dint of its humanist character, is *explicitly normative*. His account of *normative humanism*—based on the assumption that there are better and worse, more satisfactory and less satisfactory solutions to the problem of human existence—is the crux of his account. This is not a thick prescriptivism, as some claim, but a *thin normativism*, in which many varied ways of living are consistent with human flourishing. It is prescriptively normative in only one sense: that living in certain ways will lead to certain psychological and practical consequences for self and others, these consequences mapped by Fromm in their individual and social manifestations so as to guide us toward a better world. It is here that that the *prophetic* nature of Fromm's thought comes to the fore. Fromm's prophetic orientation foregrounds the elementary alternatives that structure human existence—and particularly human existence under conditions of modernity and late modernity, working so as to provide us with the evaluative and motivational tools for appraising the social relations that structure our lives. Central to the prophetic element of Fromm's critical theory is a stress on *hope for* and *faith in* our capacity to make the kind of individual and social changes that will ensure human creative and solidaristic flourishing at the highest level. This hope and faith is not marked by passivity but, rather, by activity, ever aligned as it is to the humanist conviction in the possibility of change while remaining wary of overoptimistic adventurism in relation to the determinate possibilities for change.[43]

Fromm's notion of *pathological normalcy* is also central to his critical theory. The observation that normalcy itself can be (and is) pathological—that certain social relations that obtain and may be considered normal or even desirable are damaging—is the analytical basis of any truly critical theory: the grounds from which to appraise the world in its immanent and emancipatory relationships. The first step in moving toward social change is to acknowledge the widespread social pathology that characterizes so much of our lives, and that is instantiated at various levels of the social structure. Crucially, Fromm's account of pathological normalcy is related, and points back, to his account of normative humanism, and to the prophetic character of his theory. It is here that the stress on objective norms assumes its particular importance, being leveraged against his account of the structural forces that are mediated through ideological and characterological factors. The notion that we can, and need to, speak *at some level* in objective terms in relation to the existence of social pathology and alternatives to this state of affairs goes against the extreme constructivism and sociological relativism that often obtains in the social sciences and humanities. These bifurcated social-theoretical paths are coming into sharper focus in the present moment, with developments in the world outside of academia, such as the rise of right-wing authoritarianism, heightened racism, sexism, heterosexism, and related forms of xenophobia.[44]

Importantly, Fromm's critical theory is set up with the intention of encouraging *critical reflexivity* and *mutual recognition*: what Fromm terms "productive relatedness." Fromm places a central stress on embracing positive freedom: that is, overcoming narcissism (both individual and group narcissism) and replacing hateful for loving, destructive for creative, and sadomasochist for humanist forms of relationship. The religious analogy of overcoming idolatry-alienation is important here—the idols to be overcome are those of flag, state, identity, race, ethnicity, and status, as well as productive and political relations that leave human individuals beholden to powers beyond their rational and empathetic control. The central pathological feature in Fromm's critical theory is of course capitalism, with the elementary alienation and other reifying effects that result from its dehumanized structures; but Fromm approaches this in a manner that focuses on experiential aspects and emotions and values pitched at the level of the ideological superstructure as well as material forms of development in the base. This is a focus that brings the individual and the societal together: a concern for the "art of living" indexed to a wider social platform for the humanization of institutions and structures.[45] Prefiguration is thus a central part of Fromm's critical theory: a theory is critical in its fullest sense because it *also* concerned with the steps between the present and the future. These steps in Fromm's critical theory are doubly important as intermediate revivifications—praxis altering, radical reformist steps toward realistic utopias hewed out in the midst of a society that works hard to deny the possibility of transcendence.[46]

The lynchpin of Fromm's critical theory is his account of *social character*. The fruits of his synthesis of Marx and Freud, Fromm's account of social character attempts to explain the *dynamic process* whereby socially shaped needs and desires for characteristic human forms of relationship are fostered in a particular society (and for particular groups of that society in similar and different ways). The social character for Fromm is the *intermediary* (in both directions) between the socioeconomic structure and the ideas and ideals prevalent in a given society or subsection of that society. It is through this theory that Fromm is able to account for the dynamics of the psychological process operating within the individual *as well as* the role of the wider cultural forces on that individual, and the relationship between each aspect. Fromm's stress on the deep, varied, and dynamic psychological processes that characterize social life means that this account of the social shaping of subjective being is able to extricate itself from a closed structural-functionalist analysis without losing connection to structural and functional elements that nevertheless circumscribe this reality. The role of emotions, repression, and other unconscious processes interacts with the process of socialization, never being fully reduced to it. In this way, Fromm's critical theory can account for ideology as filtered through and channeled into characterological drives, opposing the anti-agentic depictions of social reality found in the structuralist tradition.[47]

The Structure of This Book

This collection is divided into three parts, reflecting what we feel are the three central areas of study pertaining to Fromm's critical social theory today. As with the nature of Fromm's writings, there is considerable overlap between each area—a fact that is reflective of the deeply integrated texture of Fromm's thought.

Part I of the collection focuses on the social-theoretical, philosophical, and religioethical bases of Fromm's critical theory. Michael Thompson's contribution stresses the ontological nature of Fromm's theorizing, a feature which he claims marks Fromm out from the third-generation Frankfurt School theories of thinkers such as Jürgen Habermas, Karl-Otto Apel, Axel Honneth, and Rainer Forst. In contradistinction to the "neo-Idealism" of these theorists, who pay insufficient attention to the structuralist and functionalist aspects of the social process, Thompson praises Fromm's position for its incorporation of the affective and cognitive *along with* the structural and functional. This approach, Thompson argues, avoids the "reductive noumenalism" of the third-generation Frankfurt School thinkers that "reduces social relations to the noumenal structures of consciousness." Fromm's thinking, on the contrary, for Thompson, grows out of a theory of freedom and judgment that also takes into consideration the deep ontological shape of social relations that possess a constitutive power over not only the individual self but society as a whole. Central to Thompson's argument is Fromm's account of humanistic ethics—an account which Thompson contends is not severed from the functional-structural part of Fromm's analysis but, rather, explicitly drawn out of it. On this reading, Thompson makes the case for the deep normativity that exists in Fromm's thought that has been missing in critical social theory in its more contemporary manifestations.

Michael Löwy's contribution engages a discussion of Fromm's earliest writings—those dating from the period between 1922 and 1930, and which have historically been the least studied of all Fromm's works. As Löwy demonstrates, these early writings were marked by the intersection of Fromm's Judaic, social-psychological, and Marxian interests, all of which Löwy contends were unified through Fromm's "messianic/revolutionary spirituality." Löwy places Fromm in relation to the late nineteenth- and early twentieth-century renaissance of Jewish thought and culture, describing him as a romantic Jewish "pariah intellectual," related to but distinct from thinkers such as Gustav Landauer, Ernst Bloch, the young Georg Lukács, Manès Sperber, and Walter Benjamin. As with these other thinkers, Löwy identifies in Fromm a strong romantic antipathy to capitalist civilization and a related nostalgia over the loss over certain aspects of premodern society. Löwy identifies aspects of this Jewish romanticism intermingling with methodological and conceptual borrowings from Max Weber in Fromm's earliest works, although he points out that Fromm belongs, like Walter Benjamin, Ernst Bloch, and others, to a group that developed "anti-capitalist interpretations" of Max Weber, quite opposed the *wertfreiheit* definition. In this connection, Löwy traces the evolution of Fromm's thought into more outwardly Freudo-Marxist terrain in works such as *The Dogma of Christ*.

George Lundskow's contribution focuses on a later manifestation of Fromm's engagement with religion, specifically, with the potential that Fromm's social-psychological of an "object of devotion" has to play in progressive social change. Primarily referencing the US context, Lundskow identifies the dominance of a reactionary "religious nationalism" that he implicates in the manifest racism, sexism, and general xenophobia that characterizes support for Donald Trump. Lundskow draws on Fromm's distinction between *humanistic* and *authoritarian* religion, as well as his distinction between revolutionary and rebellious character, to make the case for a concept of "productive transcendence." This account is expanded through a discussion of Black Panther Huey Newton's call for a "spiritual humanism" in which revolutionary religion and spiritual morality are united. From these sources, Lundskow puts forward a Frommian account in which progressive social change can only happen if social movements are able to "articulate and practice an inspirational spirituality that elevates progressive moral imperatives above mundane concerns." The "vision of becoming" that Lundskow has in mind is one that merges faith and reason, and that draws motivation from a transcendent and sacred urgency into a practice that is based on mutual respect and love.

In Part II, we look at the integration of sociology and psychology that is the methodological cornerstone of Fromm's account. Roger Foster's contribution explores the potential that Fromm's social psychology possesses to explain the contemporary rise of nationalism and xenophobia. Noting the parallels between the present social and political crisis of the postindustrial democracies and the crisis of laissez-faire capitalism that formed the backdrop to the first generation of the Frankfurt School in the 1920s and 1930s, Foster draws on Fromm's psychosocial perspective to explain how it is that capital has been able to weaponize the fears and anxieties that arose in the fast-paced socioeconomic change of the *Trentes Glorieuses* and the neoliberal era. Through a reading of Boltanski and Chiapello's thesis in *The New Spirit of Capitalism*, and the humanistic psychoanalysis of the mid-twentieth century (of which Fromm was among the most notable), Foster posits a deep-seated "structural conflict between progressive and regressive tendencies and forces" at the heart of the dynamic of capitalism in which we have seen the systematic alienation of increased potentials for autonomy and personal growth. Posing the question as to how we overcome "the neoliberal colonization of humanist aspirations," Foster is clear as to the need to identify and rescue the emancipatory tendencies that underlie the social and cultural change and that are the cornerstone of Fromm's account of an unalienated social character.

Lynn Chancer's contribution is concerned with the relationship between feminism and humanism in Fromm's work. Chancer focuses on texts such as *Escape from Freedom* and *The Art of Loving*, and the tools that they provide for analyzing psychosocially caused gendered effects which have been somewhat neglected by leading feminist thinkers. She demonstrates how Fromm's accounts of sadomasochism and love offer related insights into the subtleties and dynamics of unequal power, as well as, and at the same time, cultural discourses and ideologies of romance and sexuality. As part of this discussion, Chancer interrogates Fromm's social psychology, laying bare some significantly gendered and even biologist lapses in Fromm's writings, but nevertheless making the case for the overall progressiveness of Fromm's work for feminist and queer theorizing. She points out Fromm's humanism operates on the basis of "common psychosocial dynamics at the same time differing by gender, class, race, sexualities, and other social categories," and that thus, in spite of his biologist lapses, Fromm's overriding concern in his writings was with the rise of cultural and gendered norms that led to psychosocial harms and alienated/alienating personalities and character structures within capitalistic and patriarchal societies. In so doing, Chancer stresses the degree to which "feminist and humanist ideas are compatible in ways beneficial for feminist and social theories overall," and that critiques of sadomasochism, or of alienated love, are, in Fromm's writings, "interconnected with prefigurative visions of what non-sexist relationships would look like on both individual and social levels."

Michael Maccoby's and Neil McLaughlin's contribution explores the intellectual relationship between Fromm and influential French sociologist Pierre Bourdieu. Their comparative analysis charts the respective careers of both thinkers, exploring the dynamics that led to two very different positions within the sociological field, and to the relative sociological inertia that can be said to hold in the case of Fromm relative to Bourdieu. They highlight broad areas of convergence between both thinkers: their shared sociological heritage, strong critiques of positivism, and opposition to the structure/agency dualism, but also the relatively unexplored commonalities (and divergences) between their respective "sociopsychoanalytic" and "socioanalytic" accounts. As part of this discussion, Maccoby and McLaughlin explore commonalities between Fromm's and Bourdieu's most closely comparable empirical works, and between their respective accounts of "social character" and "habitus." What they particularly want to highlight is the productive relationship between the two thinkers over the issue of depth psychology, and the unrealized potential of a research agenda that is able to synthesize Fromm's psychoanalytical account with Bourdieu's more cognitivist framing. Such a synthesis, they point out, which would deepen mainstream contemporary sociological accounts of the emotions, has assumed greater importance in our contemporary political and cultural climate, and would thus possess the potential to rejuvenate sociological research and theorizing into areas that are pivotal to the lives of millions today.

Part III of the volume is primarily concerned with the issue of authoritarianism and the ways in which we can monitor and transcend it. David Norman Smith's contribution looks at Fromm's anti-authoritarian Marxism as it developed in the 1920s and 1930s, in the context of political developments in Germany and the USSR. Smith details Fromm's concerns during this period as they intersect with other Institute members and leading socialist and communist figures, including Karl Wittfogel, Otto Rühle, and Hilde Weiss. Smith devotes particular attention to Weiss—"one of the truly neglected figures in the history of the Frankfurt School"—and her role in the German workers study. Weiss is shown by Smith to have been, in many senses, the principal architect of the study, and a very influential but tragically unsung figure in the Institute in general. Through his discussion of Fromm's friendships with Weiss, Rühle, and Wittfogel, Smith is able to shed new light on Fromm's positions in relation to the defining politics of the age. Particularly at issue is the figure of Leon Trotsky, and the crossroads facing the USSR under Stalin's rule. Fromm's relationship to Georg Lukács, Karl Korsch, and Eduard Bernstein is also touched upon. In this connection, Smith reveals how Fromm's revision of Freud during this period is integrally related to his radical humanist concerns for human emancipation that he unequivocally held in the face of the battle between humanism and authoritarianism that came to define the middle part of the twentieth century.

Charles Thorpe's contribution engages in an intertextual reading of Fromm and Anthony Giddens on the issue of anxiety and reflexivity. Outlining the development of political economy in the United Kingdom and the United States in the last thirty years, Thorpe charts the role Giddens's account of the Third Way played in "creat[ing] the social and psychological conditions for the authoritarian backlash against reflexivity" in the United States and the United Kingdom. Central to his argument is the way in which structural economic changes, and related changes toward a "politics of lifestyle," have threatened demarcations of identity that have destabilized ontological security. Global economic turbulence and the anxiety associated with that and other forms of insecurity (in terms of status and cultural identity) have become interiorized, according to Thorpe, "creating susceptibility to authoritarian forces offering escape from this anxiety." Common to both Fromm and Giddens is the notion that modernity calls for social transformation toward a higher form of individuality—that which Giddens calls "reflexivity" and which Fromm termed "positive freedom." But whereas Giddens's account of reflexivity is somewhat restricted to a politics of lifestyle, unconnected to a structural account of market dynamics, Fromm's account of positive freedom is "connected to the structural question of the social control over economic forces." Thorpe draws upon Ronald Inglehart's notion of existential security, developing a response to it in which emphasis is placed on Fromm's conception of "humanistic planning" as the basis for a program for the institutional articulation of life politics in which existentially rooted moral questions are answered alongside, and as part of, the need for economic security.

Langman's and Lundskow's contribution applies Fromm's notion of social character to the differentiated process of characterological change taking place at the present juncture in advanced capitalist countries, such as the United States. Developing on the Gramscian theme of our present moment as one of "interregnum," when the old values are dying but the new values are still to fully emerge, Langman and Lundskow identify a battle between reactionary movements and progressive movements. As with Foster in Part I, their analytical lens focuses on the changes that have taken place in US society since the 1960s. Central to their discussion here are the developments toward "liquid selfhood" and increased degrees of mutual recognition (if not always strong ideological commitment) found among large sections of younger cohorts, especially among later Gen X, Millennials, and Gen Z. Evoking Fromm and Maccoby's notion of "social selection," Langman and Lundskow pit this "new, emerging and growing form of social character" against the more authoritarian and reactionary older social character, which they note often erupts in "desperate attempts to halt, and in some cases reverse . . . the social changes giving rise to more a democratic and even productive social character." In light of this struggle, and movements such as the Arab Spring, the Indignados, Occupy Wall Street, Black Lives Matter, and that behind the candidacy of Bernie Sanders, they pose the vital question: "Is the flexible, multiple self capable of effecting social transformation and working towards a 'sane society'?"

Notes

1 Wilde, *Erich Fromm and the Quest for Solidarity*; Wheatland, *Frankfurt School in Exile*; Braune, *Erich Fromm's Revolutionary Hope*; Durkin, *The Radical Humanism of Erich Fromm*; Miri, Lake, and Kress, *Reclaiming the Sane Society*; Langman and Lundskow, *God, Guns, Gold, and Glory*; Funk and McLaughlin, *Towards a Human Science*; Thorpe, *Necroculture*.

2 There is scant reference to Fromm in Schroyer, *The Critique of Domination* and Tar, *The Frankfurt School*, and even those works that accord Fromm a greater degree of recognition—such as Jay, *The Dialectical Imagination*, Held, *Introduction to Critical*

Theory, and Wiggershaus, *The Frankfurt School*—fail to really see Fromm in his true significance.
3   This is apparent in McLaughlin, "Origin Myths in the Social Sciences"; Wheatland, *Frankfurt School in Exile*; and Abromeit, *Max Horkheimer and the Foundations of Critical Theory*.
4   Durkin, "Erich Fromm and Theodor W. Adorno Reconsidered"; and Abromeit, *Max Horkheimer and the Foundations of Critical Theory*.
5   Fromm, "Psychoanalysis and Sociology," 37.
6   Fromm, *Dogma of Christ*, 20, 21.
7   Ibid., 35.
8   Ibid., 8.
9   Fromm, "The Method and Function of an Analytic Social Psychology"; and "Psychoanalytic Characterology."
10 Fromm, "Psychoanalytic Characterology," 150, 158.
11 Ibid., 148.
12 Abromeit, *Max Horkheimer and the Foundations of Critical Theory*, points out that it is highly likely that it played a significant role in influencing Horkheimer's early formulation of critical theory and in the development of certain of his essays from the period.
13 At this point in time, this document remains unpublished in English.
14 Wolfgang Bonss stresses role of Hilde Weiss—who largely executed the study, and who brought an extensive knowledge of Weberian tradition—in his introduction to *Working Class in Weimar Germany*, 24. David Norman Smith elaborates upon Weiss's contribution to the study in his chapter in this volume.
15 Questions pertaining to whether or not women should wear lipstick and to admirable historical figures were used to elicit responses that revealed less radical societal attitudes.
16 Fromm, "Man's Impulse Structure and Its Relation to Culture."
17 Quoted in Funk, *Erich Fromm*, 93.
18 Fromm, "Man's Impulse Structure and Its Relation to Culture," 23.
19 Durkin, *The Radical Humanism of Erich Fromm*; Durkin, "Erich Fromm and Theodor W. Adorno Reconsidered"; McLaughlin, "Origin Myths in the Social Sciences."
20 Horkheimer to Leo Löwenthal, October 31, 1942, quoted in Funk, *Erich Fromm*, 99.
21 In response to a question on his connection to the culturalist school in an interview given in 1966, Fromm expressed his differences with that school thusly: "Rather more emphasis [than is given by the culturalist] should be placed on social structure, class structure, economic structure, the impact these elements have on the development of the individual, and the practice of life which follows from each of these," *Dialogue with Erich Fromm*, 58.
22 Libido theory is far less dominant in the current psychoanalytical tradition, surpassed by a more relational form of psychoanalysis as seen by thinkers such as Nancy Chodorow and Jessica Benjamin. As Lynn Chancer demonstrates in this volume, Fromm's position was markedly more progressive for the feminist agenda.
23 See Durkin, *Radical Humanism of Erich Fromm*, 72–77, 93–101.
24 Funk, "Erich Fromm and the Intersubjective Tradition."
25 See Durkin, "Erich Fromm and Theodor W. Adorno Reconsidered," and *The Radical Humanism of Erich Fromm*.
26 See Durkin, "Erich Fromm and Theodor W. Adorno Reconsidered."
27 Adorno, *Minima Moralia*, 60; Marcuse, *Eros and Civilization*, 6.
28 See Knapp, *The Art of Living*; and Jacoby, *Social Amnesia*.
29 Fromm, *Escape from Freedom*, 2.

30 See Durkin, *The Radical Humanism of Erich Fromm*, Chapter 2 for a defense of this position.
31 Fromm, *Psychoanalysis and Religion*, 34–37.
32 Fromm's doctoral dissertation was concerned with a comparative analysis of the Jewish sects in early twentieth-century Germany, and his first publication was an analysis of the Sabbath. See Braune, Erich *Fromm's Revolutionary Hope*, and Michael Löwy in this volume on these writings.
33 Fromm, *Psychoanalysis and Religion*, 21.
34 Fromm, *The Working Class in Weimar Germany*, 209.
35 Fromm, *Man for Himself*, 14.
36 Lynn Chancer in this volume points to Fromm's stubborn retention of the gendered use of "man" despite awareness of strong feminist arguments to the contrary, as well as some regrettable biologistic lapses. She also points to his otherwise progressive position in relation to gender, something that should not be forgotten.
37 See Durkin, *The Radical Humanism of Erich Fromm*, 80, fn 6, for a partial defense of Fromm.
38 What should be stressed is that Fromm's works in this period—from *The Sane Society*, to *Marx's Concept of Man*, to *Let Man Prevail*, to *Beyond the Chains of Illusion, Socialist Humanism*—also demonstrated a renewed engagement with Marx. While this engagement tends at times toward what might be called an "existential" analysis, and certainly with almost no engagement with issues of class, it was a notable contribution to the dissemination of Marxist theory in the United States in this period. For a discussion of this influence, see Anderson, "Fromm, Marx, and Humanism."
39 Jacoby, *Social Amnesia*, 77.
40 See Durkin, "Erich Fromm and Theodor W. Adorno Reconsidered," as well as the contributions by Thompson and by Foster in this volume.
41 It should be pointed out that books such as *You Shall Be as Gods, Social Character in a Mexican Village*, and *The Anatomy of Human Destructiveness* were significant academic accomplishments that resemble Fromm's earlier Institute works. It is a great shame that these publications have not been given the attention they deserve, not even today, in this period of relative renaissance.
42 Fromm speaks of needs for relatedness, identity, and transcendence in *The Sane Society*.
43 See Fromm, *The Revolution of Hope*, but also Braune, *Erich Fromm's Revolutionary Hope*, and Michael Löwy in this volume.
44 See Foster, Lundskow, Thorpe, and Langman and Lundskow in this volume.
45 In books such as *The Sane Society, The Revolution of Hope*, and *to Have or to Be?* Fromm develops a form of practical philosophy that speaks to the need to interpersonal and collective engagement in terms of groups, clubs, and town hall meetings.
46 See Lundskow in this volume on aspects of this.
47 See Thompson and Maccoby and McLaughlin in this volume.

References

Abromeit, John. (2011). *Max Horkheimer and the Foundations of Critical Theory*. New York: Cambridge University Press.
Adorno, Theodor W. (2005). *Minima Moralia: Reflections on a Damaged Life*, translated by E. F. N. Jephcott. London: Verso.

Adorno, Theodor, W., Else Frenkel-Brunswick, Daniel J. Levinson; R. Nevitt Sanford, in collaboration with Betty Aron, Maria Hertz Levinson, and William Morrow. (1969). *The Authoritarian Personality*. New York: W.W. Norton & Company.

Anderson, Kevin B. (2015). "Fromm, Marx, and Humanism." In Rainer Funk and Neil McLaughlin (eds.), *Towards a Human Science: The Relevance of Erich Fromm for Today*, 209–18. Giessen: Psychosozial-Verlag.

Bonss, Wolfgang. (1984). "Introduction," to Erich Fromm *The Working Class in Weimar Germany: A Psychological and Sociological Study*, edited by Wolfgang Bonss. Cambridge, MA: Harvard University Press.

Braune, Joan. (2014). *Erich Fromm's Revolutionary Hope: Prophetic Messianism as a Critical Theory of the Future*. Rotterdam: Sense Publishers.

Durkin, Kieran. (2014). *The Radical Humanism of Erich Fromm*. New York: Palgrave Macmillan.

Durkin, Kieran. (2019). "Erich Fromm and Theodor W. Adorno Reconsidered: A Case Study in Intellectual History." *New German Critique* 46, no. 1: 103–26.

Fromm, Erich. (1936). "Sozialpsychologischer Teil." In Max Horkheimer (ed.), *Studien über Autorität und Familie*. Paris: Felix Alcan.

Fromm, Erich. (1950). *Psychoanalysis and Religion*. London: Yale University Press.

Fromm, Erich. (1955). *The Sane Society*. New York: Rinehart and Winston.

Fromm, Erich. (1956). *The Art of Loving*. New York: Harper and Row.

Fromm, Erich. (1960). *Let Man Prevail: A Socialist Manifesto and Program*. New York: Call Association.

Fromm, Erich. (1966a). *Dialogue with Erich Fromm*. Interview with Richard Evans. New York: Harper and Row.

Fromm, Erich. (1966b). *You Shall Be as Gods: A Radical Interpretation of the Old Testament and Its Traditions*. New York: Holt, Rinehart, and Winston.

Fromm, Erich. (1967). *Socialist Humanism*. London: Allen Lane, The Penguin Press.

Fromm, Erich. (1968). *The Revolution of Hope: Toward a Humanized Technology*. New York: Harper and Row.

Fromm, Erich. (1969). *Escape from Freedom*. New York: Farrar and Rinehart.

Fromm, Erich. (1970 [1932]a). "The Method and Function of an Analytic Social Psychology." In Erich Fromm (ed.), *The Crisis of Psychoanalysis: Essays on Freud, Marx and Social Psychology*, 110–34. New York: Holt, Rinehart and Winston.

Fromm, Erich. (1970 [1932]b). "Psychoanalytic Characterology and Its Relevance for Social Psychology." In Erich Fromm (ed.), *The Crisis of Psychoanalysis: Essays on Freud, Marx and Social Psychology*, 135–58. New York: Holt, Rinehart and Winston.

Fromm, Erich. (1984). *The Working Class in Weimar Germany: A Psychological and Sociological Study*. Cambridge, MA: Harvard University Press.

Fromm, Erich. (1989 [1929]). "Psychoanalysis and Sociology." In Stephen Eric Bronner and Douglas Kellner (eds.), *Critical Theory and Society: A Reader*. London: Routledge.

Fromm, Erich. (1992 [1963]). *The Dogma of Christ and Other Essays on Religion, Psychology, and Culture*. New York: Henry Holt.

Fromm, Erich. (1997 [1973]). *The Anatomy of Human Destructiveness*. London: Pimlico.

Fromm, Erich. (2003 [1947]). *Man for Himself: An Inquiry into the Psychology of Ethics*. New York: Farrar and Rinehart.

Fromm, Erich. (2004 [1961]). *Marx's Concept of Man*. London: Continuum.

Fromm, Erich. (2009 [1976]). *To Have or to Be?* London: Continuum.

Fromm, Erich. (2010). "Man's Impulse Structure and Its Relation to Culture." In Rainer Funk (ed.), *Beyond Freud: From Individual to Social Psychology*, 17–73. New York: American Mental Health Foundation.
Fromm, Erich, and Michael Maccoby. (1996). *Social Character in a Mexican Village: A Sociopsychoanalytic Study*. London: Transaction.
Funk, Rainer. (2000). *Erich Fromm: His Life and Ideas—An Illustrated Biography*. New York: Continuum.
Funk, Rainer. (2013). "Erich Fromm and the Intersubjective Tradition." *International Forum of Psychoanalysis* 22, Issue 1: 5–9.
Funk, Rainer, and Neil McLaughlin, eds. (2015). *Towards a Human Science: The Relevance of Erich Fromm for Today*. Glissen. Psychosozial-Verlag.
Held, David. (1980). *Introduction to Critical Theory: Horkheimer to Habermas*. London: Hutchinson.
Horkheimer, Max, ed. (1936). *Studien über Autorität und Familie*. Paris: Felix Alcan.
Jacoby, Russell. (1977). *Social Amnesia: A Critique of Conformist Psychology from Adler to Laing*. Sussex: Harvester Press.
Jay, Martin. (1996). *The Dialectical Imagination: A History of the Frankfurt School and the Institute of Social Research, 1923–1950*. London: Heinemann.
Knapp, Gerhard P. (1993). *The Art of Living: Erich Fromm's Life and Works*. New York: Peter Lang.
Langman, Lauren, and George Lundskow. (2016). *God, Guns, Gold, and Glory: American Character and Its Discontents*. Boston: Brill.
Marcuse, Herbert. (1966). *Eros and Civilization: A Philosophical Inquiry into Freud*. Boston, MA: Beacon Press.
McLaughlin, Neil. (1999). "Origin Myths in the Social Sciences: Fromm, the Frankfurt School and the Emergence of Critical Theory." *Canadian Journal of Sociology* 24, no. 1: 109–39.
Miri, Seyed Javad, Robert Lake, and Tricia M. Kress, eds. (2014). *Reclaiming the Sane Society: Essays on Erich Fromm's Thought*. Rotterdam: Sense.
Schroyer, Trent. (1973). *The Critique of Domination: The Origins and Development of Critical Theory*. Boston, MA: Beacon Press.
Tar, Zoltan. (1977). *The Frankfurt School: The Critical Theories of Max Horkheimer and Theodor W. Adorno*. New York, NY: John Wiley and Sons.
Thorpe, Charles. (2016). *Necroculture*. New York: Palgrave Macmillan.
Wheatland, Thomas. (2009). *The Frankfurt School in Exile*. Minneapolis: University of Minnesota Press.
Wiggershaus, Ralph. (1994). *The Frankfurt School, The Frankfurt School: Its History, Theories and Political Significance*. Cambridge: Polity Press.
Wilde, Lawrence. (2004). *Erich Fromm and the Quest for Solidarity*. New York: Palgrave.

Part I

RADICAL AND PROPHETIC HUMANISM

Chapter 1

ERICH FROMM AND THE ONTOLOGY OF SOCIAL RELATIONS

Michael J. Thompson

Once central to critical theory was the thesis that critical reflection on social reality was only possible via a capacity to grasp the whole, the social totality, within which the subject and social phenomena occurred. Beginning with Hegel's dictum in the *Phenomenology of Spirit* that only the whole was true to Marx's exhaustive project to demonstrate the coherence of capitalism as a total system, the first generation of critical theorists took this as a basic paradigm of thought from which to develop their own critical projects. At the core of the Hegelian-Marxist structure of thought therefore is the axiomatic premise that we take human beings as essentially associative, social beings. The social totality was therefore seen as a concrete totality of social relations and processes that was constitutive of the development of individuality, consciousness, and reflective capacities. Whether expressed in terms of Hegel's conception of a sociality of reason via metaphysical relations of interdependence or Marx's *Theses on Feuerbach* that maintains the essentially social nature of human activity, a central concept emerges capturing the idea that social-relational structures are active in shaping human life and culture.

Recently, a new generation of critical theorists has taken the concept of social relations in a very different direction. This move toward Kantian and pragmatist themes has meant thinning the conception of human sociality and interdependence. Reconceived as intersubjectivity, or a conception of social relations that stresses cognitive and symbolic forms of interaction, this paradigm shift has all but eclipsed the Hegelian-Marxian structure of thought that was once the infrastructure for critical theory. This new paradigm, heralded by Jürgen Habermas, Karl-Otto Apel, Axel Honneth, Rainer Forst as well as a myriad of others, essentially reduces social relations to cognitive structures of consciousness. Whether it be in linguistic, pragmatic, communicative, or recognitive terms, what unites these neo-idealist theories is the premise that our relations with others are essentially cognitive and affective. What they are not is in any sense ontological with causal powers or in possession of structures and functions that circumscribe them.

The reductive intersubjectivity that characterizes these approaches should be contrasted to what Erich Fromm saw as distinctive about human sociality. For Fromm, our relations with others have an ontological ballast in that they are structures that constitute both our social reality and the psychic structures of the self. The ontological thickness of our relations with others is not meant to be interpreted as some form of communitarianism, but rather in the Marxian sense of a structure of relations that have constitutive force on our social reality. This is in stark contrast to the intersubjectivist-pragmatist approach that currently characterizes critical theory in that relations cannot be simply made and remade via our capacities for communication or recognition. They have a deep embeddedness in the way we have organized our relations with nature as well as the power relations that are inherent in the control over the institutions that reproduce those relations. In this sense, Fromm's conception of human relations is historical as well as critical. We must be able to discern those forms of relations and relational activity that promote human flourishing—the creative, active, nondestructive, and emancipated manifestation of self that can only thrive and in fact be instantiated by a particular kind of social-relational ontology.

My thesis in this chapter is that Erich Fromm's work evinces a distinctive way of thinking about the nature of social relations and the ways that these relations possess causal powers over the development of the self as well as the social world more generally. More concretely, I want to argue that Fromm's conception of critical theory is rooted in a theory of freedom and judgment that takes into account the ontological shape of social relations that have constitutive power over the self and the society as a whole. As I see it, Fromm's distinctive take on a critical theory of society takes the social ontology of our relational sociality as the primary source of social and personal pathologies. In this sense, he is in line with the evolution of the Hegelian-Marxist paradigm that takes the ontological-material structures of human sociality as having causal powers over the phenomenological and cognitive structures of consciousness and self. Comprehending these relations is central in the sense (i) that they antecede the self and thereby are active in the shaping and contouring of psychological structures and drives of the self; and (ii) that it is only through the overcoming of pathological social forms (i.e., structures of relations) that a more concrete, total reality of freedom be achieved. After pointing to how Fromm unfolds this argument and exploring its implications, I will then explore how Fromm develops a distinctively Marxian conception of freedom as well as an objective ethics that can help reconstruct critical theory as well as a more humane, rational form of critical politics.

Robust and Defective Relations and the Nature of the Self

Fromm is insistent that Marx's conception of human being contains a crucial dimension lacking in Freudian theory. Whereas Freud saw the individual as self-contained, Marx sees that the nature of human psychology is dynamic, functionally related to the relations in which the individual is embedded: "Marx's dynamic psychology," Fromm writes, "is based on the primacy of man's relatedness to the world, to man, and to nature, in contrast to Freud's, which is based on the model of an isolated *homme machine*."[1] Fromm notes in his psychological interpretation of Marx that Marx's theory of needs and drives is dependent on this sociality. We need our relations to others, to the world and to nature. This need, in turn, provides the basis for our drives: "Man's 'drives,' then, are an expression of a fundamental and specifically human need, the need to be related to man and nature, and of confirming himself in this relatedness."[2]

This relatedness is not a merely structural reality; it is also an active one. Fromm's Marxism is expressed in the notion that our relations with others are not only ontologically prior to us as subjects but also enacted by us through our activities. The essence of any social relation is therefore constituted by practices, by conscious activity. But it is also structured by the patterns of relations shaped by forms of social power as well as norms, values, and functional roles that these patterns of social power exhibit. The relations of parent and child, teacher and student, husband and wife, owner and worker, and so on are not simply reified social scripts that we take on. They are enacted by practices. Our active social relations with others are essential to grasping the ways that pathological forms of character and consciousness emerge. Fromm is adamant that, in contrast to idealist and neo-idealist theses about human social relations that see them as "intersubjective," we return to Marx's concept of the human being "with his physical and psychic properties, the real man who does not live in a vacuum but in a social context, the man who has to produce in order to live."[3] The kinds of social relations that Fromm points to here are the thick relations of the totality of human sociality. It therefore encompasses intersubjective as well as material, structural, and functional layers of social relations and sociality. It is this that gives causal power to social relations and makes them the primary object of critique and the aim of social transformation.

To say that these relations possess an ontological character means that they are *objective* in nature and, although not material in nature, they also have the capacity to shape the subject via socialization, which means they also possess a *causal power*. Relations are therefore real in a distinctively social sense in that they are not the property of our subjectivity alone, but rather of the shared structures that we inhabit, reproduce, and which also shape us. The term "ontological" therefore contains an important difference from material or natural forms of reality in that a social-ontological relation is constituted by human intentions. The very concept of social character, for Fromm, is an example of the way that forms of existential, subjective being is shaped by the nature and structure of social relations. The reification of these relations over time—their stabilization and persistence through different social cohorts—is what gives a society its permanence and coherence. The critical question is how particular societies organize and legitimate the social-ontological structure that is constitutive of their social reality as well as their subjectivity. It is Fromm's thesis throughout his work that these social-ontological relations can be evaluated based on the kinds of ends that they promote. Defective forms of relations are organized according to ends that are non-fulfilling in terms of the human potentialities or powers (potencies) that can be developed by any agent. Human beings should be conceived as ontological as opposed to natural insofar as what powers they can realize are dependent on the social-relational structures that shape and form them.

Socialization is the process whereby the structures, and the norms and values that undergird them, of the predominant society are absorbed by each individual within the community. Of course, this process is always insecure in that each person may not take to the absorption of the norms, resulting in neuroses or other forms of "pathological" behavior. But what Fromm sees as crucial is that the dialectic between the innate drives of the individual and the mediating powers of socialization produce our social being. These "drives," Fromm argues, "are an expression of a fundamental and specifically human need to be related to man and nature, and of confirming himself in this relatedness."[4] The nature of our social being is therefore a product of the ways that these relations are able to enhance our real needs rather than the artificial needs that the predominant reality principles both defines for us and organizes our drives to seek.[5] The problem is that, drawing from Marx, Fromm sees that true human needs are to be understood as a particular kind of active-relational life. As Fromm notes,

> Marx's concept of socialism is a protest, as is all existentialist philosophy, against the alienation of man; if, as Aldous Huxley put it, "our present economic, social and international arrangements are based, in large measure, upon organized lovelessness," then Marx's socialism is a protest against this very lovelessness, against his exploitiveness toward nature, the wasting of our natural resources at the expense of the majority of men today, and more so of the generations to come. The unalienated man, who is the goal of socialism as we have shown before, is the man who does not "dominate" nature, but who becomes one with it, who is alive and responsive toward objects, so that objects come to life for him.[6]

Relations are therefore not only between human beings but between humans and nature. Alienation—seen as those forms of life that actively negate healthy relations and states—is the product of defective relations in that they root within us artificial needs and drives: drives to power, dominance, exploitation, and destructiveness. The pathological origins of these kinds of character structure are therefore traced back to the structure of the relational nexus of society.

It is important to emphasize that social character is distinct from individual character. It is the social character that must be shaped and organized by the functional imperatives of society; it is the site where social-relational structures and functions intersect and shape the inner drives of the individual. As Fromm sees the matter, "It is the social character's function to mold and channel human energy within a given society for the purpose of the continued functioning of this society."[7] But the nature of social character is also a function of the relations that shape it and which shape the drives of the individual toward creating certain kinds of self- and other-relations. This is because Fromm's distinction between what he calls "neurotic" and "healthy" personalities has at its core an implicit ontology of social relations. Indeed, the neurotic's tendency is to seek the creation and maintenance of primary bonds in order to assuage the alienating feeling of loneliness. In primary bonds, one seeks "to give up the independence of one's own individual self and to fuse one's self with somebody or something outside of oneself in order to acquire the strength which the individual self is lacking."[8] The very concept of "independence," it must be stressed, would seem to fly in the face of any relational conception of psychic or human health. But independence, for Fromm as it was for Marx, is rooted in the Aristotelian category of "self-sufficiency" (αὐτάρκης) which does not denote a *separateness* from or literal non-dependence on others but, rather, conversely, the state of having what one needs as a result of one's associations with others.[9] One is "self-sufficient," in Aristotle's sense, when ensconced in a nexus of interdependent relations with others that fulfill his needs. I achieve self-sufficiency, in other words, by living within the thick relations that interdependent sociality provides. Hence, independence is an emergent property of associational life. But only an associational life that has as its aim the common good of its members.[10]

Once this model of human sociality is corrupted, pathologies begin to emerge. Social organization is the root cause of the way that character is formed and the formation of social character is also highly determinative of the values that underwrite consciousness, cognition, and the moral-evaluative powers of practical reason. The damaged self, the crippled self, is unable to develop its fully human powers. The alienation that is a result of this process stunts the development of these powers, the most important of which is the power of self-creation, creativity, and productivity itself. The independent person is truly independent, as was noted earlier, not when literally nondependent on others, but when existing within a certain kind of relations with others that would enable and empower the self. It is only the weakened ego that seeks destructiveness, dominance, or submission. And this weakened ego is a function of the particular relations that are constitutive of capitalist society—a society that increasingly privileges the narrowest forms of need and desire and deprives the self of its own autonomous power for self-mastery, for freedom.

From Fromm's exploration of the healthy and neurotic characters, we can infer an implicit ontological theory about the kinds of relations that I will call here *robust* and *defective* relations. A society possesses *robust* social relations when these relations are interdependent, mutually beneficial for the members of the community, and oriented toward the development of each person's individuality. By contrast, *defective* relations would be those defined by exploitive, extractive, or instrumental forms of relational activity. These relations constitute a kind of *abuse of the social bond*; they warp what could potentially be an interdependent relation where mutual needs are met and fulfilled in order for healthy individuality to develop and attain self-mastery and self-creation. Once I use others for my own gain, once I exploit them, see myself in competition with them for gain, glory, attention, or whatever, I am in the midst of defective relations that will only achieve neurotic, alienated, and crippled manifestations of subjectivity.

A central pathology of capitalist society therefore consists in the kinds of relations or even absence of relations that constitute it. With the predominance of exploitive, alienating forms of life and activity—the hierarchical, regimented modern workplace, the atomization of the modern family, competitive acquisitiveness, technological reification, and so on—we are confronted with the shredding of the social relations requisite to nourish and build free personhood. This shredding of our relations, the diminution of their thickness into brittle forms of dependency, creates anxiety within the subject. This anxiety leads to the search for alternative forms of self- and other-relations. Since the primary bonds that granted security in childhood are no longer available, in its place individuals search to find others that can buttress their weakness of self.[11] But the key idea here is that freedom—whether as an achievement of the individual or of society—cannot be realized within the nexus of such perverse and pathological relations. The very ontology of those relations must be transformed and reshaped in order to help in the realization of freedom.

Expanded Autonomy: Social Structure and Self-Development

So we are moving toward a thesis about the nature of social-ontological relations that serves as the ground for the diagnostic and normative ideas that Fromm will call "normative humanism." But the key insight that he wants to press is that there exists a crucial dialectic between social relations and the nature of freedom. Fromm is developing a distinctly Marxian conception of freedom with the help of Freud. Essentially what Fromm wants to argue is that a conception of freedom that transcends the liberal eighteenth- and nineteenth-century conception is constituted by a specific structure of social relations that, in turn, grants the subject with powers of self-mastery. This is because Fromm is working with a conception of autonomy that is capable of providing the ego with a character structure that can live a self-developing, creative form of life. But this also entails, via the dialectic, that the society that will produce such a character structure will also be one that receives the benefit of that new kind of self. A free society does not exist, in this sense, for the purpose of articulating the creative, free self. Rather, the society that creates such selves *will also be constituted by them*, and a reflexive interplay between the ontology of social relations and the ontology of the self merges into a higher structure of freedom.

I want to develop this idea that social relations have causal powers over the development of self. Fromm sees Marx's thesis of the base and superstructure here as determinative in this sense, but not in terms of an orthodox reading of that thesis. Social relations shape and orient the development of self because of their capacity to organize the inner drives of the individual. This is done through the ways that social relations shape the structure of needs within the community. What we can call "expanded autonomy" is the idea that social relations are properly shaped so as to create individuals whose freedom will not be in tension with the community but, rather, be activated by it. Individuals are not autonomous in the classical Kantian sense where they reflect as individuals on the abstract principle of morality. Rather, the thesis here is that—following from Rousseau, Hegel, and Marx—an expanded conception of the self emerges that takes into account and is self-conscious of the fact that one's own good is dialectically related to the good of others. The truly, concretely free being will now see others and nature as constitutive of his own good and freedom.

This thesis has a long pedigree. In many ways, it was initiated by Jean-Jacques Rousseau and his thesis of the "general will" (*volonté générale*) that posited an expanded conception of subjectivity that would be able to take into account its own relatedness to others as a dimension of the individual's good. In his *Emile*, Rousseau explores the way that a subject can be shaped to think in a new, expanded way rather than narcissistically.[12] The self, as Rousseau saw it, was to be enlarged so as to encompass the interdependent practical reality of one's being, culminating in a kind of moral-political cognition, the general will, which would serve as the basis for a legitimately free republic. But this idea also appears in the work of Hegel and his attempt to build an alternative framework for self-consciousness. In the *Phenomenology of Spirit*, the well-known thesis of the struggle for recognition is used to expose the idea that selfhood is dialectically tied to the recognition by the other. Hegel uses this idea to expand beyond the Kantian and Fichtean models of consciousness to articulate a model of mind that is socially embedded and relationally dependent. Hegel's development of this model can be seen also in the *Philosophy of Right*, where he explores the ways that different structures of relations, from the family to the market to the state, all entail a socialization of our practical reason. Finally, Marx, too, sought to recreate this thesis in his early writings where he uses the concept of "producing for another" as the basis for understanding a more material ontology of our interdependent relations with others. The key idea that unites these three arguments—and constitutes what I think we can call a distinct structure of thought—is that only a self-awareness and self-consciousness of this ontological reality of mutual interdependence will grant us the critical capacity for social transformation. The reason for this is that it is the substantive social-ontological basis from which we can diagnose social pathologies and inquire into more humane, more developmentally just forms of social life, institutions, and norms. Only once we are able to hold in view the idea that our own individuality is dependent on our social relations with others, that these relations constitute structures that can be organized either according to mutual benefit or for a particular benefit (i.e., dominance), can we become truly aware of the pathological shapes and forms that our social reality manifests.

I think this is a powerful idea that Fromm probes in his writings from various perspectives. It is, in a sense, the normative vantage point from which his critical-diagnostic account of modern society and individualism is constructed. Whereas Rousseau uses the education of the child for non-domination, Hegel the struggle of recognitive relations between master and slave, and Marx the idea of producing for mutual benefit, Fromm explores this thesis in his paradigmatic case of the concept of love. Loving relationships can be characterized either by pathological or by healthy bonds between the lovers. Pathological bonds are shaped by the drive to re-create primary bonds; in this sense, the lovers become *symbiotic*. Since the weakened, crippled ego seeks out primary bonds that will grant the ego a primitive sense of security, the relation created with the other is defective in that it wants that other to assuage the anxiety brought on by loneliness and separateness. The masochistic and sadistic drives that emerge from this quest for primary bonds create a defective bond between the lovers, and their egos become trapped within this doomed quest. Development, growth, and self-mastery become frustrated since the interdependence of each on the other descends into dependence of one on the other.

Fromm contrasts these pathological forms of love with the concept of "mature love" which he describes in the following passage:

> In contrast to symbiotic union, mature *love* is *union under the condition of preserving one's integrity*, one's individuality. *Love is an active power in man*; a power which breaks through the walls which separate man from his fellow men, which unites him with others; love makes him overcome the sense of isolation and separateness, yet it permits him to be himself, to retain his integrity. In love the paradox occurs that two beings become one and yet remain two.[13]

This supposed "paradox" that Fromm points to is, in fact, no paradox at all; it is the very description of the expanded form of autonomy in mutual, interdependent relations. In mature love, "Love is the active concern for the life and growth of that which we love."[14] But the essence of this relationship of mature love is that each individual is expanded through the interdependent relation that is activated by the desire for the other to grow and develop. One's selfhood is thereby expanded and deepened by this unique structure of interpersonal relations.

It seems clear that Fromm's discussion of the concept of love can be seen to have social-theoretical salience. First, it involves more than mere recognition of the other. It is, in fact, a productive activity in that, as mature love, it seeks to give to the other all that is needed to be able to achieve free, creative individuality. Second, it is an inherently relational concept in that it is dependent on the structure of the relationship. We cannot achieve this form of free, developed selfhood outside of the robust relationship between those in the relation. What Fromm calls a "paradox" is in fact only *seemingly* a paradox. In reality, it is precisely the kind of dialectic between robust social relations and the development of ego-individuality that is in view here. We can now see that robust social relations entail specific kinds of structures and features. Those relations are robust only when they are motivated by the intention of mutual benefit and mutual good—and mutual good can only be valid if that good entails each individual's good. Robust, healthy forms of relations are those that evince mutual interdependence as well as reciprocity. And finally, such robust relations can only be seen to be successful if they are able to permit the individuals involved in those relations to achieve a kind of individuality that is self-conscious of this interdependence and use their self-mastery and creative powers to enhance those relational goods and ends rather than narcissistic needs or instrumental ends.

Enlarging the scope of the discussion, we can see that this thesis about how relations shape and structure forms of individuality can be used to capture more than just intimate relations. Society need not be characterized by relations of love for them to exhibit the structural characteristics Fromm discusses. The distinction between defective and robust social relations described earlier now can be read through this understanding of the concept of expanded autonomy. The reason for this is that the dialectical relation between individual and society operates with the relative capacity of any subject to create, maintain, and sustain the robust relations that give rise to self-mastery and genuinely free individuality. This becomes a central criterion for how relations are structured and maintained. Fromm points to several different polarities that relations can take. In one instance, the polarity of brotherliness and incest is used to describe how relations can maximize mutual respect between the individuals involved (brotherliness or rootedness) versus those relations that squash the egos involved (i.e., incest). In this instance, the problem of incest emerges when the egos involved are unable to have sufficient personal space for development and enrichment, whereas "brotherliness" denotes a kind of relation-with-others that allows for that space while allowing one's relation-with-others to serve as a means for self-expansion and development. The key difference here, again, is the causal power of the ontological relation itself: the way any *relatum* is constructed has consequences on the *relata* involved. The emergence of symbiotic forms of relations therefore results in relations of domination and submission, where "both persons involved have lost their integrity and freedom; they live on each other, satisfying their craving for closeness, yet suffering from the lack of inner strength and self-reliance which would require freedom and independence."[15]

Fromm is aware that this is also a premise that underlies Marx's vision of a postcapitalist world. Marx is clear that the nature of self-development is dependent on the interdependent relations between subjects. Their individuality can only come to fruition through a bond where each is dependent on the other but nevertheless remain individual. In his early notes on James Mill's *Elements of Political Economy*, Marx notes this in detail:

> Our mutual value is the value of our mutual objects for us. Man by himself therefore is mutually valueless for us. Suppose we had produced things as human beings: in his production each of us would have twice affirmed himself and the other. (1) In my production I would have objectified my individuality and its particularity, and in the course of the activity I would have enjoyed an individual life.... (2) In your satisfaction and your use of my product I would have had the direct and conscious satisfaction that my work satisfied a human need.... (3) I would have been the mediator between you and the species and you would have experienced me as a reintegration of your own nature and a necessary part of your self.... (4) In my individual life I would have directly created your life; in my individual activity I would have immediately confirmed and realized my true human and social nature.[16]

The parallel here with Fromm's model of mature love is not difficult to discern. In a kind of materialist twist on Hegel's cognitive model of the struggle for recognition between master and slave, Marx's thesis is that the end of any kind of mutual production for the good of the other results not only in the satisfaction of the other's need but, more importantly, in the realization of the one's true human nature. The reason seems to be that only in realizing mutual interdependence can our true individuality be realized—an individuality that is cognizant of one's interlacing with others as the precondition for his own freedom and self-development.

For both Marx and Fromm, the optimal structure for robust relations therefore seems to be that they are shaped according to the essential reality of our interdependence as members of a society, but also an interdependence that has as its aim the mutual development of each member of the interdependent relation. Indeed, all human association is, in some basic sense, based on forms of dependency. Each of us needs others to complement our own existence, to somehow provide basic needs, whether physical, emotional, or productive. But dependence, in its pure form, is a pathological form of relation; it is a relation of need, but a relation that does not have mutual benefit as its aim. Egyptian pharaohs needed, were indeed dependent on, the mass of workers to build their temples and pyramids just as a capitalist depends on his or her workers to produce the commodities that will be the basic mechanism for surplus value. Similarly, the workers depend on the capitalist to be able to provide their wages and livelihood. But these dependent relations are pathological because they are not aimed at a common interest: they are not aimed at the common good of the members of the associative relations. A modern theory of the common interest is one that has in view the development and welfare of each member of the community; it has as its goal the development and freedom of each member of the association. Each individual therefore has an interest in the community being organized toward those ends not only for instrumentally self-interested reasons but *reflexively* because that developed free individuality is also *mutually beneficial for all*. And this mutual benefit for all becomes, in turn, an enhanced benefit for the self insofar as it has a more developed context within which to develop and enrich itself. In *robust* relations, those that exhibit the features of interdependence, each of us is cognizant of the mutuality of our bonds and that these bonds, these relations, are constitutive of the kind of self- and other-relations that form our world.

The concrete form of freedom that Marx had in view, especially in the early manuscripts, but also in *Capital*, is illustrative of this thesis. Freedom can only become real in the world when it becomes concrete. And it can only become concrete when it is thoroughly *social*. The practical interdependence that characterizes the basis of human existence must be shaped in such a way that its end product is a social context that will be able to shape and realize *free individuality*. As Marx says in the *Grundrisse*,

> Relations of personal dependence (entirely spontaneous at the outset) are the first social forms, in which human productive capacity develops only to a slight extent and at isolated points. Personal independence founded on *objective* [*sachlicher*] dependence is the second great form, in which a system of general social metabolism, of universal relations, of all-round needs and universal capacities is formed for the first time. Free individuality, based on the universal

development of individuals and on their subordination of their communal, social productivity as their social wealth, is the third stage.[17]

Both Fromm and Marx are articulating a thesis about the concrete nature of social freedom. It is only through the enrichment of the social context within which individuality emerges that genuine freedom can also emerge.[18] We move through different social-developmental phases, from relations of dependence to a narrow form of independence, and finally to a phase of "free individuality" once we subordinate our collective productive powers toward the ends of self-development. What this indicates is a need for social relations and institutions to be oriented toward and organized for the development of free individuality. For Marx, this will require that the institutions of society are organized around common goods and needs, and that these common needs are understood as absorbing the development of individuality as a constitutive basis of any rational expression of the common good.

What Fromm adds to this discussion is a detailed account of the way that the psychic structure of the self is also involved in this process. Free individuality requires robust, interdependent relations that have as their end, their telos, the development of each members' individuality; at the same time, each members' individuality and creativity will be reflexively oriented toward common concerns and not considered merely an end in itself. In this new kind of free individuality, which will be social as well as individual, self-interest becomes common interest without ever sacrificing the drive toward the individual. Only those that can self-consciously perceive their cooperative interdependence on and with others will be capable of grasping their own freedom as interlaced with others rather than at their expense. Fromm makes this very point when he says: "Freedom does not imply lack of constraint, since any growth occurs only within a structure. What matters is whether the constraint functions primarily for the sake of another person or institution, or whether it is autonomous—i.e., that it results from the necessities of growth inherent in the structure of the person."[19]

A society that is able to achieve these robust relations in the complex, overlapping structures that constitute its totality—that is, the family relations, economic relations, political, and so on—is one that is able to maximize a concrete form of freedom. This concrete concept of freedom is in stark contrast to the liberal, negative conception of freedom in that it places emphasis on the nature of social relations and their structures. Whereas liberal theories of freedom emphasize subjective preferences and freedom of opportunities or freedom as absence of constraint, along with a negative liberty to refrain from the harm of others, Fromm's concrete form of freedom has in view the totality of real human life and activity. It is concrete, in this sense, because it is made objective in the world; it becomes not only an ideal or a form of practice but an ontological reality. In this sense, it constitutes a valid critical theory of society in that it is able to capture elements of the social totality and the idea that human individuality is essentially social and hence relational in nature. We can now move on to see how this can also lead to a distinctively critical theory of ethics as an objective ethics.

The Objectivity of Ethical Value

Once we see social relations as having a thick ontological quality, we can then begin to inquire about the extent to which values can be articulated to help guide critical consciousness as well as maintain the creation of alternative forms of life that can promote robust social relations. For Fromm, these values would not be mere "oughts," they would not be abstract normative postulates, but rather be *objective value premises*. This points to the possibility of a theory of objective ethics which, for much of contemporary moral philosophy, violates the concern with the idea of value pluralism and the Kantian idea of a constructivist ethics. But Fromm is arguing that there are certain objective things that we know about the way human development proceeds. He maintains throughout his work that the structure of social relations, the character structure of the self, and the states of personal and social pathology are not constructs of norms, but rather of the concrete ways that we organize our social institutions. In this sense, we can speak of an objective ethics to the extent that these known variables are ontological. They are not objective in the same way that natural kinds are objective. The key idea here is that our values and our moral-evaluative concepts are neither arbitrary nor derive any normative force of power because of some sense of agreement through rational discourse or justification. Rather, our moral-evaluative concepts must be framed by the way that social-relational structures shape drives and character and how both can be arranged to realize a concrete form of social and individual freedom.

Fromm does not advocate some outmoded expression of natural law, nor does he see the objectivity of value as somehow rooted in cultural beliefs, norms or traditions, or static understanding of nature. This is an historical understanding of value in that it grasps the capacity of modern society to articulate the interdependent forms of robust social relations requisite for free individuality. Fromm's ideas about the mechanisms of social and personal development grant us an ontological ballast to normative concepts of freedom. Against the neo-idealist prejudices of contemporary theory, Fromm proposes that our normative concepts can have an objectivity that transcends the arbitrariness of our agreement with others or our phenomenological experiences of what we deem to be right and wrong, or good and bad. Fromm maintains that a truly humanistic ethics would be derived from the objective criteria of what kinds of relations will be able to foster the development of our powers and potentialities for free, creative self-mastery. This is why Fromm says that "if ethics constitutes the body of norms for achieving excellence in performing the art of living, its most general principles must follow from the nature of life in general and of human existence in particular."[20] If we reference the expanded conception of autonomy that I suggested earlier, then we can see that the referent for objective value propositions must be the way that social structure and personal development relate dynamically. We have to talk about the socio-developmental structures that exist and inquire into the extent to which they promote healthy or pathological relations. An objective ethics is one that has actual relations and the self-development of their constituents as its substance, its content: "If ... psychology and anthropology are to make valid propositions about the laws governing human behavior, they must start out with the premise that *something*, say X, *is reacting to environmental influences in ascertainable ways that follow from its properties.*"[21]

What is suggested here is that ethical premises that are oriented toward humanistic ends cannot be abstracted from some feature of human life (say reason, utility, pleasure, pain, or whatever), nor can they be formalized and emptied of content (such as in the categorical imperative). Rather, the content is the *social-relational nexus that constitutes social reality* and the ways the organization of social-relational structures affects the development of personhood. It is not a cognitive conception of value, nor is it rooted in a thin conception of social practice, such as linguistic communication, recognition, or whatever. Rather, as I have sought to demonstrate earlier, it is content that has ontological ballast in that it refers to the actual ways that social forms shape and affect individual development. As opposed to the precritical philosophical doctrine of natural law theory, Fromm follows a modern, critical understanding of ethical value as tied to the ontological structure of human life.[22] The features of such ontological relations would have to be understood as *reflexive* between individual and common goods; *non-dominating* in the sense that they do not seek to extract some benefit from one for another; as well as *nonsymbiotic*, in the sense that their purposes is the mutual development of each individual within the relations and instead seek their development as productive, self-mastered agents. An objective ethics therefore concerns the ways that what we consider a valid moral proposition or value proposition achieves this validity not via the agreement of intersubjective reason-exchange, but rather to the extent that it is able to promote the development of those distinctively human powers that are aimed at self-mastery and expanded autonomy. In this respect, the objectivity of any ethical proposition must have as its referent the ontological shape of the social-structural reality that shapes and orients our existence.

The objectivity of our value propositions therefore is related not to the *value* itself, but rather to the social-structural ways that human life is manifested. If a consequentialist places the emphasis of how we judge a moral proposition based on its *effect*, and a deontologist on our *duty* to an abstract, rational principle, an objective theory of ethics judges a moral or ethical proposition based on how social relations and institutions should be organized and how these relate to the promotion of free individuality. It therefore violates the sterile "fact-value" dichotomy in that ethical principles are derived not from an abstract consensus on values, but rather from the actual, concrete social life. An example of this is in the basic theory of neurosis that Fromm defends: "All neuroses can be understood as the result of unconscious strivings which tend to harm and to block a person's growth."[23] This kind of critical reasoning possesses a logical structure that we can express as follows: "*To know X is to know the good expression of X.*" Any rational, factual knowledge of any given thing also grants us knowledge of the normative criteria for its healthy or good manifestation. If I have a good nose, as Socrates once argued, it is because it performs its nose-ness well, that is, it can smell better than other noses. "Neurosis" cannot be understood as a value-neutral term without doing violence to the concept of neurosis itself. Critique is effectively built into the structure of true, rational knowledge.

Human values should be seen as rooted in the actual conditions of life and the ways that the forms of life can either inhibit or promote free individuality in a real, genuine sense. Fromm seems to have this concept in view when he writes: "Humanistic ethics, for which 'good' is synonymous with good for man and 'bad' with bad for man, proposes that in order to know what is good for man we have to know his nature. Humanistic ethics is the applied science of the 'art of living' based upon the theoretical 'science of man.'"[24] This "science of man" is provided by the enquiry into the social-relational nature of human psychic development as well as the ways that individual development is a function of social-relational structures. Norms and values are therefore objective when they reference the ways that social structures of relations are organized to shape the full development of the individual.

The criterion for judgment now becomes the extent to which any given norm, institution, practice, or whatever is able to instantiate robust social relations and healthy self-development; it must be judged, in other words, according to a concrete conception of freedom. The insight here is that ethics are *embodied* and *ontological*; they are not simply ideas or norms that govern behavior. Rather, they are instantiated objectively and *ontologically* in the very substance of our existence. The ontological therefore embraces the idea that these relations and subjective states are objectively real, but nevertheless pliable, transformable, and also determined by our own will. It is only as we developed an increasingly conscious awareness of the intentional nature of our social reality—that is, that it is constituted by our own practices and norms and not according to some natural, chemical, or biological substrate—that the power of human social and personal transformation increases. This conception is what Marx, too, was pursuing in his materialist critique of Hegel's idealism: a concrete conception of what the good or what freedom actually was. Indeed, what is significant for Fromm's critical diagnosis of defective, pathological, and neurotic forms of social relations and personality is that the actual personality structure of the self and his or her experience of it can be traced to the defective social arrangements of the society itself. We need to have not only an objective referent for our diagnosis of social pathologies but also an objective conception of the good grasped as a quality of the social-individual nexus that enables the productive growth or our potentialities.

Fromm and Contemporary Critical Theory

This now brings us back to the question of the dynamics of critique itself. How is a critical strategy to be developed from this thesis of an objective ethics? First of all, on Fromm's account, the emergence of critical consciousness and awareness will always be present because no social system, no matter how powerful or how efficient its means of control and dominance, can assuage the forms of neurotic frustration that emerge from pathological social relations. Social and self pathologies will continue to make themselves evident. But he also argues that we have the theoretical equipment to process and mediate the experience of these pathologies. We have, in other words, the capacity to be able to reflect and analyze our neuroses and trace them back to the relational (i.e., social) context that produced them. Hence, the cause of the neurotic personality not only is a product of defective social relations and forms of socialization, in a descriptive-diagnostic sense but also allows us to follow the pathology that is instantiated in the individual due to the ontological social structures and processes to which it is a response. Fromm's hypothesis here is that an objective ethics is not only a form of intellectual, philosophical mode of critique but a *practical* one as well—it can illuminate for us new ways of acting, relating, and new norms and value-complexes that can facilitate and guide social change.

But this does not address what is perhaps a more pernicious problem: namely, the extent to which the theory is able to provide actual agents with the capacity for judgment as well as the requisite will-formation for advancing critical attitudes. The question, therefore, of the formation of a political subjectivity can be derived from Fromm's theory in the sense that an objective ethics forces us to see the connection between pathological forms and states and the social-organizational context that produces them. Neurosis is the very defect within individuals that continues to make social critique relevant and call into question the objective, ontological ways that our social world is organized.

Since Fromm's thesis places emphasis on the idea that the good is an ontological category, it is therefore not an empty formalism nor can it be articulated via any proceduralist account. It is generally argued that the paradigm shift to communicative and intersubjective models of critique—via discourse ethics, recognition or justification, and so on—is the solution to this problem that remained from the first generation of critical theorists. According to this view, a theory of social action was needed that could bridge the gap between theory and practice and to fulfill Max Horkheimer's thesis that critical theory's distinctiveness concerns the capacity of agents to become critical of their own social reality. Habermas is insistent that our moral ideas possess cognitive content, but this cognitive content is bereft of any kind of substantive, ontological weight. Indeed, the neo-idealism of these approaches that rely on the pragmatics of intersubjective social action sacrifice any substantive content for the development of the good.

One compelling reason for this is that such an approach is not sufficiently *immanent* in terms of critique. For neo-idealists, the immanence of critique emerges from the experience of injustices that require some sense of justification or which contradicts one's sense of integral selfhood through a denial of recognition. But this is really only viable if we assume that the egos involved are not affected by the kinds of neurotic pathologies that Fromm points to and that these neurotic pathologies do not undermine the cognitive and moral-rational capacity for critical judgment—which is a markedly problematic assumption. Fromm's theory, in contrast, provides us with a more immanent form of critical awareness. As the incidence and experience of neuroses become more acute and prevalent within society, it is possible to make these into the substance of political critique and an account of the need for change. The orientation for change, following Fromm's theoretical vantage point, brings us into contact with the social-structural relations that constitute our reality. We are therefore brought to a social-theoretical critique and moral-evaluative critique at once, since Fromm urges us to see that valid (i.e., objective) ethical concepts are rooted in the ontology of social forms.

Fromm's approach provides a theoretical way to think through social and personal pathology as the objective, ontological ways that social relations are constructed. On such an approach, critical consciousness can therefore be short-circuited only when the search for security or primary bonds is assuaged through submersion in alternative identities and communities that in fact take energy away from direct social transformation and instead force the search for primary bonds and existential comfort away from the source generating the pathologies. Hence, newer approaches in the critical theory of ethical life such as Axel Honneth's "theory of recognition" fail to the extent that the mechanism of recognition can be coopted by these escapist forms of group narcissism—forms of group identity that proliferate modern culture. But by holding to an objective theory of ethical value, we can retain a vantage point of critique despite the ways that social and personal pathologies affect the possibility for a change in consciousness. As Fromm puts the matter, "The more crippled a society makes man the sicker he becomes, even though consciously he may be satisfied with his lot. But unconsciously he is dissatisfied, and this very dissatisfaction is the element which inclines him eventually to change the social forms that cripple him."[25] The moment of critical awareness and consciousness here is captured in the neurotic problems that one experiences phenomenologically. The key critical moment, what gives awareness of the ontological primacy of our relations with others and their varying shapes and forms critical power, is therefore contained in our ability to cognize the dialectic between subject and object, between the subjective state of the self and the objective relations and processes that constitute it. Only then can we begin to talk about a critical theory that has transformative potential, that is, a critical theory with political valence.

The problem for contemporary critical theory is therefore twofold. First, Fromm warns us that the nature of defective social relations, specifically those under capitalist-market-consumer society, may indeed manifest in a crippled form of subjectivity, but also that it has the ability to form the kinds of subjectivity that will "take" to the prevailing power relations and orient their own consciousness toward that reality principle. The problem lies in the nature of social character, namely its conformity to highly efficient forms of socialization. As Fromm notes, "A dynamic psychological theory can show that society produces the social character, and that the social character tends to produce and to hold onto ideas and ideologies which fit it and are nourished by it."[26] Herein lies a crucial weakness in the intersubjective and pragmatist reconstruction of critical theory that has taken place since Habermas's turn to communicative action. Since it emphasizes the intersubjective-cognitive dimensions of consciousness, it does not penetrate to the level of social character and instead relegates critique to the procedures of discourse and rational justification. But this has the real danger of merely reproducing many of the social structures of power that already exist, either because agents have been too thoroughly socialized by the predominant norms that regulate the institutions of society and moral cognition or because they have exited from the rational participation with the society as whole.

This leads to the second major problem confronting the project of critical theory in contemporary society. This can be described as the extent to which contemporary culture—especially the deep proliferation of a commodified and technologically mediated form of popular culture—has been able to create forms of identity or cultural practices that render critique inert and provide crippled subjectivities (to borrow Fromm's terminology) with communities of relations that provide ego comfort and protection from the frayed relations of the society at large. The problem here is that, as Fromm tirelessly points out, the crippled ego will search for ways to escape confrontation with the reality principle rather than engage it. It is clear that since the period when Fromm was writing, the increase in this search for identity and the kind of narcissism it creates has only proliferated. Identity politics, ethical nihilism, and group narcissism are all on the rise and they nourish and perpetuate the withered ego that is formed by defective social relations. Group narcissism, Fromm points out, "furthers the solidarity and cohesion of the group and makes manipulation easier by appealing to narcissistic prejudices."[27] This can distort political consciousness by orienting the discussion of politics toward group rights and interests. But it also further serves to weaken the ego by submerging it in primary bonds that buttress the withered ego: "It is extremely important as an element giving satisfaction to the members of the group and particularly to those who have few other reasons to feel proud and worthwhile ... there is compensation for one's miserable condition in feeling 'I am a part of the most wonderful group in the world.'"[28]

Of course, this group narcissism can be either benign or aggressive and destructive, but the point is that the crippled ego will search out those forms of cohesion and primary bonds that will enable it to support and protect itself from the anxiety produced by modern society. Recognition and inclusiveness of misrecognized groups is clearly an important and positive dimension of identity. But it can also serve to submerge the self into a protective sphere of incestuous relations as well. The critical moment is to discern when these identities and their recognition expand and enrich our social-relatedness as a whole and when they serve to fragment those relations and embalm the withered ego. Modern culture evinces a plurality of mechanisms for the protection of the self through masochistic strivings and, increasingly with the rise of nationalism and populism, sadistic strivings as well. The issue of social character therefore is an important issue for any critical theory of society to take seriously since it has effects on consciousness and ego-formation that undermine the rationalist and recognitive layers of self-development that neo-idealist critical theorists assume as basic. In this sense, an objective theory of ethics can not only help us in the judgment of value propositions and their legitimacy but also serve as a means for the development of a critical theory of society that will provide a more concrete form of political agency.

Conclusion

Fromm's ideas can be seen to evince a deep structure that makes his overall critical theory of salience to contemporary social critics. If we are to take away some semblance of hope in an age of neoliberalism, populism, and aggressiveness, it is that these neuroses can be understood as rooted in the defective social forms that have been developing since the advent of industrial society. In this sense, the hope emerges once we grasp that there is no teleological structure to history, that it is imperative for us to enhance the formation of critical-political agency by providing theories of society and self that actually cultivate critical awareness. Fromm's critical theory of society is an essential building block for any such theoretical endeavor. If indeed critical theory is to have any impact on fostering critical consciousness and agency, it will have to depart from the neo-idealist system building characteristic of contemporary academic critical theory and set its sights on the living reality of our social world. It will also need to provide a sense of normative hope in the light of such criticism. Fromm's work does both. And although his ideas are not taken seriously enough by the academic mandarins of our time, one thing is increasingly clear as their ideas become more technical, abstruse, and impotent: we dismiss him at our peril.

Notes

1. Fromm, *The Crisis of Psychoanalysis*, 64.
2. Ibid., 66.
3. Fromm, "The Application of Humanist Psychoanalysis to Marx's Theory," 207.
4. Fromm, *The Crisis of Psychoanalysis*, 66.
5. Fromm explains that Marx, too, has a theory which distinguishes between "constant" and "relative" drives: "His most general and yet very fruitful concept of drives consists in the differentiation between 'constant' or 'fixed' drives, and 'relative' drives. The constant drives 'exist under all circumstances and . . . can be changed by social conditions only as far as form and direction are concerned'; the relative drives 'owe their origin only to a certain type of social organization.'" *The Crisis of Psychoanalysis*, 64.
6. Fromm, *Marx's Concept of Man*, 63; emphasis in original.
7. Fromm, *The Sane Society*, 79.
8. Fromm, *Escape from Freedom*, 141. Also see the rich discussion of this theme by Benjamin, *The Bonds of Love*, 51ff.
9. See Aristotle, *Politics*, book I; emphasis in original.
10. Marx resonates with this classical idea when he writes: "As long as a cleavage exists between the particular and the common interest man's own deed becomes an alien power opposed to him, which enslaves him instead of being controlled by him." Marx, *The German Ideology*, 220.
11. See Fromm, *Escape from Freedom*, 136ff. Also cf. Slater, *The Pursuit of Loneliness*.
12. I have explored this thesis elsewhere in my paper "Rousseau's Post-Liberal Self: *Emile* and the Formation of Republican Citizenship." *The European Legacy* (forthcoming).

The term "expanded autonomy" was first used by Christopher Yeomans in his discussion of Hegel. See his *The Expansion of Autonomy: Hegel's Pluralist Philosophy of Action*.

13 Fromm, *The Art of Loving*, 20–21; emphasis in original. Elsewhere Fromm notes that "love is union with somebody, or something, outside oneself, under the condition of retaining the separateness and integrity of one's own self. It is an experience of sharing, of communion, which permits the full unfolding of one's own inner activity." *The Sane Society*, 31.

14 Fromm, *The Art of Loving*, 26.

15 Fromm, *The Sane Society*, 31. Jessica Benjamin also notes on this issue that "domination and submission result from a breakdown of the necessary tension between self-assertion and mutual recognition that allows self and other to meet as sovereign equals." *The Bonds of Love*, 12.

16 Marx, "Notes on James Mill's *Elements of Political Economy*," 280–81.

17 Marx, *Grundrisse*, 158; emphasis in original. Fromm sees that for Marx, an initial form of alienation, in this sense, is not problematic, but necessary: "Socialism, in Marx's sense, can only come, once man has cut off all primary bonds, when he has become completely alienated and thus is able to reunite himself with men and nature without sacrificing his integrity and individuality." *Beyond the Chains of Illusion*, 61.

18 As Iring Fetscher insightfully remarks, "Marx looked ahead to a co-operative civilization in which each man would take satisfaction in his own accomplishments because they contributed to the gratification of others and would accept the work of others as contributing to his own gratification. Instead of dissolving the mutual relations which corresponded to the idea of the city-state, Marx preferred their universalization, and a radical transformation of their character." "Marx's Concretization of the Concept of Freedom," 239.

19 Fromm, *The Anatomy of Human Destructiveness*, 225.

20 Fromm, *Man for Himself*, 28–29.

21 Ibid., 31; emphasis in original.

22 I have discussed the epistemological dimensions of Fromm's unification of facts and values in my *Domestication of Critical Theory*, 151ff.

23 Fromm, *Man for Himself*, 183.

24 Ibid., 27.

25 Fromm, "The Application of Humanist Psychoanalysis to Marx's Theory," 213.

26 Ibid., 212. Also cf. Fromm's discussion of "authoritarian conscience" in *Man for Himself*: "In the formation of conscience, however, such authorities as the parents, the church, the state, public opinion are either consciously or unconsciously accepted as ethical and moral legislators whose laws and sanctions one adopts, thus internalizing them." 148 and *passim*.

27 Fromm, *The Anatomy of Human Destructiveness*, 230.

28 Ibid.

References

Aristotle. (1964). *Politics*. Oxford Classical Texts. Oxford: Oxford University Press.

Benjamin, Jessica. (1988). *The Bonds of Love: Psychoanalysis, Feminism and the Problem of Domination*. New York: Pantheon.

Fetscher, Iring. (1964). "Marx's Concretization of the Concept of Freedom." In Erich Fromm (ed.), *Socialist Humanism: An International Symposium*, 238–49. New York: Doubleday.
Fromm, Erich. (1941). *Escape from Freedom*. New York: Henry Holt.
Fromm, Erich. (1947). *Man for Himself: An Inquiry into the Psychology of Ethics*. New York: Holt, Rinehart and Winston.
Fromm, Erich. (1955). *The Sane Society*. New York: Rinehart and Co.
Fromm, Erich. (1962a). *The Art of Loving: An Enquiry into the Nature of Love*. New York: Harper and Row.
Fromm, Erich. (1962b). *Beyond the Chains of Illusion: My Encounter with Marx and Freud*. New York: Pocket Books.
Fromm, Erich. (1964a). "The Application of Humanist Psychoanalysis to Marx's Theory." In Erich Fromm (ed.), *Socialist Humanism: An International Symposium*, 207–22. New York: Doubleday.
Fromm, Erich. (1964b). *Marx's Concept of Man*. New York: Frederick Ungar.
Fromm, Erich. (1970). *The Crisis of Psychoanalysis: Essays on Freud, Marx, and Social Psychology*. New York: Henry Holt and Co.
Fromm, Erich. (1973). *The Anatomy of Human Destructiveness*. New York: Henry Holt.
Marx, Karl. (1967). "Notes on James Mill's *Elements of Political Economy*." In Lloyd Easton and Kurt Guddat (eds.), *Writings of the Young Marx on Philosophy and Society*. New York: Anchor Books.
Marx, Karl. (1973). *Grundrisse*. London: Penguin Books.
Marx, Karl. (1998). *The German Ideology*. New York: Prometheus Books.
Slater, Philip. (1970). *The Pursuit of Loneliness*. Boston: Beacon Press.
Thompson, Michael J. (2016). *The Domestication of Critical Theory*. London: Rowman and Littlefield.
Thompson, Michael J. (2020). "Rousseau's Post-Liberal Self: *Emile* and the Formation of Republican Citizenship." *The European Legacy* (forthcoming).
Yeomans, Christopher. (2015). *The Expansion of Autonomy: Hegel's Pluralistic Philosophy of Action*. New York: Oxford University Press.

Chapter 2

JEWISH MESSIANISM AND REVOLUTIONARY UTOPIAS IN CENTRAL EUROPE: ERICH FROMM'S EARLY WRITINGS (1922-30)[1]

Michael Löwy

Central Europe, *Mitteleuropa*, is a geographic entity but above all a cultural entity. The Central European Jewish intellectuals think and write in German, not only in Berlin and Vienna but also in Prague, Budapest, or even Chernowitz. Next to the *Yiddishland*—Poland and Russia, where the Jewish language and culture is Yiddish—there exists a *Deutsch-Jüdischland*: the Jewish-German culture of Central Europe, which still persists in the years that follow the First World War, in spite of the demise of the Austro-Hungarian Empire. From the mid-nineteenth century to the 1930s, there is an extraordinary upsurge of this German-speaking Jewish culture, in all areas of cultural life: Heinrich Heine and Karl Marx, Sigmund Freud and Albert Einstein, Franz Kafka and Stefan Zweig, Georg Lukács and Walter Benjamin are only a few among the best-known figures of this "golden age," comparable only to the Jewish culture in Spain during the Middle Ages.

The social condition of Jewish-German intellectuals in Central Europe is quite different from their counterparts in Western or Eastern Europe. To the West (France, England), the Jewish intellectual is—at least in appearance (see the Dreyfus affair)—integrated in bourgeois society, while in the East (Russia, Poland) he is excluded, and treated as a social pariah. In Mitteleuropa, the situation is an intermediary one: there is a feeling of exclusion; the Jewish intellectual feels himself as a sort of "semi-pariah," in spite of his desperate attempts at assimilation to the dominant (German) culture.

The concept of "pariah intellectual" has mainly been discussed by Hannah Arendt. Her proposition, inspired by the brilliant insights of the French romantic socialist (anarchist) Bernard Lazare, distinguishes the Jewish pariah intellectual, bearer of a critical (Jewish) viewpoint, from the parvenu Jews, which deny their identity and adapt themselves to the social dominant forces.[2] Enzo Traverso discusses, in his remarkable essay on Jews and Germany, these two ideal-typical figures, as defined by H. Arendt: on one side, the lineage of the parvenus—the Jews who have grown rich, utterly conformist, and are craving "respectability," from Bleichröder, Bismarck's banker, and Rothschild to Walter Rathenau, Jewish capitalist and (ephemeral) foreign affairs minister; on the other side, the "hidden tradition" of the pariahs, excluded and persecuted, who rebel against the bourgeois society, such as Heinrich Heine, Franz Kafka, and Rosa Luxemburg. However, unlike Arendt, Traverso defines the rebel pariah by his social consciousness, and not, necessarily, by a strong Jewish self-assertion.³

What are the different sorts of radical Jewish intellectuals in Central Europe? Rather than a classical political typology (anarchists, socialists, communists, Left Zionists, etc.), I propose a different approach, which transcends these political distinctions:

(I) The Enlightened (*Aufklärer*) intellectuals, partisans of Western modernity and of rationalism, unreligious, and believers in progress, whether social democrats, Marxists, or communists: Eduard Bernstein, Paul Singer, Max Adler, Otto Bauer, Paul Levi, Paul Frölich, among many other examples.

(II) The romantics, who share a critical view of the industrial/capitalist *Zivilisation*, responsible for the disenchantment of the world; their protest against bourgeois society is inspired by a nostalgia for some aspects of the premodern past. Among the romantic radicals, the anarchist Gustav Landauer or the Marxists Ernst Bloch and Erich Fromm are among the most influential.

In other words: radical Jewish intellectuals in Mitteleuropa are attracted by the two main poles of German cultural life, which one could define by referring to two famous personae of Thomas Mann's novel *The Magic Mountain* (1922): Settembrini, the liberal, democratic, and republican philanthropist—in part inspired by his own brother, Heinrich Mann—and Naphta, the strange romantic conservative and revolutionary Jewish Jesuit (!), probably inspired by Georg Lukács. Trying to understand why so many Jews supported socialism, Walter Laqueur wrote, in his book on the Weimar Republic:

> They gravitated towards the left because it was the party of reason, progress and freedom, which had helped them to attain equal rights. The right on the other hand, was in varying degrees anti-Semitic because it regarded the Jew as an alien element in the body politic. This attitude had been a basic fact of political life throughout the nineteenth century and it did not change during the first third of the twentieth.⁴

This hypothesis is certainly relevant and it helps us to understand why so many Jews joined social democracy in Germany and even more so in Austria. However, it is not adequate to understand the radicalization of the romantic Jewish generation, who distrusted rationalism, industrial progress, and liberalism, and who will be rather attracted to the anarchist utopia—or to communism—rather than social democracy.

In the specific context of Central European Judaism, a complex network of links, of "elective affinities"—to use a concept (*wahlverwandtschaft*) borrowed from Goethe by Max Weber, in his sociology of religion—will be established between romanticism, Jewish messianism, anti-bourgeois cultural rebellion, and revolutionary (socialist and/or anarchist) utopias. This messianism is not the one of Jewish orthodoxy, but a new, highly political version, seen through the lenses of German romanticism.

One can distinguish two poles in this vast romantic/messianic galaxy of the Central European radical Jewish culture. The first is composed of religious Jews with radical/utopian leanings: Rudolf Kayser, Martin Buber, Gershom Scholem, Hans Kohn, the young Leo Löwenthal. The rejection of assimilation and the assertion of a religious and/or cultural Jewish identity is the dominant aspect of their thought. Most of them were Zionists, but soon left the movement (Hans Kohn, Leo Löwenthal) or remained but were marginalized because of their anti-nationalist stance (Buber, Scholem). And all share, to various degrees, a universal utopian perspective, a sort of libertarian (anarchist) socialism, which they articulate with their messianic religious faith.

The other pole is made up of the assimilated, religious-atheist Jews, with anarchist and/or Marxist sympathies: Gustav Landauer, Ernst Bloch, the young Georg Lukács, Manès Sperber, Walter Benjamin. Unlike the others mentioned above, they distance themselves from Judaism, without breaking all the links, especially with the messianic tradition. The term "religious atheism" used by Lukács in reference to Dostoyevsky is relevant to understand this paradoxical spiritual figure, who seems to search, with the energy of despair, for the point of messianic convergence between the sacred and the profane. Erich Fromm also belongs to this religious/atheistic pole, but with the peculiarity that his first writings are those of a believer strongly committed to traditional orthodox Jewish law.

Some of these romantic/messianic intellectuals received in their youth a religious Jewish education—Fromm, Sperber—but most of them discovered Judaism later in their life. Independently of this individual trajectory, they have in common this strange and contradictory attitude, which combines the rejection of traditional religious beliefs with a passionate interest for the mystical, heretical, and chiliastic Jewish and Christian currents. They share a messianic/revolutionary spirituality, which weaves, in an inextricable way, the threads of religion and those of radical utopias. Sympathetic to the anarchist ideals during the years 1914–23, most will progressively be drawn to Marxism in the following years.

The Case of Erich Fromm

Erich Fromm (1900–80) is well known for his essays on social psychology, most of them written after his exile in the United States at the end of the 1930s. But his lesser-known early works—from 1922 to 1930—are very creative, as well as politically radical, and deserve to be discussed. They have some common aspects: a messianic understanding of Judaism; a Freudian-Marxist rejection of capitalism as a socioeconomic system; and the revolutionary aspiration for a socialist utopia with religious roots. These elements together shaped an original and subversive thought.

After participating, with Martin Buber and Franz Rosenzweig, at the foundation of the Free House for Jewish Studies in Frankfurt, in 1922 the young Fromm—at that time still a believing Jew—presented his doctoral thesis, under the title "The Jewish Law: Contribution to the Sociology of Diaspora Judaïsm," directed by the sociologist Alfred Weber at the University of Heidelberg. Probably for personal reasons—his loss of faith a few years later—the book will not be published during his lifetime; it will appear seventy years later in an edition of his complete works.

In spite of the title, the work does not have much in common with a sociological monography on the diaspora Jewish communities (demography, institutions, family). It belongs rather to the classical school of the German sociology of culture and religion, as practiced by the Weber brothers, Alfred and Max. In other words, at the center of the research are the relations between socioreligious cultures and economic ethics. To these methodological references one has to add other ingredients, less conventional and less academic: the ideas of his master in Talmud, Rabbi Salman Baruch Rabinkow, partisan of a socialist Judaism influenced by the Russian intelligentsia, and of Martin Buber, the romantic socialist who rediscovered Hassidism. The most astonishing aspect of this doctoral thesis is its strong anti-capitalist and anti-bourgeois edge, which seems to belong to the realm of Jewish religious socialism.

The first chapter, "The Significance of Law in Judaïsm," is an attempt at a socioreligious analysis inspired by Alfred Weber's sociology of culture.[5] According to Fromm, the loss of state, language, and territory did not prevent diaspora Judaism from keeping its social and religious identity. By destroying Judea, the Romans only dealt with a shell (*Gehäuse*), without importance for the Jewish historical body. There is probably a sort of anarchist tendency in this negative attitude toward the state. In Fromm's understanding, Jewish religion, which assured the continuity of the Jewish people in the diaspora, was not a theological system, a body of dogmas, but a collection of laws and rules, the *Halacha*, which did not manifest itself so much in the Kingdom of Ideas, but rather in "value-rational actions" (*wertrationalen Handeln*) (Max Weber).[6]

This first chapter includes an interesting section called "Labor and Vocation (*Beruf*) in Rabbinical Judaism," directly inspired by Max Weber. Fromm tries to demonstrate that, unlike Protestant ethics, the Jewish ones are not favorable to the spirit of capitalism. Jewish economic ethics are, in Weber's terminology, "traditionalist": knowledge, not labor, is the supreme value; not by accident, in the biblical narrative on the expulsion from Paradise, is work presented as a malediction. Alternating biblical, Talmudic and, Weberian quotations, Fromm argues that "in direct contradiction to the Puritan conceptions," Jewish ethics do not at all consider the acquisition of wealth as a duty toward God; they represent, therefore, "a *non-capitalist* attitude towards the economy." For sure, one can find, in modern times, Jewish capitalists, but, as Weber has shown, this is a "pariah capitalism," speculative, political, and adventurous, in contrast to the Puritan ethos of the rational bourgeois enterprise, with its rational organization of labor.[7]

Fromm rejects—again, referring himself to Max Weber—Werner Sombart's attempt to present the Jews as the first modern capitalists, and his definition of

Judaism as a purely rationalist religion: the ethic line that goes from the biblical prophets until Hassidism, passing by the Mishna and the Kabbala, is anything but rationalist. The nineteenth-century German rabbis quoted by Sombart in support of his thesis do not represent the authentic Jewish religion—which remained alive among the Jewish masses of Eastern Europe—but rather the modern "capitalist culture."[8]

The chapter called "Reform Judaïsm" is precisely a critique of the currents that attempted to re-elaborate the tradition, from Moses Mendelssohn, at the end of the eighteenth century, to the Reform Judaism of the nineteenth century. The reformers—which include for Fromm not only Abraham Geiger, founder of the enlightened Wissenschaft des Judentums but even Raphael Samson Hirsch, the initiator of a would-be neoorthodox movement—tried to adapt Judaism to the requirements of the new times, and to the needs of the German bourgeois society: they wanted to reconcile the ethics of Judaism with the spirit of capitalism, at the price of sacrificing the laws and moral principles of historical Judaism. Reform Judaism, adopted by the capitalist/bourgeois social layers, led, therefore, to the dissolution of the Jewish "popular body" (*Volkskörper*), rendering the Jewish law, the unifying element of this body, useless and superfluous.[9] Obviously, this violent attack on Reform and liberal Judaism went against the grain of the dominant Jewish opinion in Germany.

The last chapter of the book is devoted to Hassidism, the mystical popular movement founded in Poland by Rabbi Isaac Ben Eliezer (1700–60), the Baal Shem Tov (in Hebrew: "Master of the Good Name"), which Fromm defines as a "social-religious movement of self emancipation," radically opposed to the bourgeois/capitalist spirit. By its radical democratism, its mysticism of community, it represents a "social-religious revolutionary principle." Finally, by its joyous and anti-ascetic spirit, its practice of fraternity and mutual help, and by its traditionalist economic frame of mind (*Gesinnung*), Hassidism develops an "entirely anti-capitalist attitude."[10]

The orthodox rabbinical circles, who refused to join Hassidism—known as the Mitnagdim (in Hebrew: "the Opponents")—had, in contrast, ascetical practices, which are reminiscent of those of the Protestant Puritan sects described by Max Weber. This explains, concludes Fromm, why German Judaism, hostile to Hassidism, could so easily be won by the spirit of capitalism.

After discussing, also, Karaism—an "heretical" Jewish current founded by Anan Ben David in the eighth century, which developed mainly in the Muslim world—Fromm compares the historical significances of the two great socioreligious movements of modern Judaism: Hassidism, which refused any change in the religious tradition aiming to satisfy economic requirements, and Reform, which led to the triumph of the spirit of capitalism over the spirit of Judaism.

What is striking in this essay—obviously written by a believing Jew, attached to the spirit and the letter of the law—is not only the strongly idealized vision of Hassidism, and the equally one-sided demonization of Reform Judaism but above all the emphasis on the opposition between the Jewish tradition and capitalism, with frequent references to Max Weber's writings. Erich Fromm belongs, like

Buber and others, to the religious romantic anti-capitalist—not Marxist—current, well represented among the Central European Jewish intelligentsia. More specifically, he belongs, like Walter Benjamin, Ernst Bloch, and others, to a group that developed "anti-capitalist interpretations" of Max Weber, quite opposed to the noncommitted—"free of value judgements" (*Werfrei*)—attitude of the author of *The Protestant Ethic and the Spirit of Capitalism*.[11]

In 1924, Erich Fromm settled in Heidelberg where he was psychoanalyzed by Frieda Reichmann, an orthodox Freudian with whom he fell in love and married in 1926. It was probably the impact of his analysis that made him lose his religious faith—even if his thinking remained always deeply tinged with religiosity. Freud and later Marx became the guiding lights of his work. In 1926, Gershom Scholem, his former teacher at the Free Institute of Jewish Studies, met him in Berlin and was astonished by the fact that his "Zohar pupil" had become "an enthusiastic Trotskyite."[12] This is a curious assertion, not documented in Fromm's writings from these years or in other witness accounts.[13] We shall return to this question later.

In 1927, Fromm published his first psychoanalytical work in the journal *Imago*, edited by Sigmund Freud. The article "Der Shabbath" is quite an astonishing piece with a powerful messianic impetus, in spite of the scientific language. According to Fromm, the interdiction of work during the Jewish Sabbath means a suspension of man's violation of Mother Earth. By strictly and harshly prohibiting any form of labor during the Sabbath, Jewish religion sought the reestablishment (*Wiederherstellung*) of the paradisiacal state without work: the harmony between man and nature. According to Fromm,

> The prophets regarded messianic time as a condition in which the struggle between man and nature would reach an end. . . . If man was expelled from Paradise because he wanted to be like God—that is, the father's equal, capable of conquering the mother—and if work was punishment for that primal breach (*Urverbrechen*), then, according to the prophets, in the messianic period human beings would live once more in complete harmony with nature, in other words, without having to work, in Paradise—the equivalent of the mother's womb.[14]

Once more, Jewish religion is being opposed to the Protestant ethic of labor, as in his doctoral thesis, but this time with a specific Freudian argument, and a messianic/utopian horizon.

During the 1920s, Fromm becomes increasingly interested in Marxism; he meets Freudian-Marxists such as Wilhelm Reich and Siegfried Bernfeld, and he establishes close links with the Marxists of the Frankfurt School, such as Leo Löwenthal and Max Horkheimer. In 1930, he is appointed by Max Horkheimer—the head of the Institute for Social Research (the Frankfurt School)—director of the Social Psychology section of the Institute. Fromm's attempt to combine Marxism and Freudism lies at the heart of his works in the following years. His first major work in this field—first published as a large essay in Freud's journal *Imago*—was the book *The Dogma of Christ* (1931): this new interest in the Gospels is not at

2. Jewish Messianism and Revolutionary Utopias in Central Europe

variance with his previous Jewish concerns, since he considers early Christianity as the direct successor of Jewish messianism struggling against the Roman Empire.

One cannot understand Christianity, argues Fromm, without taking into account the socio-historical conditions of its appearance. In order to give a brief overview of the economic, social, cultural, and psychical situation of the first Christians, he will borrow from Eduard Meyer's book on ancient slavery; from Max Weber's essay on the social foundations of the decline of ancient civilizations; and from Karl Kautsky's book on the origins of Christianity. How could one define sociologically the social layers attracted by the first Christian groups? Fromm speaks of the subaltern and oppressed classes, of the uneducated poor peasants, the illiterate masses—those that were designated by the Hebrew scornful term *Am Ha'aretz* (the people of the land)—the Jerusalem proletariat. However, while using the Marxist method, he nevertheless dissociates himself, in a long footnote, from Karl Kautsky's analysis—in *The Origins of Christianity* (1896)—which he considers flawed by his reduction of the motivations of the religious actors exclusively to economic and social reasons, as well as by his "contempt for the historical importance of religious ideas."

Kautsky's interpretation of historical materialism is so superficial that it was easy for academic sociologists such as Ernst Troeltsch to refute him. What neither of the two sides in this polemic understood is that class relations did not find expression only in the economic and social program of the first Christians, but precisely in their religious ideas, in what Kautsky calls, in a contemptuous way, their "pious sweet daydreaming" (*frommen Schwärmerei*). While rejecting Kautsky's narrow approach, Fromm nevertheless defends, against academic social science (Troeltsch), the Marxist sociology—the class analysis: "The real issue was missed by Kautsky, but the class origin of primitive Christianity is so obvious that the tortuous attempts which have been made to deny it—such as Troeltsch in his book on the Social Teachings of the Christian Churches—betray in a very visible way the political tendency of the authors defending this thesis."[15]

In Fromm's view, Christianity was originally "a messianic revolutionary movement," bearing the message of eschatological expectation, the imminence of the Kingdom of God. The early Christian community was "a free brotherhood of the poor," intensely hostile to all authority or "paternal" power. The original Christian myth depicted Christ as the suffering Messiah, who was elevated to the dignity of God; it bore a concealed hostility to God the Father, the emperor and authority in general. Christianity was the expression of the revolutionary tendencies, the expectations and longings of the oppressed masses—first Jewish and then gentile—who grouped together in a "community organization without authorities, statuses or bureaucracy," based on economic mutual help, and "love communism," a concept proposed by Adolf von Harnack and adopted by Max Weber.[16]

From the third century onwards, however, the social foundations of Christianity were transformed, when it became the religion of the upper classes of the Roman Empire. Beliefs about Christ were then deeply modified: man elevated to the dignity of God became the Son of Man who had always been God (dogma of consubstantiation). At the same time, the eschatological hope for real historical deliverance was gradually replaced by the idea that salvation would be an internal, spiritual, nonhistorical, and individual liberation. Finally, in close association with this disavowal of messianism, a growing reconciliation took place between the church and the state. In other words, "Christianity, which had been the religion of a community of equal brothers, without hierarchy or bureaucracy, became 'the Church,' the reflected image of the absolute monarchy of the Roman Empire." Together with this transformation of a free confraternity into an authoritarian, hierarchical organization, there was also a psychic change: hostility toward the father, and the early Christian contempt for the rich and the powerful, for all authority, was replaced by reverence and subordination to the new clerical authorities. Aggressive impulses, originally directed against the father, were then turned against the self in a manner that posed no danger for social stability; they thereby induced a general feeling of guilt—along with a masochistic need for atonement.[17]

Fromm is also interested in the theological confrontations until the Council of Nicaea (AD 325): he perceived in Montanism and Arianism tendencies of hostility to the authority of God the Father; in his viewpoint, they were the true inheritors of primitive Christianity, which would explain their persecution by the official church, which branded them as "heretics." The Gnostics, instead, were intellectual representatives of the prosperous middle classes of the Hellenistic period who favored the suppression of the eschatological dimension of Christianity.[18]

The Dogma of Christ owes much to Theodor Reik's essay "Dogma and Compulsion" (1927), which had already suggested the interpretation of the primitive Christian faith as the expression of hostility to the Father. The difference between the two works is precisely the socio-historical dimension. According to Fromm, Reik's mistake was to neglect the diversity of social and psychical interests of social groups. The different dogmas are the expression of social conflicts, and the triumph of a dogma against others is not the result of a purely internal psychic conflict like in an individual, but of historical developments that lead to the victory of one side and the defeat of the other.[19]

The Dogma of Christ was hailed by Franz Borkenau in the *Zeitschrift für Sozialforschung*—the *Journal of the Institute for Social Research*—as the first concrete example of a synthesis between Freud and Marx.[20] What is striking about his interpretation of Marxism and Freudianism is its strong anti-authoritarian, anti-bureaucratic revolutionary orientation. The book is both a scholarly research of church history and theological theory and a powerful political statement. Could it be that his presentation of the history of early Christianity as the transformation of a free confraternity into an authoritarian, hierarchical organization is an implicit reference to the disappointing evolution of the Soviet Union under Joseph Stalin, during the 1920s? The frequent use of the term "bureaucratic" seems to hint at such an historical parallel; could it be that, after all, Scholem's memories of a "Trotskyite" Fromm had some foundation? The question remains open, but it is clear that Fromm's own political views in 1930 are an important background for his study of early Christian dogmas.

Notes

1. First appeared *European Judaism* 50, no. 1 (Spring 2017): 21–31.
2. Arendt, *The Jew as Pariah*.
3. Traverso, *Les Juifs et l'Allemagne*.
4. Laqueur, *Weimar, A Cultural History, 1918–1933*, 73.
5. Fromm refers to Alfred Weber's article "Prinzipielles zur Kultursoziologie," published in 1921 in his brother's Journal, *Archiv für Sozialwissenschaft und Sozialpolitik*.
6. Fromm, *Das jüdische Gesetz*, 16–21.
7. Ibid., 41–54.
8. Ibid.
9. Ibid., 121–23, 155.
10. Ibid., 161–84.
11. It is interesting that neither Marx nor any Marxist authors are mentioned in Fromm's thesis, not even in the bibliography.
12. Scholem, *From Berlin to Jerusalem: Memories of My Youth*, 156.
13. It is only much later, in 1958, that Fromm will write a piece on Trotsky: a (not published at the time) review of his *Diary in Exile*. The review is highly sympathetic to Trotsky and his writings, characterized by "objectivity and courage and humility." (Fromm's "Trotsky's Diary in Exile—1935" was preceded by an essay by Anderson, "A Recently Discovered Article by Erich Fromm on Trotsky and the Russian Revolution," 272.) However, it is difficult to deduce from this piece of 1958 which were Fromm's ideas in 1926.
14. Fromm, "Der Sabbath," 226, 228, 233.
15. Fromm, *Das Christus-Dogma und andere Essays*, 192–93.
16. Fromm, *The Dogma of Christ and Other Essays on Religion, Psychology and Culture*, 35–49.
17. Ibid., 56–65.
18. Ibid., 71–79.
19. Ibid., 85.
20. Ibid.

References

Anderson, Kevin. (2002). "A Recently Discovered Article by Erich Fromm on Trotsky and the Russian Revolution." *Science and Society* 66, no. 2, Summer: 266–73.

Arendt, Hannah. (1978). *The Jew as Pariah: Jewish Identity and Politics in the Modern Age*. New York: Grove Press.

Fromm, Erich. (1927). "Der Sabbath." *Imago*, XIII: 235–46.

Fromm, Erich. (1963). *The Dogma of Christ and Other Essays on Religion, Psychology and Culture*. New York: Holt, Rinehart and Winston.

Fromm, Erich. (1965). *Das Christus-Dogma und andere Essays*. Munich: Szczesny.

Fromm, Erich. (1989). *Das jüdische Gesetz: Zur Soziologie des Diaspora-Judentums*. Basel: Heyne.

Fromm, Erich. (2002 [1958]). "Trotsky's Diary in Exile—1935." *Science & Society* 66, no. 2 (Summer): 271–73.

Laqueur, Walter. (1974). *Weimar, A Cultural History, 1918–1933*. New York: Transcation Publishers.

Scholem, Gershom. (1980). *From Berlin to Jerusalem: Memories of My Youth*, translated by H. Zohn. New York: Schocken Paperbacks.

Traverso, Enzo. (1993). *Les Juifs et l'Allemagne: De la 'symbiose judéo-allemande' à la mémoire d'Auschwitz*. Paris: La Découverte.

Chapter 3

THE NECESSITY OF PROPHETIC HUMANISM IN PROGRESSIVE SOCIAL CHANGE

George Lundskow

This chapter calls for a new religion to play a social-psychological role in progressive social change to challenge the dominance of reactionary religion in the United States, and also to inspire movements toward a progressive future. Recently, Lauren Langman and I[1] argued that Donald Trump represents a reassertion of white male ethnonationalism, a direct extension of Erich Fromm's assertion from forty-two years ago that the true religion of the United States early on morphed from Christianity into what Fromm similarly understood as religious nationalism.[2] To counter this, I propose a prophetic humanism, a culture that views the present critically in order to envision (prophesy) the future using spirituality, science, and other ways of knowing in order to elevate human existence beyond violent acquisition and domination and toward an ongoing spirit of enlightenment and mutual benefit as moral imperatives.

Extensive empirical research since the 2016 US presidential election shows that misogyny[3,4] and racism[5,6,7,8] most strongly predict support for Trump, especially violent attitudes toward Blacks and Hispanic immigrants[9,10] and racism and sexism combined.[11] Empirical research also reveals that anti-Islamic attitudes as central to "true" American values, also predicts strong support for Trump[12] as well as authoritarianism—of which racism and misogyny are particular aspects.[13] In other words, empirical research supports my interpretation that the dominant religion has been and is still for the moment white male ethnonationalism. Despite its apparently secular components, I update Fromm's concept of American religious patriotism to include a racial and gender component, to argue that the white male nation is the dominant and oppressive God of the United States, and that whether emancipatory or oppressive, all societies require religious faith for human fulfillment. Progressive forces need to discover a counter faith, and it cannot be just a comforting personal faith or a couple of hours on weekends, but an active faith that worships humanism and inclusion, and challenges oppression.

For Fromm, collective human endeavor shapes both a material world and a transcendent spiritual world, which in turn shape the individual human experience. Natural reality places physical requirements on the human body, but ever since we became self-aware, we needed to construct a social reality to fulfill our intellectual and emotional needs. In order to unify our biological and social existence, we must develop a spiritual life as well, so as to envision and legitimize a meaningful moral system to guide our actions. This spiritual life takes two basic forms, a xenophobic idolatry and a universalist emancipation,[14] that each inspires and legitimates two different types of social character that each connects the individual to the world around them with different moral codes of behavior. Fromm regards the universalist type as mentally healthy, and the xenophobic type as fundamentally unhealthy and antisocial. Universalism breaks down exclusionary identities and empowers people through collective reinforcement and broad social progress rather than through personal gain and domination. Universalism reinforces a cooperative and compassionate social character while xenophobia reinforces a competitive and hostile character. In this chapter, I argue that progressive change will only happen if any associated movements articulate and practice an inspirational spirituality that elevates progressive moral imperatives above mundane concerns. To sustain a living experience that challenges power, a progressive movement requires a morality that obligates people to risk their own well-being for a greater good in which they also envision themselves, and to unite within a transcendent faith that inspires individual commitment to and through collective good.

Our particular moral faith depends on the object of worship. Do we worship power, wealth, and status embodied in a judgmental and punitive god? Do we worship peace and love embodied in a forgiving and empowering god? In *To Have or to Be?* and elsewhere, Fromm argues that human evolution replaced instincts with self-awareness, reason, and creativity, and so all humans inherently require "a frame of orientation and an object of devotion in order to survive."[15] No society or individual has ever existed without an object of devotion or frame of reference which together constitute a worldview, and even the most cynical or the most exuberant free spirits have a goal (object of devotion) and guidelines (frame of reference) on how to get there. Whether the individual consciously avows such commitments, and whether they freely accept them or must submit through force, a worldview nevertheless inhabits all people. A love of god, nature, spontaneous expression, the nation, money, power, violence, community, commodity fetishism—people can devote their thoughts and emotions to nearly anything, and once devoted, the object determines behavior appropriate to turning faith in that object into worldly reality. Fromm focused on the god of the Jewish and Christian religions as the dominant object, and institutionalized Christianity as the dominant moral frame of reference in the West, although he also lauded the spiritual leadership of Muhammad, Nanak, Confucius, Jesus, and others—and often separated the life and teachings of these people from the institutionalized religions that followed.[16]

Prophetic Social Character

In *You Shall Be as Gods*, Fromm argues that Judeo-Christian religion initially steered Western civilization away from the oppressive hierarchy and elitist clan lineage of Greco-Roman paganism, but later itself fell to the service of empire and consequently imposed its own oppressive moral codes. Infused with the lust for power and wealth, Christianity transformed from its universalist origins into a dogma of domination and conquest, and thus abandoned the genius of the prophetic tradition of the loving god that consistently challenged domination, and instead elevated a judgmental and unforgiving god who punished dissent as immorality in order to defend wealth and power. Fromm argues that opposition to power and domination is the one and only prophetic message that "the prophets spoke in the name of the God of justice and love, and they foretold the downfall of the state and of priestly power. They did not compromise with expediency, nor hide their attack behind courteous words."[17] The prophets constituted a living revolution, the ideals of universal humanism in living example and practice, which explains why the priests and kings persecuted and often executed them in the most horrible ways. Far more than critics of power, the prophets fundamentally condemned devotion to power and wealth in general, and evoked instead devotion to universal humanity as both a moral and practical requirement for peace and prosperity without resort to force. While conventional Marxists and others see history as class struggle or in other ways a struggle for material dominance, Fromm also sees a related spiritual struggle to condemn wealth and thus escape the morbid systems of acquisition and hoarding that deify luxuries and privilege. The prophets did not seek to replace one ideology with another, but rather to subvert all ideologies with a critical orientation, so that questions rather than answers become the essence of the new faith: What should we do, and how should we live? The prophetic vision "rested upon the tension between what existed and was still there, and what was becoming and yet to be," and crucially, "this world to come is not a world within history but an ideal world above that will fulfill history."[18] In this view, no God dictates how to live nor descends from the heavens and remakes existence; instead, grassroots humans ascend to godhood through an exemplary life to inspire others. For the first 150 years or so, early Christians embraced the radical Jesus who, as a common person, embodied service to the common good and rejected the authority of priests and the state. Most importantly, Fromm argues, the oppressed Jews could only embrace a messiah who rose from the bottom of society, and this early vision of the messiah could only appeal to the oppressed because faith only carries meaning for the oppressed when they see themselves in the divine.[19] The revolutionary Jesus challenged both a corrupt priesthood within Judaism and imperial Roman occupation, direct action that reinforced a revolutionary social character and which eventually led to an open revolt (which the Romans crushed in 70 CE). Whether a person participates in dramatic revolutionary upheaval misses the point, but rather that the revolution occurs in every action, that we challenge all the smaller injustices, exorcise the demons of domination in everyday routines, as well as confront the hierarchies of power. Whatever the form of revolutionary practice, it must contribute to the larger vision and common good. This "vision of becoming" distinguishes mere rebellion from revolution, because a person can rebel against convention and authority for any number of reasons but usually for personal satisfaction or gain.[20]

In contrast to rebellion, Fromm calls for a revolutionary social character that consists, first, of commitment to humanity and that transcends the "parochial worship of the culture" in which people were born, which is nothing more than a happenstance of time and place. Second, the revolutionary character cultivates a deep love for life, and third, they "think and feel in a critical mood"[21] at all times. This type of person transcends the doctrines and platitudes of nations, of religious demagoguery, actively engages with the real world, and critically evaluates claims to truth and claims to power.[22] The revolutionary character can thus exist in all areas of human endeavor, including politics, but no less importantly in art, science, and religion. Most people in most areas of life are not revolutionary but overwhelmingly conformist, with some admixtures of authoritarianism and some destructiveness.[23,24] For the multitudes to transcend the pathologies of social-psychological dysfunction, to become revolutionaries, and simultaneously to reclaim a democratic society, Fromm believes that humans must socially and collectively both create the "horizontal" utopia that materially unmakes the sociohistorical lineage of class power and wealth and simultaneously achieve the "vertical" salvation that spiritually transcends the desire for power and wealth as compensation for emotional and intellectual vacancy. The so-called end of history will not be a climactic moment and ever after a celebration of perfection but, rather, an ongoing reinvigoration of peace and love that relies on collective affirmation of responsibility, and not simply on an individual sense of triumph over personal imperfections (sins) which cannot happen anyway without a social morality that exalts the ideal of goodness and also shows the way. For Fromm, sin is not an offense against god but, rather, the will directed toward action that violates the collective good of which the individual is a part. The personal response to sin should be a return to the collective good rather than acts of contrition or submission to authoritative punishment[25] that separates people from each other as good and bad. This "return" to the collective good means to once again actively improve the lives of others, and so sin is not a matter of offense and punishment, but rather recognition of error and a corresponding effort to improve the collective good. People may envision the divine in diverse ways (a singular God, a pantheon, spirits of our ancestors, reason, nature, the universe, and many other ways) but always as a living practice of the collective good that preserves the sanctity of the individual. In this way, Fromm argues that a progressive spirituality does not accumulate knowledge about god but, rather, seeks to imitate god's inspiration and universal love of each individual (and life in general) as part of the collective good. Of course, if a society envisions a domineering, judgmental, and unforgiving god, then the way of life becomes one of aggression and ruthless gain as moral imperatives. As individuals, we face a basic choice between a faith in life and a faith in death—faith in love and joy of living that derives from collective experience, or faith in lifeless objects and power that derives from control and destruction. Again, we should ask questions: Do we cherish the decrepit death-culture of inanimate objects and systems of control, which Charles Thorpe brilliantly elucidates in *Necroculture*[26] ("necrophilia," in Fromm's typology), or the hearty and exuberant ("biophilic") culture of shared experience as equals?

The artist and socialite Andy Warhol once said that the worst person to invite to a party is someone who first asks: Who else is going to be there? Warhol had a point: such people have nothing to say and nothing to contribute, or they seek only personal gain—"face time" with the right people, business connections, and so on—what's in it for me? They are dead; they do not create; they consume somebody else's interesting conversation and talent. For those engaged in life, the greatest satisfaction derives from curiosity, learning, knowing, and doing. They do not seek thrills or material gain; they seek adventure through discovery, through meaningful moments that make them feel closer to others, closer to nature, closer to the divine. They do not submit to religious or scientific ideologies; they embrace a critical orientation, complexity, and paradox, and solve problems. The more their work helps other people, the more gratification they feel. In short, this is the productive (or biophilic) character that Fromm cherished as "sensitivity to the realms of thinking and feeling, to give soul to one's surroundings"[27] and to evoke productive qualities in others. This social character of mutual affirmation creates a union among authentic selves and thus counters all forms of alienation, and in turn resolves the contradictions between the roles that people must play as social actors and the types of experiences that bring fulfillment. In short, we must achieve what I call productive transcendence.

The Progressive Left and Social Change

One reason the left has struggled in the United States is that it has no animating vision working toward a productive transcendence. It has no object of devotion (ideological thinking maybe), no transcendent purpose and thus nothing to inspire action of any type except, at best, esoteric intellectual discussions; carnivalized festivals of loud music, public drunkenness, and sexuality; and angry spectacles against Trump; guns; and many other social problems. Capitalism readily sells pleasures and rebellion in contained spaces and thus easily negates the spirit of revolution. Personally, I like the loud music and the class-conflict lyrics of Lemmy Kilmister (RIP) and Motörhead, but the music alone will not change society. Before and after the show, most people find employment satisfactory. Pay and benefits could always be better, but some kind of job is better than no job at all, and for most people, capital provides enough compensation in the form of consumer goods and diversionary entertainment (I like NCAA basketball and NFL football) to stave off any consistent revolutionary spirit.

Although the United States is descended predominately from European culture, Europe is not a model for the United States. The left has significantly more influence in European politics, but this derives mostly from institutionalization achieved during the rebuilding process after the devastation of the Second World War. Only such a cataclysm could force European capital and its entrenched premodern traditions to incorporate some degree of leftist politics, but much of this arose from practical concerns, namely, the immense costs of rebuilding and the inherent concerns about public welfare in devastated countries, especially

Germany. Let us remember that even before the Second World War, Bismarck instituted national healthcare, not as a progressive initiative but as a means to generate a central national identity in order to make Germany an imperial power. The driving motivation was efficiency and the quest for global power, not humanist concerns about decency or the quality of life.

Practicality is essential to a progressive future, but by itself, inadequate. The first question is this: What *can* we do? After that we must ask: What *should* we do? That answer decides our path, and that answer depends on religion. Everyone has some object of devotion, according to Fromm, something that motivates them and directs them to live a certain way and pursue certain means and objectives rather than others:

> Religion is any group-shared system of thought and action that offers the individual a frame of orientation and an object of devotion. . . . In this broad sense, it seems that no culture of the past or present, or indeed of the future, can exist without religion. . . . People may worship animals, trees, idols of gold or stone, an invisible god, a saintly person, or a diabolical leader; they may worship their ancestors, their nation, their class or party, money or fame . . . so the question is not whether one has religion or not, but what kind of religion.[28]

Without a progressive spirituality, the left has offered only political and economic critiques, often limited to some notion of a more equitable distribution of wealth. This has produced some important reforms, but without an animating transcendent vision, socialism and the left rarely inspire the emotions necessary to sustain mass movements and more extensive social change. For socialism to succeed, it must overcome its attempts to be the first society ever to exclude religion. Even atheists worship something, and logic or rationality will not supplant the gods of commodities and capital, nor white male ethnonationalism.

The Gods of White Male Ethnonationalism

On their own version of a global Mount Olympus live the idle mega-rich, lords lavishly separated from the minions they rule. As Chris Hedges discovered through personal experience,

> the rich are different, because when you have that much money, then human beings become disposable. Even friends and family become disposable and are replaced. And when the rich take absolute power, then the citizens become disposable, which is in essence what's happened. There is a very callous indifference. . . . I mean, these people—and C. Wright Mills wrote about this in "The Power Elite"—they're utterly cut off. I mean, the only people they ever meet who are members of the working class are people who work for them—their gardeners or their chauffeurs. They live in self-encased bubbles. They have no

real contact with reality. I mean, they don't even fly on commercial airlines. And yet they have absolute power.²⁹

Heartless and ruthless, economic elites lobby legislators and provide support through PACs—billionaire and corporate sugar daddies who want and need conservative legislators in order to minimize regulations on production and transportation, maintain low wages, cut healthcare benefits, and protect unlimited pollution rights in order to maximize profits, but also to disinvest in education, cut food benefits, and enact draconian mass incarceration to punish the poor and to excite the white ethnonationalist population that embraced, for example, Brett Kavanaugh's angry self-defense that persuaded senators to elevate his misogyny and vows of revenge against liberals to the Supreme Court. Similarly, voters rewarded Donald Trump with sufficient electoral votes, although not the popular vote, to take his racism and misogyny to the presidency, such that conservative evangelicals above all support Trump more strongly two years into his first term to a new high of 71 percent for conservative evangelical women and 81 percent for men.³⁰ On the surface, it seems incongruous that morally repressive evangelicals would support Blackout drunks like Kavanaugh and fast-food gluttons like Trump who both bragged openly about their predatory sexual assaults. However, conservative religious morality parallels a social-psychological justification for domination in general, such as misogyny and racism. Conservative evangelicals love Trump because he puts women and ethnic minorities in their place. They embrace a domineering and punitive god and neglect the loving and forgiving god who gradually frees his people by teaching the righteousness of inclusion and forgiveness. See, for example, 1 Tim. 6:6-10 and Mt. 5:38-48.

Punitive righteousness may feel good, but it doesn't pay the bills. A great deal of contemporary malaise stems from the policies of the ruling classes which vastly increase their incomes and wealth, but these same policies foster ever greater hardships for the majority. For the multitude, the dream of the modern age has been that ever more production, an ever-growing economy is the one sure way of improving the material quality of life. As the saying goes, a rising tide allegedly lifts all ships (unless many of the ships are stuck in the mud). So, the material promise can only succeed if actual prosperity reaches broad segments of the population, and today it reaches ever fewer segments and thus loses the practical ability to meet needs and wants and therefore the entire system loses legitimacy. Yet even before the alleged golden age of American prosperity in the 1950s and 1960s, before the massive debt of today,³¹ at the advent of modern expansion in the late nineteenth and early twentieth centuries, Emile Durkheim argued that modern capitalism offers its own very tangible deities of purely social creation. They do not exist in nature (or in the heavens). Although some people have more than others, the pursuit of the blessings of white male ethnonationalism—money, status, thrills, and power—is available to everyone. These riches are inherently unlimited; there is always more money, fame, thrills, and power to accumulate. Only society can set a limit on such socially created desires, which it has done historically through religion. Unfortunately, religion has used the force of ideology, law, and arms to establish and maintain boundaries and limits, especially on the lower classes. This is alienated religion, and not the type I am talking about.

Prophetic Revolution

Instead, we need meaningful and legitimate limits on desires, not just formal limits. We must believe that limits are good and just, not just laws that forbid something. Institutions can force limits on people, but no institution or person can force meaningful limits. People must find satisfaction and fulfillment, not just locate barriers. They must accept limits willingly because they believe it is the right thing to do, and the requirements and restrictions on behavior should be whether action or inaction harms other people, harms society, or harms the natural world.

We have no such meaningful expectations or limits today, at least none that we all accept. The special problem in modern society is unlimited desire. In contemporary capitalist society, more is always better. Bigger—better—faster—more. However, "unlimited desires are insatiable by definition, and insatiability is rightly considered a sign of morbidity. Being unlimited... they cannot be quenched. Inextinguishable thirst is constantly renewed torture."[32] We find ourselves in a state of perpetual unhappiness, and "a thirst arises for novelties, unfamiliar pleasures, nameless sensations, all of which lose their savor once known."[33] We want it all, and we want it now. The more we want, the more we seek. The more we get, the less satisfaction we find. This vicious circle produces feelings of desperation, despair, and self-destruction, and yet, we accept no limits. Instead, we sanctify unlimited desires, "and by sanctifying them this apotheosis of well-being has placed them above all human law. Their restraint seems like a sort of sacrilege."[34] We worship money, fame, thrills, and power without limit. We celebrate them with every thought, every breath, every effort to accumulate them, possess them, and gain ever more of them, any way we can and admire those who have amassed the most. Regulation of any kind becomes a kind of sacrilege, the demented ravings of a jealous lunatic. Whether for status or power, or capital accumulation or anything else, all the things I feel that I need are socially created, and so our needs are both highly subjective yet correlate to social impositions. Do I need a muscle car that puts out 535 horsepower with a few aftermarket mods? No. Is it fun to drive? Yes. Does that 392 CI (6.4 liter) hemi motor sound cool? Absolutely. Does it blow the doors off almost everything else on the road? Yes, it does. Maybe I appreciate the human art and science that developed and produced this very complex machine at a price I can afford, with massive power, cool looks, and even decent gas mileage, all together a celebration of human ingenuity and imagination in material form—an American experience of freedom and autonomy. Maybe all of the above.

Continuing with the theme of the absence of limits: Do I need to eat at foodie restaurants? Wouldn't boiled turnips, soybeans, and a salad with no dressing meet nutritional requirements? I could be a raw-food vegan, but do we really want to live like Puritans? We have attempted to extend a higher material quality of life to more people by endlessly increasing production, and in the process, we assumed that ever increasing quantity and sometimes quality of consumption is adequate for a full life. In the past, population increases generally coincided with increases in production, the massive industrial armies cranking out ever more of everything. Standardization, mechanization, and automation have greatly enhanced the productive capacity of human labor, such that in the automotive industry, for example, one worker today can do the work of about 500 workers in 1960, and this technological displacement accounts for 88 percent of jobs lost since 1990, with only about 8 percent to outsourcing and 4 percent to consolidation.[35] As technology phases out workers, they are supposed to find jobs somewhere else. What happens when all sectors of the economy phase out workers? The economy as a system of labor exploitation and private accumulation doesn't need as many workers, nor as many consumers. For example, as fewer people can afford new cars, the auto industry can make profit from lower volume, higher-priced premium cars and phase out the entry-level vehicles.[36] Here again we see an inherent limit in capitalism: as wealth concentrates at higher levels, the precariat and the unemployed cannot afford the commodities made for them to consume, no matter how efficiently a business can exploit the remaining workers. No type of regulation can fix this problem. It also means that what I think of as needs appear as a pure luxury to those with less earning power, and even a tasty and nutritious meal every day seems like a dream of avarice in a world that offers high-calorie, low nutritional processed junk to low-income people. No doubt a more equitable distribution of resources would improve the quality of life for billions of people, and yet, like our application of technology, it would only delay the inevitable day when food, water, energy, clean air, green space, and space to live all run out because the planet has finite resources, a finite capacity to handle waste, and a finite renewal system. Unity must transcend all existing divisions and conventional expectations, and that unity must reset expectations within the moral imperatives of sustainability and social justice.

Unfortunately, no established religion today can unify the global multitude, because they all descend from the material conditions and cultures of particular times and places and along particular historical trajectories. Consequently, they serve some people but inherently exclude others unless they are willing to adopt the corresponding cultural values, which become more of an imposition and duty than a productive connection to community. Yet, the faith I envision must also include, not negate, existing religions. The solution depends on the social character of revolutionary faith, and not on creeds or institutions, so a revolutionary faith may arise rather quickly and globally—wherever modern media reaches the multitudes of precariat and oppressed classes. Fromm argued that the search for meaning is inherent in humans as an outcome of self-awareness.[37] As sociologist Peter Berger concluded long ago, every religion must answer four central existential questions: Who am I, why am I here, how should I live, and what happens when I die?[38] Taken together, the answers instill a sense of meaning in the individual, but religion as a source of meaning is not a thing, but shared experience. As Lauren Langman and I argued,[39] Puritan beliefs in New England created a meaningful community of believers, as did the austere individualist beliefs of the Appalachians when they fought bouts of personal honor or labored in coal mines or opposed state and governmental regulation on whiskey. Whites in the Old South reinforced their supremacist beliefs and identity when plantation owners bought and sold human beings, lashed backs with whips, and poor whites scratched out a living on tenant farms. They fought side by side against the Union in the Civil War because of a perceived sacred bond of rich and poor whites united by faith in racial supremacy and the tradition of patrimonial fealty. Elements of these regional collective beliefs remain as central elements of American social character. In the past, they held communities together in meaningful identity and purpose, which enabled them to survive and prosper, even if that prosperity depended on conquest, exploitation, and enslavement.[40] These same identities today exist only as fragments, as the glorification of guns and the military but with no more frontier or enemy, of wealth but without the studious work ethic and commitment to the common good, of white supremacy without the plantation and patrimonial obligations. These relics no longer function for the nation, and no longer build communities or shared meaning. They create only conflict and division. This social dysfunction paralyzes government, and allows unscrupulous entrepreneurs and big money elites to dominate policy as the country and the lives of the multitude decline.

We still have religion. We have churches, synagogues, mosques, temples, groves, and shrines. Freedom of religion is a major freedom that not only reduces social conflict but empowers people to live as they see fit, and the freedom of religion in the United States was a crucial foundational right and a principle of advanced civilization. At the same time, the great diversity of religious belief means that all of us collectively around the world have no universally accepted system of human rights, and therefore no basic and automatic respect for each other, and no common basis to stop ourselves from running over each other, as Stephen Prothero argues.[41] He is partially correct. We highlight the differences because the world's religions are each attached to particular systems of power, cultural history, and other forms of domination, and consequently we fail to realize the similarities among the world's religions and the people alive today. Even when religion is not the source of conflict, it cannot bring us together because we have lost a sense of obligation to people in general, and to society. We need only follow the rules on a daily basis, formal or informal, that we feel like following or which might result in negative sanctions. We throw trash along the side of the road because it's convenient and we won't get caught. We tolerate torture of people "over there" (somewhere), or let the police shoot unarmed Black men. We don't care about things that don't affect us personally because we identify as individuals and not as members of a society. Only religion can unite humanity, because nothing else can speak to the one reality that transcends all people—the universal experience of death. The inescapable reality of death could and should be the basis for making life better for everyone, because we all die and take nothing with us. If we cling to possessions, we will obsess with death as the ultimate dispossessor that will rob us of property—even our life becomes a possession rather than an experience. In order to live, we must share life through love of living and let go of property—a wisdom that Fromm sees in people such as Master Eckhart, the Buddha, Jesus, and others.[42]

Existing religions have some sense of productive transcendence. For example, Christian theologian Brian McLaren argues that the Gospels reveal that the logos of power are false—just as we saw with Fromm. The true logic of the universe is truth and love. Jesus thus does not fit into any scheme of power or inequality and does not fit any conventional notion of god or meaning. In contrast, "Jesus presents us with a radically new vision of God, a non-violent God, a suffering and serving God, descending and disrupting categories, opening up previously unrealized possibilities"[43] of inclusiveness, mutual progress, and fulfillment.

Theologians of other religions see the same conflict between authoritarian and humanistic faith. Muslim theologian Tariq Ramadan argues similarly that Islam needs a radical redevelopment of its sources of authority. Ramadan argues that for too long, Islam has drawn exclusively from scripture, and then only from official and elitist interpretations often reinforced by state power. Instead, he proposes that "the Universe, history, and human societies should become sources of authority in their own right"[44] in order to shift the center of authority away from religious and political elites and into the communities and realities of the contemporary world. Much of the Islamic world has reached a point of desperation where its people often react to events with reactionary emotional defensiveness instead of free and open public debate, which stifles critical, constructive, and especially, dissenting thought. The Islamic world has no lack of leaders, but a severe lack of leadership "nurtured by a collective aspiration and very concretely expressed through a common movement in which all those involved take part intellectually and practically, transversally, and from the grassroots to the top."[45]

How should we live? Islam teaches The Way (shariah), the principles of which govern the conduct of daily life, which many inaccurately equate with the brutal, medieval punishments of Saudi Arabia and some elements of Iranian political or cultural life. Shariah also calls for higher and universal global pursuits (maqasid ash-shariah), particularly dignity, welfare, freedom, equality, and justice. Again, many elites claim exclusive authority over The Way and usually impose it as some sort of austere lifestyle, strict gender codes for women, and theological purity. Ramadan argues that The Way is not supposed to be a fixed set of laws but, rather, a spirit of interaction that seeks "norms aimed at fulfilling the higher goals of the global message"[46] yet developed and applied locally as an ongoing discovery. Think globally, act locally.

Most consistent with my concept of revolutionary faith and Fromm's revolutionary social character, which often conflicts with institutionalized religion, Thomas Paine argues that The Way cannot be found in any scripture or formal system of belief. As God created everything in elaborate magnificence, the world of God is vast and eternal, while the word of people is finite and changeable. Therefore, enlightenment and the solutions to social problems are out there in the real world, in what Paine calls creation (his word for "all that exists"). "It is only in the creation," Paine writes, "that all our ideas and conceptions of a word of God can unite. The Creation speaketh a universal language. . . . It is an ever-existing original which every person can read."[47] Reading and comprehension are not automatic, however. Each of us possesses the skills, but institutions, doctrines, and ideologies often beat the desire for enlightenment out of us. In contrast, reason follows from active observation and active contemplation of observation. As we learn the universal truths of the universe, so we become qualitatively better people—"everything of agriculture, of science, and of the mechanical arts"[48] all follow the same truth of the real world. The basic Deism that Paine proposes is in other words a combination of faith and science, an empirical religion directed at solving the problems of the day in order to create broad and equitable benefits. As he sees it, Deism was really the first and will likely be the last religion humans create, because it preceded all formal doctrines and governments, and will outlive them all because "pure and simple Deism does not answer the purpose of despotic governments." Politicians, priests, and the rich and powerful must mix religion "with human inventions and make their own authority a part" and by "incorporating themselves and their functions with it, and becoming, like the government, a party to the system"[49] they can then wield religion as a bludgeon of domination. Mixing in petty human agendas of wealth and power creates an apparently seamless unity of government, religion, and authority, but all have been corrupted. In Paine's view, the unity of church and state makes "the church human, and the state tyrannic."[50] In reality, eternal truths are open to everyone, for the benefit of everyone.

Furthermore, Paine notes that the universe as we know it is vast, and given the immense diversity of life on earth, in every corner, little universes on every leaf, in every drop of water, he concludes that God created all the people and cultures of the world as essential parts of a glorious whole. Therefore, each one of them is equally legitimate; only our provincial arrogance claims exclusive legitimacy and rightness. Similarly, we can reasonably conclude that the earth is only one of many globes suspended in space, that each sun harbors worlds, millions of them, and unfortunately, millions of miles apart—advanced thinking for 1795 and which we now know is true. Paine believes that all of existence has meaning, equally in the miniscule and in the vast, in each moment and in eternity. Anyone can read the real world if they take the time and utilize their inherent powers of reason, because a natural (and perhaps God-given) right to understand and the inherent ability to learn make everyone equally deserving of the world's bounty, since everyone must enjoy a decency of life that enables them to pursue the higher abilities of their humanity.

Today, white male ethnocentrism is the religion of the United States; capitalism is its god. The invisible hand of the market divinely rewards the smartest, the hardest-working, the best products and services. Right-wing Christianity equates this divine adjudicator with god and class hierarchy, the "magic of the market," and "meritocracy" to the will of God. Faith in US greatness serves as a loyalty test because not everyone can be a rich white male, but everyone must declare allegiance and fealty to their domination. In actuality, I think the right would prefer atheism. They are god-fearing, not Jesus loving, so consequently their god is judgmental and unforgiving, oppressive rather than empowering. They submit to his authority because they fear not to. Yet with their God so firmly dominant, why then does the white right feel so aggrieved, and by whom? They feel aggrieved by a combination of authoritarianism,[51,52] and white male status decline,[53,54,55] ethnic invasion paranoia, wild conspiracies, and what Pfattheicher and Schindler analyzed as "bullshit intellectualism"[56] that collectively appear as profound insight to explain the ill-favored fortunes of white people whose ethnonationalist allegiance seems to confer fewer automatic benefits. Rather than retreat into fantasy, let's consider an example of a living and progressive faith to inspire life in the real world.

Faith and Death as the Basis of Life

Born in Monroe, Louisiana, to a sharecropper, Huey Newton taught himself how to read as a teenager and discovered a classic work that changed his life: *The Republic* by Plato. He agreed with Plato's assumption that Reason could produce a fair and just government. Condemned to several years in prison and many months in solitary confinement, which both the prisoners and the guards called "the soul breaker," he realized that the legal system served mainly to protect the private property rights of wealthy white people through the police and courts, and through wars against indigenous people earlier in North America and wars abroad in the present. Drawing mainly from Plato and Marx, he realized that systematic injustice and exploitation were not just found in the deep South but throughout the country, and indeed, the entire world.

First with his friend Bobby Seale and then with many others, they built the Black Panther People's Party organization and social movement in 1966 to establish food kitchens, homeless shelters, educational centers, health clinics, and to provide free legal services.[57] However, many of the individuals and the organization itself became highly controversial. They called for radical reforms in land, food, housing, education, justice, and an end to wars. As Newton explains, the Black Panthers and every other revolutionary movement, as well as one's personal life, must unite spirituality with worldly implementation, "to conceptualize, articulate, and share."[58] Otherwise, great ideas remain only abstract concepts. Abstractions and hopelessly complex intellectual language are both useless and meaningless because they fail the test of social change. Newton believed that revolution must have a soul and can only succeed if it draws motivation from a sense of higher and sacred urgency turned into practice. Consequently, the Black Panthers were an attempt to address both the spiritual and the material oppression of Black people, but quickly expanded its mandate to include all oppressed people, whites as well. Officially, The Black Panther Party was both a Black Liberationist movement and a Marxist-Leninist organization that sought much broader change:

> We see a major contradiction between capitalism in this country and our interest. We realize that this country became very rich upon slavery and that capitalism is slavery in the extreme. We have two evils to fight, capitalism and racism. We

must destroy both capitalism and racism.... The Black Panther Party is not a Black racial organization, not a racial organization at all.... We realize that the only way we are going to be free is to wipe out once and for all the oppressive structure of America. We realize we cannot do this without a popular struggle, without many alliances and coalitions ... we need to get as many alliances as possible of people that are equally dissatisfied with the system.[59]

This was the real threat to the Establishment in the United States. COINTELPRO could infiltrate and undermine a militant organization easily enough. The Establishment, both the FBI and local police, murdered at least twenty Black Panther leaders.[60] As long as Black ghettos remained isolated from the larger world, the revolution posed no threat to rich white domination. The larger fear was that organizations like the Black Panthers might successfully unite the interests of Black people in urban ghettos with the interests of white people disillusioned with the Vietnam War, the state of the environment, and working for women's liberation. Most significantly, they might bring a credible challenge to the military-industrial system that dominated American life and drove the United States ever onward in the quest for world domination.

Attacking racism and capitalism challenged two essential and dominant systems of power in the United States. Later, the Panthers in general and Huey Newton in particular called for the full and unbiased acceptance of women and gay people, and thus opened yet a third front by challenging sexual and gender hierarchy in the United States. On the issue of women's and gay rights, Newton wrote that

> we want to hit the homosexual in the mouth because we are afraid we might be homosexual; and we want to hit the woman in the mouth or shut her up because we are afraid she might castrate us or take the nuts that we might not have to start with. We must gain security in ourselves and therefore have respect and feelings for all oppressed people. ... I do not remember ever constituting any value that said that a revolutionary must say offensive things towards homosexuals, or that a revolutionary should make sure that women do not speak out about their own particular kind of oppression. As a matter of fact, it is just the opposite: we say we recognize the women's right to be free. ... I know through reading and through my own life experience and observations that homosexuals are not given freedom and liberty by anyone in society. They might be the most oppressed people in the society.... But there is nothing to say that a homosexual cannot also be a revolutionary. ... Quite the contrary, maybe a homosexual could be the most revolutionary because they are the most oppressed.[61]

Newton does not dismiss anyone, because he recognizes that any one form of oppression tends to interlock with others in mutual reinforcement. In order to accept women and gays as equals, Newton expects men to develop a masculine identity that does not depend on the subordination of others, a sense of security that stands *with* others because we can see ourselves *in* the Other. In order to unite such presently disparate identities, Newton calls for a spiritual humanism, not a secular humanism. While he may not be deistic, he is definitely spiritual. He describes his own life as a moment in a long history of struggle, a brief moment on the stage of life when one's own actions might make a difference, however large or small. In the early 1970s, he wrote,

> I do not think that life will change without an assault on the Establishment—the power structure based on the economic infrastructure, propped up and reinforced by the media and all the secondary educational and cultural institutions—which goes on exploiting the wretched of the earth. . . . It is better to oppose the forces that would drive me to self-murder than to endure them. Although I risk the likelihood of death, there is at least the possibility, if not the probability, of changing intolerable conditions. . . . I say with hope and dignity; if premature death is the result, that death has meaning and is the price of self-respect. Revolutionary suicide does not mean that I and my comrades have a death wish; it means just the opposite. We have such a strong desire to live with hope and human dignity that existence without them is impossible.[62]

This view transcends practical concerns and speaks to a larger motivating vision in the form of the revolutionary prophet that Fromm finds necessary for a better future. We are all players in history, and consequently, everyone's life matters. For good or for evil, the choices we make shape the world. Actions that contribute to freedom, peace, and love are good; actions that deny these to others are evil.

Despite their reputation, the Panthers tried to work within the law.[63] Unfortunately, many law enforcement agencies did not work within the law. Amid the violence, community organizing continued. Without further summarizing the complete history of the Black Panthers, it is enough to say that nearly all the leaders ended up dead, in prison, or in exile, and the organization's assets seized or destroyed without search warrants or a trial.[64] Huey Newton and Bobby Seale survived the tumultuous 1960s and early 1970s. Huey Newton earned a PhD from the University of California Santa Cruz, and he continued work to set up homeless shelters and food kitchens. While walking home on the night of August 22, 1989, a drug dealer named Tyrone Robinson pointed a gun at Huey's face. They stood on a corner in Oakland where Huey had once established a social services center for poor people. The moment had arrived. He couldn't run. He was alone. He did what he had done all his life; he stood his ground, and stood up for his beliefs. He said to Robinson, "You can kill my body, but you can't kill my soul. My soul will live forever!"[65] Already filled with rage, Robinson shot Newton three times in the face, which killed him on the spot.

This reveals a story that is seldom told about Huey Newton or the Black Panthers. In addition to their special programs and confrontations with law enforcement, I suggest that none of their activism would have been possible without a larger vision of a better world and faith in a cause beyond themselves. While the Panthers drew extensively from leftist political theory such as Karl Marx and Mao Zedong, many of them personally, including Huey Newton, also lived with faith, just as Martin Luther King (a pastor) was part of the Southern Christian Leadership Conference and Malcolm X was a Muslim. While not all the Panthers were people of faith as such, their activism was a type that benefited themselves very little, and sought to benefit other people a lot more. I think this is Fromm's notion of a life of spiritual humanism—the revolutionary prophet becomes such through service to others—leadership by example that awakens the inherent curiosity, life-loving emotions, and commitment to others. These commitments need not be religious as such, but they do need to include faith. Newton could not prove that the soul is real, although he seems to believe that. Instead of a doctrine of the soul or of immortality, he relied on a practical faith that our lives matter and we can become more than we are assigned by our birth or society, and so he dedicated his life to the future. In the 1960s, he could have simply finished college and pursued a career, but he didn't. In the 1980s, he could have become a college professor and he could have lived in a better neighborhood, but he didn't. He refused to give up or run away. Whether we live more or fewer years, Newton believed that our lives only matter if we make the world a better place. The stress of ongoing activism drove him to drug addiction, which eventually ended in his murder on the streets of Oakland. "I do not expect to live through our revolution, and most serious comrades probably share my realism," he wrote. Yet his optimism remained undiminished. "I have no doubt that the revolution will triumph. The people of the world will prevail, seize power, seize the means of production, wipe out racism, capitalism" and all forms of what he calls "reactionary suicide," which is sacrificing one's life for people and institutions who only exploit and oppress them. Huey believes that in the end, "the people will win a new world." However, "if the world does not change, all its people will be threatened by the greed, exploitation, and violence of the power structure that is the American empire." Like Fromm, myself, and many others argue, Newton writes, "The United States is jeopardizing its own existence and the existence of all humanity. If Americans knew the disasters that lay ahead, they would transform this society tomorrow if for no other reason than their own preservation."[66] Yet many prefer the comfort of fantasy and smugness of power like a Pharaoh, king, plutocrat, or the vacancy of jingoism—America is the greatest country ever and offers the most opportunity; climate change is a mistake or a hoax; all our problems result from lazy and criminal immigrants; "if we just elect enough Democrats . . . ." We refuse to see the disasters ahead. Faith is necessary but by itself, insufficient.

Newton also realized that practical action is necessary, and in the course of practical action, confrontations with power can mean violence and death, so faith doesn't mean that people should walk blindly into their actions. A person would only flail about and never accomplish anything productive. Faith requires a companion—reason. At the moment of an action, a person must decide how much they are willing to risk and the likelihood of success. Newton realized that to get results, a person must believe that change is possible, but also that change will only happen with organization and rational planning. Faith and reason must strengthen and temper each other because the Establishment can deploy exceptional violence to defend itself, as we see in the streets every day and the endless wars abroad. Newton died in order to sustain a life with meaning and a life worth living. Today, even the 1960s seems to many like ancient history (at least to my students). Newton's prophetic humanism aspired to transcend culture and nation, and to encourage a life of productive transcendence as the way forward. We can take the best of history and of today's religions, but in order to break the oppressions grounded in the past, progressive movements must construct a revolutionary religion, unite the multitude in common morality, and transform the world where each improves the lives of all.

Notes

1. Lundskow and Langman, "Erich Fromm and Contemporary American Politics."
2. Fromm, *To Have or to Be?*, 96
3. Bock, Byrd-Craven, and Burkley, "The Role of Sexism in Voting in the 2016 Presidential Election."
4. Ratliff, Redford, Conway, and Smith, "Engendering Support: Hostile Sexism Predicts Voting For Donald Trump Over Hillary Clinton In The 2016 U.S. Presidential Election."
5. Baker, Cañarte, and Day, "Race, Xenophobia, and Punitiveness among the American Public."
6. Major, Blodorn, and Blascovich, "The Threat of Increasing Diversity."
7. Knowles and Tropp, "The Racial and Economic Context of Trump Support."
8. Smith and Hanley, "The Anger Games."
9. Hooghe and Dassonneville, "Explaining the Trump Vote."
10. Swain, "Negative Black Stereotypes, Support for Excessive Use of Force by Police."
11. Cassese and Barnes, "Reconciling Sexism and Women's Support for Republican Candidates."
12. Whitehead, Perry, and Baker, "Make America Christina Again."
13. Ludeke, Klitgaard, and Vitriol, "Comprehensively-Measured Authoritarianism Does Predict Vote Choice."
14. Fromm, *You Shall Be as Gods*, 84–85.
15. Fromm, *To Have or to Be?*, 112.
16. Ibid., 109–40.
17. Fromm, *You Shall Be as Gods*, 132–33.
18. Ibid., 133.
19. Fromm, *The Dogma of Christ*, 48–49.
20. Ibid., 150.
21. Ibid., 158–59.
22. Ibid., 160–61.
23. Fromm, *The Anatomy of Human Destructiveness*, 295–97.
24. Fromm, *Social Character in a Mexican Village*, 83–109.
25. Fromm, *You Shall Be as Gods*, 169–70.
26. Thorpe, *Necroculture*.
27. Fromm, *Social Character in a Mexican Village*, 70–71.
28. Fromm, *To Have or to Be?* 111.
29. Hedges, "The Pathology of the Rich."
30. Jones, "White Evangelical Support for Donald Trump at All-Time High."
31. US national debt is currently $21.6 trillion, personal debt is $19 trillion, and total US debt from all sources is $71 trillion. http://www.usdebtclock.org/
32. Durkheim, *Suicide*, 247.

33 Ibid., 256.
34 Ibid., 255.
35 Hicks and Deveraj, *The Myth and the Reality of Manufacturing in America*.
36 Rendell, "Global New Car Sales: The Key Trends and What They Mean for the Future."
37 Fromm, *The Sane Society*.
38 Berger, *The Sacred Canopy*.
39 Langman and Lundskow, *God, Guns, Gold and Glory*.
40 Ibid.
41 Prothero, *God Is Not One*.
42 Fromm, *To Have or to Be?*, 102.
43 McLaren, *Why Did Jesus, Moses, the Buddha, and Muhammad Cross the Road?*, 143.
44 Ramadan, *Islam, the West and the Challenges of Modernity*, 259.
45 Ibid., 261.
46 Ibid., 269.
47 Thomas Paine, *The Age of Reason, Parts I and II*, 316–17.
48 Ibid., 450.
49 Ibid., 448.
50 Ibid., 449.
51 Lundskow, "Authoritarianism and Destructiveness in the Tea Party Movement."
52 Lundskow and Langman, "Erich Fromm and Contemporary American Politics."
53 Hetherington and Weiler, *Prius or Pickup?*
54 Marc and Weiler, *Authoritarianism and Polarization in American Politics*.
55 Whitehead, "Cops and the Performance of White Masculine Decline."
56 Pfattheicher and Schindler. "Misperceiving Bullshit as Profound Is Associated with Favorable Views of Cruz, Rubio, Trump and Conservatism."
57 Hilliard and the Huey P. Newton Foundation, *The Black Panther Party*.
58 Newton, *Revolutionary Suicide*, 68.
59 Newton, *To Die for the People*, 51.
60 Churchill and Wall, *Agents of Repression*.
61 Newton, *Revolutionary Suicide*, 153–54.
62 Ibid., 3.
63 Haskins, *Power to the People*.
64 Bloom and Martin, *Black against Empire*.
65 Newton and Hilliard, *Huey: Spirit of the Panther*, 247.
66 Newton, *Revolutionary Suicide*, 4–6.

References

Baker, Joseph O., David Cañarte, and Edward L. Day. (2018). "Race, Xenophobia, and Punitiveness among the American Public." *The Sociological Quarterly* 59, no. 3: 363–83.

Berger, Peter L. (1990 [1967]). *The Sacred Canopy: Elements of a Sociological Theory of Religion*. New York, NY: Random House.

Bloom, Joshua, and Waldo E. Martin. (2016). *Black against Empire: The History and Politics of the Black Panther Party*. Berkeley and Los Angeles: The University of California Press.

Bock, Jarrod, Jennifer Byrd-Craven, and Melissa Burkley. (2017). "The Role of Sexism in Voting in the 2016 Presidential Election." *Personality and Individual Differences* 119, no. 1 (December): 189–93.

Cassese, Erin C., and Tiffany D. Barnes. (2018). "Reconciling Sexism and Women's Support for Republican Candidates: A Look at Gender, Class, and Whiteness in the 2012 and 2016 Presidential Races." *Political Behavior*, https://doi-org.ezproxy.gvsu.edu/10.1007/s11109-018-9468-2

Churchill, Ward, and Jim Vander Wall. (2002 [1988]). *Agents of Repression: The FBI's Secret Wars Against the Black Panther Party and the American Indian Movement*. Cambridge, MA: South End Press.

Durkheim, Emile. (1998 [1897]). *Suicide: A Study in Sociology*. New York, NY: The Free Press.

Fromm, Erich. (1990 [1955]). *The Sane Society*. New York, NY: Henry Holt.

Fromm, Erich. (1991 [1966]). *You Shall Be as Gods: A Radical Reinterpretation of the Old Testament and Its Traditions*. New York, NY: Henry Holt.

Fromm, Erich. (1992 [1973]). *The Anatomy of Human Destructiveness*. New York, NY: Henry Holt.

Fromm, Erich. (1992 [1963]). *The Dogma of Christ*. New York, NY: Henry Holt.

Fromm, Erich. (1996 [1970]). *Social Character in a Mexican Village*. New Brunswick, NJ: Transaction Publishers.

Fromm, Erich. (1997 [1976]). *To Have or to Be?* New York, NY: Continuum Publishing.

Gould, Stephen Jay. (1999). *Rocks of Ages: Science and Religion in the Fullness of Life*. New York, NY: Ballantine Books.

Haskins, Jim. (1997). *Power to the People: The Rise and Fall of the Black Panther Party*. Washington DC: Ebooks for Students.

Hedges, Chris. (2013). "The Pathology of the Rich." https://www.opednews.com/articles/Chris-Hedges-on-The-Patho-by-Chris-Hedges-Class_Dehumanization_Rich-People_Wealth-131207-825.html

Hetherington, Marc, and Jonathan Weiler. (2009). *Authoritarianism and Polarization in American Politics*. New York, NY: Cambridge University Press.

Hetherington, Marc, and Jonathan Weiler. (2018). *Prius or Pickup?: How the Answers to Four Simple Questions Explain America's Great Divide*. New York, NY: Houghton Mifflin Harcourt Publishing.

Hicks, Michael J., and Srikant Deveraj. (2017). *The Myth and the Reality of Manufacturing in America*. The Center for Business and Economic Research. Muncie, IN: Ball State University Press.

Hilliard, David, and the Huey P. Newton Foundation. (2008). *The Black Panther Party: Service to the People*. Albuquerque, NM: University of New Mexico Press.

Hooghe, Marc, and Ruth Dassonneville. (2018). "Explaining the Trump Vote: The Effect of Racist Resentment and Anti-Immigrant Sentiments." *Political Science & Politics* 51, no. 3: 528–34.

Jones, Robert P. (2018). "White Evangelical Support for Donald Trump at All-Time High." PRRI Report. Washington DC, https://www.prri.org/spotlight/White-evangelical-support-for-donald-trump-at-all-time-high/

Knowles, Eric D., and Linda R. Tropp. (2018). "The Racial and Economic Context of Trump Support: Evidence for Threat, Identity, and Contact Effects in the 2016 Presidential Election." *Social Psychological and Personality Science* 9, no. 3: 275–84.

Langman, Lauren, and George Lundskow. (2016). *God, Guns, Gold, and Glory: American Character and Its Discontents*. Boston, MA: Brill Publishing.

Ludeke, Steven G., Camilla N. Klitgaard, and Joseph Vitriol. (2018). "Comprehensively-Measured Authoritarianism Does Predict Vote Choice: The Importance of

Authoritarianism's Facets, Ideological Sorting, and The Particular Candidate." *Personality and Individual Differences* 123, no. 1: 209–16.
Lundskow, George. (2012). "Authoritarianism and Destructiveness in the Tea Party Movement." *Critical Sociology* 38, no. 4: 529–49.
Lundskow, George, and Lauren Langman. (2012). "Down the Rabid Hole to a Tea Party." *Critical Sociology* 38, no. 4: 589–99.
Lundskow, George, and Lauren Langman. (2018). "Erich Fromm and Contemporary American Politics." *Free Associations: Psychoanalysis and Culture, Media, Groups, Politics* 73, no. 3: 1–15.
Major, Brenda, Alison Blodorn, and Gregory Major Blascovich. (2018). "The Threat of Increasing Diversity: Why Many White Americans Support Trump in the 2016 Presidential Election." *Group Processes and Intergroup Relations* 21, no. 6: 931–40.
McLaren, Brian. (2012). *Why Did Jesus, Moses, the Buddha, and Muhammad Cross the Road?* New York, NY: Jericho Books.
Newton, Fredrika, and David Hilliard. (2006). *Huey: Spirit of the Panther*. Philadelphia, PA: Perseus Group.
Newton, Huey. (1972). *To Die for the People*. New York, NY: Random House.
Newton, Huey. (2009 [1973]). *Revolutionary Suicide*. New York, NY: Penguin Group.
Paine, Thomas. (2010 [1795]). *The Age of Reason, Parts I and II*. No City Given: Merchant Books/Amazon Publishing.
Pfattheicher, Stefan, and Simon Schindler. (2016). "Misperceiving Bullshit as Profound Is Associated with Favorable Views of Cruz, Rubio, Trump and Conservatism." *PLoS One* 11, no. 4, https://doi.org/10.1371/journal.pone.0153419.
Prothero, Stephen. (2010). *God Is Not One: The Eight Rival Religions That Run the World—and Why Their Differences Matter*. New York, NY: HarperCollins.
Ramadan, Tariq. (2009). *Islam, the West and the Challenges of Modernity*. Markfield, Leicester: The Islamic Foundation.
Ratliff, Kate A., Liz Redford, John Conway, and Colin Tucker Smith. (2017). "Engendering Support: Hostile Sexism Predicts Voting for Donald Trump over Hillary Clinton in the 2016 U.S. Presidential Election." *Group Processes and Intergroup Relations*, https://doi-org.ezproxy.gvsu.edu/10.1177%2F1368430217741203
Rendell, Julian. (2018). "Global New Car Sales: The Key Trends and What They Mean for the Future." MSN Online: https://www.msn.com/en-us/autos/news/global-new-car-sales-the-key-trends-and-what-they-mean-for-the-future/ar-BBJfUkK
Smith, David Norman, and Eric Hanley. (2018). "The Anger Games: Who Voted for Donald Trump in the 2016 Election, and Why?" *Critical Sociology* 44, no. 2: 195–212.
Swain, Randall D. (2018). "Negative Black Stereotypes, Support for Excessive Use of Force by Police, and Voter Preference for Donald Trump During the 2016 Presidential Primary Election Cycle." *Journal of African American Studies* 22, no. 1: 109–24.
Thorpe, Charles. (2016). *Necroculture*. New York, NY: Springer Nature America.
Torry, Harriet. (2018). "U.S. Workers Get Biggest Pay Increase in Nearly a Decade." *The Wall Street Journal*, October 15, https://www.wsj.com/articles/u-s-employment-costs-rose-in-the-second-quarter-1533040473
Whitehead, Stephanie Nichol. (2014). "Cops and the Performance of White Masculine Decline." *Race, Gender & Class* 21, no. 3/4: 174–88.
Whitehead, Andrew L., Samuel L. Perry, and Joseph O. Baker. (2018). "Make America Christian Again: Christian Nationalism and Voting for Donald Trump in the 2016 Presidential Election." *Sociology of Religion* 79, no. 2: 147–72.

Part II

SOCIAL AND PSYCHOLOGICAL ASPECTS

Chapter 4

ERICH FROMM AND THE PROSPECTS FOR RENEWING CRITICAL THEORY IN THE NEOLIBERAL ERA

Roger Foster

In many ways, the political and social crisis that appears to be enveloping postindustrial democracies at the tail end of the neoliberal era recalls the crisis of laissez-faire capitalism that formed the backdrop to the "first generation" of the Frankfurt School in the 1920s and 1930s. In Germany, hyperinflation had destroyed the economic and social cohesion of the nation's middle class, contributing to the legitimacy crisis of the Weimar regime. The gradual collapse in support throughout the 1920s for parties supportive of the Republic intensified the sense of the regime's extreme fragility. The decline of the neoliberal era, as Nancy Fraser has recently argued, has brought with it a clear impression that we are once again faced with a deep-seated crisis of democracy.[1] Fraser's topology of capitalist crisis draws on Karl Polanyi's account of how capitalism destabilizes its own conditions of possibility by threatening to overwhelm the work of social reproduction and the health and sustainability of the natural environment (as well as, on Fraser's reading, overwhelming its political sphere). A structurally similar reading can be found in the work of sociologist Wolfgang Streeck, who argues that because capitalism has done such a thorough job of weakening and eliminating the countervailing powers that provide stability, we are faced with a situation in which "capitalism may undermine itself by being too successful."[2] There are reasons to believe that we have returned to the default condition of capitalist society, in which the interminable conflict between the levels of growth and profitability required to power capitalist markets, and the demands of democratic citizens for social protections, abundant well-paying jobs, and protection of the natural environment once again threatens the stability of democratic societies. Without the distorting lens of the postwar period of managed capitalism, the *Trentes Glorieuses* that provided robust economic growth and social stability, and that gave credence to the comforting but misplaced belief that capitalism had been successfully tamed by social engineering, today's crisis recalls the political and social instability that capitalism has generated throughout its brief history.

While I am in broad agreement with these readings of a renewed crisis of capitalism and democracy, I believe there is an important story to be told about how we arrived at this point. Indeed, telling this story is essential to the task of identifying and rescuing the emancipatory tendencies that have generated sweeping social and cultural change in the neoliberal era. What I have in mind is a theory about the dynamic of social change in capitalist society that I derive from Erich Fromm. The basis of the theory is the idea of a structural conflict between progressive and regressive tendencies and forces in the dynamic of capitalism. In order to establish a viable regime of accumulation, capitalism must draw on the prevalent emancipatory energies in society in order to forge paths for higher growth and profits.[3] In the neoliberal era, these energies centered on notions of personal autonomy, self-expression, and authenticity that drove a profound transformation of work relations and personal life. At the same time, those progressive forces accompanying these social and cultural changes were ultimately directed to serve the interests of capital accumulation. This is where, on Fromm's reading, the regressive tendencies of capitalism appear, with the aim of making the emerging emancipatory trends serve the needs of the current class structure and the current configuration of social power.[4] What is most powerful about Fromm's account, however, is that it is able to diagnose this problem from the psychosocial perspective, in which it is individuals' anxiety-driven response to social transformation that motivates popular sympathy with the regressive tendencies of capitalism. In Fromm's most famous formulation of this problem, individuals faced with new possibilities for growth opened up by socioeconomic change often succumb to a "fear of freedom" that impels them to look for security in various, often archaic, forms of collective or tribal identity.[5] At the psychosocial level, there is a deep-seated economic, social, and cultural struggle between the progressive forces that represent emancipatory tendencies in the present, and the regressive movement that emerges to defend the current constellation of wealth and power. This is not only a battle of ideas, since the forces at work themselves shape the human substance of individuals into the social identities that Fromm calls "social character."

While Fromm has long been a marginal figure in the story of the Frankfurt School, I believe that Fromm's work manages to avoid the core problems that tainted both the canonical version of "first generation" critical theory associated with Theodor Adorno and Max Horkheimer, as well as subsequent second- and third-generation formulations associated with Jürgen Habermas and Axel Honneth. Fromm's split with the Frankfurt School in the late 1930s and disagreements with Marcuse and Adorno have obscured the crucial role he played in developing with Horkheimer what John Abromeit calls the "most important" current of first-generation critical social theory.[6] When Horkheimer sought an intellectual alliance with Adorno in the late 1930s, the idea of a psychoanalytically informed Marxism was supplanted by an interpretation of emerging, mid-twentieth-century-managed capitalism as the culmination of the collapse of Western reason into instrumental reason. It is obvious today that mid-twentieth-century-managed capitalism was not the end point of a historical process, but a temporary and unstable solution to the insuperable problems that had developed in the disastrous collapse of nineteenth-century liberal capitalism into world war and recession. By the 1970s, however, when Habermas was constructing the mature form of his social theory, it seemed to many that capitalism had finally tamed its wild, laissez-faire nature, and could simply be harnessed as a tool for producing mass prosperity. In Habermas's theory of communicative action, capitalism is assigned the role of a self-sustaining technical subsystem.[7] On Habermas's view, as Albrecht Wellmer points out, emancipatory processes "cannot question the internal logic of capitalist economy."[8] The focus of Axel Honneth's theory on normative relations of recognition also has difficulty giving an account of the forms of class-based power that pervade advanced liberal democracies.[9]

The deep-seated, long, and mutating conflict between emancipatory trends and reactive forms of escape that has plagued neoliberal societies has today morphed into the form of a nationalist and nativist reaction against those very globalizing forces that have undermined the security provided by various forms of fixed identity. As the fixed and stable social identities anchored in class, race, ethnicity, gender, sexuality, and nationality have become more fluid and uncertain, the capacity of those identities to signify social status and identity has waned. In the era of postwar-managed capitalism, these fixed identities were central to the mechanisms by which the state structured the postwar economy, for example, through the "family wage" that male breadwinners were expected to earn for their families. At the same time, the global reach of capital has allowed it to discipline the expectations of the wage-earning inhabitants of postindustrial democracies. Rural, less-educated segments who have had most to lose from the unwinding of postwar collectivism have also lost the most from global economic changes. In the present moment, a section of the owners of capital and the segments of the population for whom the neoliberal era has meant perceived economic decline and sociocultural disorientation have entered into a political alliance with the purpose of opposing those trends that undermine existing status differentials of wealth and power. Whereas nationalists are concerned with the decline of traditional identity markers, and especially their capacity to guarantee forms of social privilege and economic status, the owners of capital are concerned to redirect emancipatory trends toward the support of existing circuits of wealth and power. As I shall argue, the latter project takes the form of a depoliticization of emancipatory forces, seeking to ensure their domestication by turning them into private claims for new forms of consumption and lifestyle. This was realized in large part through certain structural economic shifts in the neoliberal era. What Fromm's psychosocial understanding of the binding force of capitalist society gets right is that capitalism, in its urgency to restore or repair a functioning regime of accumulation, weaponizes the fears and anxieties that arise in the course of rapid socioeconomic change, molding those reactions into a putative democratic opposition to the threats to wealth and power harbored by new emancipatory possibilities, while in reality seeking to lock those possibilities into consumerism and other depoliticized forms.[10]

The Original Idea of Critical Theory

Erich Fromm's association with the Frankfurt School began through his work with the Frankfurt Institute of Psychoanalysis, where Fromm, who had already previously opened his own private psychoanalytic practice, worked as a lecturer. The Institute was accommodated in Frankfurt in the building housing the Institute of Social Research, and Fromm gave a lecture on the opening of the Institute for Psychoanalysis in 1929.[11] Fromm's essay "Psychoanalysis and Sociology" grapples with the problem of the role of psychoanalysis in understanding social phenomena, a problem that would occupy Fromm throughout the 1930s.[12] While arguing that the common task of psychoanalysis and sociology is the investigation of how the psychic apparatus determines the development and organization of society, Fromm's essay already shows his intention to move beyond the explanation of social processes by way of analogical reasoning from the psychoanalysis of the individual. Human beings, Fromm argues, do not have an individual psyche and, in addition, a mass psyche that springs into being whenever they act collectively. This view might, for example, try to explain the social phenomenon of war through the existence of human aggressive drives, or revolution as hatred toward the father. Instead of understanding the connection between individual and society through direct analogical relationships, Fromm suggests that it is necessary to understand the individual as a "socialized person."[13] The implication here is that the analysis of how common experiences of individual members of society lead to the formation of similar character traits is crucial to overcoming the misleading psychologizing of social phenomena. Social phenomena do not have a psychic basis because they are individual psychological phenomena writ large; rather, they implicate psychology because they reflect the common structure that individuals, under the same social influences, have adopted with regard to the satisfaction or disappointment of their essential needs.[14]

That such a line of thought was congenial to Horkheimer's own development toward an empirically grounded social philosophy is clear from Horkheimer's 1931 inaugural address.[15] In this essay, Horkheimer begins with an account of the shortcomings of Kantian idealism. He argues that Hegel transformed idealism into the social-philosophical investigation of the structures of objective spirit, which mediated the transformation of empirical individuals into the vehicles of the historical realization of human freedom. Horkheimer charged that idealism, prior to Hegel, had tried to derive the organization of society from the analysis of the modes of activity of the autonomous ego. Horkheimer argues that Hegel decisively shifted "the question of our essence—the question of the autonomous culture-creating subject—to the work of history, in which the subject gives itself objective form."[16] The autonomous ego, on Horkheimer's interpretation, was therefore subject to a misreading similar to the one Fromm had discerned with reference to the mass psyche. This meant that the autonomous subject of idealism, like the mass psyche on Fromm's reading, was the result of a confusion about the relation between individual subjects and the collective structures that give expression to the life lived in common and sustained by the daily activity of individuals. The solution, in both cases, was to investigate how individuals come to sustain and reproduce social structures through their inculcation into a particular way of life. The social totality is not the subject writ large; it is formed from the way individuals are shaped by their experiences to embody the beliefs, understandings, and justifications that structure the terms of social interaction. Individual psychology, as Fromm saw, merges with social psychology.

In his 1931 inaugural lecture, Horkheimer had argued that social philosophy's charge was to examine "the question of the connection between the economic life of society, the psychical development of individuals, and the changes in the realm of culture."[17] This, according to Fromm, would involve understanding how individuals develop emotional investments in social and economic structures through the channeling of individual needs into designated patterns of work and social relationships. These investments provide a kind of mortar that protects a class-stratified society from the radical social change that seemed to be called for by its economic basis. Social character was therefore the crucial switching point between the economic structure and the beliefs and commitments circulating in the cultural field. In *Escape from Freedom*, this threefold interpretive scheme is employed in a social and economic history of capitalist society. In his account of the Reformation, Fromm argues that the doctrines of Lutheranism and Calvinism offered a solution to problems thrown up by profound socioeconomic change. The dissolution of the social ties of feudalism, Fromm argues, left many people feeling threatened and anxious at the prospect of the loss of status, as well as by the related rise of a new monied class. The socially typical character of that era would have sensed the freedom from socially binding ties as provoking great anxiety and feelings of insignificance. Lutheranism and Calvinism emerged in response to this situation, but the effect of their doctrines, Fromm argued, was not to assuage the individual's fear and anxiety but to radically intensify feelings of fear and anxiety in order to channel the individual's response away from the search for collective solutions and toward subordination of the self to powerful authorities

> Thus Luther and Calvin psychologically prepared man for the role which he had to assume in modern society: of feeling his own self to be insignificant and of being ready to subordinate his life exclusively for purposes which were not his own. Once man was ready to become nothing but the means for the glory of a God who represented neither justice nor love, he was sufficiently prepared to accept the role of a servant to the economic machine.[18]

This argument is readily recognizable from Horkheimer's 1936 essay on "Egoism and Freedom Movements." Horkheimer had also, in this essay, sought to derive idealist morality from the prevailing economic situation of the high bourgeois age.[19] The function of bourgeois morality, according to Horkheimer, was to license the principle of competition within the restricted social space of private interests, but at the same time to repress the possibility of collective action to improve social and economic conditions. What morality sought to restrict, Horkheimer claims, was not private enterprise, but "common action," in other words, the recognition of shared interests transcending their private identity as economic subjects.

The idea that religious and political doctrines exercise a social function through their psychological significance for the individual furnished a powerful psychosocial account of the capacity of capitalist society to absorb and deflect radical opposition in spite of its continual failure to secure the basic economic interests of the majority. Fromm and Horkheimer developed a common materialist position that saw new possibilities for human freedom emerging in the bourgeois era, but they also drew on the new discipline of psychoanalysis in order to explain how capitalist society is able to harness human energy for the purpose of fortifying existing divisions of class while deflecting the nascent emancipatory tendencies that emerge in the course of socioeconomic change. The crucial insight emerging from the Horkheimer-Fromm collaboration is this very notion of a perpetual social and cultural struggle between emancipatory tendencies which, for instance, in the bourgeois age, are trying to push through the class barriers of bourgeois society to realize a classless society, and the forms of reaction which, rising up in defense of the class structure and its distribution of wealth and power, seek to redirect those emancipatory tendencies toward purposes that do not threaten the current social order. I shall make the case in the rest of this chapter that Fromm remained faithful to this idea through his mature works of the postwar period.[20] In the next section, I want to reconstruct this idea, drawing broadly on Fromm's corpus. Then, in the following section, I argue that Fromm's theory proffers a powerful explanation of the intensifying political, economic, and ecological crisis of neoliberalism.

Fromm on Humanism and Historical Materialism

In his rich and informative work on Fromm's humanism, Kieran Durkin notes that Fromm drew many of his principal themes and ideas from his lifelong immersion in the Judaic tradition.[21] It was from his encounter with Judaism that Fromm derived his principle of universalism, the idea of the unity of the human race beyond divisions of tribe and nation. In *You Shall Be as Gods*, Fromm conceives the opposition between progressive movement and reactionary response in the terms of the difference between the universalism of Judaic monotheism and practices of idol worship that subordinate human activity to the service of material objects. Fromm writes that the idol serves "man's central passion: the desire to return to the soil mother, the craving for power, fame, possession, and so forth."[22] Idol worship is essentially a form of alienation, in which human beings transfer their most exalted qualities into an object external to them, which then becomes an object of worship. Idol worship therefore follows the same logic as the phenomenon that Fromm often describes as the development of incestuous ties. This is clear from Fromm's catalog of contemporary "idols" that have replaced the symbols of tribal religion, namely "honor, flag, state, mother, family, fame, production, consumption."[23] Fromm's understanding of Jewish theology in this work as fundamentally preoccupied with the negation of idols associates monotheism with the historical process of humanity's liberation from its thrall to nature, the clan, and nation. Monotheism therefore enables humanity's progress toward freedom and self-determination through its permanent vigilance in rooting out and rejecting the collapse of religion into idol worship. Fromm writes in *The Sane Society* that "we are never free from two conflicting tendencies": one is to "emerge from the womb," from bondage to freedom; the other to return to "nature, to certainty and security."[24] Fromm's theory of civil disobedience tells the same story in secular form.[25] Fromm conceives disobedience—saying "no" to and refusing authority that doesn't serve our interests—to be essentially a process in which humans realize their collective freedom through the rejection of social arrangements that bind the self to the service of a preexisting group, entity, or institution. One becomes free in the *via negativa* that proceeds through the rejection of attempts to prematurely bind the self to a fixed identity before it has actualized itself through its own self-directed development.

In *The Sane Society*, Fromm opposes idolatry—in which the individual worships the alienated products of his or her own activity—to the idea of being a "center" of experience that relates to the world through acts of love and reason.[26] Idolatry prevents this experience of centering because it involves projecting all one's powers into another person or object. In idolatry, Fromm writes,

> It is the fact that man does not experience himself as the active bearer of his own powers and richness, but as an impoverished "thing," dependent on powers outside of himself, unto whom he has projected his living substance.[27]

Fromm, speaking at the height of the postwar boom in the mid-1950s, argues that this experience of alienation has become ubiquitous in modern society. He cites the experience of repetitive and meaningless work in modern industry, as well as the organization of leisure time according to similar, industrially conceived spheres of consumption that place the individual in the position of a passive recipient of the forms of enjoyment fabricated for mass appeal and distribution.

These themes were picked up more broadly in postwar psychological humanism. Maslow's discussion of self-actualizers emphasizes the importance of autonomy, in the sense of coming to one's own decisions, instead of being manipulated by others. Self-actualizers are said to be "self-movers" who are internally motivated, giving them a certain insulation from the wider culture's judgments about the value of different activities and ways of life.[28] Maslow hypothesized that self-actualizing individuals were at the opposite end of the spectrum to authoritarian types, among whom a "passive yielding" to cultural shaping was the norm.[29] Fromm had also picked up on the resistance of self-determining individuals to social norms, emphasizing the importance of rejecting the social categories that seek to channel the expression of self into established group patterns. In taking these positions, Fromm, Maslow, and other humanist psychologists were taking a stand in the conflict around authority in the postwar era, which manifested itself through religion, sex, gender, and youth culture. Petigny argues that a social liberalization occurred when the value of self-mastery was broadly replaced by the value of self-discovery. Important developments on this path included "a rejection of the belief of the innate depravity of mankind, the celebration of spontaneity, and a pronounced turn towards self-awareness."[30] Conservative cultural critics saw in these developments the emergence of a permissive society that threatened to dissolve moral and social constraints on individual behavior. Philip Rieff spoke of the "triumph of the therapeutic," which meant the rejection of the possibility of organizing collective life through a system of controls and prohibitions that imposed a sacrifice on the individual for the sake of the collective. Hence the lesson of midcentury society, for Rieff, was "how not to pay the high personal costs of social organization."[31]

For Fromm and the humanists, the gradual shift in social authority from authoritarian control of individual behavior to more therapeutic attitudes promoting individual initiative and self-determination opened up important new possibilities for human freedom.[32] Social and economic changes in the postwar era made it possible for individuals to be the "active bearers" of their own powers, rather than the executors of a social role that left little scope for free self-determination. The assumption of the postwar humanists that increasing scope for autonomy and self-control allows for human growth and self-development has been carried further in recent decades by Self-Determination Theory (SDT). SDT explains why personal autonomy and self-expression are so crucial to human well-being. Actions that are autonomous and felt to be intrinsically motivated serve three underlying psychological needs that are vital to psychic growth and development.[33] First, competence refers to the feeling that one is exercising and expressing one's capacities, leading to the search for appropriate challenges for using one's talents and abilities. Relatedness, second, involves feeling connected to others and involved in mutual relationships of caring. Third, the notion of autonomy, involving the experience of one's behavior as an active expression of the self, is closely related to Fromm's humanist idea of being the "active bearer" of one's capacities. The important point is that the self's activities and engagements must be experienced as intrinsically motivated, which comprises elements of spontaneity and volition.[34] Intrinsic motivation is focused on goods intrinsic to the activity itself, whereas extrinsic motivation focuses on external outcomes, such as rewards, praise, or blame, which may be attached to the activity through social institutions, but are not part of what makes the activity itself intrinsically rewarding.

The therapeutic transformations sweeping postwar society brought about a definitive cultural and moral shift, one that Fromm and the humanists, and later, SDT, captured in terms of a contrast between authentic, intrinsically motivated experiences in which the self is immersed in rewarding activities that promote autonomy, self-expression, and relatedness, and practices that bind the self to the service of some external value. The latter might take the form of living out a social role, in which one acts as the agent of society by subordinating one's own inclinations and needs to the greater imperative of survival and reproduction. It might also involve service to external goods, money, and power, and the single-minded focus on their accumulation, to the detriment of one's own psychological need for growth and development.

The idea that changing socioeconomic circumstances can cause radical shifts in culture and moral values is, for Fromm, a crucial assumption of historical materialism. In his treatment of this idea, Fromm is always concerned to differentiate his own view from a certain economistic misunderstanding of Marx. In *The Sane Society*, Fromm expresses this difference in terms of psychological or sociological understandings of the importance of the economic system:

> Marx's concept of the significance of the economic factor was not a *psychological* one, namely, an economic motivation in a *subjective* sense; it was a *sociological* one, in which the economic development was the *objective* condition for the cultural development. His main criticism of Capitalism was exactly that it had crippled man by the preponderance of economic interests, and Socialism for him was a society in which man would be freed from this domination by a more rational and hence productive form of economic organization.[35]

It can be readily discerned from this quote that Fromm's Marx is essentially a humanist who is concerned with the crippling of human potential in capitalist society. Marx is materialist, according to Fromm, not because he believes that all human motivation can be reduced to its economic kernel of material interest. Rather, his materialism concerns the crucial role played by the level of socioeconomic development in setting the stage for moral and cultural progress. Marxism for Fromm is therefore not a reductivism in which mental and spiritual phenomena are traced back to their self-interested motivations. They are seen rather as resulting from the "whole practice of life," the manner in which society as a whole organizes economic production, and the consequences of this organization for cultural and moral self-understandings. Marx, according to Fromm, "is not concerned primarily with the equalization of income. He is concerned with the liberation of man from a kind of work which destroys his individuality."[36]

Fromm is clear that the socioeconomic conditions for the development of human powers of self-realization have been lacking in the vast sweep of history. In the attempt to improve social conditions, Fromm writes, "man is constantly limited by the material factors of his environment."[37] For most of human history, he suggests, "the productive forces were not sufficiently developed to permit the coexistence of both technical and cultural progress *and* freedom, to permit uncrippled development for all." This is an argument that Thomas Piketty picks up in the work of nineteenth-century novelists who were highly sensitive to what different levels of income meant for one's life and prospects. Without extreme inequality in the nineteenth century, "it would have been impossible for a very small elite to concern themselves with something other than subsistence."[38] Extreme inequality is simply a precondition, in this society, of the possibility of a tiny minority having access to the high culture of musical instruments, ball gowns, and French lessons. In such a society, as Horkheimer knew, humanism would be little more than the "Reformation for the wealthy."[39] At the same time, Fromm argues that humanity has an "immanent goal" that, given the right material conditions, will manifest itself as a striving for growth and individual development. The full development and growth of humanity are possible, he argues, "*provided the external conditions that are given are conducive to this aim.*"[40] In *Escape from Freedom*, Fromm sketches what such a society would look like:

> The victory of freedom is possible only if democracy develops into a society in which the individual, his growth and happiness, is the aim and purpose of culture, in which life does not need any justification in success or anything else, and in which the individual is not subordinated to or manipulated by any power outside himself, be it the State or the economic machine, finally a society in which his conscience and ideals are not the internalization of external demands, but are really *his* and express the aims that arise from the peculiarity of his self. These aims could not be realized in any previous period of modern history, because the material basis for the development of genuine individualism was lacking.[41]

Sweeping changes in socioeconomic conditions, on this view, call out certain human capabilities and desires that fit with the forms of production and relationships sustained by the social order. Fromm, as Michael J. Thompson has argued, shared with Aristotle, Hegel, and Marx the view that "human development is grounded in the social conditions that form human beings, largely through the nature of social relations."[42]

The plausibility of Fromm's humanism depends upon the coherence of this view of socioeconomic change as the motor of human development. Inglehart and Welzel have offered an interpretation of modernization that in many ways is supportive of Fromm's account. They argue that social change in contemporary postindustrial societies like the North Atlantic democracies is increasingly a process of human development, producing "increasingly humanistic societies with an emphasis on human freedom and self-expression."[43] Inglehart and Welzel note an important shift from the industrial to the postindustrial phase of modernization. The industrial phase resulted in the process of secularization of authority, the increasing eclipse of religion as a source of meaning. But the mechanistic, standardized world of industrial society only shifted the source of authority without abolishing it. However, the postindustrial phase brings an emancipation from authority, inaugurating a decisive shift from survival values to self-expression values. The result, according to Inglehart and Welzel, is that "emerging self-expression values transform modernization into a process of human development, giving rise to a new type of humanistic society that promotes human emancipation on many fronts."[44] Emancipatory themes, it is suggested, have entered into all domains of life in postindustrial societies, including gender relations, religious orientations, civic engagement, and work relations. The ability to make autonomous choices is said to be so important to human development that it is likely to become an ever more central feature of modern societies.[45] The growth of self-expression values, which have prospered on the basis of the existential security made available to citizens in advanced postindustrial societies, has driven a process of individualization that has resulted in a weakening of pressures for group conformity, the kind of "incestuous ties" that Fromm saw blocking the progress to a society of free individuals. As the new values take root in society, they drive a transition from a more collectivist society in which individuals fill standard social roles and perform standardized tasks, to a more individualistic society in which there is considerable scope for the expression of individuality in daily life.

This theory of modernization provides robust support for Fromm's grounding of humanism in the material basis of socioeconomic development. But there appears to be a glaring problem. We can put this by asking: How does this theory make sense of the gathering political crisis of neoliberalism? Why are antidemocratic sentiments, and variants of authoritarian populism on the rise in a society that is increasingly approximating a humanistic culture devoted to self-expression values? The answer must be sought in the phenomenon that barely merits a mention in modernization theory: capitalism. Fromm saw clearly that an attention to progressive socioeconomic developments and their emancipatory trajectory in capitalist society can only be a part of the story. The new possibilities for freedom generated by socioeconomic change must be institutionalized and anchored in a stable regime of accumulation that, temporarily at least, is successful enough to satisfy claims to profit of capital owners and also to avoid exhausting beyond repair the demands of social reproduction and environmental sustainability. Regimes of capital arise in order to exploit the new possibilities for accumulation that emerge with shifts in values, lifestyle, and general levels of existential security. But regimes of capital are also, over time, destabilized by the continual buildup of new potentials for growth that cannot come into their own until the regime is dismantled and replaced by one more congenial to the new possibilities. At some point, the contradiction between the structural requirements of the current regime and the institutional demands of the new potentials for human development becomes too great. Economic and political contradictions began to hit the regime of postwar-managed capitalism in the 1960s, centering on militarism, imperialism, and asymmetries of race, ethnicity, and gender, and the distorting effects of bureaucracy and mass production on the lifeworld.[46] However, the emancipatory currents seeking to push state-managed capitalism toward an institutional form more congenial to self-expression and autonomy triggered a powerful countermovement that began to perceive the progressive social currents as a threat to existing divisions of wealth and power. Fromm correctly saw that these reactionary countermovements are able to mobilize a pseudo-populist base of citizens by drawing on fears and anxieties associated with social change. These countermovements draw on the competitive and exploitative social relations that are required by a capitalist economy to generate psychological anxieties and insecurities. The latter, in turn, work to block and redirect the emancipatory tendencies welling up from the trajectory of socioeconomic change. Fromm's concept of social character explains how this process works at the psychosocial level. Rapid social change is likely to be particularly destabilizing to individuals habituated to social conditions that are becoming obsolete or dysfunctional through the dynamic of social change. Fromm explains that

> the past puts a stamp on the present by the fact that the character of the individual is formed through the established patterns; only through a much longer process do the new economic conditions weaken the old character structure and reduce the weight of the traditional value structure so that the new economic practice can exercise its full influence on the development of character.[47]

The fact that it takes a significantly longer time for new economic conditions to have an effect of social character is responsible for what Fromm calls the "lag" between changing economic conditions and personality. Over time, socioeconomic change will adjust individuals' emotional investments in social life such that the social character will align with economic developments, leading individuals to take pleasure in (and hence perform voluntarily) the type of activities required for sustaining the economic trajectory of the regime. But before this readjustment happens, the lag between social character and new socioeconomic conditions turns the former from social mortar, stabilizing the social order, into a kind of dynamite that is prepared to destroy it. In the mid-1970s, Donald Warren wrote about the increasing political and social radicalization of an important swath of the lower middle class, a group he referred to as "middle American radicals."[48] By the 1970s, they had come to see themselves as an exploited and dispossessed group, squeezed between the tax and economic policies of the elite, on the one hand, and the efforts to dismantle the structures of white, patriarchal privilege, which Middle American Radicals interpreted as an attack on their own rights and status, on the other. This group had been a bulwark of the postwar regime, responding to the invocations of God, Family, and Country that induced them to sacrifice for the higher purposes of the regime. But when it began to appear as though society was being pulled by socioeconomic changes toward a drastic reevaluation of the centrality of religious values, the white, patriarchal family, and national sacrifice, Middle American Radicals entered the political arena as reactionaries determined to preserve the privileges conferred upon them by the postwar order.

Neoliberalism was birthed in the United States in the struggle between these two movements of emancipation and reaction. For a new regime to take hold, it must find a way of making use of the new human and technological potentials for economic growth and innovation, while at the same time ensuring that those new potentials do not constitute a threat to existing stratifications of wealth and power. The claims for autonomy and self-determination would have to be institutionalized in forms that promote consumerism, and the monetization of new self-expressive capacities. In the next section, I want to show how the neoliberal regime, emerging in the 1970s, was able to draw on the political strength of the forces of reaction in order to channel these demands into social spaces in which personal autonomy was rendered compatible with vast inequalities of power and wealth.

The Neoliberal Turn

Our current postindustrial capitalist societies seem to be obsessed with questions of happiness and well-being. William Davies notes that since the 1960s, capitalist societies have come to depend more on individuals' emotional and psychological engagement with their work, health, and own well-being, while at the same time they appear to lack any real sense of how to achieve these things.[49] The sense of burnout, pessimism, and the prevalence of clinical signs of depression are, as Davies explains, part and parcel of the way in which neoliberalism has turned the need for personal growth and self-development into a private imperative upon individuals in a social order in which there are very few limits to the scope of competition and measurement. The problem afflicting neoliberalism is in fact no different from the problem afflicting every capitalist regime when it has to confront the physical, psychological, and cultural problems caused by its distinctive manner of extracting value from workers. Taylorization in the early twentieth century extracted value by treating workers like machines, controlling their movements down to the smallest units of measurement. Neoliberalism, in contrast, was able to draw upon the discourses of growth and authenticity welling up from the consequences of socioeconomic change in the postwar period and has managed to put those ideas to work in framing the private and personal dimensions of individual existence as corporate resources to be monetized in the accumulation process. The concept of authenticity, Murtola and Fleming note, seems to have shifted "from a problem of the humanist revolutionary left to one that is now at home in glossy corporate training manuals, team-building exercises of investment firms and advertising agencies."[50] What neoliberal economists genuinely admired about markets, Davies notes, was not so much the idea of a framework of fair competition, but rather the competitive psychology that sought to distinguish, compare, and rank individuals according to their productivity and contribution.[51] This was the crucial insight that enabled the transformation of the humanistic discourse of growth and authenticity into the terms of competition for the spoils of success. In order to structure this winner-takes-all competition throughout the social body, neoliberalism had to construct a new vision of government. There arose a new breed of expert, stripped down of moral notions of care and traditions of professionalism, and rooted "in a dispassionate ability to measure, rank, compare, categorize, and diagnose."[52] The neoliberal self, Mirowski writes, "lives in an invisible grid of FICO gradients."[53] Government is required to establish the terms of competition and to measure and quantify the results. But since the injunction to develop and improve oneself has been privatized, government has no interest in preferring any particular outcome over others, even when the consequences actually undermine the very idea of competition that is supposed to justify the whole framework in the first place. At this point, neoliberalism discards its ideological covering and reveals its true interest: the licensing of private ambitions to unlimited wealth and power.

This reading of neoliberalism is compatible with Boltanski and Chiapello's argument concerning neoliberalism's absorption of the "artistic critique" directed against capitalism in the 1960s. The artistic critique, they argue, was focused on claims for individual creativity and authenticity, and emerged when the standardized, methodical, and hierarchical work arrangements of the era of managed capitalism became radically out of alignment with the needs and expectations particularly of young workers who had most fully imbibed the ethos of self-expression and self-development that had emerged during the security and prosperity of the postwar period. However, the corporate assimilation of the values of authenticity and self-expression has enabled the development of new and more extensive forms of control over workers' subjectivity. In the neoliberal era, they argue, the subordination of entire dimensions of the artistic critique to the demands of capital accumulation has "emptied the demands for liberation and authenticity of what gave them substance."[54] In the world of managed capitalism, the control of labor through standardization and surveillance allowed for the extraction of value in an age of institutionalized class opposition. Instead of directly controlling the worker's operations, the new, neoliberal forms of control simply record and quantify workers' contributions and allow the structural framework of private competition to assign rewards. In this way, the worker's personal qualities and capacities, which are the foundation of personal growth and self-development, are turned into competitive advantages in the general struggle for control of social resources. Instead of illuminating a path to a society that takes individual self-development and self-expression seriously for their own sake, the neoliberal colonization of humanist aspirations has turned those elements into quantifiable, competitive performances for the apportionment of material rewards.[55]

In the postwar era, as Robert Castel argues, the idea of citizenship became associated with specific conditions that integrated wage earners into the political body, and associated citizenship with a status that was a collective responsibility of society as a whole.[56] The neoliberal era has brought about what Margaret Somers describes as a "contractualization of citizenship."[57] The solidarities and noncontractual obligations that characterized social relationships in the postwar era have been eviscerated by the remodeling of social relations on the idea of market exchange. The consequences of this depoliticization of social relations can be seen in the radical shifts in power relations among different social classes in the neoliberal era. The shareholder value revolution that surged through corporate institutions in the 1980s was itself conceived as a rebellion against the sclerotic and bureaucratic institutions that had (supposedly) neutered the capitalist class in the postwar era. Returning control of corporations to the shareholders, the alleged "owners" of these corporations, was portrayed as a way of unleashing the creative energies of the individual, which had been smothered by the collectivist institutions of postwar society.

Underlying these changes in social relations in the interests of concentrated wealth and power is a significant depoliticization in the understanding of what it means to be a citizen. In the postwar era, the state maintained a significant (if insufficient) role in marrying economic growth to the demands of social progress. As noted earlier, individuals in the postwar era benefited from social solidarities and noncontractual obligations that set out a robust role for the state in guaranteeing social citizenship. The neoliberal state, however, has come to view its citizens merely as a resource for enterprises, seeking to "maximize the population's utility" through increasing readiness to work and decreasing the social costs of labor.[58] Neoliberalism, as Wendy Brown argues, has sought to transform notions of equality, freedom, and sovereignty from a political to a purely economic register.[59] As liberty is relocated to the economic from the political sphere, it undermines the very idea of social equality in its tying of social status exclusively to market performance. Freedom also gets tied to the idea of participation in markets, in a way which ultimately radically constrains individual choices and possibilities. The suppression and marginalization of the political capacities of citizens gives free reign to the pre-political relations of socioeconomic power, leaving no institutional space that might form a counterweight to that power. It is the reduction of aspirations to freedom and self-expression to a purely economic significance that allows neoliberalism to align these aspirations with notions of competition and preexisting social inequalities, turning them into means for the extraction of value.

The consequences of the evacuation of political capacities and understandings from economic life can be seen in the history of antitrust policy in the neoliberal era. During the "Second New Deal" of the 1930s, through legislation such as the Packers and Stockyards Act and "fair-trade" laws, there was a concerted effort to dismantle the heavy concentration and monopolization of industry that characterized the Gilded Age.[60] In the postwar era, the state played an active role in blocking corporate mergers, attacking price fixing, breaking up monopolistic concentrations, and preventing aggressive anticompetitive practices. This began to change in the 1970s, in large part under the influence of a group of neoliberal economists. Neoliberals began to push the argument that what matters was not the structure of competition per se, but rather the idea of "consumer welfare." In providing value to the consumer, it was argued, monopoly might in fact turn out to be more efficient than competition. Actions of corporate entities were now to be judged not in terms of their effects on the health of market structure but in terms of how they affected the welfare of the consumer. The most significant consequence of this shift from a political language of preservation of market structure to a purely economic language of efficiency, Will Davies argues, was to ensure "far greater freedom for dominant competitors within the overall contest of capitalism."[61] Behind the idea of efficiency, then, lay an ideological campaign to exclude economic life entirely from political questions about market structure and the design of institutions able to promote common purposes. The idea of monopolistic power was no longer seen as a threat to freedom, since individuals were recast as consumers who wanted first and foremost greater utility, rather than as citizens concerned with the fairness or justice of underlying structures of economic life.[62]

The measure of neoliberalism's evisceration of political life is to be found in its reduction of autonomy to its purely economic significance, while excluding the social and political dimension of autonomy, which involves the capacity of citizens to organize a society according to values to which they adhere. The ideas of shareholder value, core competence, and the dismantling of antitrust policy have eviscerated the preexisting moral-political meanings embedded in economic life, leaving the symbolic vacuum to be filled by the raw power of antagonistic class interests. While corporations have acquired considerable governmental power to set policy, to regulate, and to tax, domination has been written into the structure of contemporary corporate institutions through the suppression of the citizen's power to set the terms of engagement in economic life through common principles of fairness and justice.

Conclusion

Throughout his life, Fromm remained committed to a form of democratic socialism that would establish democratic power over the course of economic life. Only in a planned economy, he argued, in which "the whole nation has rationally mastered the economic and social forces," can individuals share responsibility and enable their collective creativity.[63] Fromm argues that such power necessitates far more than sporadic political participation. Modern democracy must be extended far beyond the political sphere if it is going to challenge the "economic insignificance" of the average individual. Far more than a formal procedure for electing leaders, then, democracy is, on Fromm's view, "a system that creates the economic, political, and cultural conditions for the full development of the individual."[64] Fromm believed that substantive democratic control over the economic system was a fundamental aspect of what makes a genuinely democratic society different from an authoritarian one. The active control and cooperation of individuals through radical decentralization of decision-making furnishes the social conditions for the flourishing of autonomy and individuality, transforming citizens from passive and alienated consumers to the active creators of the form of democratic life they share in common. After decades of neoliberal anti-politics, in which the common habits of political life have been left to atrophy, if not deliberately destroyed, it is vital for critical social theory to recover a perspective on capitalism as a site of untrammeled political, social, and economic power. The deep problems of heavily concentrated economic power, massive social and economic inequality, and the corporate takeover of democratic life and society have now reached a stage which is bound to make the ameliorative efforts of later critical theories, whose worldviews were nurtured in the collectivist era of managerial capitalism, appear to be wholly inadequate.

Honneth's idea in *Freedom's Right* of rebuilding the pre-contractual moral background to a free-market economy clearly harks back to the successes of postwar liberalism. But it is questionable today whether any attempt to tame capitalism through regulation, management, and elite planning can claim intellectual and strategic plausibility. Capitalism has demonstrated a tremendous capacity to transcend whatever limits and restrictions political institutions have placed on them, drawing on the anxieties and insecurities generated by rapid social change to alter its trajectory in ways favorable to existing configurations of wealth and power. The solution must involve the radical dismantling of the structural inequalities that continue to furnish the motivational energy for large-scale, reactionary opposition to the traditions of democracy, universality, and equality. But this can only succeed as a social project of deep democratization rather than a managerial project seeking to tame capitalism from above. The resurgence of capitalism in the neoliberal era has shown that managerial solutions to problems of concentrated economic power are deeply vulnerable to sustained attack when they are unable to challenge the fundamental structure of the system and its generation of social and economic inequalities. Over time, if it fails to challenge that structure, such a system will be judged simply on its capacity to deliver the goods. Breaking that cycle will require what K. Sabeel Rahman terms a thicker notion of freedom; not the passive freedom of enjoying security provided by experts and policymakers, but "shared authorship and self-rule, over matters both economic and political."[65] The idea of democracy as a force for the fundamental restructuring of social relations is essential to prevent the emergence of reactionary countermovements that can be deployed by the capitalist class to restore archaic forms of class power and to undermine the notions of equality and universality.

Notes

1. Fraser, "Legitimation Crisis?"
2. Streeck, *How Will Capitalism End?*, 58.
3. This idea was argued most influentially by Boltanski and Chiapello, *The New Spirit of Capitalism*.
4. Fromm's most systematic account of the dynamic between these two tendencies is in Fromm, *Escape from Freedom*.
5. See Fromm, *Escape from Freedom*, 39–122.
6. Abromeit, "The Origins and Development of the Model of Early Critical Theory," 47, 55. The story of Fromm's marginalization in the history of the Frankfurt School is told in Mclaughlin, "Origin Myths in the Social Sciences."
7. On this argument, see Sitton, "Disembodied Capitalism."
8. Wellmer, "On Critical Theory," 713.
9. I have argued this case in depth in my paper "Freedom's Right: Critical Social Theory and the Challenge of Neoliberalism." See also Thompson, *The Domestication of Critical Theory*, 63–88.
10. I believe this is the essential insight behind Fromm's idea of the "escape" or "fear" of freedom. Anxieties about social change are exploited by powerful authorities in order to reinforce a libidinal attachment to the existing order.
11. Fromm worked on a study of the psychological profile of members of the German working class during his years in Frankfurt, which would remain unpublished until the 1980s: Fromm et al., *The Working Class in Weimer Germany*.
12. Fromm, "Psychoanalysis and Sociology," 37–39.
13. Ibid., 38.
14. In *The Sane Society*, Fromm argues that these essential needs include healthy, loving relations with others, creative expression, a rootedness in community, a sense of individuality, and an understanding of our place in the world. See pp. 33–66.
15. Horkheimer, "The Present Situation of Social Philosophy and the Tasks of an Institute for Social Research."

16 Ibid., 1.
17 Ibid., 10.
18 Fromm, *Escape from Freedom*, 131.
19 Horkheimer, "Egoism and Freedom Movements," 49–110.
20 Horkheimer began to move away from this position in the late 1930s, at a time when he was beginning a new collaboration with Theodor Adorno. Horkheimer came to adopt a version of Friedrich Pollock's notion of state capitalism, and also became much more pessimistic about the prospects for social change. See Abromeit, "The Origins and Development of the Model of Early Critical Theory," 61. His collaboration with Adorno became the canonical model of "first generation" critical theory, sowing the seeds for Fromm's marginalization in the history of the Institute.
21 Durkin, *The Radical Humanism of Erich Fromm*, 43. This tradition's influence on Fromm is also discussed from a different perspective in Funk, *Erich Fromm: The Courage to Be Human*, 157–90.
22 Fromm, *You Shall Be as Gods*, 36.
23 Ibid., 40.
24 Fromm, *The Sane Society*, 33.
25 Fromm, "Disobedience as a Psychological and Moral Problem," 16–24.
26 Fromm, *The Sane Society*, 112.
27 Ibid., 114.
28 Maslow, *Motivation and Personality*, 161.
29 Ibid., 171.
30 Petigny, *The Permissive Society*, 226.
31 Rieff, *The Triumph of the Therapeutic*, 239.
32 Petigny suggests that in its focus on growth and autonomy, "humanistic psychology helped cultivate the very attitudes that helped spawn the feminist movement," *The Permissive Society*, 159. See also Eva Illouz, *Saving the Modern Soul*, 105ff.
33 Ryan and Deci, "Overview of Self-Determination Theory," 7.
34 See Ryan and Vansteenkiste, "On Psychological Growth and Vulnerability," 266.
35 Fromm, *The Sane Society*, 219; emphasis in original.
36 Fromm, *Marx's Concept of Man*, 40.
37 Fromm, *The Anatomy of Human Destructiveness*, 293.
38 Piketty, *Capital in the Twenty-First Century*, 415.
39 Horkheimer, "Egoism and Freedom Movements," 99.
40 Fromm, *The Anatomy of Human Destructiveness*, 291; emphasis in original.
41 Fromm, *Escape from Freedom*, 297; emphasis in original.
42 Thompson, "Normative Humanism as Redemptive Critique," 45.
43 Inglehart and Welzel, *Modernization, Cultural Change, and Democracy*, 2.
44 Ibid., 47.
45 Ibid., 137.
46 Fraser, "Legitimation Crisis?" 169.
47 Fromm and Maccoby, *Social Character in a Mexican Village*, 127.
48 Warren, *The Radical Center*.
49 Davies, *The Happiness Industry*, 9.
50 Murtola and Fleming, "The Business of Truth," 2.
51 Davies, *The Happiness Industry*, 146.
52 Ibid., 147.
53 Mirowski, *Never Let a Serious Crisis Go to Waste*, 127.
54 Boltanski and Chiapello, *The New Spirit of Capitalism*, 420.

55 It is interesting to compare this thesis with Fromm's account of the marketing character, which performs a similar function in postwar-managed capitalism. See *The Sane Society*, 129–37.
56 Castel, *From Manual Workers to Wage Labourers*.
57 Somers, *Genealogies of Citizenship*, 2.
58 Dardot and Laval, *The New Way of the World*, 225.
59 Brown, *Undoing the Demos*, 41.
60 Lynn, "Killing the Competition."
61 Davies, *The Limits of Neoliberalism*, 83.
62 See Teachout and Khan, "Market Structure and Political Law."
63 Fromm, *Escape from Freedom*, 299.
64 Ibid., 301.
65 Rahman, *Democracy against Domination*, 173.

References

Abromeit, John. (2014). "The Origins and Development of the Model of Early Critical Theory in the Work of Max Horkheimer, Erich Fromm, and Herbert Marcuse." In David Ingram (ed.), *Critical Theory to Structuralism*. New York: Routledge.
Boltanski, Luc, and Ève Chiapello. (2005). *The New Spirit of Capitalism*. New York: Verso.
Brown, Wendy. (2015). *Undoing the Demos: Neoliberalism's Stealth Revolution*. New York: Zone Books.
Castel, Robert. (2003). *From Manual Workers to Wage Laborers: Transformation of the Social Question*, edited and translated by Richard Boyd. New Brunswick, NJ: Transaction.
Dardot, Pierre, and Christian Laval. (2013). *The New Way of the World: On Neoliberal Society*, translated by G. Elliot. New York: Verso.
Davies, William. (2014). *The Limits of Neoliberalism*. London: Sage.
Davies, William. (2015). *The Happiness Industry*. New York: Verso.
Durkin, Kieran. (2014). *The Radical Humanism of Erich Fromm*. New York: Palgrave Macmillan.
Foster, Roger. (2017). "Freedom's Right: Critical Social Theory and the Challenge of Neoliberalism." *Capital and Class* 41, no. 3: 455–73.
Fraser, Nancy. (2015). "Legitimation Crisis? On the Political Contradictions of Financialized Capitalism." *Critical Historical Studies* Fall: 157–89.
Fromm, Erich. (1941). *Escape from Freedom*. New York: Avon.
Fromm, Erich. (1955). *The Sane Society*. New York: Rinehart and Co.
Fromm, Erich. (1966). *You Shall Be as Gods*. New York: Ballantine Books.
Fromm, Erich. (1973). *The Anatomy of Human Destructiveness*. New York: Henry Holt.
Fromm, Erich. (1984). *The Working Class in Weimer Germany: A Psychological and Sociological Study*, translated by Barbara Weinberger and edited by Wolfgang Bonss. Cambridge, MA: Harvard University Press.
Fromm, Erich. (1989). "Psychoanalysis and Sociology," translated by Mark Ritter. In Stephen Bronner and Douglas Kellner (eds.), *Critical Theory and Society: A Reader*. New York: Routledge.
Fromm, Erich. (2004). *Marx's Concept of Man*. New York: Continuum.

Fromm, Erich. (2011). "Disobedience as a Psychological and Moral Problem." In Lawrence Behrens and Leonard J. Rosen (eds.), *On Writing and Reading across the Curriculum*, 11th ed. New York: Longman.

Fromm, Erich, and Michael Maccoby. (1966). *Social Character in a Mexican Village*. New Brunswick: Transaction.

Funk, Rainer. (1982). *Erich Fromm: The Courage to Be Human*. New York: Continuum.

Horkheimer, Max. (1993a). "The Present Situation of Social Philosophy and the Tasks of an Institute for Social Research." In *Between Philosophy and Social Science: Selected Early Writings*, translated by G. Frederick Hunter, Matthew S. Kramer, and John Torpey, 1–13. Cambridge, MA: MIT Press.

Horkheimer, Max. (1993b). "Egoism and Freedom Movements." In *Between Philosophy and Social Science: Selected Early Writings*, translated by G. Frederick Hunter, Matthew S. Kramer, and John Torpey, 49–110. Cambridge, MA: MIT Press.

Illouz, Eva. (2008). *Saving the Modern Soul*. Berkeley, CA: University of California Press.

Inglehard, Ronald, and Christian Welzel. (2005). *Modernization, Cultural Change, and Democracy*. Cambridge: Cambridge University Press.

Lynn, Barry. (2012). "Killing the Competition: How the New Monopolies are Destroying Open Markets." *Harpers Magazine*. Retrieved from https://harpers.org/archive/2012/02/killing-the-competition/ (accessed June 3, 2017).

Maslow, Abraham. (1954). *Motivation and Personality*. New York: Harper and Row.

Mclaughlin, Neil. (1999). "Origin Myths in the Social Sciences: Fromm, the Frankfurt School and the Emergence of Critical Theory." *Canadian Journal of Sociology* 24, no. 1: 109–39.

Mirowski, Philip. (2013). *Never Let a Serious Crisis Go to Waste*. New York: Verso.

Murtola, Anne-Marie, and Peter Fleming. (2011). "The Business of Truth: Authenticity, Capitalism and the Crisis of Everyday Life." *Ephemera* 11, no. 1: 1–5.

Petigny, Alan. (2009). *The Permissive Society: American 1941–1965*. Cambridge: Cambridge University Press.

Piketty, Thomas. (2014). *Capital in the Twenty-First Century*. Cambridge, MA: Belknap Press.

Rahman, K. Sabeel. (2017). *Democracy against Domination*. Oxford: Oxford University Press.

Rieff, Philip. (1966). *The Triumph of the Therapeutic*. Chicago: University of Chicago Press.

Ryan, Richard M., and Maarten Vansteenkiste. (2013). "On Psychological Growth and Vulnerability: Basic Psychological Need Satisfaction and Need Frustration as a Unifying Principle." *Journal of Psychotherapy Integration* 25, no. 3: 263–80.

Ryan, Richard M., and Ryan L. Deci. (2002). "Overview of Self-Determination Theory: An Organismic Dialectical Perspective." In Ryan L. Deci and Richard M. Ryan (eds.), *Handbook of Self-Determination Research*, 3–26. Rochester, NY: University of Rochester Press.

Sitton, John. (1998). "Disembodied Capitalism: Habermas's Conception of the Economy." *Sociological Forum* 13, no. 1: 61–83.

Somers, Margaret. (2008). *Genealogies of Citizenship*. Cambridge: Cambridge University Press.

Streeck, Wolfgang. (2016). *How Will Capitalism End?* New York: Verso.

Teachout, Zephyr, and Lina Khan. (2014). "Market Structure and Political Law: A Taxonomy of Power." *Duke Journal of Constitutional Law & Public Policy* 9: 37–74.

Thompson, Michael J. (2014). "Normative Humanism as Redemptive Critique." In Seyed Javad Miri, Robert Lake, and Tricia M. Kress (eds.), *Reclaiming the Sane Society*, 37–58. Rotterdam: Sense.

Thompson, Michael J. (2016). *The Domestication of Critical Theory*. London: Rowman and Littlefield.

Warren, Donald L. (1976). *The Radical Center: Middle Americans and the Politics of Alienation*. South Bend, IN: University of Notre Dame Press.

Wellmer, Albrecht. (2014). "On Critical Theory." *Social Research* 81, no. 3: 705–33.

Chapter 5

FEMINISM, HUMANISM, AND ERICH FROMM

Lynn S. Chancer

In recently writing about Erich Fromm's work having greater relevance to contemporary feminist thought than usually recognized, I criticized Fromm's use of the word "man."[1] My assumption was that Fromm was living in places and circumstances that did not expose him to the sharp explosion of ideas happening with second and later waves of feminisms; otherwise, he would have changed his conventional but historically sexist usage. However, evidence from later Fromm texts shows that Fromm continued to use "man" purposely.[2] It is possible that something was lost in translation from German to English; more likely he could have changed the linguistic habit but did not. Why? And what does Fromm's persistence bode, if anything, about the compatibility of his ideas and feminist theories broadly speaking?

Fromm may have stubbornly held onto using "man" out of conviction that this was part of clear writing; his work is admirable for its characteristically strong writing and wonderful accessibility that led to virtually all his books becoming bestsellers in the one to many millions of copies. Indeed, in one place, he argued that "to say 'he or she' each time would be awkward" and that "it would be somewhat pedantic to avoid the word ['man'] in order to make the point that the author does not use it in the spirit of patriarchalism."[3] But Fromm may have also persisted from a sense that using "man" had enough of a history of generic associations as to keep his meaning firmly focused on people—on "everyone"—as was his humanistic intention.

Toward the very end of his career, in *To Have or to Be?*, Fromm makes explicit reference to such supposedly undifferentiated usage in the humanist tradition, citing also the fact that in his native German the word *Mensch* (as opposed to *Mann*) is set aside for precisely this function. While I respect these explanations, it needs also be emphasized that language—as theorists from Foucault through Derrida and Butler well understood—matters. To write and refer to "man" rather than "people" is arguably to perpetuate, rather than undermine, the sexist and male-dominated history of social theorizing itself. Perhaps stubbornly myself, I suspect that Fromm would have changed this practice had he been closer to and participating in passionate feminist debates from the 1960s through the 1980s— that is, intensely involved with day-to-day discussions that did eventually alter the lens and writing of many (male) theorists. Yet whether he made the change or not, Fromm scholars in contemporary contexts ought to remedy the usage issue themselves/ourselves. Otherwise, Fromm's ideas may remain alienating and relatively removed from, rather than seen as compatible in some important ways with, feminist theorists.

My purpose here, though, diverges slightly: if Fromm meant "man" (even mistakenly) to stress the humanism that was intended by his work, this begs an interesting question as to whether feminist and humanist ideas are compatible in ways beneficial for feminist and social theories overall—both, not either/or. I wish to argue that humanistic frameworks, tending to be demeaned from the 1980s onward as essentialist and insensitive to differences between people, are nonetheless worth looking at again—a theoretical recuperation already begun in Kieran Durkin's work,[4] and reiterated here through a simultaneously feminist and Frommian lens.

For even if such connections were not made by Fromm in his own time, combining humanistic and feminist perspectives taps non-essentialist *analytic* categories. These categories can be reinterpreted to show gender categories in ways that contemporary post-structural and intersectional feminists can appreciate, that is, as highly flexible and also encompassing commonalities as well as differences between people. For instance, in my own work *Sadomasochism in Everyday Life: Dynamics of Power and Powerlessness*, I borrowed from Fromm's use of masochism and sadism as processes that involve common psychosocial dynamics at the same time differing by gender, class, race, sexualities, and other social categories. Something similar can also be seen in Fromm's *The Art of Loving*, in which love is treated as a psychological phenomenon that has universal characteristics, which are nevertheless experienced divergently across the different social categories in line with their attendant social inequalities. In other words, in this originally best-selling work, which is no longer read or cited frequently,[5] Fromm made universal claims that can also be interpreted with sensitivity vis-à-vis differences. Nothing about his analysis was "essentially" limited to particular gender, sexual, class, racial, or ethnic categories—such social differences affecting but not obviating humanistic arguments about the mutually respecting traits of love that he elaborated.

Consequently, and pursuant to these two examples, combining feminism and humanism points to precisely the kind of multidimensional thinking-and-feeling about commonalities-and-differences (again both, not either/or)[6] that twenty-first-century theorizing—and, more importantly, life—demands. Moreover, by highlighting love and a wide range of emotions, including anxiety and insecurity (which lead people, for example, to want to "escape from freedom"), Fromm reveals himself as an early "psychosocial" theorist. Both sociologically and psychoanalytically trained, Fromm's work calls attention to how emotionality and rationality function inseparably in day-to-day life for most of humanity.

Where, then, does this leave us? This chapter looks at Fromm's thought and its implications for feminist theorizing from the perspective of both understanding gender dynamics *and* generalizing beyond them to non-essentialist conclusions.

For I contend that despite its problems, Fromm's work in the contemporary context emerges as (perhaps surprisingly) compatible with developments in feminist and queer theorizing. Because I believe advantages as well as disadvantages can be culled from his ideas, I turn now to what is strikingly relevant about Fromm's work, before turning to places where essentialist thinking about gender sometimes crept in, nonetheless. The former ideas are well worth developing while the latter merit corrective. Overall, I argue that while not necessarily obvious or generally recognized, the work of Erich Fromm is much more consonant with feminist theories and thought than usually recognized.

Advantages of Fromm's Thought for Combining Feminism and Humanism

Fromm's work is helpful for overcoming still frequent assumptions that Freudian-influenced psychoanalytic theories are incompatible with feminist beliefs. First and foremost, feminists are not always aware that some of Fromm's analyses sound like they could have been written by radical feminists of the American second wave. Two important examples can be cited, the first relevant to the practice of psychoanalysis, and to the critique of the patriarchal assumptions that mar its classical statement. In what is an incisive critique of Freud's famous *An Analysis of a Case of Hysteria* at the very end of his life, Fromm sheds light on Freud's sexist use of power in that psychoanalytic situation.[7] In Fromm's hands, Dora was not so much a "case study in hysteria" as an example of a therapist/patient reproduction of patriarchal inequalities of power and powerlessness. Fromm showed himself an astute social observer while never letting go of his belief in unconscious and psychoanalytically attuned processes. He perceived Dora's rebellion from the sexist psychoanalytic situation in which she had been cast as unequal (Dora had been placed in a subordinated position within the therapeutic "couple," whether or not Freud was taking the psychoanalytic encounter in a direction that made sense and was resonant for her). Indeed, Fromm was able to perceive that for Dora leaving her analysis with Freud could be an act of liberation, a means of exiting the patriarchal and unequal relationship that *prevented* her from freeing herself.

As previously suggested, one can reinterpret *The Art of Loving* as consistent with radical feminist critiques of unequal sexist relationships and of marriage and romance (to the extent the latter depend on notions of women needing men to have fulfilling lives). Indeed, traditional romantic ideologies have conventionally portrayed women as "incomplete" unless "completed" by romance, by a partner, by—historically—a "man." As Simone de Beauvoir described in *The Second Sex*, young girls' daydreams and musical lyrics become filled with the supposed benefits of "merging" for women: take "someday he'll come along—the man I love," a seemingly bygone lyric that nonetheless still accords with fairy tales of Cinderella and Rapunzel as well as songs across a range of music styles. But images of women incomplete without love and romance is quite at odds with Fromm's notion of love in *The Art of Loving*. For Fromm, and in many later feminist critiques from de Beauvoir to Shulamith Firestone, love is impossible unless between two people who are wholes—not parts—each loving themselves or, in whatever combination and permutation applies, loving her and him, him and her, her and her, him and him, and so on. In this regard, Frommian and feminist ideas appear parallel in both insisting that the very idea of love needs revision if gender equality is to be experienced and achieved.

If a first advantage of Fromm's thought thus involves feminist-consistent insights into the subtleties and dynamics of unequal power—whether in quotidian interactions (including psychoanalysis) and/or as embedded in cultural discourses and ideologies of romance and love—a second compatibility returns us to the benefits of humanism. Again, Fromm's categories of analysis were and remain radically humanistic and anti-essentialist. More to the point, his discussions of character structure, biophilia and necrophilia, and of productive and nonproductive orientations, are neither affected nor broken down according to the binaries of a gender-skewed world. In other words, such Frommian concepts have nothing to do with biological determinism and everything to do with human capacities and possibilities across men and women, races, nationalities, and sexualities. They are not intrinsically gendered at this historical moment (the almost 2020s) when deterministic thought—about women, races, and particular groups such as immigrants—remain widespread and often the basis of ongoing modes of dominance and subordination.

A specific example of this radically anti-essentialist character of Fromm thoughts pertains to my own doctoral dissertation that later became the book *Sadomasochism in Everyday Life*. My own thought was very much inspired by Fromm's, especially by *Escape from Freedom*, wherein Fromm discusses the process whereby individuals seek to defend themselves against the loneliness and anomie of modern gesellschaft societies. Here Fromm points out the fact that this need to defend oneself against these stresses can take the form of submission to a more powerful being (masochism) or of exerting controls over a relatively powerless party (sadism). Thus, masochism and sadism emerge in this conceptualization as social defense mechanisms. Noteworthy about this for the feminist "appropriation" of Fromm is how non-essentialist renderings of sadomasochism free such psychosocial understandings of power-and-powerless relationships from essentialist ideas like those of Helene Deutsch.[8] In Deutsch's much more deterministic psychoanalytic treatment, with which Fromm would have been familiar, women are innately masochistic by virtue of biology and their/our connection with birth. According to Deutsch, biology trumps social construction, an association that has made the use of masochism by social theorists badly in need of revision.

On the other hand, and indeed helping with such progressive revision, Fromm's *Escape from Freedom* provides no indication whatsoever that sadism is inherently the province of men nor masochism that of women; this, too, influenced me in *Sadomasochism in Everyday Life*. One of the real strengths of Fromm's theorization here is that it allows for seeing that society pushes people into skewed gendered directions (men toward sadism, women toward masochism) but not in such a way that is biologically based nor essentialist. For women can be sadistic or men masochistic, depending on the nature of the situation. Rather, sadism and masochism can be present in the same individual: someone who is a woman may be socialized into, say, submissiveness toward a male partner or husband while enacting masochism toward a relatively less powerful person in her life. On the other hand, anyone familiar with literary and popular cultural depictions of sadomasochism is likely to recall depictions of powerful men whose dominant sadism (during the day) may transpose (at night) into sexual desires to be beaten and dominated. Socialized patterns exist then, as Fromm indicates, but they are not biologically given and can reverse under certain existential circumstances and at differing historical moments. Moreover, and again, this is a non-essentialism that is very much consonant with feminist insistence—not only with de Beauvoir's classic work but extending through the recent "classic" writings of Judith Butler about gender fluidity and the post-structural character of socially (not biologically based) oppressions.

But I also see third and fourth advantages of utilizing Fromm in the ongoing process of feminist theorizing. Third: whereas this is not always the case with progressive theorists, Fromm is marked out by his insistence on offering positive (one might even say, with a Foucauldian nod, productive[9]) alternatives to the sadomasochistic social arrangements he saw around him. Whether in *The Sane Society* or going back to *The Art of Loving*, Fromm envisioned personal and political relationships of exactly the kind—that is, entailing interdependence between self and others—that feminist object relations theorist Jessica Benjamin more recently dubbed "mutual recognition" in her now well-known, Frankfurt School-influenced work *The Bonds of Love*. Both Fromm and Benjamin— the latter a feminist sociologist who received her PhD in Sociology from New York University before becoming a full-time psychoanalyst—understood how mutual recognition differs from master/slave or sadomasochistic dynamics, wherein one person takes away the freedom of another so as to render himself (or herself) more secure. For Benjamin, the philosophical underpinnings of mutual recognition—so consonant with Fromm's ideas—is that individuals are necessarily social beings while simultaneously endowed with individual, psychic, and psychoanalytic uniqueness. Consequently, people are both independent and connected—an apparently paradoxical, but phenomenologically recurring, diagnosis of human interdependence that also inspired other dynamic thinkers from G. F. W. Hegel through Fromm. Most relevant to this chapter, though, is that for Fromm, like psychoanalytically oriented feminists including Benjamin, critiques of sadomasochism became themselves interconnected with prefigurative visions of what nonsexist relationships would look like on both individual and social levels.

Finally, a fourth compatibility between Frommian and feminist theories strikes me as particularly interesting and promising for concerns about "toxic" forms of masculinities with which current feminists are, of course, also deeply concerned. One reason for the relative neglect of Fromm's thought may be that books like *The Art of Loving* can seem, in retrospect, as though merely psychological self-help books; they may be perceived as "soft" or "touchy feely" reactions that ignore their deeply sociological insights into the importance of transcending gender-based dichotomies between reason and emotion, affect and instrumentality. With Fromm, one aptly draws on the language of caring, love, sanity, and reason, as well as art and joy. In other words, "macho" categories of thought that may socially construct divides between "hard" and "soft" emotions and experiences, tend to be surpassed in the very process of "doing" and "talking" about both Frommian and feminist theories and practices. By extension, Fromm's ideas can be deduced to be consistent with recent critiques of masculinity and masculinities as found in the work of Raewyn Connell, C. J. Pascoe, and Michael Kimmel.[10] This is because, arguably, not only sexism but also heterosexism presupposes masculinities steeped in maintaining rather than transcending rigid emotional dichotomies that are inconsistent with contemporary feminist ideas, and which have coercive consequences by limiting people's gender and sexual freedoms.

From Thesis to Antithesis: Problems of Fromm's Analyses for Feminists

Moving along this argument, if there are so many relationships of compatibility, of intellectual and theoretical and philosophical affinity between Frommian and feminist thought, why do feminists rarely if ever associate themselves with the Frommian tradition? What are reasons that may help to explain why Fromm and feminism have not been perceived as consonant? With this, I now turn to three disadvantages that feminists in contemporary context may associate with Fromm and ideas.

A first problem, and possible contradiction, one that distances Fromm and feminists despite the theoretical advantages just elaborated, involves—indeed—language and discourse. For despite his penetrating critiques of sexist power and inequalities, Fromm continued to use the gendered noun "man" to describe all of humanity. This is clearly evident even in the title of his book *Man for Himself* (1990) and is something that recurs throughout many of his writings about the human condition. This is something I noted long ago when initially reading Fromm, and it is an observation that can easily be passed over and ignored relative to the intellectual power of his ideas. On the other hand, and certainly in this context, the usage is arguably quietly, subliminally, even unconsciously sexist, especially in our contemporary context and in its English language usages. Let us assume that the problem is not primarily or entirely one of translating German into English: ought Fromm to have known better insofar as other of his contemporaries were not making quite so much use of "man" in their writings around the same period? Arguably so, since Fromm lived until 1980, passing away when he was close to eighty, he ought to have had time, by then, to have become familiar with early feminist classics from *The Second Sex* (itself published in the United States in 1951) through well-known liberal and radical feminist books published by Kate Millett[11] and Shulamith Firestone,[12] among others, in the 1960s and 1970s. Again, however much he was accustomed to using the species-oriented term "man," perhaps having feminist theorists closer at hand would have influenced Fromm to change this linguistic habit so as to be more in line with the entirety of his other clearly feminist beliefs and insights.

But a second disadvantage also helps to explain why Fromm's ideas are not generally seen as relevant to feminist thought: this one involves how, despite his overall social constructionist and anti-essentialist leanings (ironically enough, this comprising one of the previously alluded to "advantages" of Fromm for feminists), in other contexts and places, Fromm referred rather contradictorily to "feminine nature." For example, in *Love, Sexuality and Matriarchy: About Gender*, Fromm discussed the anthropological ideas of Bachofen, writing approvingly of Bachofen's "discovery of mother right" and of this notion's ongoing relevance for social psychology (Fromm 1997). As Lawrence Wilde described this aspect of Fromm's thought, "During his years as a member of the Frankfurt School, Erich Fromm developed a strong interest in the idea that there were distinctive male and female character orientations," and drew on the "positive evaluation of matriarchy" made by Bachofen in the nineteenth century.[13] Interestingly, as Fromm also knew, Bachofen's idea—to wit, matriarchy having (allegedly) existed prior to its destruction with the rise of patriarchal societies—had been cited by Friedrich Engels, too, the latter describing an historical progression whereby matriarchal societies were overturned and replaced by patriarchal (and also property-based capitalistic) rule. According to Bachofen, Engels, and later Fromm, then, patriarchy is relatively recent "and was preceded by a state of culture in which the mother was the head of the family, the rules in society, and the Great Goddess."[14]

Why does this matter, though, so much to Fromm? Unlike Engels's theorization, which links the overthrow of "mother right" to forced monogamy and the beginnings of property, Fromm's concern is with the rise of cultural and gendered norms that led to psychosocial harms and alienated/alienating personalities and character structures within capitalistic and patriarchal societies. In Fromm's words,

> As a further consequence, the basic principles of the mother-centered culture are those of freedom and equality, of happiness and the unconditional affirmation of life. In contrast to the motherly principles the fatherly principle if that of law, order, reason, hierarchy; the father has his favorite son, the one who is most like him, the most suited to become the heir and successor to his property and worldly functions. Among the father-centered sons, equality has given way to hierarchy, harmony to strike.[15]

Significant to underscore here is the fact that a deterministic stance is thereby suggested, going back to Bachofen. The "essence" of differences between motherly and fatherly love are biologically based insofar as they are linked with women's role in reproduction.[16] Fromm quotes Bachofen to the effect that "maternity pertains to the physical side of *man*" [my emphasis], concluding that "two traits, therefore, characterize the relationship of matriarchal society to nature: passive surrender to nature; and recognition of natural and biological values, as opposed to intellectual ones. Like the mother, nature is the center of matriarchal culture; and mankind ever remains a helpless child in the face of nature."[17]

With this, though, an explanatory clue emerges about this obvious contradiction between Fromm's typically social constructionist (and feminist) writings and the biologism evident from his endeavors to understand how the system socialist feminist Zillah Eisenstein dubbed "capitalist patriarchy" evolved.[18] For possibly, through Bachofen's allusions to a matriarchal past and the concept of "mother right," Fromm tried to reconcile the sadomasochistic, deeply oppressive inequalities of capitalism (and the pathological deviation he witnessed arise in Fascist Germany) with his own anti-patriarchal sympathies. The "reconciliation" for Fromm might have been to posit a "feminine" principle through which the possibilities of a different society based on love, caring, compassion, and mutually recognizing human beings could be envisioned as more than simply utopian—a notion which is surely fantastical given the anthropological documentation Bachofen proffered.

By way of evidence for this interpretation, note how Fromm complains in *Love, Sexuality and Matriarchy* that previous arguments for women's equality in bourgeois society were based on presuming men and women to be biologically equal. Making a case resonant of critiques by radical and socialist feminists of liberal feminists who wanted nothing more than formal equality with men, Fromm writes, "The theory that woman and man were identical formed the basis for demanding her political equality. But whether it was expressed or only implied, woman's equality meant that she, in her very essence, was the same as man in bourgeois society. . . . The 'human' emancipation of woman really meant her emancipation to become a bourgeois male."[19]

Does this justify Fromm's essentialism? Not persuasively. More to the point is that it explains this out-of-sync biologism while also providing insight into why Fromm may have thought himself progressive—and even consistently feminist (if socialist/radical, not liberal feminist!)—when excavating an allegedly matriarchal history to ground imaginings of a humanistic future. But I would argue that Fromm did not need to theorize matriarchal roots, thereby veering into essentialist territory, in order to comprehend the strength of gender differences that empirically separate men and women so that the former often becomes/became, say, more "aggressive" and the latter often becomes/became, say, more "nurturant." Alternatively, Fromm could have stayed consistent with his usually admirable social constructionist leanings by attributing divergent characteristics to the deeply sociological enculturation that bequeaths and reproduces gendered patterns from generation to generation as well as from country to country. Clearly, gender socialization differs not only according to class/national background but along racial, sexual, and other intersectionally divergent lines—as Fromm, too, was not known for noting—while still creating clusters of behaviors and practices *across* race and class through broad personality patterns of "masculinity" (and masculinities) and "femininity" (and femininities). From this, persistent patterns of gender-divided "habituses"—to tap Pierre Bourdieu's own creative and solidly sociological concept[20]—can be derived so as to render biologistic allusions superfluous. Moreover, it is literally impossible to know what is biological or culturally caused so long as the two are overdetermined. Ironically enough, social determinants of gender discrimination would have to "wither away" entirely to know, for sure, what was or was not biologically caused: nothing of the kind, that is, elimination of gender's social concomitants, has yet happened in Fromm's time or our own.

However, whereas feminists can still arguably benefit from Fromm's thought is in relation to the psychological/psychoanalytic part of "psychosocially" caused gendered effects, which have been relatively less explored or expanded upon by movements from the second wave until now. Obviously, as Fromm understood even better than Freud, given the former's far more explicit critiques of patriarchy and sexism, gendered patterns create terrible harms for both men and women. These patterns are at once "objective" and "subjective," and social as well as psychological; as such, they bequeath emotional as well as rationalistic reactions, including anger and guilt, at both conscious and unconscious levels. For this reason, in concluding, I turn to whether and how Fromm's ideas can be rediscovered not only in the present context of rising political authoritarianism but that of persistent sexist subordination also. How can Fromm's ideas regarding feminism be reconciled post facto even if this happened only partially (albeit significantly) in his own time, place, and space?

A first disadvantage of using Fromm pertains to his use of sexist language (and, thereby, his ignoring power inequalities, even though he usually otherwise acknowledges them). A second, related disadvantage, which I have discussed, is Fromm's veering into essentialism via Bachofen (and Bachofen interpreted too biologically), even where Fromm is arguably admirably and radically anti-essentialist. A third disadvantage—and one that may have contributed to Fromm being a *forgotten intellectual not just in general but for feminists*—may have to do with the fact that Fromm was not as interested in libido theory as much as stressing human relatedness, which can be considered "pre-oedipal" in its developmental importance. In so doing, while Fromm gained much, it is nevertheless the case that he did stop analyzing sexuality in the ways that contemporary feminist theorists, influenced by Butler among others, are now very concerned about, and which involves talking about pleasure, desire, and taking on the socially constructed and imposed, and often discriminated against, character of diverse sexuality and sexualities. Here, as with the advantages, it seems possible to revise Fromm back toward a reconciliation between his ideas and feminisms. It is no longer necessary to use "man" when writing about Fromm unless when (of course and reasonably) quoting him directly. It is possible to use Bachofen in a way that refers to how patriarchal societies mandated divisions between matriarchal and patriarchal parts of ourselves so that they are perceived as biologically based when they are actually deeply cultural. (In other words, one can revise Fromm's interest in Bachofen so that it is interpreted culturally and sociologically rather than biologically and essentialistically—since to smack of "essentialism" seems overall anti-Frommian.) And finally, the fact that Fromm shifted away from libido does not have to mean—and I do not think it *would* mean—that he did not understand the joys of sex as well as the joys of love and creativity and productivity in all other spheres of life. Nor do contemporary discussions of Fromm and feminism have to focus only on sexism rather than also—and importantly in feminist theories of the present—about heterosexism as well. There is nothing that ought to make us think that Fromm would not understand and be willing to embrace these levels of complexity—especially as he did not rule out physicality (and may have also been ahead of his time in understanding the limits of social constructionism when taken to an extreme).

Coming Full Circle Then: Why Does "Fromm and Feminism" Matter?

Perhaps the greatest value of Fromm's thought for contemporary feminism is its centrality in any body of work purporting to demonstrate the compatibility—rather than incommensurability—of sociological and Freudian-influenced psychoanalytic ideas. As Rainer Funk has underscored,[21] Fromm maintained a deep psychological reliance on unconscious defense mechanisms but, again, saw human beings as structured by social as opposed to primarily biological forces. Moreover, reflecting the influence of Karen Horney within psychoanalytic (if not more anti-Freudian feminist) circles,[22] Fromm's concerns about anxiety and relatedness led him to anticipate object relations theory of precisely the kind further developed within psychoanalysis by Melanie Klein[23] and within sociology (and psychoanalysis) by Jessica Benjamin[24] and Nancy Chodorow.[25]

But is it possible to see beyond the essentialism that nonetheless appears in some, though by no means all, of Fromm's writings on gender and sexuality? By now, Fromm's essentialist view of maternalism seems historically obsolescent, as men as well as women more commonly parent and co-parent as single parents, in different types of couples, or in group settings from kibbutzim to other communes. And, by now, it seems obvious that nurturance is and can be provided to babies such that non-patriarchal modes of relating empathetically, with oneself as well as others (as, in *The Art of Loving*, Fromm so clearly and well understood) can result: apparent at this point is that what matters most is not gender but the presence of absence of compassion, love, and respect in parent/children as well as adult relationships. But yet, one wonders if biological as well as psychological differences between people are matters that extreme social constructionism has rendered as though unbroachable. Without resorting to gender essentialism, are there realms of biological differences (of, say, weight or height as pertains to—perhaps—what one person or another can carry or a space that can be fitted into) that can be referred to without judgment but detachedly? Is biology still something that can be discussed (even if theories of biological origins are not at all close to being easily ascertained) insofar as even conceivably a dimension of life—and death—not reducible to the social? While this was not what Fromm had in mind, sociologists and feminists may still find his work interesting insofar as allowing complexity and multidimensionality to be debated, examined, investigated, and explored without fear of sadomasochistic repercussions and punishments—and in the spirit of mutual recognition, at once potentially intellectual and psychic and cultural, that Fromm so brilliantly and ahead of his time advocated.

Notes

1. Chancer, "Sadomasochism or the Art of Loving."
2. Fromm has an explicit discussion of the usage of "man" in the preambles to both *The Anatomy of Human Destructiveness* and *To Have or to Be?*
3. Fromm, *The Anatomy of Human Destructiveness*, 18.
4. Durkin, *The Radical Humanism of Erich Fromm*.
5. A notable exception being bell hooks, who approvingly quotes *The Art of Loving* on numerous occasions in her *All About Love: New Visions*.
6. See Chancer, *After the Rise and Fall of American Feminism*.
7. Fromm, *The Greatness and Limitations of Freud's Thought*.
8. See Deutsch, *The Psychology of Women*.
9. See Foucault, *Discipline and Punish*.
10. See Connell, *Masculinities*, Pascoe, *Guyland*, and Kimmel, *Dude, You're A Fag*.
11. Millett, *Sexual Politics*.
12. Firestone, *The Dialectic of Sex*.
13. Wilde, "The Significance of Maternalism."
14. Fromm, *Love, Sexuality and Matriarchy*, 4.
15. Ibid., 6.
16. Ibid., 5.
17. Ibid., 23.
18. Eisenstein, *Capitalist Patriarchy and the Case for Socialist Feminism*.
19. Fromm, *Love, Sexuality and Matriarchy*, 26.
20. Bourdieu, *Distinction*.
21. Funk, "Erich Fromm and the Intersubjective Tradition."
22. See Horney's *Our Inner Conflicts*.
23. See Klein, *Envy and Gratitude and Other Works*.
24. See Benjamin, *The Bonds of Love*.
25. See Chodorow, *The Power of Feelings*.

References

Benjamin, Jessica. (1988). *The Bonds of Love: Psychoanalysis, Feminism, and the Problem of Domination*. New York: Pantheon Books.

Bourdieu, Pierre. (1986). *Distinction*. New York: Routledge.

Butler, Judith. (2006). *Gender Trouble: Feminism and the Subversion of Identity*. New York: Routledge.

Chancer, Lynn. (1992). *Sadomasochism in Everyday Life*. New Brunswick: Rutgers University Press.

Chancer, Lynn. (2017). "Sadomasochism or the Art of Loving: Fromm and Feminist Theory." *Psychoanalytic Review* 104, no. 4: 469–84.

Chancer, Lynn. (2019). *After the Rise and Stall of American Feminism: Taking Back a Revolution*. Palo Alto, CA: Stanford University Press.
Chodorow, Nancy J. (2001). *The Power of Feelings*. New Haven: Yale University Press.
Connell, Raewyn W. (1995). *Masculinities*. Cambridge: Polity Press.
De Beauvoir, Simone. (2011). *The Second Sex*. New York: Vintage Press.
Deutsch, Helene. (1944). *The Psychology of Women*. New York: Grune & Stratton.
Durkin, Kieran. (2014). *The Radical Humanism of Erich Fromm*. New York: Palgrave Macmillan.
Eisenstein, Zillah. (1978). *Capitalist Patriarchy and the Case for Socialist Feminism*. New York: Monthly Review Press.
Firestone, Shulamith. (2003). *The Dialectic of Sex: The Case for Feminist Revolution*. New York: Farrar, Straus & Giroux.
Foucault, Michel. (1991). *Discipline and Punish: The Birth of a Prison*. London: Penguin.
Freud, Sigmund. (1997). *Dora: An Analysis of a Case Study of Hysteria*. New York: Touchstone.
Fromm, Erich. (1980). *The Greatness and Limitations of Freud's Thought*. New York: Harper and Row.
Fromm, Erich. (1990a). *Man for Himself: An Inquiry into the Psychology of Ethics*. New York: Holt Paperbacks.
Fromm, Erich. (1990b). *The Sane Society*. New York: Holt Paperbacks.
Fromm, Erich. (1992). *The Anatomy of Human Destructiveness*. New York: Holt Paperbacks.
Fromm, Erich. (1997). *Love, Sexuality and Matriarchy: About Gender*, edited and with an Introduction by Rainer Funk. New York: Fromm International.
Fromm, Erich. (2006). *The Art of Loving*. New York: Harper Perennial Modern Classics.
Fromm, Erich. (2013a). *Escape from Freedom*. New York: Open Road Media.
Fromm, Erich. (2013b). *To Have and To Be*. New York: Bloomsbury Academic.
Funk, Rainer. (2013). "Erich Fromm and the Intersubjective Tradition." *International Forum of Psychoanalysis* 22, Issue 1: 5–9.
Hooks, Bell. (2000). *All about Love: New Visions*. New York: William Morrow and Company.
Horney, Karen. (1992). *Our Inner Conflicts: A Constructive Theory of Neurosis*. New York: W.W. Norton & Co.
Kimmel, Michael. (2009). *Guyland: The Perilous World Where Boys Become Men*. New York: Harper Perennial.
Klein, Melanie. (1975). *Envy and Gratitude and Other Works*. New York: Delacorte Press and Seymour Lawrence.
Millett, Kate. (2016). *Sexual Politics*. New York: Columbia University Press.
Pascoe, C. J. (2011). *Dude, You're A Fag: Masculinity and Sexuality in High School*. Berkeley, CA: University of California Press.
Wilde, Lawrence. (2004). "The Significance of Maternalism in the Evolution of Fromm's Social Thought." *The European Legacy* 9, no. 3: 343–56.

Chapter 6

SOCIOPSYCHOANALYSIS AND RADICAL HUMANISM: A FROMM-BOURDIEU SYNTHESIS

Michael Maccoby and Neil McLaughlin

Mainstream social science has been blindsided by the rise of Trumpism and broader growth of authoritarian populism around the world. Despite the methodological sophistication of our research, our theories have not been able to fully account for the emotions and passions so obviously central to political and cultural conflict. Erich Fromm was unique among twentieth-century social scientists in putting emotions, comparative-historical analysis, and a structural sociological imagination together. But his synthetic combination of Marx, Freud, and popular public intellectual writing helped consign him to the margins of mainstream sociology and social theory by the 1970s. We believe that Fromm's theory is needed inside the core of contemporary social science theorizing. We will make this argument by examining social character theory up against and alongside the concept of habitus developed by French sociologist Pierre Bourdieu,[1] the dominant social theorist in contemporary critical social science.

Bourdieu and Fromm were very different types of thinkers even though they shared many similarities. Bourdieu rose to fame and influence as a French sociologist in the twilight of Fromm's career and they did not directly engage each other's ideas, so we must reconstruct what a conversation or dialogue between these two traditions might look like. The similarities and differences between the ideas and research traditions of both Fromm and Bourdieu are worth serious examination and comparison with an eye toward synthesizing their theories. As David Swartz puts it, "Bourdieu thinks of the practice of sociology as *socioanalysis* where the sociologist is to the 'social unconscious' of society as the psychoanalyst is to the patient's unconscious,"[2] a vision that has obvious links with Fromm's own combination of sociology, psychoanalysis, and social criticism. Fromm also thought of his work as socioanalysis, and Fromm and Maccoby considered using the concept in the title of what was eventually published as *Social Character in a Mexican Village* (1970).

Fromm scholars can learn much from Bourdieu's structural and historical sociology and methodological sophistication, but little has been written about how Fromm's vision complements Bourdieu's theoretical weaknesses. Bourdieu offers us insights into how social class dynamics, organizational mechanisms, and cognitive schemas operate in reproducing inequality, and he tells us much about how society shapes people's practices through the reproduction of what he calls the habitus in various professional and political fields. But he says little about the social psychology of healthy human living and the emotions that are internalized into human beings shaped by the combinations of capitals, fields, and habitus central to his theory. The current political and cultural moment we are living in highlights for us the necessity of grappling with sociopolitical issues with psychological depth and sophistication Bourdieu did not possess but which was central to Fromm's social theory.

Bourdieu certainly did a better job than Fromm in developing a successful school of social science research and theorizing rooted in the modern research university. The road forward, we suggest, does not involve replacing Bourdieu's paradigm with Fromm's scholarship or even a broader psychoanalytic sociology. Fromm did not see himself as an academic social scientist partly due to his critique of the hyper-professionalism and narrowness of modern social research. And psychoanalysts, even those with sociological training, have not succeeded in creating a paradigm that can compete with the analytic power and empirical rigor of the Bourdieu school of sociology, whatever one thinks of the limitations of orthodox "reflexive sociology."[3] Research universities have access to enormous resources and it is extremely difficult (although not impossible, of course) to carve out a research program without access to tenured academic positions, graduate student collaboration, and the research grants established academics have better access to. And Bourdieu, even though he began his career very much on the margins of both the academy and the French elite, was a master of learning and performing the rules of the scholarly game while Fromm wrote insights from the margins of the social science. This institutional marginality gave Fromm a valuable independence from social science orthodoxy, but he also paid an intellectual as well as reputational price for his exclusion from the mainstream. We believe that Fromm's vision of a humanistic social science will only succeed if it gains more legitimacy for its ideas and research agendas within contemporary social science; we thus argue here for dialoguing more with mainstream social science, something that will be facilitated by engagement with Bourdieu's work.

In order to facilitate this engagement with Bourdieu, we will first outline the basic contours of Bourdieu's social science career, comparing the reception of his work within mainstream social science with the story of Fromm's marginalization and contemporary revival. Both Fromm and Bourdieu were concerned with the human costs of social change and economic development: Fromm with his work with Michael Maccoby on Mexican village life in the 1960s and 1970s, and Bourdieu with his extended studies of peasants in Algeria during the French colonial war of the 1950s and early 1960s. In theoretical terms, however, both Fromm's social character theory and Bourdieu's concept of habitus have unique strengths and weaknesses for dealing with these case studies as well as the broader sociological and social-psychological issues.[4] With the possibilities for synthesis in mind, we will compare and contrast the theory of social character developed in the Mexican study with Bourdieu's concept of habitus, and discuss what Fromm's ideas can add to Bourdieu-influenced critical social science. We will end with some thoughts on the need for a research agenda that synthesizes Fromm's and Bourdieu's broader agenda on social character and habitus, respectively. But first, let's start with the story of how Bourdieu become a dominant social scientist, in contrast to the story of how Fromm's social science and radical humanist political engagement was assigned, at least for a time, to the margins of academic social science.

Two Social Science Careers: Fromm and Bourdieu

Erich Fromm and Pierre Bourdieu were both trained as sociologists but their relationship to the discipline is dramatically different. Fromm did his PhD at Heidelberg in the early 1920s under the supervision of Alfred Weber, Max Weber's younger brother, and he was widely cited in the mid-twentieth century by noted sociologists, yet he became marginal to the core of discipline, especially in North America and the English-speaking world.[5] Fromm was not primarily interested in being an academic, although he did empirical research in the mid- to late 1920s on authoritarianism among the German working and middle classes while a member of the Horkheimer circle of critical theorist based in Frankfurt.[6] Fromm then helped shape the reception of Marx's ideas in America in the immediate postwar period and the early 1960s, and did social character research again in the 1950s and 1960s in Mexico. Fromm made his living, however, as a therapist, lecturer, and author of popular books, not a sociology professor, only very occasionally publishing in core sociology or other academic journals.

Bourdieu's relationship to professional sociology was very different. Bourdieu finished his graduate work in the late 1950s, in contrast, thirty years later than Fromm, and in France not Germany. The major difference between the two, however, is that Bourdieu was centrally identified and involved in professional sociology and was focused on producing theoretical and empirical contributions to the field that he hoped would come to dominate the discipline. Sociology as an organized disciplinary project ended up being peripheral to Fromm's intellectual vision even though he drew extensively from the tradition (Marx, Weber, Durkheim, and Simmel, in particular) while Bourdieu's intellectual self-concept, as Neil Gross would later theorize the concept,[7] was as a critical sociologist and interdisciplinary thinker. Disciplinary academic politics was at the very core of Bourdieu's intellectual self-concept, and while he started on the periphery of the French intellectual elite, he gained access, over time, to a coveted appointment at an elite French institution that allowed him the space and resources to produce an enormous amount of high-quality social science research. Given this context and the intellectual creativity of both thinkers, it is not at all surprising that Bourdieu would arguably become the dominant sociologist of the late twentieth century and that his work would become central to graduate education while Fromm would become a forgotten sociologist read only occasionally on the margins of the discipline in undergraduate studies while retaining a dedicated following among a wide general audience.

Bourdieu is the dominant theorist in the sociology of culture and education in the discipline, and he has helped shape debates in studies of inequality, reflexive methodologies, media, professions, and political sociology. Every trained sociologist in the discipline will be broadly familiar with Bourdieu's core concepts of field, capital, and habitus, and there is a very powerful and well-networked school of Bourdieu scholars active in European and North American sociology as well as in emerging sociologies around the world. Fromm, on the other hand, is largely a figure in intellectual history in sociology with very little influence on debates in the discipline connected to his core research concerns in social character and his social theory. There is a revival taking place of research inspired by Fromm, some of it in sociology,[8] but there is very little chance his work will enter the core of the discipline at Bourdieu's level of dominance.

Despite these obvious differences in their relationship to the field of sociology, Fromm and Bourdieu share much politically and intellectually. Both Fromm and Bourdieu viewed themselves as critical and left scholars, and they each engaged the Marxist tradition in substantial ways without being orthodox Marxists. Each was deeply schooled in the classical sociological tradition, drawing on Marx, Weber, and Durkheim. Fromm was influenced by Simmel just as Bourdieu's approach was shaped by Goffman, Simmel's American heir to the micro tradition. Both Fromm and Bourdieu were synthetic thinkers who rejected the simplistic agency versus structure dichotomy. They each articulated powerful critiques of positivism and both were militant opponents of colonialism and American imperial dominance of the world. Moreover, both Fromm and Bourdieu were committed to political action outside of the ivory tower, even though their careers as public intellectuals and public sociologists were very different. As Swartz puts it, "Bourdieu's sociology would be critical though not prophetic, theoretical though empirically researchable, and scientific though not positivist,"[9] a summary that highlights one major difference along with two core similarities. Fromm was a critical, non-positivist theorist deeply committed to empirical analysis, as was Bourdieu, but as Michael Maccoby has reminded us, there was a powerful prophetic voice in Fromm's intellectual vision.[10] For most of Bourdieu's career he was purely academic in ways Fromm never was, but we need to remember that in the last ten years of his life, Bourdieu lifted his earlier self-imposed ban on signing petitions and political involvement, allowing him to take on the role of critical-left public intellectual in various interventions in the 1990s on issues of public concern. But even then, Bourdieu spoke in public as a scientist never as a prophet, a role Fromm sometimes slipped into and even embraced.[11]

A second difference, more central to our present analysis, involves their very different relationship to Freud and psychological theory. Before his public intellectual years, Fromm was a relatively obscure psychoanalyst and social researcher, but he was well networked as a core member of the Frankfurt School of critical theorists led by Max Horkheimer during this period. It was in these years that Fromm developed the concept of the authoritarian character that Adorno would make famous as the authoritarian personality, and the methodology of interpretive questionnaire he would later use in *Social Character in a Mexican*

Village[12] in order to test his broader theory of social character. Yet, for the most active years of Fromm's career between his time in the Frankfurt School network and the publication of *Social Character in a Mexican Village* (1970) and *The Anatomy of Human Destructiveness* (1973), he operated outside of standard disciplinary norms and the academic field, largely writing books such as *Man for Himself* (1947), *The Sane Society* (1955), *The Art of Loving* (1956), and *May Man Prevail?* (1961) addressed to the general reading public. As a classic public intellectual in the era after the creation of the paperback book and before the rise of the internet, Fromm spent the bulk of his intellectual energy focused on developing his own radical humanist theoretical ideas. Fromm was not contributing to mainstream sociological research for most of his career but instead was critiquing the outdated and patriarchal elements of orthodox Freudian theory, engaging in political interventions in Cold War era politics, and contributing to the upsurge of left-wing politics during the 1960s, particularly around questions of nuclear disarmament and the Vietnam War.

After Fromm's initial burst into fame and academic stature with the critically acclaimed *Escape from Freedom* (1941), he was largely uninterested in sustaining a record and reputation as an academic social scientist. It was only in the last decade of Fromm's life, when he returned to scholarly work with *The Anatomy of Human Destructiveness* (1973), an attempt to synthesize his Freudian inspired social theory with new developments in neurosciences, archaeology, and historical anthropology/comparative sociology and, most importantly *Social Character in a Mexican Village* (1970), an empirical test of his social character theory written with Michael Maccoby, that he moved farther in this direction. Perhaps too little too late to overcome decades of attacks on his social theory lead by both critical theorists and mainstream social scientists, Fromm's most rigorous and scholarly works written in the 1970s never gained academic legitimacy and have largely been ignored in sociology, anthropology, and the broader behavioral and human sciences. As a consequence, Fromm is known today primarily as a popular writer and his enormous theoretical contributions have been largely forgotten in social science.

While Bourdieu is also known as a public intellectual and public sociologist, the majority of his career was given over to developing what he would later call academic capital, almost exclusively writing for peers within the social sciences until the last decade of his life. Bourdieu was marginal in his own way, but after having risen from the margins of the intellectual world as a lower-middle-class provincial to the very top of the French academic hierarchy with his election to the College de France in 1981, he became the dominant empirical researcher in sociology of his generation. Bourdieu had also developed a theoretical framework for a scientific sociology based on the concepts of fields, capital, and habitus, establishing theoretical dominance as well as an empirical research agenda. It was only then that Bourdieu would spend a decade writing more accessible books critiquing neoliberalism and American culture in France, offering his thoughts on gender inequality, attacking mainstream media and the French socialist party for their conformism, and contributing his intellectual stature to the anti-globalization movement of the period. Despite the fact that there are many sociologists who do not share Bourdieu's radical politics and that his more popular books were not always well received among his peers, Bourdieu's academic reputation was not damaged by his popular writing in the way that Fromm's was. Bourdieu's public intellectual period, in fact, could be read as a capstone accomplishment, as the French intellectual field is shaped by norms that encourage top scholars to contribute to public dialogue and debate in a nation whose culture was shaped by figures such as Voltaire, Zola, and Sartre.

While Fromm and Bourdieu were politically active as radicals, the nature of this engagement was quite different. Fromm's *Escape from Freedom* (1941) was a theoretical text with a political subtext—he was making the argument for the American entry into the Second World War to defeat the Nazis. Some of Fromm's other books had clear political intent: *The Sane Society* (1955) was partly a polemic for a communitarian socialism, *May Man Prevail* (1961) was a critique of both American militarism and Soviet-Chinese communism, *The Revolution of Hope* (1968) initially came out of his intervention in the movement against the Vietnam War and his political campaign work within the Democratic Party primaries, and *To Have or to Be* (1976) was a call to arms for a green radical humanist revival. Outside his writing, Fromm was active at various times in the antinuclear weapons movements (the antinuclear organization SANE bears the name of his book) and was involved for a time in the American Socialist Party. He helped fund Amnesty International in its early days and was successful at times in giving concrete policy advice to government officials around the Berlin crisis during the Cold War, not to mention his high-profile principled criticism of Israel's dispossession of Palestinian land. Furthermore, Fromm saw his book *Social Character in a Mexican Village* (1970) as partly an attempt to give back to the Mexican society that had hosted him for two decades from 1950 to the early 1970s. In the end, however, Fromm's political activism was secondary to his major focus as a psychoanalyst, writer, and social theorist. Fromm was aware that he was temperamentally not suited to political activism and electoral politics. Michael Maccoby's critique of Fromm as a prophetic thinker as well as an analytical scholar can also be applied to understanding his political activism,[13] where he was far better at prophetic visioning than political strategy. A well-informed intellectual with principled anti-Stalinist left politics, Fromm operated best on the margins of real-world politics, as a visionary and a critic not a pragmatic political actor.

The same was true with Bourdieu. Bourdieu's initial involvement in politics and scholarship were linked, as was the case with Fromm and his analysis of the Nazi threat, but in Bourdieu's case the issue of the day was the French colonial war in Algeria. As a young man from a lower-middle-class background, Bourdieu was in the military when the Algerian revolution against French colonial rule dominated politics in his nation, and he believed he was sent to Algeria in a noncombat role because of his vocal opposition to the war. After a couple of years of service, Bourdieu went back to start his career as a researcher and academic teacher in Algeria, and his first publications were rooted in his anthropological observations of Algerian peasant life in the context of modernization and colonial violence.

The Sociologie de L'Algerie (1958) (in English as *The Algerians* [1962]) was a fairly traditional work of anthropology, albeit informed by Bourdieu's anti-colonial sensibility, and his series of publications on Kabyle society in northern Algeria provided the empirical material during the 1960s and early 1970s that was to be used when he developed his theoretical breakout framework in *Outline of a Theory of Practice* (1972 in French and then 1977 in English). From then on, Bourdieu was primarily an academic social scientist intensely focused on preserving his scientific credibility—he did not sign petitions, involve himself in protests, or take sharp positions on political issues until the last decade of his life.

Bourdieu did share with Fromm, however, an anti-colonial politics and their *The Algerians* (1958) and *Social Character in a Mexican Village* (1970) represent the most directly comparable works, something we shall return to after first outlining the theoretical framework that shaped their respective careers. One major difference between the empirical work that their respective theories were built on, however, is that Bourdieu's Algerian work was done before he developed his theory of habitus while Fromm and Maccoby's *Social Character in a Mexican Village* (1970) was written as a test of a theory developed in the 1920s and 1930s. Let's turn now to Fromm's theory of social character, talk about its development and testing in the Mexican study, before we compare the concept of social character to Bourdieu's notion of habitus.

Social Character versus Habitus: Competing and Complementary Theoretical Traditions

The concept of social character was Fromm's most original and important contribution to social theory, and it can be understood as an earlier version of Bourdieu's theory of habitus. While Fromm was a psychoanalytic theorist and Bourdieu was a sociologist generally hostile to psychoanalysis, the concept of social character does not refer to unique character structure or psychological personality as it exists in an individual and thus cannot be dismissed as psychologically reductionist. Social character relates to what Fromm termed a character matrix—a syndrome of character traits that has developed as an adaptation to the economic, social, and cultural conditions, common to that group. Fromm's theory emerged and developed in the 1930s, 1940s, and 1950s, around the same time as the development of various national character theories, and his work during this period was loosely associated with the culture and personality research agenda that is now unfashionable. Fromm rejected, however, in *Escape from Freedom* (1941), *The Sane Society* (1955), and elsewhere, the view that Nazism can be explained by German character or that modern conformism and alienation is exceptionally American. Furthermore, *Social Character in a Mexican Village* (1970) was explicitly framed as a critique of modernization theories that highlighted culture in uncritical ways, and thus would explain poverty in Latin America as partly caused by Catholic or Mexican traits. Fromm's theoretical roots went deeper, and his synthetic vision was more imaginative. Distinct from national character theories, Fromm's social character theory has more affinity to Bourdieu's theory of habitus, with more psychoanalysis, less cognitive psychology, and a different history and set of analytic goals. Fromm critically integrated what he viewed as core insights from both Karl Marx and Sigmund Freud while rejecting orthodox dogma from the theoretical systems of Marxism and psychoanalysis, respectively.

In 1962, he described the basis of his theory:

> Marx postulated the interdependence between the economic basis of society and the political and legal institutions, its philosophy, art, religion, etc. The former, according to Marxist theory, determined the latter, the "Ideological superstructure." But Marx and Engels did not show, as Engels admitted quite explicitly, *how* the economic basis is translated into the ideological superstructure. I believe that by using the tools of psychoanalysis, this gap in Marxian theory can be filled, and the economic basis structure and the superstructure are connected. One of these connections lies in what I have called the *social character*.[14]

The core of the theory was expressed clearly in "The Social and Individual Roots of Neurosis," in the *American Sociological Review*, the only time Fromm published in the most prestigious journal in the field:

> The particular ways in which a society functions are determined by a number of objective economic and political factors, which are given at any point of historical development. Societies have to operate within the possibilities and limitations of their particular historical situation. In order that any society may function well, its members must acquire the kind of character which makes them want to act in the way they have to act as members of the society or of a special class within it. They have to desire what objectively is necessary for them to do. Outer force is to be replaced by inner compulsion, and by the particular kind of human energy which is channeled into character trait.[15]

One can see the Marxist roots of Fromm's social character theory in these quotes, but it is important to emphasize that he also rejected the inattention to emotions, morality, and human nature in orthodox versions of Marxism in the twentieth century. Moreover, although Fromm used Freud's dynamic character types to describe the nucleus of social character in ways that Marxists never could with their focus on economic and class relations, he also rejected Freud's theory of character development based on libidinal ties as well as what he viewed as Freud's historical commitment to patriarchal and nineteenth-century bourgeois values embedded in the theory. In its place, Fromm proposed a theory of character formation based on a Marxist-influenced analysis of the social relationships rooted in the form of economic development and class relations of a particular historical period.

As Fromm created his social character theory, his purpose was not only to understand social behavior like major twentieth-century sociologists such as Bourdieu but also to describe what it would require for developing a healthier, more productive social character (for what Fromm meant by productive, see

Durkin 2014).[16] Fromm was openly normative in a way that Bourdieu never was. Bourdieu had a commitment to the scientific field of sociology as he envisioned it while Fromm saw himself as a radical interdisciplinary intellectual even though his theoretical framework was deeply sociological. Let us look closer at Fromm's most detailed account of social character theory, before considering Bourdieu's theory of habitus.

Social Character in a Mexican Village

Fromm initiated this study in 1957 after having lived in Mexico since 1950, when he had been invited to establish the Mexican Institute of Psychoanalysis and to train psychiatrists to be psychoanalysts. He had two main reasons for this study. Unhappy with criticism of *The Sane Society* as unscientific in major social science and intellectual journals, Fromm wanted to establish scholarly support for his concept of social character. The second purpose was to discover data that might be useful for prediction and planning of positive social change in peasant society, something Fromm especially wanted to do in Mexico to give back to the society that had welcomed him in the 1950s.

Although Fromm was often attacked as a mystical thinker or a radical polemicist, it would be a mistake to ignore his roots in nineteenth-century utopian radicalism and the traditions within sociology concerned with designing a better society through the use of science. While Fromm, like Bourdieu, was a critic of positivism, he shared with Comte and St. Simon a vision that looked to gather social science data, use theory to predict the future based on the laws of human nature, and thereby design a better society. Before writing *Social Character in a Mexican Village* (1970), he had argued for the creation of a committee of respected scientific and humanistic intellectuals who could be consulted on social and political issues, so his commitment to helping design a better Mexico was rooted in a long-standing vision of democratic social engineering. In this way Bourdieu and Fromm were similar, as Bourdieu would call, in the 1990s, for the establishment of a committee of intellectuals to shape social change very much in the French social engineering tradition of what Marx once called "utopian socialism."[17]

The Mexican Study

The conventional wisdom among many scholars that Fromm left serious social science after he left the Frankfurt School is clearly wrong and ignored a major funded empirical research project he led in Mexico in the late 1950s through to the late 1960s. Fromm had a fair amount of resources at his disposal for the Mexican character study, far more than Bourdieu did as a young graduate student/junior scholar in Algeria around the same time (late 1950s), although far less than Bourdieu would later command in the 1980s and 1990s from his position at the College de France. Fromm had the cooperation of the national and regional

Mexican government, local elites in the village, Father William Wasson, the founder of a large orphanage in the surrounding area, and some American Friends Service volunteers. Fromm was also able to get volunteers from the Mexican Psychoanalytic Institute he had founded as well as significant funding from the American Foundations Fund for Research in Psychiatry. He selected a small village, called Chiconcauc, made up of 280 families that were typical of villages where some of the *campesinos* who had been *haciendo peons* were given *ejidos* after the revolution of 1910–20. By interviewing every villager over the age of sixteen and half the children, using economic surveys, statistical analysis, psychological tests, and participant observation, he sought to demonstrate with scientific rigor that his sociopsychoanalytic concept of social character could explain relationships between economic, social, and psychological factors.

Fromm engaged a Mexican internist who was living in the village to interview adult villagers using a questionnaire that elicited responses that could be interpreted according to character types. Mexican psychologists administered Rorschach tests and TATs. From 1958 to 1960, two American anthropologists named Theodore and Lola Schwartz, who were linked to Fromm's old friend Margaret Mead, carried out participant observation and an economic survey of village families. There were conflicts between the Schwartz couple and Fromm, partly over theoretical differences (Fromm felt they were not committed to the psychoanalytic theoretical frame for the study) and questions of ethics (Fromm wanted to preserve the confidentiality of the village while Lola Schwartz, in particular, wanted to use the data for her dissertation in ways that Fromm felt was compromising his promise to the villagers).[18]

In 1960, Michael Maccoby, then a young Harvard trained scholar, joined the project as an eventual replacement for the Schwartz's who left in 1961. Maccoby—who was funded by a research and training fellowship from the US National Institute for Mental Health—interpreted all of the questionnaire responses and projective text material in terms of social character types and, at regular project meetings with Fromm, he discussed many of the interpretations and results. Together with an anthropologist and psychologist, Maccoby studied the children[19] and led an agricultural club for adolescent boys with help from the American Friends Service Committee. Maccoby organized the statistical analysis and wrote all the book's chapters that reported the study's results, and was responsible for the history chapter that framed the study in the context of the colonial destruction of traditional culture and the oppressive nature of Spanish economic rule. He also interviewed *campesinos* in another village for comparison.[20]

Fromm recognized that the study would be strengthened with illustrative descriptions of individuals and families, but he had promised the villagers that they would remain anonymous. Fromm believed that in a small village in which some of the inhabitants suffered from alcoholism and were prone to physical violence, it would be ethically unacceptable to identify the village or include detailed case studies on individuals. There is a strong methodological objection to the way the study makes claims about the prevalence of individual characters without detailed qualitative evidence on individual people and families, but there simply was no reasonable way to present this evidence without breaching obvious ethical obligations for social research. It was unfortunate, moreover, that there was an unpleasant professional conflict between Fromm and the Schwartz's that extended for some years after despite the (unsuccessful) attempts of David Riesman (close friend to both Margaret Mead and Fromm) at mediation, since if they had been more involved, the final study might well have provided more ethnographic data and certainly this would have served to moderate Fromm's tendency to do his social science outside of dialogue with more mainstream anthropologists. This incident may well have been unavoidable given the real ethical issues at stake, but it is worth noting that while Bourdieu also tended to demand theoretical loyalty from his students and collaborators, he was more successful than Fromm at keeping research teams together. Some feel that Fromm's prophetic tendencies sometimes led to a certain level of authoritarianism in his behavior, something that is debated in the literature.[21]

Results of the Study

The most important contributions of *Social Character in a Mexican Village* to knowledge concern the relationship between social character and behavior and the interaction between economic, social, cultural, and psychological factors. At the start of the study, Fromm raised the following question: What happened to the *campesino* after the Mexican Revolution? Despite the fact that they were given land, many *campesinos* failed to take advantage of their opportunities. Alcoholism appeared to increase, and there was a high incidence of violence. Why did this happen?

The study showed the importance of social character in explaining this failure of development. Those villagers brought up before the revolution in the culture of the semifeudal hacienda lacked the self-confidence and the self-directed, hard-working character associated with successful peasants throughout the world. Their submissive, receptive, unproductive character, which was adapted to life in the hacienda, made them vulnerable to alcoholism and exploitation after the revolution. Furthermore, the children of these villagers were apt to share some of these character traits. In contrast, the villagers who had been landowners did demonstrate adaptive productive hoarding traits. They farmed their land effectively, and they attempted to maintain conservative, patriarchal values and traditions. Those few villagers with a modern outlook and an entrepreneurial character, the productive exploitative types, proved best able to take advantage of the new opportunities, and they also took advantage of the unproductive villagers. They opened small businesses, and they rented land from alcoholics. They took the lead in transforming the culture, getting rid of costly fiestas, while building roads and schools.

The study thus demonstrated that although the revolution left the villagers in a state of relative equality, a class system emerged partly because of differences in social character. One of the most significant findings of the study is the relationship between character and the actual farming behavior of the *campesinos*. Those who were psychologically more productive, as interpreted from the questionnaires, were also economically more productive. They planted the major part of their land in cash crops, such as rice and vegetables, which demanded much care and hard work. While some of the psychologically receptive unproductive landholders rented out their land, the others farmed it with sugarcane which produced a much lower profit but greater security. Cane required fewer days of work and less care. The difficult, dirty job of harvesting the cane was done by migrant workers who occupied the lowest class in Mexican rural society and were hired by the sugar refinery, the "cooperative" which took on the paternalistic role of the old hacienda. Some landholders who tried to escape the control of the cooperative found their crops ploughed under. The most astute villagers planted a small percentage of their land in sugarcane, just enough to satisfy the cooperative, gain its benefits (scholarships for their children, health care, low-cost loans) and avoid trouble, while optimizing their income.

Fromm and Maccoby's *Social Character in a Mexican Village* (1970) was a remarkable piece of work for its time, which succeeded in its core goal of providing an empirical test of social character theory while largely being ignored in the academic literature. There are a range of reasons for the marginalization of *Social Character*, including the ways in which the argument came up against the polarized debates in the United States about the "culture of poverty" in the late 1960s, the ways in which it was caught between the competing intellectual logics and research methods of economics, psychology, anthropology, and sociology, and the broader reputational decline of Fromm that occurred in the English-speaking intellectual and academic world in the late 1960s through to recent years. Fromm's broader intellectual decline was due to his conflicts with orthodox Marxists, Freudians, neoconservatives, anti-humanist thinkers of various ideological stripes and a bitter feud between Fromm and various intellectuals in the network around the German Frankfurt School particularly as mediated by an influential Fromm-Marcuse debate in the mid-1950s.[22]

One additional factor, however, that helps explain the ignoring of the book has to do with the career directions Fromm's intellectual followers took after working with him. Many of Bourdieu's students went on to take leadership roles in the social sciences after training with him, while Fromm's major students did not become professors. *Social Character*'s coauthor Michael Maccoby never entered the academic profession but instead went on to develop social character theory outside the university in a series of best-selling and carefully researched works of applied social science directed at business leaders and executives.[23] There was also a small network of Mexican scholars and psychoanalysts[24] and a German based international Erich Fromm society led by Fromm's former assistant Rainer Funk who did work on social character,[25] but all of the major promoters of social character theory built careers as therapists[26] and thus were marginal to the modern research university, especially in leading American, French, German, and British universities. Bourdieu, on the other hand, was anything but marginal in academic institutions by Fromm's death in 1980, and from this institutional platform he developed and diffused his version of these ideas in the form of habitus theory, to which we now turn.

Bourdieu's Theory of Habitus

Bourdieu's equivalent theoretical construct to Fromm's notion of "social character" is habitus, a key part of his conceptual framework alongside capital and field. Bourdieu does not focus so much on cultures as anthropologists do or on societies as sociologists tend to, but on fields. As Swartz puts it, fields are "arenas of production, circulation, and appropriation of goods, services, knowledge, or status, and the competitive positions held by actors in their struggle to accumulate capital."[27] There are various forms of capital in Bourdieu's theory—primarily economic, social, cultural, and symbolic capital[28]—and there are various ways in which individuals can accumulate, exchange, and transform each form of capital into one of the other three. Paying for private schools for your children, for example, is a way economic capital can be exchanged for social and cultural capital, as one purchases networking with more privileged people and the learning of more prestigious ways of talking, writing, and consuming cultural commodities.

This constant competition within fields for gaining capital is mediated and facilitated by what Bourdieu calls an internalized habitus. As Swartz describes it, "Habitus derives from the predominately unconscious internalization—particularly during early childhood, of objective chances that are common to members of a social class or status group."[29] Habitus, as Swartz put it, "transforms social and economic 'necessity' into virtue" by leading individuals to a "kind of immediate submission to order,"[30] or as Fromm would put it, people learn to want to do what they have to do, in order to survive and prosper in the particular society they live in given their own class position. Bourdieu shared Fromm's Marxist proclivities, moreover, because Bourdieu saw the habitus as something that "legitimates economic and social inequality by providing a practical and taken-for-granted acceptance of the fundamental conditions of existence."[31] For Bourdieu, as for Fromm, class habitus happens early in life, and does not change easily.

As important as Bourdieu theory of fields and capital has been in contemporary sociological work, the notion of habitus was particularly pivotal to his massive influence in contemporary sociology of culture and education. Bourdieu's single most important book was *Distinction* (1984), an empirical masterwork that laid out an agenda on class habitus that transformed the modern sociology of culture and broader studies of cultural consumption. Bourdieu's writings on education were more diffuse, focusing as they did on both schools and higher education with an agenda shaped by his insights into how the class habitus of teachers interacts with the class habitus of students. Educational social processes were mostly about, for Bourdieu, the re-enforcement and reproduction of inequality.

Bourdieu developed the empirical basis for his theory in his late 1950s and early 1960s research in Algeria and only fully developed the conceptual model in the 1970s and 1980s. In Bourdieu, habitus theory developed in a largely anthropological descriptive way in the Algerian work that was both similar to and different from Fromm's social character work written only a few years later. As is well known by scholars of Bourdieu, the notion of habitus came out of his observations and research in Algeria.[32] Bourdieu became convinced from his military experience in Algeria during the colonial war of the importance of academic and scientific autonomy as he defined his intellectual self-concept against military intelligence operatives, government officials, and right-wing professors and students at the University of Algiers. Bourdieu's work on Algeria was in French in *Sociologie de l'algerie* (1958) and in English in *The Algerians* (1962), and the theoretical work came out in *Outline of a Theory of Practice* (1997) and *The Logic of Practice* (1990). There is an extensive secondary literature on Bourdieu's Algeria writing and a number of works, particularly on his photography in the area taken at the time,[33] have been published after Bourdieu's death.[34]

Bourdieu's concern with understanding Algerian underdevelopment has significant overlap with Fromm and Maccoby's Mexican study. French supporters of the colonial war in Algeria always stressed France's positive contributions to a less than efficient and productive local culture, a perspective Bourdieu did not share. As Steinmetz puts it, "In his earliest publications, Bourdieu blamed Algerian underdevelopment not on the Algerians' own shortcomings but on the 'shock effect' of a clash between an archaic economy and a modern one."[35] Both *Social Character in a Mexican Village* (1970) and *Sociologie de L'Algeria* (1958) placed the lives of the peasants they were studying in the context of colonialism and conquest (by both Europeans and Arabs, in the Algerian example) but in Bourdieu's case he was writing about the issue during the French-Algerian colonial war. As George Steinmetz's points out, "the second edition of *Sociologie de L'Algeria* included a discussion of French land annexation and settlements, which produced a 'tabula rasa of a civilization that could no longer be discussed except in the past tense.'"[36] And Bourdieu would later return to what Steinmetz describes as the "uprooting, resettlement, and war" in a coauthored book with a former Algerian.[37] Despite the similar critical anti-colonial assumptions of both *Social Character* and Bourdieu's various writings on Algeria, there were significant theoretical differences in their respective frameworks, something to which we now turn.

Bourdieu on Algeria

In the early Algeria work in the 1950s and early 1960s, Bourdieu was working on his definition of habitus, which he modified again in the later part of the 1960s and 1970s. By 1980, he had developed the more commonly used one in the current literature in the sociology of culture and education where he suggests that the habitus is

> a system of durable, transposable dispositions, structured structures predisposed to function as structuring structures, that is, as principles which generate and organize practices and representations that can be objectively adapted to their

outcomes without presupposing a conscious aiming at ends or an express mastery of the operations necessary to attain them.[38]

In various other places in what is his considerable scholarly output Bourdieu, as Swartz has documented, had used the wordings of "cultural unconscious," "habit-forming force," "set of basic, deeply interiorized master-patterns," "mental habit," "mental and corporeal schemata of perceptions, appreciations, and actions," and "generative principle of regulated improvisations" to designate his key concept.[39] The connections and similarities between social character theory and the notion of habitus are obvious, but it is clear that Bourdieu relies on sociological and cognitive frames, downplaying an explicit psychoanalytic analysis of emotions which is the core strength of Fromm's social character theory. Before discussing the implications of this difference for contemporary work, we will look at Bourdieu's relationship to the study of emotions and his intellectual relationship to psychoanalysis in greater detail.

Bourdieu and Feelings

Bourdieu shared Fromm's early interest in the sociology of emotions. Like Fromm, Bourdieu had also been deeply influenced by the early Marx, and, unlike many Parisian intellectuals, he never adopted an Althusserian structuralist or an orthodox Marxist position. Here, Fromm and Bourdieu were very similar, as Fromm was a strong critic of Althusser and Althusserian Marxism as well as Stalinism and other mechanical forms of Marxism.[40] Fromm and Bourdieu also were critical of the Frankfurt School, for some similar reasons. As Bourdieu puts it, "I've always had a pretty ambivalent relationship with the Frankfurt School: the affinities between us are clear yet I felt a certain irritation when faced with the aristocratic demeanor of that totalizing critique which retained all the features of grand theories, doubtless so as to not get its hands dirty in the kitchens of empirical research."[41]

The major difference between Fromm's concept of social character and Bourdieu's theory of the habitus revolves around their relationship to psychoanalysis. Despite the claims of Fromm's critics within the orthodox psychoanalytic traditions, his work was always anchored by a commitment to the insights of a depth psychology that emphasizes the emotional power of unconscious motivations. As a consequence, Fromm's analysis of both Nazism and Mexican peasant life was grounded in an understanding of how internalized oppression and irrationality can shape political, economic choices and, indeed, the most intimate aspects of people's personal lives. Social character theory was created and designed precisely to help us understand how our social analysis must give an adequate weight to authoritarian impulses, feelings of humiliation and despair, and passions for control, destruction, and revenge, as well as feelings of love, empathy, compassion, and desires for transcendence, solidarity, and productive living. It is precisely with respect to these emotional dynamics where Bourdieu's theory of habitus falls short.

There is a deep ambivalence in Bourdieu with regard to the psychoanalytic tradition. Throughout most of his career, Bourdieu was known to be a strong and unyielding critic of the psychoanalytic tradition, viewing it as unscientific and insufficiently sociological. Near the end of his career, however, Bourdieu came to recognize, as Steinmetz puts it, that "psychoanalysis was intrinsic to his own project," and over time his writings "accumulated a growing and ever more elaborate psychoanalytic vocabulary" including the following terms: "projection, reality principle, libido, ego-splitting, negation (denegation), compromise formation, anamnesis, return of the repressed, and collective phantasy."[42]

Steinmetz has played a leading role in trying to bring out and develop the psychoanalytic aspects of Bourdieu's thought, drawing on the Lacanian tradition, but he has not directly addressed the two core flaws in Bourdieu's theory of the habitus that Fromm's theory of social character can help illuminate: (1) the need for a theory of both self-destructive/undermining character traits and productive character development that can complement a structural theory of oppression-exploitation and (2) a less theoretically abstract version of psychoanalytic theory that would put emotions centrally into the dynamics of the habitus.

It is understandable, of course, that Bourdieu did not want to emphasize how the social psychology of the Algerian peasants played a role in their own oppression as Fromm carefully attempted to do in *Social Character in a Mexican Village*; Bourdieu was sent to Algeria as part of the French army, speaking nothing of the local languages during studying at the time of what was a brutal colonial war. Bourdieu, moreover, did not believe there was much value in exploring the concept of internalized oppression and he was openly dismissive of Franz Fanon who is the most important theorist of this idea along with the Brazilian theorist Paulo Freire. Bourdieu felt that Fanon's ideas were "false and dangerous."[43] Bourdieu's contested concept of "symbolic violence" was both influential and controversial precisely because it focused attention almost exclusively on the actions and agency of the powerful, leaving little room for a psychoanalytic entry-point into the contribution of psychological mechanisms that might make it difficult for the marginalized to create productive lives.

The habitus internalized by the oppressed, in Bourdieu's theory, leaves actors unfamiliar with the rules of the game they need to succeed in the particular field they are competing in. It provides a mental map and perceptual frame that makes it harder for the lower classes to move through and up the class structure, resulting in a social and cultural deficit that is difficult to overcome relative to the position of advantaged elites. Bourdieu's theory of habitus, however, says nothing explicit about how feelings of low self-worth, emotional passivity created by society and existing family dynamics, or how comfort with or adaptation to unhealthy and exploitative emotional relationships can make it difficult for the oppressed to overcome their disadvantages. Fromm and Maccoby's *Social Character* study explicitly addressed and showed how social character factors, partly rooted in historical economic relations of oppression, shaped rates of alcoholism and violence against women, dynamics that generally have not been addressed by Bourdieu's habitus theory. The theory of habitus tends to downplay the emotional mechanisms created in families and fields and almost exclusively highlights the role of structures and elites with little attention to these kinds of internalized then externalized forms of oppression and abuse-self-abuse. Decades of research has since been done on alcoholism and what we now call gender-based violence that any attempt to address these issues with social character theory would have to deal with, but Bourdieu's approach is far less open to the dialogue.

The kind of research carried out by Fromm and Maccoby is extremely sensitive, being done by outsiders to the communities under study, and runs the risks of being weaponized to "blame the victims" of oppressive structures. In such a situation, the researchers might well be attacked as proponents of white or colonial and/or male social science and not always unfairly. This is especially true since the rise of social media, where the results would quickly enter circulation in decontextualized ways that lose the nuance and care that would be required to contextualize them. To do this kind of research, even more effort would be required to ensure community engagement, and it might also require an explicit commitment to conduct the research with scholars across a range of political views sponsored by well-trusted intellectual representatives of diverse political traditions. The problems may well be insurmountable given justified fears of the weaponization of this kind of research and the history of colonial social science research, but that is a discussion for another time.

Toward a Social Character and Habitus Synthesis

It may well be that the most practical use of a social character/habitus synthesis will not come from research on the descendants of those colonialized, invaded, and enslaved, but from raising questions and designing research projects that look at the emotional dynamics of modern nationalism, populist authoritarianism of both the left and right, and the psychological consequences of digital and social media on the emotional life of the middle and professional classes. Bourdieu's habitus theory has little to say about the emotional and irrational aspects of nationalism although his structural analysis of fields, his focus on different forms of circulating capital (economic, social, cultural, and symbolic), and more nuanced attention to social class provides a framework that Fromm's social character theory could sharpen and improve. Bourdieu's theory of symbolic violence has had a rather negative consequence as it has played out in mass politics, leading to inflationary dynamics that define all potentially offensive language speech while saying very little about actual violence and the human emotions of hatred, destructiveness, pathological forms of control and the desire to humiliate, something Fromm's theory has more to say about.[44] While Bourdieu had little to say about actual violence after his Algerian studies, the sociologist Michael Mann has pioneered the sociological study of fascism, Stalinism, and ethnic cleansing,[45] but he has produced a theoretical framework that says little about the social character elements of sadism and genocide and has nothing to offer with regard to the social psychology of genocidal-violent leaders, as Fromm did in his studies of Stalin, Hitler, Himmel, and Mao.[46] In less dramatic contexts, moreover, a synthesis of habitus with social character theory offers a way into understanding the appeal of Trumpism. This kind of research agenda, which raises critical questions about mass character in modern societies, would not be easy and would be challenging and risky given our current polarization. It will not be enough to suggest that liberal America is a culture of narcissism or that Trump's base is rooted in the authoritarian personality. The goal of highlighting both sociological and psychodynamic mechanisms, however, is worth aiming for in a world being torn apart by political conflict and violence partly created by emotional logics that Bourdieu's original theory did not predict and cannot fully explain or understand.

Notes

1 Grillo, "Revisiting Fromm and Bourdieu."
2 Swartz, *Culture and Power*, 10; emphasis in original.
3 Bourdieu and Wacquant, *An Invitation to Reflexive Sociology*.
4 Grillo, "Revisiting Fromm and Bourdieu."
5 McLaughlin, "How to Become a Forgotten Intellectual."
6 Burston, *The Legacy of Erich Fromm*; Funk, *Erich Fromm*.
7 Gross, *Richard Rorty: The Making of an American Philosopher*.
8 Durkin, *The Radical Humanism of Erich Fromm*.
9 Swartz, *Culture and Power*, 26.
10 Maccoby, "The Two Voices of Erich Fromm."
11 Ibid., 72–82.
12 Fromm and Maccoby, *Social Character in a Mexican Village*.
13 Maccoby, "The Two Voices of Erich Fromm," 72–82.
14 Fromm, *Beyond the Chains of Illusion*, 17; emphasis in original.
15 Fromm, *Individual and Social Origins of Neurosis*.
16 Durkin, *The Radical Humanism of Erich Fromm*.
17 Swartz, *Symbolic Power, Politics, and Intellectuals*.
18 Friedman and Schreiber, *The Lives of Erich Fromm*.
19 Maccoby, Modiano, and Lander, "Games and Social Character in a Mexican Village"; Maccoby and Modiano, "On Culture and Equivalence."
20 Maccoby and Foster, "Methods of Studying Mexican Peasant Personality."
21 Friedman and Schreiber, *The Lives of Erich Fromm*.
22 McLaughlin, "How to Become a Forgotten Intellectual," 215–46.
23 Maccoby, *The Gamesman*; Maccoby, *The Productive Narcissist*; Maccoby, *Narcissistic Leaders*; Maccoby, *The Leaders We Need*.
24 Gojman de Millán and Millán, "Understanding Social Motivation for Encouraging Children's Development."
25 Funk, *The Clinical Erich Fromm*.
26 Cortina, "The Greatness and Limitations of Erich Fromm's Humanism."
27 Swartz, *Symbolic Power, Politics, and Intellectuals*, 35.
28 Bourdieu, "The Forms of Capital."
29 Swartz, *Culture and* Power, 104.
30 Ibid., 105.
31 Ibid.
32 Steinmetz, *Sociology and Empire*.

33 Bourdieu and Schultheis, *Picturing Algeria*.
34 Bourdieu, *Algerian Sketches*.
35 Steinmetz, *Sociology and Empire*, 37, citing Bourdieu, "La Logique Interne de la Civilisation Algérienne Traditionnelle."
36 Steinmetz, *Sociology and Empire*, 37; emphasis in original.
37 Ibid., 37.
38 Swartz, *Culture and* Power, 100–1.
39 Ibid., 101.
40 Anderson, "Fromm, Marx and Humanism."
41 Bourdieu, *The Logic of Practice*, 19.
42 Steinmetz, "Bourdieu's Disavowal of Lacan," 443.
43 Bourdieu, *Sketch for a Self-Analysis*, 17.
44 Cheliotis, "For a Freudo-Marxist Critique of Social Domination."
45 Mann, *The Dark Side of Democracy*.
46 Fromm, *The Anatomy of Human Destructiveness*.

References

Anderson, Kevin B. (2015). "Fromm, Marx and Humanism." In Rainer Funk and Neil McLaughlin (eds.), *Towards a Human Science: The Relevance of Erich Fromm for Today*, 209–18. Giessen: Psychosozial-Verlag.
Bourdieu, Pierre. (1959). "La Logique Interne de la Civilisation Algérienne Traditionnelle." *Le sous-développement en Algérie*, 40–51.
Bourdieu, Pierre. (1962). *The Algerians*. Boston: Beacon Press.
Bourdieu, Pierre. (1986). "The Forms of Capital." In Pierre Bourdieu and J. G. Richardson (eds.), *Handbook of Theory and Research for the Sociology of Education*, 241–58. New York: Greenwood Press.
Bourdieu, Pierre. (1990a). *The Logic of Practice*. Stanford: Stanford University Press.
Bourdieu, Pierre. (1990b). *In Other Words: Essays towards a Reflexive Sociology*. Stanford: Stanford University Press.
Bourdieu, Pierre. (2007). *Sketch for a Self-Analysis*. The University of Chicago Press.
Bourdieu, Pierre. (2013). *Algerian Sketches*. London: Polity Press.
Bourdieu, Pierre, and Franz Schultheis. (2012). *Picturing Algeria*. New York: Columbia University Press.
Bourdieu, Pierre, and Loïc J. D. Wacquant. (1992). *An Invitation to Reflexive Sociology*. Chicago: University of Chicago Press.
Burston, Daniel. (1991). *The Legacy of Erich Fromm*. Cambridge, MA: Harvard University Press.
Cheliotis, Leonidas. (2011). "For a Freudo-Marxist Critique of Social Domination: Rediscovering Erich Fromm." *Journal of Classical Sociology* 11, no. 4: 438–61.
Cortina, Mauricio. (2015). "The Greatness and Limitations of Erich Fromm's Humanism." *Contemporary Psychoanalysis* 51: 388–422.
Durkin, Kieran. (2014). *The Radical Humanism of Erich Fromm*. New York: Palgrave.
Friedman, Lawrence J., with Anke M. Schreiber. (2013). *The Lives of Erich Fromm: Love's Prophet*. New York: Columbia University Press.
Fromm, Erich. (1941 [1969]). *Escape from Freedom*. New York: Holt, Reinhart & Winston.
Fromm, Erich. (1944). "Individual and Social Origins of Neurosis." *American Sociological Review* 9, no. 4 (August): 380–84.

Fromm, Erich. (1947). *Man for Himself: An Inquiry Into the Psychology of Ethics*. New York: Rinehart.
Fromm, Erich. (1955). *The Sane Society*. New York: Holt, Reinhart, & Winston.
Fromm, Erich. (1961). *May Man Prevail?* New York: Doubleday.
Fromm, Erich. (1962). *Beyond the Chains of Illusion: My Encounter with Marx and Freud*, 17. New York: Simon & Schuster.
Fromm, Erich. (1973). *The Anatomy of Human Destructiveness*. New York: Holt, Reinhart & Winston.
Fromm, Erich. (1976). *To Have or to Be?* New York: Harper & Row.
Fromm, Erich, and Michael Maccoby. (1970). *Social Character in a Mexican Village: A Socio-Psychoanalytic Study*. Englewood Cliffs, NJ: Prentice-Hall.
Funk, Rainer. (1982). *Erich Fromm: The Courage to Be Human*. New York: Continuum.
Funk, Rainer, ed. (2009). *The Clinical Erich Fromm: Personal Accounts and Papers on Therapeutic Technique*, vol. 9. Amsterdam and New York, NY: Rodopi.
Gojman de Millán, Sonia, and Salvador Millán. (2015). "Understanding Social Motivation for Encouraging Children's Development: Social Character Studies in Mexico." In Rainer Funk and Neil McLaughlin (eds.), *Towards a Human Science: The Relevance of Erich Fromm for Today*. Psychosozial-Verlag.
Grillo, Carmen M. (2018). "Revisiting Fromm and Bourdieu: Contributions to Habitus and Realism." *Journal for the Theory of Social Behaviour* 48, no. 4: 416–32.
Gross, Neil. (2008). *Richard Rorty: The Making of an American Philosopher*. Chicago: The University of Chicago Press.
Maccoby, Michael. (1976). *The Gamesman*. Simon and Schuster.
Maccoby, Michael. (1995). "The Two Voices of Erich Fromm: Prophet and Analyst." *Society* 32, no. 5: 72–82.
Maccoby, Michael. (2003). *The Productive Narcissist: The Promise and Peril of Visionary Leadership*. New York: Broadway Books.
Maccoby, Michael. (2007a). *Narcissistic Leaders: Who Succeeds and Who Fails*, 2nd ed. Harvard Business School Press.
Maccoby, Michael. (2007b). *The Leaders We Need: And What Makes Us Follow*. Harvard Business School Press.
Maccoby, Michael, and George M. Foster. (1970). "Methods of Studying Mexican Peasant Personality: Rorschach, TAT, and Dreams." *Anthropological Quarterly* 43: 225–43.
Maccoby, Michael, and Nancy Modiano. (1966). "On Culture and Equivalence." In Jerome S. Bruner, R. Oliver, and P. Greenfield (eds.), *Studies in Cognitive Growth*, 257–69. New York: Wiley and Sons.
Maccoby, Michael, Nancy Modiano, and Patricia Lander. (1964). "Games and Social Character in a Mexican Village." *Psychiatry* 27: 150–62.
Mann Michael. (2004). *The Dark Side of Democracy*. Cambridge: Cambridge University Press.
McLaughlin, Neil. (1998). "How to Become a Forgotten Intellectual: Intellectual Movements and the Rise and Fall of Erich Fromm." *Sociological Forum* 13: 215–46.
Steinmetz, George. (2006). "Bourdieu's Disavowal of Lacan: Psychoanalytic Theory and the Concepts of 'Habitus' and 'Symbolic Capital.'" *Constellations* 13, no. 4: 445–64.
Steinmetz, George, ed. (2013). *Sociology and Empire: The Imperial Entanglements of a Discipline*. Duke University Press.
Swartz, David L. (1997). *Culture and Power: The Sociology of Pierre Bourdieu*, 10, 26. The University of Chicago Press.
Swartz, David L. (2013). *Symbolic Power, Politics, and Intellectuals: The Political Sociology of Pierre Bourdieu*. The University of Chicago Press.

Part III

AUTHORITARIANISM, FASCISM, AND THE CONTESTED FUTURE

Chapter 7

ANTI-AUTHORITARIAN MARXISM: ERICH FROMM, HILDE WEISS, AND THE POLITICS OF RADICAL HUMANISM

David Norman Smith

Erich Fromm is traditionally depicted as the architect of an attempted synthesis of Marx and Freud which culminated in a "revised," desexualized psychoanalysis. That outcome is often characterized as a retreat from the full radicalism of Sigmund Freud's original vision, which did not avert its eyes, as Fromm is said to have done, from the facts of libidinal life. I will argue that, in fact, what Fromm achieved by his attempted synthesis of Marx and Freud was quite different—an anti-authoritarian Marxism, leavened with psychoanalytic insight, which was more radical than either traditional Marxism or traditional Freudianism. Fromm's several successive versions of this critical theory were never wholly or equally satisfactory, but they sprang from a genuinely radical impulse—the wish to complement Marx's critique of political economy with a humanist critique of political psychology. In today's age of unbridled capital and authoritarianism, that double critique remains as necessary now as ever.

Fromm began his work of synthesis in the decisive years from 1928 to 1939. His wish to merge Marx with Freud led him, initially, into the Frankfurt Institute and into collaboration with the Institute's director Max Horkheimer. Ultimately, his pursuit of that same wish led him away from Horkheimer and out of the Institute. This reflected changes not only in Fromm's worldview but, ultimately, in politics and the economy. In 1919, Max Weber had forecast that, within a decade, reactionary backlash to socialism and democracy could bring the world to the eve of "a polar night of icy darkness" and dictatorship.[1] That prediction now seemed prescient. The year 1929 was not only Year 1 of the Great Depression but Year 1 of Stalin's unchallenged hegemony in Bolshevik Russia. In 1930, the Nazis scored their first major electoral gains. Less than three years later Hitler came to power, sending Fromm and his colleagues into exile and imprisoning thousands of socialists and communists. In 1936, Stalin's purge trials began. Given German rearmament, Hitler's bellicose rhetoric, and the *Anschluss* of Austria, war clouds clearly hovered on the horizon.

These fateful events were, of course, significant for everyone; but they held special meaning for Marxists. Capitalist crisis had been expected, but the degree to which that crisis sparked a fascist response was (or should have been) startling. And Stalin's new course—which entailed the violent expropriation of the peasantry, the intensified exploitation of workers, and the eradication of opposition—was a sharp reversal of Marxian doctrine, provoking cognitive dissonance in many left-wing circles.

Victor Serge, one of the first and most influential anti-authoritarian Marxists, said the expropriations reminded him of "the pages of *Capital* where Marx describes the relentless mechanism of primitive capitalist accumulation."[2] Trotsky's left opposition in exile quoted the same pages from *Capital* to oppose what, echoing Marx, they described as yet another "grotesquely terroristic" expulsion of farmers from the land.[3]

How were Marxists to make sense of this rapidly inverting world? A great many, resisting cognitive dissonance, acted as if nothing surprising had happened—as if socialist movements and doctrines had been expected to turn into their opposites. This was particularly true of leaders with a vested interest in defending their positions and reputations. Vague recourse to triumphalism—"our time will come, we have history on our side!"—displaced analysis. One of the most damaging effects of this kind of denial, as Fromm said in 1937, is that it transfers agency from people to personified history: "Quite characteristic in this respect, in Germany in 1918, was the slogan that was most visible on posters and in the press: 'Socialism is on the march.' In this formula people are eliminated as active and consequential subjects." Instead, "socialism" figures as an invincible metaphysical force, and all threats posed by the incalculability of the future, by the unknown, are denied in advance. Faith in the march of time permits even defeated leaders to retain their *autoritären Ideologie*.[4]

Fromm's goal, in this phase above all, was to better understand working people as active and effective agents. If the achievement of authentic socialism requires the self-emancipation of the working class, wage earners cannot be an afterthought in emancipatory theory. Embracing that premise led Fromm to begin his affiliation with the Institute in 1930 by collaborating on a survey of working-class consciousness. At first that project simply accompanied his ongoing theoretical project but, ultimately, it played an important role in complicating and changing the tenor of that project. Fromm's Marxism, orthodox to begin with, grew increasingly unorthodox.

Among the Orthodox

Fromm's work in the decade from 1928 to 1937 can be analytically bisected into two periods: an initial phase of orthodox Marxism blended with orthodox Freudianism, followed by a phase in which Fromm distanced himself from the authoritarianism and "bourgeois materialism" he found problematic in each of these orthodoxies. The orthodox phase preceded Fromm's reading of Marx's *Economic and Philosophic Manuscripts of 1844*, which first appeared in 1932; the second phase ripened after his arrival in the United States on May 31, 1934.

Fromm's ultimate challenge to Freud, in *Escape from Freedom* (1941) and later writings, is well known. Less familiar, however, is the path that led him to this challenge, and the degree to which this paralleled his challenge to Marxian orthodoxy. In each arena, Fromm became increasingly critical of tendencies to reify people, to treat them as manipulable objects, as bodies to be disciplined.

Fromm sought, in his first phase, to work out a *rapprochement* between psychoanalysis and Marxian materialism. He made that attempt in a series of provocative essays on the interpenetration of class interests and libidinal drives.

Three of those essays loom large for our purposes. The first, written in 1929 for Freud's journal *Imago*, probed the psychodynamics and social psychology of the Christ doctrine in messianic early Christianity. The other two essays, both of which were written for the inaugural issue of the Institute's new journal, the *Zeitschrift für Sozialforschung* (1932), extended Fromm's effort to integrate psychoanalysis with Marxian social psychology.

Fromm's colleague Franz Borkenau praised "Die Entwicklung des Christusdogmas" in the inaugural issue of the *Zeitschrift* in 1932 as "the first concrete example" of a study successfully "integrating Marxism and Freudian psychoanalysis." Several earlier thinkers had anticipated a synthesis of this kind—Federn, Bernfeld, and others—but Fromm was the first, Borkenau wrote, who went beyond statements of principle to show, "brilliantly," that psychoanalytic thinking, merged with Marxism, could yield a rich harvest.[5]

The very idea of integrating Marx with Freud was, in itself, unorthodox. But Fromm took pains to stress his fidelity to orthodoxy. In the first of the two essays that appeared in the *Zeitschrift* in 1932, "The Method and Function of an Analytic Social Psychology," he said that his psychoanalytic stance was strictly Freudian.[6] But he differed with Freud sociologically, most notably with respect to class analysis. Freud, like Theodor Reik, assumed a universal human nature, untouched by status or class.[7] But in reality, Fromm stressed, character is not fate, but social. And historical materialism is the sociology that enables us to understand the origin and differentiation of social character over time.

Fromm's Marxism, at this stage, was decidedly orthodox, practically as well as theoretically. His starting point was a thesis about psychological barriers to change which echoes one of Marx's most critical observations in *Capital*. In the passage immediately after he indicts the expulsion of the peasantry, Marx offers this sobering point about the proletariat:

> The advance of capitalist production develops a working class which, by education, tradition, and habit, looks upon the conditions of that mode of production as self-evident laws of nature. The organization of the capitalist production process, once fully developed, breaks down all resistance.... Direct force [is] still used, but only exceptionally. In the usual run of things, the [worker's compliance] can be entrusted to the "natural laws of production," *i.e.*, to his dependence on capital.[8]

Fromm makes an equivalent point: "Social stability depends relatively little upon the use of external force. It depends for the most part upon the fact that men find themselves in a psychic condition that roots them inwardly in an existing social situation."[9] This "psychic condition" is rooted in character, which includes but goes beyond mere rational self-interest.

> Consider first a relatively stable social constellation. What holds people together? What enables them to have a certain feeling of solidarity, to adjust to the role of ruling or being ruled? . . . To be sure . . . rational and egotistic interests . . . contribute to structural stability. But neither the external power apparatus nor rational interests would suffice to guarantee the functioning of the society, if the libidinal strivings of the people were not involved. They serve as the "cement," as it were, without which the society would not hold together.[10]

What, then, permits change? On this point, too, Fromm echoes Marx, stressing that the unfolding of objective social contradictions and conflicts has destabilizing effects. Traditional ties dissolve and "there is change in traditional emotional attitudes. Libidinal energies are freed for new uses, and thus change their social function. They no longer serve the preservation of the society, but contribute to the development of new social formations. They cease to be 'cement,' and turn into dynamite."[11]

Social dynamite, exploding the bourgeois order, could clear the path for socialism, but it could also precipitate what Marx once called "the common ruin of the contending classes," or, as Rosa Luxemburg warned, lay the groundwork for barbarism.[12] With the polar night of Hitlerian barbarism already beginning to darken Weimar skies, Fromm wanted the revolutionary libidinal energies freed by disintegrating capitalism to usher in an era of working-class socialism. That wish was, of course, consonant with the revolutionary Marxism which rejected reformism *à la* Bernstein and Kautsky. A hint of this position had appeared in *Christusdogmas*, when Fromm alluded knowingly to the "revisionism" of the second-century Christians, who attempted to promote a "slow, gradual" shift "from the hope in a revolutionary Jesus to faith in a state-supporting Jesus."[13] Similarly, but in less veiled ways, Fromm indicted Kautsky et al. in his later essays, decrying Kautsky's "complete lack of understanding" of messianic radicalism and his banal interpretation of historical materialism.[14] And he criticized "Marx's petit-bourgeois interpreters"—citing Bernstein as well as Kautsky—for failing to see that Marxists would need more than superficial inferences from economics if they hoped to successfully fight barbarism.[15]

Fromm's Marxism was orthodox in other respects, too. Intellectual historians could easily assume that he had been influenced by György Lukács, who had opened the door to the study of subject-object dialectics in *History and Class Consciousness*. That celebrated book, which appeared in print a year later, had been the focal point of discussion in 1922 at the small summer conference, the *Erste Marxistische Arbeitswoche*, which led directly to the founding of the Frankfurt Institute.[16] And Lukács personally had won the sympathy of many independent radicals when he was censured by Communist Party leaders for overstepping the bounds of orthodoxy. But Fromm was not among Lukács's admirers. In a show of loyalty to traditional historical materialism, he praised the work of two of Lukács's most prominent communist critics, his Institute colleague Karl August Wittfogel and the Bolshevik leader Nikolai Bukharin.[17] Stating his opposition to "certain idealist positions which accord unlimited power to the human will," he underscored the fact that, like Bukharin and Wittfogel, he assigned primacy to nature over mind. He depicted his own distinctive views—notably, the claim that instinctual drives are among "the 'natural' conditions that form . . . the [material] base *(Unterbau)* of the social process"—as supplementing rather than contradicting orthodoxy.[18]

A decade earlier Wittfogel, like Lukács, had played a pivotal role at the *Marxistische Arbeitswoche*, where his own book, *The Science of Bourgeois Society* (1922), had sparked lively debate. In 1923, his wife Rose Wittfogel became the Frankfurt Institute's first staff member and, in 1924, Karl affiliated with the Institute as well. Subsequently, in the journal edited by the Institute's first director, Carl Grünberg, Lukács attacked both Bukharin's Die *Theorie des historischen Materialismus* (1922) and *The Science of Bourgeois Society*.[19]

All this was well known when Fromm praised Bukharin's 1922 book and Wittfogel's article, "Geopolitik, Geographischer Materialismus und Marxismus" (1929).[20] The latter, strikingly, includes a sharp critique of Lukács, who, like the arch-idealist Kautsky, "totally denies the determining influence of the natural factor" and posits "the dominant significance of subjective factors in history," thereby standing Marx on his head.[21]

Nor was Fromm's orthodoxy merely theoretical. It was also deeply political. Today, only a handful of scholars appear to be prepared to take the political commitments of past generations fully seriously. There is a tendency to view Marxist allegiance as a personal eccentricity or a matter of academic taste—"Who do you prefer, Marx, Weber or Heidegger?" But for Fromm and his peers, his comrades and adversaries, politics was a life-and-death matter. Nazism was death incarnate, and the fight for its opposite—radical humanism—could not be more serious. But that fight was also confusing. As Fromm's survey of workers showed, the proletariat was often but not reliably socialist or anti-authoritarian. The same was true, Fromm once reflected, for the party-political left. That left was contradictory, an admixture of tendencies humanist *and* anti-humanist. What explains that contradiction, and what significance does that have for humanists today? Is humanism, *à la* Fromm and his peers, still relevant?

Paradox? Humanism and Communism

In 1967, Fromm wrote a preface for a memoir, *The Search for a Third Way*, by his cousin Heinz Brandt. Brandt, who had fought and suffered for socialism for many years, was a complex figure with an extraordinary story to tell. On the eve of Hitler's accession to power, he had belonged to the minority "Conciliator" faction of the KPD, the German Communist Party. Appalled that Stalin and his German epigones in this period treated the Social Democrats, the SPD, as "social fascists," barely distinguishable from the Nazis, and that they brooked no dissent on this score, Brandt argued instead for a united front of all-anti-fascists, including both the KPD and the SPD. Stalin ordered them to cease and desist, and he expelled those who refused. Brandt, who stayed in the KPD to fight in the underground resistance, was arrested in 1934 and spent eleven years in prison camps, ultimately including Auschwitz. After the war, he served the communist regime in East Germany led by Walter Ulbricht in a senior capacity until, disenchanted with Ulbricht's repressive *Diktat*, he fled to West Germany in 1958, where he edited the journal of the metal workers union. But Ulbricht wanted him back, and in 1961 he had Brandt drugged, kidnapped, sentenced to thirteen years in prison and thrown into solitary confinement. A campaign to free him, in which Fromm played a major role, succeeded in 1964. Earlier, Fromm had also attempted, without success, to arrange Brandt's release from Nazi prisons.

Brandt's memoir, Fromm wrote, was a priceless introduction to "the generation of authentic revolutionaries" who had lived through the First World War, the rise of Stalinism and fascism, and much more. But at that point he paused:

> As I write this I suddenly realize that my remarks may sound confusing and disconcerting, indeed nonsensical to many readers. I write about Brandt as a man of faith, a humanistic socialist who at the same time has been a Communist. How does this fit together? Didn't Stalin show that communism is the opposite of all that is spiritual and all that is even remotely concerned with humanism?

The answer, Fromm writes, is not that simple. Many SPD and KPD members had "never accepted the falsified socialism purveyed by either the right-wing Social Democrats or Stalin," and they retained their humanist impetus, even within the confines of authoritarian party politics.[22]

Karl Wittfogel was one example. In 1932, seeking to remain true to the Communist Party, he published an article in which he called the SPD "Socialist in program but Fascist in action." At that point, he belonged to a party cell that also included Walter Ulbricht. But soon he too became critical—and publicly critical— of the KPD's sectarianism.[23] He remained a friend and confidante of Fromm's for years to come.

Fromm's own political leanings in this early orthodox phase have remained somewhat obscure. The most widely noticed clue is a remark by Gershom Scholem, whose course on eschatology Fromm had taken in the early 1920s, when they were both active in the *Freies jüdischen Lehrhaus* in Frankfurt. When he met Fromm again in 1926 after an interval of some years, Scholem was bemused to learn that his former student was now "an enthusiastic Trotskyist who pitied me for my petty-bourgeois provincialism."[24]

Scholars who cite this passage are usually skeptical.[25] Fromm's anodyne image as a warm, avuncular teacher and therapist doesn't easily square with the hard-edged sectarianism conveyed by the now recondite term "Trotskyist." But Fromm was plainly a left-wing radical, and Scholem was not a political naïf. In 1925 his brother Werner, who was then one of the ruling triumvirs of the KPD, denounced Trotskyism. He then shared the leadership of the party with Ruth Fischer and Arkadij Maslow, and his close friend Karl Korsch edited the party press. In 1926, he wrote to Gershom, voicing concerns about Trotsky. But that same year, as the fog of Stalinism began to descend on German communism, Werner was expelled from the party, with Korsch and the others. In 1928, now active in the new *Leninbund*, Scholem defended Trotsky when he was sent into internal exile, and afterward he himself was widely regarded as a Trotskyist.[26]

It's unlikely that, by 1926, Fromm had become a "Trotskyist" per se, since, at that juncture, Trotsky had neither been expelled from the Bolshevik party nor exiled.[27] But many other left-socialist and left-communist groups were active in Germany in 1926, some of which were sizable. Karl Korsch, after his expulsion, had founded the "Intransigent Left" (*Entschiedene Linke*), which soon afterward merged with the ultra-left *Kommunistische Arbeiterpartei Deutschlands*. And four other ultra-left groups with at least 3,000 members were also active that year, including the *Spartakusbund linkscommunistischer Organisation* led by Franz Pfemfert and Iwan Katz.

In 1929–30, when Fromm and Hilde Weiss began the German workers' survey, many of these groups were still pillars of the left—far smaller than the SPD and KPD but hardly negligible. And the survey itself was as much a study of the Marxist left as it was of the working class, since, as Fromm explained in his report on the study, "it was certainly customary for a [German] worker, what his character traits, to belong to, or vote for, one of the two workers' parties."[28] What Fromm and Weiss learned about the workers they learned, equally, about their parties. And those parties were not simply binary. SPD voters subdivided into two camps, one of which Fromm classified as Left Socialists. In 1931, while the workers' survey was underway, the Left Socialists split to form a sizable new party, the *Sozialistische Arbeiterpartei*, which also drew in the remnants of the once-formidable USPD (Independent Social Democrats).[29] The KPD, as we learned earlier, was also subdivided into factions. And though most of the workers who responded to the survey voted for candidates from the major parties, fewer than half of KPD voters and a third of SPD voters were not registered members of either party.[30]

Was Fromm then a "Trotskyist" in this period? We will probably never know—but dismissing that possibility is naive. Even in the phase when he first knew Gershom Scholem, when he was still preoccupied with Jewish culture, his orientation was left wing. In his dissertation, as Michael Löwy notes, he extolled Hassidism as a "social-religious movement of self-emancipation" of "entirely anti-capitalist" tendency.[31] Leo Löwenthal, who was one of his closest friends in this period, later said that, "along with people such as Franz Neumann . . . I helped found the socialist student group" in Frankfurt in 1918–19.[32] In 1919, Löwenthal joined the USPD, which was one of the main tributaries leading into the KPD. Karl Korsch, Karl Wittfogel, and many others also joined the USPD in 1919. In 1920, Löwenthal became general secretary of the *Deutscher Sozialistischer Studentenbund*.[33]

In 1958, meanwhile, when Fromm was at the apogee of his fame as a public intellectual, he wrote a review of Trotsky's 1935 diary in exile. "There can be no doubt," he wrote, that Trotsky, as a person, embodied "a flowering of Western humanity." He was "unselfish," "always stimulating, always alive," endowed with "unquenchable courage" and "an uncompromising sense of truth, penetrating to the very essence of reality."[34]

Beyond Orthodoxy

Fromm's fidelity to Marx and labor became increasingly obvious in the years after his encounter with Scholem. In 1928, he hailed Marx as "the greatest sociologist"[35] and he lectured on "The Psychoanalysis of the Petty Bourgeoisie"[36]—a topic to which he would return soon after in the German workers' survey with Hilde Weiss. But what they found in that survey was disorienting. They had expected that the petty bourgeoisie and working class would stand at opposite ends of the ideological and characterological spectrum. When that orthodox Marxian expectation proved unfounded, when it became clear that workers and small entrepreneurs are not walking ideal-types of reaction and revolution, they were forced to rethink their assumptions. That rethinking ultimately led them—Weiss no less than Fromm—to a Marxism steeped in libertarianism.

Hilde Weiss is one of the truly neglected figures in the history of the Frankfurt School. But that neglect is inversely proportional to her importance. Weiss was in many ways the principal architect of the workers' survey, which built on work she had already completed in industrial sociology and laid the foundation for research she would later conduct on Marx and the history of working-class surveys and families. Politically, Weiss was among the most active and astute members of the Institute, and she was better educated in Marxian theory, sociology, and labor studies than Fromm, Horkheimer, or Adorno. She was intimately familiar with trade unions and she had direct, disillusioning experiences of both left-wing and right-wing authoritarianism.

We are indebted to Detlef Garz for most of what we now know about Hilde Weiss. In 2006 Garz printed and annotated a slender memoir that Weiss wrote about her life in pre-Hitler Germany, which, until then, had languished in an archive. Before that memoir appeared, Weiss was almost entirely unknown. Garz notes, laconically, that what Wiggershaus says about her in his standard history of the Frankfurt School is "laconic"; and in fact, Wiggershaus says only that she and Kurt Mandelbaum were among the first doctoral students at the Institute.[37] Martin Jay is even more laconic,[38] and, if we are to believe Google Scholar, Garz's volume has not yet been cited in either German or English

Hilde Weiss, like Erich Fromm, traced an arc of development that led beyond the ambiguous humanism of figures like Heinz Brandt to full-fledged, unqualified humanism. But in her earliest phase she was very much like Brandt. Just months younger than Fromm, Weiss was born in 1900 into a socially liberal bourgeois family. Her father Berthold was a philosopher and her mother, born

Lisbeth Rathenau, was the niece of Emil Rathenau, who in 1883 had founded the *Allgemeine Elektrizitäts-Gesellschaft*. Emil's son Walther was his successor and one of the most influential essayists, industrialists, and statesmen of the day. Weiss's aunts Jenny Apolant and Josephine Lévy-Rathenau were feminists who focused on the problems of working women; one of Lévy-Rathenau's books, prefiguring Weiss's later interest in white-collar workers, discussed women as white-collar workers in the technical professions.[39] Weiss's mother was also a social worker and feminist.

Weiss's childhood idyll was shattered, she wrote, by the outbreak of war enthusiasm at the start of the First World War. At school, "We had to learn by heart, I remember, and to recite in chorus the following verse: *'We love as one, We hate as one, We have only one enemy, all of us: England!'*"[40] These were lines from the wildly popular "Hate Song" (*Haßgesang*) by Ernst Lissauer which, at Kaiser Wilhelm's behest, was recited in schools, the military, and elsewhere.

Revolted by this kind of authoritarian belligerence, Weiss and her older brother Fritz joined the pacifist wing of the *Wandervogel* youth movement and, one month after the workers' and soldier's revolt in November 1918, she joined a socialist youth group as well.[41] There she befriended Helmi Liebknecht, the son of the famous socialist Karl Liebknecht who, with Rosa Luxemburg, had broken from the pro-war SPD to found the *Spartakusbund*, the tribune of anti-militarist socialism and forerunner of the KPD. Helmi walked Hilde home after every meeting: "I was so thankful to him for giving me some supplementary explanations. I began to understand the difference between the workers' living conditions and my own. I came to know that we live under the capitalist system. I felt that the capitalist should not be allowed to exploit workers, to get rich by making the workers poor."[42]

"One day," in January 1919, "the headline of the noon newspaper read: 'Karl Liebknecht and Rosa Luxemburg assassinated!' I bought the paper and found that the father of my new teacher in socialism had been murdered near our home at a bridge where I crossed twice a day. I did not know Karl Liebknecht personally, but I admired him, how he alone was courageous enough during the war in 1916 to shout on the Potsdamer Platz in the center of Berlin: 'Nieder mit dem Kriege' (Down with the war!). . . . I locked myself up in my room and cried all day long. My heart was broken by this brutal act against this hero of pacifism. I did not understand at that time that the Social Democratic Party had encouraged his murder."[43]

Weiss became increasingly radical and Germany became increasingly unstable. In January 1920, she marched in a protest that the new SPD regime met with machine gun fire. In March, a right-wing military putsch forced the SPD leaders to flee and call for a general strike. In support of the call, Weiss circulated anti-putsch leaflets outside the factory gates: "Strike! Lay aside your work and throttle this military dictatorship. With every means, fight for the preservation of the republic. Paralyze the economic life. Let no hand stir, let no proletarian help the military dictatorship. Let there be a general strike along the whole line. Proletariat, unite!"[44]

Weiss, who was still just nineteen, had chosen her path. In 1921, she moved to Jena to study with Karl Korsch, who was a *Privatdozent* at the university and had become active in the fledgling KPD.[45] Jena was also the home of the Zeiss Optical Works, which was famous for its social liberalism. That liberalism, however, was attenuating under the impact of postwar economic stress and so-called industrial "rationalization," and Weiss wanted to be part of the factory-floor resistance. A Zeiss foreman, learning that she was related to Walther Rathenau "organizer of German war economy" and now foreign minister, steered her to the personnel director, who told her: "I am very happy indeed to admit a representative of Walther Rathenau's progressive and democratic ideas to our factory."[46]

Weiss was hired to work the 7:00 a.m.–3:00 p.m. shift in the Schott glass factory, which was affiliated with Zeiss. Between them, the glass factory and the Zeiss optical plant employed fully one-tenth of the city's population, which made the relations between management and the workers the central dynamic in the city. Initially Weiss was, she said, "a bad worker" who annoyed her fellow workers by lowering the average level of productivity.[47] But she soon rallied and before long, she was invited to join the Works Council (*Betriebsrät*) which, in 1920, had consisted of twelve USPD members and three SPD members. By 1922, when Weiss became the *Betriebsrät*'s only female member, all of the USPD members had joined either the KPD or the SPD, and both parties were equally represented.[48]

Working at Zeiss was an economic necessity as well as a political choice, since Weiss's family, which had lived on inherited wealth, suffered grave losses during the hyperinflation of 1921–23. But she earned little as a *Hilfarbeiterin* at the *Glaswerk*, "not enough to eat dinner every night," and she often was invited for dinner "at the homes of comrades." In the evenings, she attended courses on social psychology and labor legislation.[49]

In 1922, when she was invited to attend summer school with 200 workers from Jena and elsewhere in Thuringia and Saxony, Weiss took a leave from May until mid-August. This *Volkshochschule* met at Schloss Tinz, a princely estate near Ilmenau in Thuringia which had been converted into a school for socialists and unionists after the November 1918 uprising.[50] Karl Korsch and Karl Wittfogel had both taught at the *Volkshochschule*, and Korsch was a mainstay.

Weiss's teachers at the summer school included both KPD members and SPD members. And unmentioned by her is the fact that, in June 1922, "at the site of the *Volkshochschule Thüringen* in an Ilmenau hotel,"[51] Korsch and several of his protégés ("men, women, and students") joined Lukács, Wittfogel, and others for the celebrated meeting of the *Erste Marxistische Arbeitswoche*, where Korsch and Lukács held center stage with a debate on party and class which prefigured their contrasting later odysseys—Lukács, into Stalinism, and Korsch into libertarian socialism.

Whether Weiss was among Korsch's students at this gathering is unknown. But the summer school, where she was given copies of *Capital* and Luxemburg's *Accumulation of Capital*, was an intellectual turning point for her—and a personal turning point as well. Just weeks after the Marxist *Arbeitswoche* concluded, while Weiss's summer school was still in session, fascist anti-Semites murdered Walther

Rathenau—who thus became, like Rosa Luxemburg in 1919, one of the first prominent victims of fascist hate.

This was the context in which Weiss returned to Jena, where, as before, she found her union work exhilarating: "Soon I was known in all departments because I held youth meetings in the factory yard almost every day. This work really thrilled me."[52] Unemployment was rife, and the union protested against overtime "by asking management to hire the unemployed." As wages fell amid the chaos of hyperinflation, the Works Council stepped up its agitation and, in September 1923 Weiss started a mimeographed newspaper for young workers, the *Zeiss-Lupe* (*Zeiss Magnifying Glass*). "Never before did you know anything about a dollar!" she wrote in one issue. "Now you are reading every day about its climbing value on the blackboard of the factory administration. One dollar = 532 million marks! The dollar is the thermometer of our misery now.... Young workers, support the demands of the adult workers. Ask for a sliding wage scale according to the changing value of the dollar!"[53]

In retrospect, though Weiss clearly took pride in her activism, she also expressed some ambivalence. She felt that she had inherited from her mother a Prussian sensibility—unrelenting, single-minded—which made her an ideal foot soldier in an authoritarian movement: "I belonged to the union with body, soul, and thought. It was this German quality of ascetic heroism and totalitarian self-surrender, demanding all I had and all I was, that had taken possession of me."[54]

In October 1923, Korsch and other communists entered the provincial governments in Thuringia and Saxony. Within days the *Reichswehr* banned the armed communist militias in the provinces and gave them three days to disarm. That order was ignored and the authorities sent in troops.[55] "In November 1923," Weiss recalled, "a general strike took place in the Zeiss plant" and elsewhere "to protect the socialist governments" *Zeiss-Lupe* issued a call to lay down tools. "The paper became political. When the police entered the factory to arrest me" her supervisor, an SPD member, "hid me in his photographic dark room and saved me from arrest." At one point, as the strike raged on, Weiss was given a rusty gun and told to guard the union office from the balcony above the street, from midnight until dawn: "Disciplined, I dared not refuse the order."[56]

When the general strike was defeated, "the clouds of reaction were hanging low over the Zeiss factory too. Hundreds of workers were dismissed." On January 1, 1924, Weiss was dismissed as well.[57] For the next few months, she traveled as a union organizer "through the small industrial villages of Thuringia full of terribly paid families who worked at home." She stayed in many of those homes, sleeping in armchairs, or in sofas, or in beds with children, dogs, and cats. "They were very poor indeed, often ill with pneumonia or tuberculosis"; but they were also, always, "generous and hospitable."[58]

In early 1924, Weiss returned to Berlin, where she reunited with her brother Fritz, who was studying medicine at the University of Berlin. Hilde enrolled in the university as well, studying sociology "under the direction of Professor Sombart" to complete her degree.[59] Fritz had been a communist youth activist for some time. In 1923, with Karl Wittfogel, he had edited the *Rundbrief der Kommunistischen Jugend*

Deutschlands.[60] At times Weiss and Wittfogel could sound almost libertarian, as Wittfogel did when he called upon youth to reject the Nietzschean "illusion of the superman" and instead seek comradeship and collective heroism as antidotes to the fetishism of a world in which "all things have become commodities." But other times they sounded entirely Bolshevik, insisting upon the historical necessity of the vanguard party, which, Wittfogel argued, would retain its legitimacy even if individual leaders were to violate party norms—much as the priesthood in the medieval Catholic Church had retained its *character indelebilis* even when "evil popes" went astray.[61]

In the spring of 1924, when Hilde joined Fritz at the university, she also joined him in the Berlin branch of a national organization led by Franz Borkenau, the *Kommunistische Studentenfraktion*.[62] Hilde and Fritz were among the signers of a flyer accusing the university of becoming a "recruiting depot" for paramilitary rightists and calling for science to be liberated from "enslavement by capital"; "we oppose a society, which, though it has money for munitions and champagne, has little for science."[63]

Soon after, when Weiss heard from "friends"—the Wittfogels?—that the freshly minted Institute for Social Research was accepting graduate students, she wrote to Carl Grünberg and "received a very sympathetic answer," including the prospect of a scholarship. She went to Frankfurt in October 1924 and became not only one of the Institute's first doctoral students but one of its very first affiliates. Fritz remained in Berlin, where he received his medical degree and played a role in Workers' International Relief (*Internationale Arbeiterhilfe*, IAH), which had been created under Comintern auspices by Willi Münzenberg in 1921. In 1925, Fritz helped Münzenberg organize a campaign to defend Sun Yat Sen's China from outside intervention which, drawing in Wittfogel as well, culminated in the formation of the Comintern's League against Colonial Oppression.[64]

At the Institute, Hilde wrote two books on the sociology of industry. *Abbe und Ford*, her doctoral dissertation, is a brilliant work about which I will write more fully on another occasion. Weiss's goal in this study was to explain the enormous popularity of Ernst Abbe, the architect of social liberalism at Zeiss, and Henry Ford, the protagonist of the "5 dollar day." Weiss offered two basic, interwoven explanations for their popularity, citing both the privileged status of monopolies, which can afford to treat their workers generously, and the ulterior influence of what Marx called capital fetishism—that is, the tendency to ascribe superhuman, charismatic strength to capital and its motley personifications. The argument in *Abbe und Ford* is artfully elaborated on both levels, especially vis-à-vis the theme of capital fetishism, which has obvious implications for the study of authoritarianism in an age, like ours, when authority orbits around capital.

Strikingly different is *Rationalisierung und Arbeiterklasse*, which Weiss wrote for the Metal Workers' Union. Published in 1926 by Führer-Verlag, which specialized in books by Solomon Lozovsky and others from the Comintern's Red International of Trade Unions, *Rationalisierung und Arbeiterklasse* is crisply written but strident. She denounced "the sabotage of profit-hungry capitalists with their never-ending plant closures" and planless production, calling (in blazing italics) *"for the revolutionary control of production by the Work Councils and the trade unions, the conquest of political power by the proletariat, the expropriation of the capitalists.*"[65] And, lest there be any doubt about her party orthodoxy, she cited Lenin to extol the "matchless" self-sacrifice and enthusiasm of the Russian proletariat, which, she said, willingly worked without pay on "communist Saturdays," content in the knowledge that they were serving "*their* economic system."[66]

Weiss, at this point, was clearly ambivalent about authority. She was strenuously opposed to the prevailing "employers' dictatorship" which, she felt, inevitably produced misery of the kind she had witnessed among the jobless in Jena and the impoverished glass-blowers in rural Thuringia. That dictatorship could not be redeemed from within, as Walther Rathenau had hoped, and the quasi-benevolence of figures like Abbe and Ford would prove short-lived, as their firms faced mounting financial troubles and ever-stronger competitors.[67] Capitalist authority, in short, was odious and unstable. But at the same time, Weiss did not hesitate to call for proletarian dictatorship "under communist leadership."[68] She was not, at this stage, prepared to oppose the rule of the worker's supposed "vanguard." But that change of heart was not long in coming, and one source of that change was what Weiss learned from the workers' survey.

Leaders versus Followers

Figure 7.1 Hilde Weiss in 1930.

Hilde Weiss returned to the Frankfurt Institute in 1930 to codirect the workers' survey, which began that year.[69] Since she had received her doctorate in 1927—after finishing *Abbe und Ford* under Grünberg's supervision and passing examinations in economics, sociology, industrial studies, statistics, and labor law—she had assisted the Institute in its collaboration with David Ryazanov's Marx-Engels Institute in Moscow. That collaboration led to the first-ever appearance, in the early volumes of the *Marx-Engels Gesamtausgabe*, of Marx's *Economic and Philosophic Manuscripts of 1844* and *The German Ideology*. Back in Berlin, Weiss worked for the liberal *Zeitschrift für Politik* and for the daily newspaper of the Council for Labor and Defense of the USSR, which, in 1928, acknowledged "Frau Dr. Hilde Weiss" for "scientific and journalistic work... with which we were wholly satisfied." And from April 1928 until 1930 she was a research associate at the *Statistischen Reichsamt*, working for Dr. Otto Nathan.[70]

Weiss was thus eminently qualified for her role in the workers' survey. She brought to the project expertise in industrial sociology, economics, statistics, and working-class culture that eluded Fromm and Horkheimer. She had direct ties to the unions that helped with the survey. She knew working-class living conditions from firsthand experience. And, according to Bonss and Friedman, she familiarized Fromm with Max and Alfred Weber's surveys of large-scale industry (*Verein für Sozialpolitik*, 1909–11) and Adolf Levenstein's survey of factory workers (1912).[71]

Besides her work on the survey per se—which was called *Arbeiter- und Angestellten Erhebung* in the short version that appeared in *Studien über Autorität und Familie* (1936)—Weiss contributed two companion studies, neither of which has yet emerged from the archives: a 190-page study of book printers, *Zur soziologischen Analyse der deutschen Buchdrucker*; and a report, of unknown length, on *Die soziale und intellektuelle Position der deutschen Arbeiterklasse*.[72] But what she found most eye-opening and alarming was the survey itself:

> The answers to the questionnaire I had sent out ... changed little by little from 1932 to the beginning of 1933. It was easy to recognize in them the reflection of the world crisis started in 1929 and the growing political and social tensions which brought about the death of the German Republic in the flames of the burning Reichstag [in] February 1933. Fear and pressure from above made the German workers think and react in the traditional Prussian way. A lot of them began to see no other way out of political and economic crises than to look for a strong hand, a man with absolute power. Bismarck, Napoleon, and Luther were [cited] as the most important personalities more and more often in the questionnaires that came back. These same names were written down by National Socialist, Catholic, Social Democratic and even communist workers. They had never come to a confidence in themselves.[73]

This finding was, of course, consistent with harsh realities that were increasingly visible on the streets and in the polling booths. When Weiss and Fromm began the *Arbeiter* survey in 1930, Hitler's ascent to power was not yet a foregone conclusion.

In 1928, the Nazis had been a minor electoral force, winning just 2.6 percent of the vote, and although they scored major gains two years later, when their vote total rose sixfold, they did not win decisive support until 1932, when Hitler capitalized on the disunity of his SPD and KPD rivals to win 37.3 percent of the vote, which made the National Socialists the largest *Reichstag* party and cleared the way for Hitler to become chancellor in January 1933 and, soon after, *Führer*.[74]

Weiss, like countless others, was repelled. But the lessons she drew from the survey went beyond Nazism alone. Hitler's triumph, she concluded, sprang not only from a visceral mass authoritarianism which crisis had sharpened and raised from the depths but also from the elitism of the workers' parties. The Communist Party, she wrote in 1939, had "taken Lenin's party theory as its basis. . . . Its members were mainly intellectuals, ruined lower middle-class, unskilled workers and unemployed who had left the factories a long time before." And since the majority of the working class wanted only gradual reforms, the KPD saw itself as "a 'Proletarian Vanguard,'" in sole, unique possession of the revolutionary truth.[75] In hindsight, Weiss now saw her *Volkshochschule* experience as a symptom of this elitism:

> The general aim of this kind of education was 1st to model a party elite, 2nd to emphasize the importance of a social revolution as opposed to the slower method of social evolution. . . . Education was to be given only to the party elite who were to lead the unconscious masses. . . . Despising more or less consciously the imperfect work of improving the workers' daily labor conditions, [the KPD approach to] education was far from the real problems and needs of the factory workers.

And, unfortunately, "some of the workers who succumbed to [this] influence felt much superior . . . to their workmates when they went back to the factories." Nor was the effect of SPD tutelage much different "than that of the orthodox communists. Upon leaving these workers' schools the newly created intellectuals would feel superior to their factory colleagues and behave like typical German trade union bosses without having their secure position."[76]

This was one side of the story. But Weiss found a silver lining in one implication of the *Arbeiter* survey. It became increasingly clear, she concluded, "that the workers did not restrict their thinking to narrow party viewpoints. Many [SPD] members . . . expressed just the same opinion as communists about war, the form of government they wanted and their estimates of [famous] personalities. It revealed that the party leaders were no longer the representatives of the working masses"—and that, in fact, the sour sectarianism of the two warring parties, each of which was dominated by an authoritarian elite, was not native to the workers but reflected the exigencies of elite Realpolitik: "The gulf between leaders and masses widened steadily until Hitler was able to benefit from those growing divergences."[77] The question, then, was why the rank and file in these parties stayed the course with their self-serving leaders—out of inertia, or deference? That question, in turn, raises the issue of authoritarianism in Fromm's sense.

About this, Weiss is very clear: "Prussian militarism and discipline had entered into every kind of activity, even into the labor movement. The members of trade unions and the students of the workers' schools had no initiative, they had to accept the leader's point of view." The consequence, she wrote, was that "the German labor movement had good followers, but poor individual leaders. Regimentation and discipline were so strong all over that no force could fight effectively against them. This lack of individual thinking [and] responsibility among the masses explains to some extent the lack of resistance to fascist aggression."[78]

No longer orthodox, Weiss left the party in 1932: "I explained my changed conviction [to the party leadership] at the time."[79] Soon after, in the wake of Hitler's *Machtergreifung* in April 1933, she fled to France, one step ahead of the Gestapo. Upon her arrival Weiss joined the Institute's Paris branch, which Horkheimer had financed not long before. She remained central to the Institute's research plans, as we learn from her job description: "For the sociological work, which will extend across three countries (Germany, France, USA, and eventually Russia) and distinct social strata (white-collar employees and manual workers), all team members will need a rough overview of economic development in the light of preexisting statistical data on the family, over roughly the last century. That overview will be provided by HW."[80]

Weiss not only produced that overview, writing a 109-page historical study, *Materialien zum Verhältnis von Konjunktur und Familie*, which she briefly summarized in the collective work *Studien über Autorität und Familie* in 1936, but embarked on several related projects as well—a research monograph on the nineteenth-century history of working-class surveys in France, which she wrote under the supervision of Émile Durkheim's old friend Céléstin Bouglé for the University of Paris; a sequel to that study, which she may not have completed; and a well-known article in the 1936 *Zeitschrift für Sozialforschung* in which she published and critiqued Marx's *Enquête ouvrière*, a workers' survey which his French followers had circulated in 1880 which she found in his papers.

What Weiss wanted most, however, was to continue in France what she had begun in Germany. On September 22, 1934, she wrote to Horkheimer in the United States, reporting that she had successfully acted as his emissary in a visit to the Institute's London office and explaining that she had begun to work with Bouglé, "who set me to work on the 1830-48 period; this historical work [is] the price of admission for the work on the mentality of the contemporary French worker which I had proposed and he had accepted as well—*after* this historical work."[81]

Nor had Weiss forgotten the *Arbeiter* survey: "May I perhaps dare to make another suggestion? You will surely recall that my first survey product, the social-psychological types (skilled, unskilled, and long-unemployed workers; civil servants, upwardly mobile white-collar employees, etc.) has never seen the light of day, though I was already encouraged in that direction in Frankfurt."[82] When, the next year, she requested a transfer to the New York office, probably to work on the survey, Horkheimer replied, "I would really like to say something positive, but I just can't do it. Oh, if we had a little more money!"[83] Two weeks later, apparently having seen Fromm's tentative typology, she told Horkheimer that "Fromm has changed the types a bit and represents them in a very abridged way. . . . But, basically, it is just a different ordering of certain answer groups, which I had already identified as typical."[84]

Rainer Funk says that, even from afar, Weiss was able to coordinate the preparation of the report on the workers' survey that appeared in *Studien* in 1936.[85] Fromm contributed a preface but Weiss explained the findings. At this point, however, she reached an impasse. Since in Paris she was unable to pursue further direct survey research, she turned, as an alternative, to the study of past workers' surveys. This led to the discovery of Marx's *Enquête Ouvrière* and to her book on workers' surveys in early industrial France. The latter, which appeared under her married name, Rigaudias-Weiss,[86] was among the first scholarly works inspired by Marx's *Economic and Philosophic Manuscripts of 1844*. The focal point of this study was Eugène Buret, an early critic of capitalism and a pioneer of workers' surveys whom Marx cited in the first of his manuscripts, "Wage Labor."

Weiss felt that Buret had anticipated Marx in some important ways, but that he fell short interpretively, not least with respect to self-alienation and what Fromm would soon call authoritarianism. Symptomatic, in this respect, was a passage cited by Marx: "The industrial war . . . demands large armies which it can amass on one spot and decimate prolifically. And it is neither from devotion nor from duty that the soldiers of this army bear the exertions imposed on them, but only to escape the hard necessity of hunger. They feel neither attachment nor gratitude towards their bosses."[87]

Weiss saw matters very differently. Workers, in conditions of alienation, are deprived "of the sense and meaning of their lives." Instead of their pursuing their own work, by means they've freely chosen, "they fall into an utter dependence on capital, in a degradation individual and moral, into a state of expropriation and brutalization."[88] But self-alienation is by no means the whole story. Here she invokes Flora Tristan, whose *Workers' Union* (1843) was strikingly Marx-like. "She declared from the start that the emancipation of the workers had to be achieved by the workers themselves"[89]—and workers retained that promise, despite everything, as Tristan had concluded in 1844 when she attempted to build that union herself. Weiss found special inspiration in Tristan's diary of that effort, which recounted a tour of industrial France that took her from factory to factory and city to city. What Tristan found was complex, and Weiss quoted her in full: On the one hand, "the workers are, most often, indifferent to social ideas, [and] when they emerge from their torpor, they show a foolish and unpleasant over-confidence which reveals their ignorance."[90] But even so, "the few organized elements"—silk workers in Lyon, and their peers elsewhere—"are the most reassuring of spectacles." "In that," Tristan wrote, "we find hope."[91]

Weiss found an echo of that hope in Marx's *Enquête Ouvrière*, which he wrote to give further impetus to the "will to emancipation" which, as the Paris Commune and other struggles had shown, accompanies the growth of industrial capitalism. That will, Weiss says, can only be the wish to overcome self-alienation, not to exchange one form of surrender for another. And that's why Marx addressed the workers directly, "since only they and not 'providential saviors' know the causes of their misery, and therefore they alone can find the effective means of eliminating them."[92]

"Lieber Genosse Fromm"

Delving further into Hilde Weiss's writings, which extended decades beyond her Institute years, would take us too far afield for present purposes.[93] The same is truer for Erich Fromm, whose writings not only map the boundary between alienation and emancipation but theorize that boundary, substantively and formally. That, in a nutshell, is what Fromm's theory of authoritarianism comprises, as I have tried to show elsewhere.[94] So, in what follows, I will focus not on the letter of Fromm's texts on authoritarianism—including, most notably, "The Psychology of Authority" (1936), which has the unique virtue of expressing his underlying theoretical premises in full and unvarnished form, unconstrained by the need to speak simply for a wide readership, as he did in most of his later writings—and instead will situate that work in the phase, between his arrival in the United States in 1934 and his break with Horkheimer and the Institute in 1939, when his psychology of authority and his Marxist anti-authoritarianism took finished form.

Hints of Fromm's anti-authoritarian concerns—perhaps Trotskyist, perhaps not—were clearly evident in his earlier writings. In his 1932 "Method" essay, he explained that he had focused mainly

> on the libidinal bonds between the ruling minority and the ruled majority.... But other social relations, too, bear their own distinctive libidinal stamp.... The relationship to the political leader is different ... in the case of a proletarian leader who identifies with his class and serves their interests ... from what it is when he confronts them as a strong man, as the great father who rules as omnipotent authority.[95]

That statement, clearly, has an anti-Stalinist ring. And in his earlier *Christusdogmas* essay he had stressed that, when rebellious oppressed classes suffer shocking defeats, they can turn, in their desperation, either to self-abasing submission or to fantasy revolution—or both. Fromm had argued, in particular, that when an oppressed class finds itself embattled, with little immediate hope of achieving its goals, it can easily turn to "phantasy satisfactions" and self-blame:

> Where were the aggressive impulses now? They were turned away from the ... fathers, the authorities, and directed back toward the individual self. The identification with the suffering, crucified Jesus offered a magnificent opportunity for this. In Catholic dogma the stress was no longer, [as it had been], on the overthrow of the father but on the self-annihilation of the son.[96]

This, allusively at least, brings us to the threshold of Fromm's later thinking about authoritarianism. But it wasn't until he arrived in the United States in May 1934 that he began to pursue the suite of projects that culminated in his full-fledged theory. Those projects included, besides the seminal papers he wrote from 1935 to 1937 (a *Zeitschrift* paper in 1935 challenging Freud's "authoritarian and patricentric" outlook, "*Psychologie der Autorität*" in 1936,[97] a *Zeitschrift* paper in 1937 on feelings of impotence, and the unpublished "fundamental paper" of 1937 which convinced Horkheimer that Fromm was no longer a Freudian), an attempt to analyze the *Arbeiter* survey psychodynamically. The combined result of those efforts was Fromm's radical new theory which, as the Institute's leaders intuited to their dismay, opposed authority so comprehensively that no prior orthodoxy was immune to challenge.

In the summer of 1936, Erich Fromm and Karen Horney went to Taxco, Mexico, to visit Otto Rühle and Alice Rühle-Gerstel, whom they visited again in Mexico the following year.[98] These visits have occasionally been noticed but their significance has gone undiscussed. Nor has Fromm's correspondence with Otto Rühle, extending from 1936 into 1940, attracted much attention. But Otto Rühle was not always so invisible. In 1914, he became famous as the most prominent Social Democratic *Reichstag* deputy besides Karl Liebknecht to vote against the authorization of war credits. Rühle was subsequently, with Luxemburg and Liebknecht, one of the defining leaders of the *Spartakusbund*, which played a major role in the uprisings of 1918 and in the formation of the Communist International—which Rühle exited almost immediately, convinced, by the Bolsheviks' centralization of authority, that it was not truly communist or proletarian. In the ensuing decade, he became a highly visible libertarian communist, advocating working-class self-activity, free of party influence.

Rühle was also a prolific writer, the author, in 1928, of an influential biography of Marx and, two years later, of a lavishly illustrated history of the proletariat. But for our purposes, the single most relevant fact about Otto Rühle and Alice Rühle-Gerstel was that they were Adlerian psychologists who probed authoritarianism psychodynamically as well as politically. In 1925, Rühle wrote "*Der Autoritäre Mensch und die Revolution*," which strikingly anticipates Fromm's later views:

> What is needed most today is the gradual dismantling of authority within people themselves, in their mode of psychic activity, in the general, daily practice of life in society. Dismantling authority in the organizational apparatus is important. Dismantling it in the theory and tactics of class struggle is more important. But most important is *dismantling authority in the human soul*, because without that it is impossible to abolish authority in either organization or tactics and theory.[99]

Otto Rühle and Alice Rühle-Gerstel both wrote extensively on this subject. Rühle, an educator by profession, wrote volumes on the psychology of working-class children and Rühle-Gerstel wrote feminist studies of working-class women (one of which, in 1932, reported the results of a miniature survey). Hence, when Otto and Alice went into Mexican exile, they were not figures to be taken lightly. Hitler's envoy to Mexico cabled the Nazi foreign office in January 1936 with this message: last month, the "communist Otto Rühle who . . . worked with Mehring, Liebknecht, Rosa Luxemburg and others in the *Spartakusbund* . . . appeared here. . . . The presence of a personality of the kind and intellectual importance of Rühle in Mexico . . . calls for an examination of the question of the importance of Communism in this country."[100]

Hundreds of orthodox German communists, including famous writers, had already taken up residence in Mexico.[101] But Rühle and Rühle-Gerstel stood out. They were, with just a few exceptions (including their son-in-law Fritz Bach, who had worked in the Comintern with Willi Münzenberg and Fritz Weiss until he was expelled, in 1929, for opposing Stalin), the only anti-Stalinists among the German exiles. When Fromm visited Otto and Alice in 1936, they had been in Mexico for only a few months. His interest in them was clearly not random. And in the ensuing years, as he continued to develop his own perspective on *Autoritäre menschen*, he deepened his acquaintance with them.

On September 9, 1936, soon after Fromm and Horney had returned to New York from their first visit to Taxco, Rühle opened what became an extensive correspondence with a cheery greeting: "*Lieber Genosse Fromm*" ("Dear Comrade Fromm"). But his message was chastened. Dismayed to find that both Alice and Fritz were already becoming forgetful about the history of the left, "I wondered: what will remain for posterity of the incalculable abundance of the working-class movement when . . . fascism has accomplished its work of destruction in the heads of men, and that epoch has moved further into the past?"[102] Given this concern, Rühle proposed a collaborative undertaking, ideally with both of them in Taxco and Institute support, to prepare a ready-reference guide to working-class and socialist history. Fromm replied encouragingly on November 11, 1936: "I think the plan is excellent and agree . . . that, as things stand, such work is necessary." He added that he had convinced the Institute to offer Rühle a monthly stipend for the project, which he would forward monthly himself. And though Fromm personally was too preoccupied with other work "(a book on social psychology and 2 empirical-socio-psychological investigations)" to contribute directly, he would help as much as he could.[103]

In December 1936, Leon Trotsky arrived in Mexico, where he too had been granted exile status. Always at risk of assassination by Stalin's agents, he arrived surreptitiously with his entourage. Fritz Bach met Trotsky at the dock and drove him to Diego Rivera's *Casa Azul* in Coyoacan, where, with Natalya, his aides and bodyguards, he remained until 1939. Otto and Alice visited often, and Otto was surprised and pleased to find that Trotsky's outlook was more democratic than he had expected. In April 1937, Rühle served on John Dewey's Commission of Inquiry into the charges that Stalin's prosecutors had leveled against Trotsky. Dewey's hearings attracted global attention and *Life* ran a photo of Trotsky talking to Otto and Alice.

Figure 7.2 Otto Rühle and Leon Trotsky in Mexico in 1937.

On April 29, less than two weeks after the hearings concluded, Rühle wrote again:

Lieber Erich Fromm! You have no doubt seen the most important news from Mexico in the papers. The Trotsky tribunal [has been] correct, decent and serious in every way ... I served on the commission, not as a Trotskyist—none of us has ever been a Trotskyist—but as a representative of the European working-class movement who has known Trotsky for 30 years and Bolshevism for twenty. My respect for Trotsky has increased and our relationship has become closer. ... He is quite close to me in his whole orientation, but he can't quite get out of his own skin. In the meantime, I've become the object of a Stalinist hate campaign, the aim of which is to force me out of my job.

One week later, in May, Fromm wrote a friendly response, updating Rühle on his own work:

I have just stopped working on my book on social psychology to devote myself to writing a survey on the political and ideological views of German blue- and white-collar workers that we undertook in 1930. The material is very interesting and I hope the work will be released in the fall. I am also writing a shorter essay in which, basically, I explain my deviations from Freud, and I'll send that to you as soon as it is available as well.

Quite a bit more could be said about Rühle, Fromm, their friendship, and their respective projects, but, for present purposes, this sketch should suffice. On March 21, 1936, Adorno had written to Horkheimer to warn against "anarchistic deviations" that had begun to creep into Fromm's work, which "I see [as] a real threat . . . to the *[Zeitschrift]* line."[104] Fromm is "sentimental and false, a blend of social democracy and anarchism." Perturbed, most immediately, by Fromm's article charging Freud with authoritarianism, he also took aim at his Marxism: "He takes far too simple a view of authority, without which, after all, neither Lenin's vanguard nor his dictatorship is conceivable. I would urgently advise him to read Lenin."[105]

Fromm, clearly, did not need to reread Lenin. What alarmed Adorno were Fromm's public objections to authoritarian orthodoxy—objections which, since they came from within the Marxian-Freudian camp, could not be dismissed as easily as if they had come from familiar adversaries. Nor was Adorno entirely wrong about the trend he perceived. Fromm, like many others of his generation, had sojourned among the orthodox but, faced with a choice between authority and humanism, chose humanism.

Karl Wittfogel, whom Fromm had shared his growing objections to Freud,[106] also broke with orthodoxy when, in a lecture at the Institute near the start of 1938, he denied that the USSR was democratic. Asked, in the ensuing "heated debate," whether Russia needed a second revolution, he replied firmly: "Yes!"[107] Franz Borkenau, the same year, published *The Communist International*, which sternly anathematized Lukács, "who was one of the first men to study, in the West, Lenin's theory of the 'vanguard,' of the organization of professional revolutionaries, and to draw [the] conclusion that [since] the proletariat [itself] had no 'proletarian class consciousness,' that consciousness must be supplied 'through the leadership of intellectuals.'" Trotsky, Borkenau added, shared responsibility for that doctrine with all the other proponents of vanguardism, however much he might have suffered in its name.[108] Otto Rühle ultimately drew the same conclusion when Trotsky, in their ongoing dialogue in Mexico, persistently defended Russia as a workers' state. Rühle, like Karl Korsch and others, including Hilde Weiss, saw Soviet Russia as the literal antithesis of a socialist society. Fromm clearly agreed. But more than that, where Weiss, Korsch, and many others offered programmatic critiques, Fromm offered psychosocial analysis. The others resisted authoritarianism—but Fromm attempted to explain it.

In 1943, when Borkenau reviewed *Escape from Freedom* in *Horizon*, he reiterated the view he had expressed a decade earlier, namely, that Fromm's "highly heretical undertaking"—uncongenial to purists of every kind, whether Marxian, Freudian, or liberal—was pathbreaking: "I believe it is no exaggeration to say that Fromm's is the first serious contribution to the problem." Fromm had exposed the equal and opposite failings of the reigning orthodoxies.[109] He had shown that Marxists, despite their ritualistic invocations of class consciousness, had overlooked psychology, while Freudians, despite their preoccupation with family dynamics, saw families as incubators of inborn biological drives, not as agencies of culture and change. The question was how to do better. Fromm's perspective, which united

Marx's critique of alienation with essential insights from depth psychology, was a step—a necessary step—in the right direction.

Acknowledgments

Many thanks to Rainer Funk, the executor of Erich Fromm's literary estate, for permitting me to cite the letter that Otto Rühle sent Fromm on September 9, 1936. Many thanks to Prof. Dr. Detlef Garz of Johannes Gutenberg University for sharing the photo of Hilde Weiss, and thanks, also, to Dr. Rainer Weiss, professor emeritus at MIT, for permitting me to reproduce that photo. Many thanks, finally, to Esteban Volkov, director of the Museo Casa de León Trotsky in Mexico City, for the permission to reproduce the photo of Rühle and Trotsky.

Notes

1 Weber, "Politics as a Vocation," 128. In what follows, I rely on standard translations whenever possible, as in this instance. But all translations from hitherto untranslated materials are my own, unless otherwise noted; and I will occasionally lightly emend standard translations as well.
2 Bois, "Opposing Hitler and Stalin," 151; emphasis in original, citing Serge, *Destiny of a Revolution*, 169.
3 See Smith, "Standing Marx on His Head," forthcoming.
4 Fromm, "Zum Gefühl der Ohnmacht," 117.
5 Borkenau, "Fromm, Erich, *Die Entwicklung des Christusdogmas*," 174.
6 Fromm approvingly cites the notions of ambivalence, the death wish, the Oedipal complex, and more. And he calls Freud's libido theory the basis of his 1932–34 papers; see "Psychoanalytic Characterology and Its Relevance for Social Psychology," 138, n. 1.
7 Fromm, "The Method and Function of an Analytic Social Psychology," 132, n. 21; he adds (n. 23) that his present concern is not Freud's failings, but his findings. On Reik, see Fromm, "The Dogma of Christ," 83.
8 Marx, *Capital*, 899; emphasis in original.
9 Fromm, "Dogma of Christ," 14.
10 Fromm, "The Method and Function of an Analytic Social Psychology," 130.
11 Ibid., 133.
12 Marx and Engels, *The Annotated Communist Manifesto*, 11. Cf. Luxemburg, *Socialism or Barbarism*, passim.
13 Fromm, "Dogma of Christ," 72.
14 Ibid., 45, n. 36.
15 Fromm, "The Method and Function of an Analytic Social Psychology," 123, 127. What is needed is "a psychology . . . and psychoanalysis is the first discipline to provide a psychology that historical materialism can really use."
16 Yagi, "Was *Sozialforschung* an Aesopian Term?," 328, citing an unpublished manuscript by Felix Weil.
17 Fromm, "The Method and Function of an Analytic Social Psychology," 126, n. 2.
18 Ibid., 127.

19 Lukács faulted Bukharin and Wittfogel for overemphasizing nature; see his 1925 reviews, "Literaturbericht, K. Wittfogel" and "Literaturbericht, N. Bucharin," both of which appear in Lukács, *Tactics and Ethics*, 134–42 and 143–46, respectively.
20 Fromm, "The Method and Function of an Analytic Social Psychology," 127. Fromm writes: "Bukharin underlines the natural factor in a clear way: *Die Theorie des historischen Materialismus*, 1922. This whole question is . . . dealt with in the illuminating work of K. A. Wittfogel, 'Geopolitik, geographischer Materialismus und Marxismus,' in *Unter dem Banner des Marxismus* III, I, 4, 5." Fromm also cites *Theorie des historischen Materialismus* on p. 129.
21 Wittfogel, "Geopolitics, Geographical Materialism and Marxism," 54. See also 48–49, where Wittfogel again equates Lukács with Kautsky and attacks him for alleging, in *History and Class Consciousness*, that in bourgeois society nature has already been subordinated. Lukács, he says, forgets "the other, material-natural side of the relation."
22 Fromm, "Foreword," xiv, xii.
23 Ulmen, *The Science of Society*, 144. And note that in 1932 Wittfogel also attempted a foray into social psychology: "Hitler: Versuch eines sozialpsychologischen Porträts," 1126–34.
24 Scholem's exact phrase (*Von Berlin nach Jerusalem*, 197–98) is that Fromm had become "ein begeisterter Trotzkist und bemitleidete mich ob meines kleinbürgerlichn Provinzialismus." Bonss says that Fromm at this stage "sympathized with Left-Socialist groups outside the SPD and KPD, without however forming any specific party-political ties" ("Critical Theory and Empirical Social Research," 32, n. 44), but doesn't give a source for this claim. On Fromm's early Kabbalah studies, see Durkin, *The Radical Humanism of Erich Fromm*, 20ff.
25 Jacobs simply says Scholem was mistaken (*The Frankfurt School, Jewish Lives, and Antisemitism*, 173, n. 185). Lundgren agrees, calling Scholem's allegation "nasty" ("Erich Fromm och Gersholm Scholem: analys av en ovänskap," 34).
26 Hoffrogge, *A Jewish Communist in Weimar Germany*, 338–39, 385, 419, 425, 425 n. 13, and 427: The KPD leadership first criticized Trotzkismus in *Rote Fahne* on 11/13/24. Fischer and Maslow remained aligned with Zinoviev after their expulsion, and Korsch became an anti-authoritarian Marxist who denied that Soviet Russia was either socialist or proletarian.
27 Trotsky and Zinoviev were expelled from the party on November 15, 1927, and Trotsky was banished in early 1928.
28 Fromm, *Working Class in Weimar Germany*, 60.
29 Ibid., 74. When he wrote this in 1937, Fromm was under the mistaken impression that the survey had been completed by the time the SAP had formed in 1931. In fact, as we learn from Weiss, below, questionnaires were still being returned as late as 1933.
30 Showing familiarity with matters even more arcane, Fromm noted that several of the survey respondents belonged to the *Revolutionäre Gewerkschafts Opposition*, which, he correctly noted, was then "newly established." The KPD formed the RGO in December 1929 to serve as a sectarian counterweight to the SPD-led unions.
31 Löwy, "Jewish Messianism and Revolutionary Utopias in Central Europe," in *Erich Fromm's Critical Theory*, 26.
32 Lowenthal, "I Never Wanted to Play Along," 35.
33 Ibid.
34 Fromm, "Trotsky's Diary in Exile—1935," 271.

35 Fromm, "Psychoanalysis and Sociology," cited by Braune, *Erich Fromm's Revolutionary Hope*, 19.
36 Friedman, *The Lives of Erich Fromm* 26; cf. n. 42.
37 Garz, *Hilda Weiss*, 107; see Wiggershaus, *The Frankfurt School*, 29. Weiss and Mandelbaum were the Institute's very first doctoral students, followed, in 1927, by Heinz Langerhans (who, after his expulsion from the KPD in 1926, joined Korsch's *Entschiedene Linke*), and the KPD's Paul Massing and Julian Gumperz. Mandelbaum, like Weiss, assisted the Institute in its collaboration with the Marx-Engels Institute.
38 Jay, *Dialectical Imagination*, cites Weiss only once (305, n. 31). Samelson, "Authoritarianism from Berlin to Berkeley," 196, n. 5, showed interest in Weiss but was able to find only a few details about her.
39 Lévy-Rathenau, *Die Frau als technische Angestellte*, 1914.
40 Weiss, "My Life in Germany Before and After January [30, 1933]," 22; emphasis in original. For further details on the *Haßgesang*, see Millington and Smith, "A Few Bars of the Hymn of Hate."
41 Weiss, "My Life in Germany Before and After January [30, 1933]," 26–27.
42 Ibid., 28.
43 Ibid., 29.
44 Ibid., 34, 35.
45 Campbell, *Joy in Work, German Work*, 163, n. 1.
46 Weiss, "My Life in Germany Before and After January [30, 1933]," 36–37. Walther Rathenau was then a beacon of bourgeois liberalism, renowned, and controversial, both for his moderately progressive employment policies and, in his influential writings, for his stress on corporate responsibility.
47 Weiss, "My Life in Germany Before and After January [30, 1933]," 37.
48 Weiss, *Abbe und Ford*, 73. She wrote in her memoir that the Zeiss factory councilors "were highly competent . . . it seemed that in time they might be able to take over the direction of the *Zeiss Werk*." Weiss, "My Life in Germany Before and After January [30, 1933]," 40.
49 Weiss, "My Life in Germany Before and After January [30, 1933]," 44.
50 Wiggershaus, *The Frankfurt School*, 20. Wittfogel, four years Weiss's senior, first taught at the *Volkshochschule* in January 1920 and soon after persuaded Korsch to teach a course there on the subject of his forthcoming study, *Arbeitsrecht für Betriebsrate*.
51 Kempe, *Der Vertrag von Versailles und seine Folgen*, 325.
52 Weiss, "My Life in Germany Before and After January [30, 1933]," 52.
53 Ibid., 52, 54. This newsletter appears in archival records as *Zeiss-Lupe. Betriebzeitung d. communist. Betriebszelle im Zeiss- u. Schott-Werk*,1924–28.
54 Weiss, "My Life in Germany Before and After January [30, 1933]," 53. I should note in passing that Weiss does not directly acknowledge her KPD membership in her memoir, which she wrote at the request of Gordon Allport and others at Harvard, who were amassing a trove of memoirs by anti-Nazi German exile. Having just arrived in the United States, this discretion undoubtedly seemed the better part of valor. But decades later, in an application for foreign travel, Weiss did formally acknowledge her communist past.
55 Sewell, "The Crisis of 1923."
56 Weiss, "My Life in Germany Before and After January [30, 1933]," 57.
57 Ibid., 58.

58 Ibid., 59.
59 Ibid., 60.
60 See, for example, *Rundbrief*, 65/66, October 1923, edited by Weiss with articles by Weiss, Wittfogel, and Alfred Kurella. The cover page is displayed online at the Deutsches Historisches Museum site, https://www.dhm.de/datenbank/dhm.php?seite=5&fld_0=D2004816
61 *Rundbrief* 63/64, 1923. See, respectively, Wittfogel, "The Saint, the Adventurer and the Hero" and "Lenin oder Mussolini?" (as cited by Ulmen, *The Science of Society*, 50). The latter, plainly, is a strikingly Lukáscian formulation.
62 Borkenau occasionally shared this role with others, including his friend Richard Lowenthal. He joined the KPD as a student in Leipzig in 1921 and, like Willi Münzenberg (below) played a big role in the youth group. On Borkenau's KPD history, see Szakolczai, "Norbert Elias and Franz Borkenau," 46–47.
63 The signers included Fritz We[?], *cand.med.* and Hilde Weiss, *rer.pol*. See Seifert, "Mediziner, 'Rassenschänder,' Interbrigadist . . .?" 79–80, n. 175, n. 176. In 1931, according to Albert Einstein's FBI file (available online; cf. Grundmann), Fritz was the first chair of the *Klub der Geistesarbeiters*. A police report in 1932 said the Klub sought to spread "communist ideas in . . . social circles that cannot be reached by usual propaganda methods." Bertolt Brecht, also in 1931, helped form a Marxist club which included, on its board, Wittfogel, Lukács, and Fritz Weiss (Parker, *Bertolt Brecht*, 43). Many of the same names (Wittfogel, Weiss, Brecht, Kracauer, and others) later appeared in a list of writers and doctors banned by the Nazis.
64 Wittfogel was surprised when KPD leaders told him to write a resolution for the campaign's founding conference since he had recently fallen afoul of the Comintern's AgitProp division. But he did in fact write the resolution, in dialogue with Fritz Weiss. See Ulmen, *The Science of Society*, 81–84.
65 Weiss, *Rationalisierung und Arbeiterklasse*, 62; emphasis in original. Fromm cites this title in his typescript of the workers' study with a brief annotation. In her memoir, Weiss translates the title of this book as *Industrial Mechanization and the Working Class*; "My Life in Germany Before and After January [30, 1933]," 60.
66 Weiss, *Rationalisierung und Arbeiterklasse*, 49; emphasis in original, quoting Lenin. Earlier (p. 17), she cited an exhortation by Lenin which Lukács had quoted in his 1924 book, *Lenin*.
67 Weiss, *Rationalisierung und Arbeiterklasse*, 22. Weiss, *Abbe und Ford*, 3 and ff. With respect to what ultimately happened with Ford and Abbe, she wrote, in her memoir: "My predictions came true just at the moment when my thesis was published. Both enterprises lost their monopoly and the workers part of their social advantages"; Weiss, "My Life in Germany Before and After January [30, 1933]," 62.
68 Weiss, *Rationalisierung und Arbeiterklasse*, 22, 62.
69 Some sources say the survey began in 1929, but that's unlikely since neither Weiss nor Fromm had yet joined the Institute staff.
70 Burkhard says that Weiss was one of those who, with Boris Nicolaevsky, Yuri Steklov, and Georg Lukács, contributed to the "brilliance" of the Marx-Engels Institute ("Ryazanov and the Marx-Engels Institute," 42). On her Berlin activities see Weiss, "My Life in Germany Before and After January [30, 1933]," 107. On the Council for Labor and Defense of the USSR, see Zaleski, *Planning for Economic Growth in the Soviet Union*, 1971 Nathan, who later taught at Princeton, was Albert Einstein's close friend and ultimately the executor of his literary estate. He was embroiled in the

1950s in a fight with the House Un-American Activities Committee, which accused him of communist sympathies. Nathan won that fight.

71 Bonss, "Critical Theory and Empirical Social Research," 24; Friedman, *The Lives of Erich Fromm*, 41. Although Friedman calls Weiss Fromm's "most valued associate," Bonss, like several others, assumes that Fromm was the project's director and Weiss was his assistant. The evidence, as we will see later, does not comport well with that assumption, as Sergio Bologna also concluded; see his "Nazism and the Working Class," online.
72 Garz, *Hilde Weiss*, 107.
73 Weiss, "My Life in Germany Before and After January [30, 1933]," 63.
74 Bois, "Opposing Hitler and Stalin," 157; Ulmen, *The Science of Society*, 143.
75 Weiss, "My Life in Germany Before and After January [30, 1933]," 47.
76 Ibid., 48–49.
77 Ibid., 49.
78 Ibid., 50.
79 Garz, *Hilde Weiss*, 128, citing Weiss's FBI file. Weiss gives a lively account of her escape from Germany, and also explains how Fritz and his wife and son escaped; "My Life in Germany Before and After January [30, 1933]," 64ff.
80 See the *Allgemeinsten Richtlinien für die Arbeit von H.W.*, as cited by Garz, *Hilde Weiss*, 108, 109. Weiss was also instructed by the Institute to draft a proposal about how to implement the study, which "will then be criticized by Pollock and possibly supplemented." Ibid.
81 "You will forgive me for my lack of awe for M. Bouglé, since he reminds me of Grünberg's famous slogan in his seminar, 'Do not try to draw me into the present, you will never succeed!'" Weiss, "My Life in Germany Before and After January [30, 1933]," 113, n. 38; emphasis in original.
82 Weiss, "My Life in Germany Before and After January [30, 1933]," 111.
83 Horkheimer, July 2, 1935, in Garz, *Hilde Weiss*, 111. Money may not have been Horkheimer's only concern. On October 29, 1935, he wrote about the study to Karl Wittfogel, who was then in China: "You know that the questionnaires used to be with Hilde Weiss, but unluckily she knew very little about that scientific capital." In fact, the only aspect of the study in which Weiss was not expert was psychoanalysis, which was becoming increasingly central to Horkheimer, as his conflict with Fromm in 1937 showed. Perhaps ironically, Weiss was herself in analysis at this point, and Fritz Weiss became a psychoanalyst; after Fromm and Horney fell out in the early 1940s, Fritz emerged as Horney's closest co-thinker.
84 Weiss, "My Life in Germany Before and After January [30, 1933]," 111.
85 Funk writes: "Hilde Weiss coordinated everything and wrote a preliminary report." *Erich Fromm: His Life and Ideas*, 90; emphasis in original.
86 In October 1935, Weiss married Louis Rigaudias, a young Trotskyist who had been faulted by Trotsky in 1934 for criticizing the Soviet Union too severely. Then as always, Trotsky maintained an equivocal stance on the USSR, which he insisted was a workers' state, however deformed. Rigaudias, after his divorce from Weiss in 1939, completed an odyssey that led him to libertarian communism after sojourns in prison, in the anti-fascist resistance, in exile in Cuba and the United States (where he remained an anti-Stalinist activist), and ultimately in France once again, where he was a strong supporter of the May events of 1968. See, for example, Casciola, "Louis Rigaudias."

87 Buret, *De la misère des classes laborieuses en Angleterre et en France*, 68–69. Marx, *Economic and Philosophic Manuscripts of 1844*, 35.
88 Weiss (writing as Rigaudias-Weiss), *Les Enquêtes Ouvrières en France*, 156.
89 Ibid., 128. This was the premise, she added, which the *Manifeste Communiste* placed "definitively" on the agenda of the workers' movement "four years later."
90 Weiss, *Les Enquêtes Ouvrières en France*, 144. The dependency is worsened, she adds, by the tyranny of "things over men." On this subject, Weiss (148) regards Buret as Marx's predecessor. It is not so much, Buret wrote, "that men fall into poverty, as that they fall under the power of things." Marx, citing this phrase, adds "that the tyranny of things ... dominates capitalists and workers alike. The power of man is shredded; he is the victim of economic laws." *Economic and Philosophic Manuscripts*, 49.
91 Weiss, *Les Enquêtes Ouvrières en France*, 125, citing Puech, *La vie et l'oeuvre de Flora Tristan*, 190.
92 Weiss, "Die 'Enquêtes Ouvrières' von Karl Marx," 85.
93 But interested readers should see Weiss, 1949, 1956 (as Hilda Weiss Parker, with Joseph Parker), 1958 (as Hilda P. Weiss), and 1964 (likewise).
94 Smith, "Surrender of the Will"; "Theory and Class Consciousness," and "The Ambivalent Worker."
95 Fromm, "The Method and Function of an Analytic Social Psychology," 132.
96 Fromm, "Dogma of Christ," 65. Fromm appreciated that, in *Theorie des historischen Materialismus*, Bukharin "cites the case where a mood of despair grips the masses or some group after a great defeat in the class struggle. . . . But," Fromm adds, "since he has no suitable psychology available to him, he cannot go on to explain the nature of this ... process"; "The Method and Function of an Analytic Social Psychology," 129.
97 In *Studien* this paper is called "The Social-Psychological Part," but Fromm, in *Escape from Freedom*, calls it "*Psychologie der Autorität*." Hence, my usage here.
98 Friedman, *The Lives of Erich Fromm*, 140 and 366, n. 45, citing contemporary interviews and Fromm's correspondence with Rühle and others.
99 Rühle, "*Der Autoritäre Mensch und die Revolution*," online; this passage is translated by Linden, "On Council Communism," 37; emphasis in original, cited in Rühle, *Zur Psychologie des proletarischen Kindes*, 141.
100 Pohle, "Otto Rühle in Mexiko," 133; emphasis in original, citing Rüdt von Collenberg to AA, 30.1.1936 (transcript report III D 6, in: Political Archive of the Foreign Office, Bonn: Dept. Ill Mexico, Politics 19, Bolshevism, Communism, etc. in Mexico, Bd. 1).
101 Gleizer cites estimates ranging from 100 to 300; she also gives political and biographical details on many of these émigrés: "International Rescue of Academics, Intellectuals and Artists from Nazism During the Second World War," 194.
102 See the index of correspondence between Rühle and Fromm in the references.
103 In the same letter, replying to Rühle's request for a psychoanalyst for Alice, who had long fought depression, Fromm recommended Barbara Lantos, who had been in the same circle with Fromm, Reich, and Fenichel in Berlin. Lantos, he wrote, "is now in London. She is very efficient and would have many political points of agreement with you."
104 Adorno, *Briefwechsel, 1927-1937*, cited by McLaughlin, "Origin Myths in the Social Sciences," 118–19.
105 Adorno, *Briefwechsel, 1927-1937*, cited by Claussen, *Theodor W. Adorno*, 233–34.
106 See Fromm's 12/18/36 letter to Wittfogel, reproduced in Bock, *Dialektische Psychologie*, 84–85, n. 48.

107 Ulmen, *The Science of Society*, 209. Horkheimer later worried, after Fromm and Wittfogel had exited the Institute, that Fromm would spearhead an opposition that would include Wittfogel and Julian Gumperz.
108 Borkenau, *The Communist International*, 172; 11.
109 Borkenau, "*The Fear of Freedom*, by Erich Fromm," 203–5.

References

In the titles below, I usually cite the original editions that appeared in the period under discussion here. But many of those books (e.g., Lukács, *Geschichte und Klassenbewusstein = History and Class Consciousness*) appear in well-known English editions as well. And many of Fromm's titles are available in versions and formats, including Kindle, edited by Rainer Funk. See, for further details, *https://fromm-online.org/werke-von-erich-fromm/*

Correspondence

International Institute of Social History, Otto Rühle Papers 1933–43
1. Otto Rühle, México, an Erich Fromm, New York, 09.09.1936
2. Erich Fromm, New York, an Otto Rühle, México, 11.11.1936
3. Erich Fromm, New York, an Otto Rühle, México, 14.01.1937
4. Erich Fromm, New York, an Otto Rühle, México, 04.03.1937
5. Otto Rühle, México, an Erich Fromm, New York, 28.04.1937
6. Erich Fromm, New York, an Otto Rühle, México, 06.05.1937
7. Erich Fromm, New York, an Otto Rühle, México, 14.05.1937
8. Erich Fromm, New York, an Otto Rühle, México, 08.06.1937
9. Erich Fromm, New York, an Otto Rühle, México, 02.07.1937
10. Erich Fromm, New York, an Otto Rühle, México, 06.08.1937
11. Erich Fromm, New York, an Otto Rühle, México, 26.09.1937
12. Erich Fromm, New York, an Otto Rühle, México, 19.10.1937
13. Erich Fromm, New York, an Otto Rühle, México, 16.11.1937
14. Erich Fromm, New York, an Otto Rühle, México, 14.12.1937
15. Erich Fromm, New York, an Otto Rühle, México, 29.12.1937
16. Erich Fromm, New York, an Otto Rühle, México, 18.01.1938
17. Erich Fromm, New York, an Otto Rühle, México, 14.03.1938
18. Erich Fromm, New York, an Otto Rühle, México, 22.12.1938
19. Erich Fromm, New York, an Otto Rühle, México, 04.04.1939
20. Erich Fromm, New York, an Otto Rühle, México, 03.05.1940 [English]

Bibliography

Adorno, Theodor. (2003). *Briefwechsel*, 1927–1937, edited by the Theodor-Adorno-Archiv. Frankfurt am Main: Suhrkamp.

Anderson, Kevin. (2002). "Introduction: A Recently Discovered Article by Erich Fromm on the Russian Revolution." *Science & Society* 66, no. 2 (Summer): 266–71.

Bock, Wolfgang. (2018). *Dialektische Psychologie - Adornos Rezeption der Psychoanalyse*. Berlin: Springer Verlag.

Bois, Marcel. (2017). "Opposing Hitler and Stalin: Left Wing Communists after Expulsion from the KPD." In Ralf Hoffrogge and Norman LaPorte (eds.), *Weimar Communism as Mass Movement*, 150–69. London: Lawrence & Wishart.

Bologna, Sergio. (1993). "Nazism and the Working Class—1933-93." A paper presented at the Milan Camera del Lavoro, June 3, 1993, translated by Ed Emery, https://libcom.org/library/nazism-and-working-class-sergio-bologna

Bonss, Wolfgang. (1984). "Critical Theory and Empirical Social Research." In Erich Fromm, *The Working Class in Weimar Germany: A Psychological and Sociological Study*, edited by Wolfgang Bonss and translated by Barbara Weinberger, 1–38. Cambridge, MA: Harvard University Press.

Borkenau, Franz. (1932). "Fromm, Erich, *Die Entwicklung des Christusdogmas*." In *Zeitschrift für Sozialforschung*, 174–75, Bd. 1. Leipzig: Hirschfeld Verlag.

Borkenau, Franz. (1938). *The Communist International*. London: Faber & Faber.

Borkenau, Franz. (1943). "*The Fear of Freedom*, by Erich Fromm." In *Horizon*, 203–9, March.

Brandt, Heinz. (1970). *The Search for a Third Way: My Path between East and West*, translated by Salvator Attanasio. Garden City, NY: Doubleday.

Braune, Joan. (2014). *Erich Fromm's Revolutionary Hope: Prophetic Messianism as a Critical Theory of the Future*. Rotterdam: Sense Publishers.

Bukharin, Nikolai. (1922). *Theorie des historischen Materialismus: gemeinverständliches Lehrbuch der Marxistischen Soziologie*. Hamburg: Verlag der Kommunistischen Internationale.

Buret, Eugéne. (1840). *De la misère des classes laborieuses en Angleterre et en France*, vols. 1 and 2. Paris: Paulin.

Burkhard, Bud. (1985). "Ryazanov and the Marx-Engels Institute: Notes toward Further Research." *Studies in Soviet Thought* 30, no. 1 (July): 39–54.

Campbell, Joan. (1989). *Joy in Work, German Work: The National Debate, 1800-1945*. Princeton, NJ: Princeton University Press.

Casciola, Paolo. (2000). "Louis Rigaudias." *Revolutionary History* 7, no. 3 (Spring): 289–97.

Claussen, Detlev. (2008). *Theodor W. Adorno: One Last Genius*, translated by Rodney Livingstone. Cambridge, MA and London: The Belknap Press of Harvard University Press.

Dewey, John, Otto Rühle, Alfred Rosmer, et al. (1937). *The Case of Leon Trotsky: Report of Hearings on the Charges Made Against Him in the Moscow Trials*. New York: Harper.

Durkin, Kieran. (2014). *The Radical Humanism of Erich Fromm*. London and New York: Palgrave Macmillan.

Friedman, Lawrence J., with Anke Schreiber. (2013). *The Lives of Erich Fromm*. New York: Columbia University Press.

Fromm, Erich. (1922). *Das jüdische Gesetz: ein Beitrag zur Soziologie des Diasporajudentums*. Dissertation, University of Heidelberg.

Fromm, Erich. (1929). "Psychoanalyse und Soziologie." In *Zeitschrift für Psychoanalytische Pädagogik*, 268–70, Bd. 3. Vienna: Internationaler Psychoanalytischer Verlag.

Fromm, Erich. (1989 [1929]). "Psychoanalysis and Sociology," translated by Mark Ritter. In Stephen Eric Bronner and Douglas M. Kellner (eds.), *Critical Theory and Society: A Reader*, 37–9. New York and London: Routledge.

Fromm, Erich. (1930). "Die Entwicklung des Christusdogmas." In *Imago*, 16, 305-73. Vienna: Internationaler Psychoanalytischer Verlag.
Fromm, Erich. (1963 [1930]). "The Dogma of Christ." In Erich Fromm, *The Dogma of Christ and Other Essays on Religion*, translated by James Luther Adams, 3-91. New York: Holt, Rinehart and Winston.
Fromm, Erich. (1932a). "Über Methode und Aufgabe einer Analytischen Sozialpsychologie: Bemerkungen über Psychoanalyse und historischen Materialismus." In *Zeitschrift für Sozialforschung*, 28-54, Bd. 1. Leipzig: Hirschfeld Verlag.
Fromm, Erich. (1970 [1932a]). "The Method and Function of an Analytic Social Psychology." In Erich Fromm, *The Crisis of Psychoanalysis: Essays on Freud, Marx, and Social Psychology*, 135-62. New York: Holt, Rinehart and Winston.
Fromm, Erich. (1932b). "Die psychoanalytische Charakterologie und ihre Bedeutung für die Sozialpsychologie." In *Zeitschrift für Sozialforschung*, 253-27, Bd. 1. Leipzig: Hirschfeld Verlag.
Fromm, Erich. (1970 [1932b]). "Psychoanalytic Characterology and Its Relevance for Social Psychology." In Erich Fromm, *The Crisis of Psychoanalysis: Essays on Freud, Marx, and Social Psychology*, 163-89. New York: Holt, Rinehart and Winston.
Fromm, Erich. (1935). "Die gesellschaftliche Bedingtheit der psychoanalytischen Therapie." In *Zeitschrift für Sozialforschung*, 365-97, Bd. 4. Paris: Félix Alcan.
Fromm, Erich. (1936a). "Sozialpsychologischer Teil." In Max Horkheimer (ed.), *Studien über Autorität und Familie*, 77-135, Schriften des Instituts für Sozialforschung, Bd. 5. Paris: Félix Alcan.
Fromm, Erich. (1936b). "Geschichte und Methoden der Erhebungen." In Max Horkheimer (ed.), *Studien über Autorität und Familie*, 231-38, Schriften des Instituts für Sozialforschung, Bd. 5. Paris: Félix Alcan.
Fromm, Erich. (1937). "Zum Gefühl der Ohnmacht." In *Zeitschrift für Sozialforschung*, 95-119, Bd. 6. Paris: Félix Alcan.
Fromm, Erich. (1984 [1937]). *The Working Class in Weimar Germany: A Psychological and Sociological Study*, edited by Wolfgang Bonss and translated by Barbara Weinberger. Cambridge, MA: Harvard University Press.
Fromm, Erich. (1995 [1937]). "A Contribution to the Method and Purpose of an Analytical Social Psychology." In *Wissenschaft vom Menschen—Science of Man. Jahrbuch der Internationalen Erich-Fromm-Gesellschaft*, vol. 6, 189-236. Münster: LIT Verlag.
Fromm, Erich. (2002 [1958]). "Trotsky's Diary in Exile—1935." In *Science & Society* 66, no. 2 (Summer): 271-73.
Fromm, Erich. (1970). "Foreword." In Heinz Brandt, *The Search for a Third Way*, xi-xvi. Garden City, NY: Doubleday.
Funk, Rainer. (2000). *Erich Fromm: His Life and Ideas. An Illustrated Biography*. New York: Continuum.
Garz, Detlef. (2006a). *Hilda Weiss—Soziologin, Sozialistin, Emigrantin. Ihre Autobiographie aus dem Jahr 1940*, herausgegeben und mit einem Nachwort von Detlef Garz. Hamburg: Verlag Dr. Kovač.
Garz, Detlef. (2006b). "Über 'Ho, Po und Wiesengrund'—ein Nachwort." In Detlef Garz (ed.), *Hilda Weiss—Soziologin, Sozialistin, Emigrantin*, 93-130. Hamburg: Verlag Dr. Kovač.
Garz, Detlef. (2006c). "Anhang." In Detlef Garz (ed.), *Hilda Weiss—Soziologin, Sozialistin, Emigrantin*, 131-47. Hamburg: Verlag Dr. Kovač.

Gleizer, Daniela. (2019). "International Rescue of Academics, Intellectuals and Artists from Nazism During the Second World War: The Experience of Mexico." In Ludiger Pries and Pablo Yankelevich (eds.), *European and Latin American Social Scientists as Refugees, Émigrés and Return-Migrants*, 181–97. New York: Palgrave Macmillan.

Grundmann, Siegfried. (2005). "Appendix: Einstein's FBI File." In *The Einstein Dossiers: Science and Politics—Einstein's Berlin Period*, 322–68. Berlin: Springer Verlag.

Hoffrogge, Ralf. (2014). *A Jewish Communist in Weimar Germany: The Life of Werner Scholem (1895-1940)*. Leiden: Brill.

Hoffrogge, Ralf, and Norman LaPorte, eds. (2017). *Weimar Communism as Mass Movement*. London: Lawrence & Wishart.

Horkheimer, Max, ed. (1936). *Studien über Autorität und Familie*. Paris: Félix Alcan, Schriften des Instituts für Sozialforschung, Bd. 5.

Institute für Sozialforschung (Erich Fromm, Hilde Weiss). (1936). "Die Arbeiter- und Angestelltenerhebung." In Max Horkheimer (ed.), *Studien über Autorität und Familie*, 239–71, Schriften des Instituts für Sozialforschung, Bd. 5. Paris: Félix Alcan.

Jacobs, Jack. (2014). *The Frankfurt School, Jewish Lives, and Antisemitism*. Cambridge University Press.

Jay, Martin. (1973). *The Dialectical Imagination: A History of the Frankfurt School and the Institute for Social Research*, 1923–1950. Boston: Little, Brown and Company.

Kempe, Hans. (2008). *Der Vertrag von Versailles und seine Folgen: Propagandakrieg gegen Deutschland*, Bd. 1. Mannheim: Reinhard Welz Vermittler Verlag e.K.

Korsch, Karl. (1922). *Arbeitsrecht für Betriebsrate*. Berlin: Franke.

Korsch, Karl. (1923). *Marxismus und Philosophie*. Leipzig: C.L. Hirschfeld.

Levenstein, Adolf. (1912). *Die Arbeiterfrage: Mit besonderer Berücksichtigung der sozial-psychologischen Seite des modernen Grossbetriebes und der psycho-physischen Einwirkung auf die Arbeiter*. Munich: Verlag Ernst Reinhardt.

Levy-Rathenau, Josephine. (1914). *Die Frau als technische Angestellte*. Berlin & Leipzig: Teubner, Schriften des Frauenberufsamtes des Bundes Deutscher Frauenvereine.

Linden, Marcel van der. (2004). "On Council Communism." *Historical Materialism* 12, no. 4: 27–50.

Löwenthal, Leo. (1987). "I Never Wanted to Play Along: Interviews with Helmut Dubiel." In *An Unmastered Past: The Autobiographical Reflections of Leo Lowenthal*, with an introduction by Martin Jay. Berkeley and Los Angeles: University of California Press.

Löwy, Michael. (2017). "Jewish Messianism and Revolutionary Utopias in Central Europe: Erich Fromm's Early Writings (1922-1930)." *European Judaism* 50, no. 1 (Spring): 21–31.

Löwy, Michael. (2020). "Jewish Messianism and Revolutionary Utopias in Central Europe: Erich Fromm's Early Writings (1922–30)." In Kieran Durkin and Joan Braune (eds.), *Erich Fromm's Critical Theory: Hope, Humanism, and the Future*. London: Bloomsbury Academic.

Lukács, Georg. (1923). *Geschichte und Klassenbewusstsein: Studien über marxistische Dialektik*. Berlin: Malik-Verlag.

Lukács, Georg. (1924). *Lenin. Studie über den Zusammenhang seiner Gedanken*. Vienna: Malik.

Lukács, Georg. (1925a). "Literaturbericht, K. Wittfogel, *Die Wissenschaft der bürgerlichen Gesellschaft*, 1922." In *Archiv fur die Geschichte des Sozialismus und der Arbeiterbewegung*, 214–18, Bd. 11. Leipzig: Verlag von C. L. Hirschfeld.

Lukács, Georg. (1925b). "Literaturbericht, N. Bucharin, *Theorie des historischen Materialismus*, 1922." In *Archiv fur die Geschichte des Sozialismus und der Arbeiterbewegung*, 218-23, Bd. 11. Leipzig: Verlag von C. L. Hirschfeld.

Lukács, Georg. (1972). *Tactics and Ethics, 1919-1929*, translated by Michael McColgan and edited, with an introduction, by Rodney Livingstone. London: New Left Review.

Lundgren, Svante. (1998). "Erich Fromm och Gersholm Scholem: analys av en ovänskap." *Nordisk Judaistik / Scandinavian Jewish Studies* 19, no. 1–2: 33–44.

Luxemburg, Rosa. (1913). *Die Akkumulation des Kapitals: Ein Beitrag zur ökonomischen Erklärung des Imperialismus*. Berlin: Buchhandlung Vorwärts Paul Singer.

Luxemburg, Rosa. (2010). *Socialism or Barbarism: Selected Writings*. London: Pluto.

Marx, Karl. (1967 [1844]). *Economic and Philosophic Manuscripts of 1844*, translated by Martin Milligan. New York: International Publishers.

Marx, Karl. (1978 [1867]). *Capital*, vol. 1, translated by Ben Fowkes. London: Penguin Books in association with New Left Review.

Marx, Karl. (1880). "Enquête Ouvrière." *La Revue socialiste*, April 20.

Marx, Karl, and Friedrich Engels. (1984 [1848]). *The Annotated Communist Manifesto*, edited by Hal Draper. London: Verso.

McLaughlin, Neil. (1999). "Origin Myths in the Social Sciences: Fromm, the Frankfurt School and the Emergence of Critical Theory." In *Canadian Journal of Sociology/ Cahiers canadiens de sociologie* 24, no. 1: 109–13.

Millington, Richard, and Roger Smith. (2017). "'A Few Bars of the Hymn of Hate': The Reception of Ernst Lissauer's '*Hassgesang gegen England*' in German and English." *Studies in 20th & 21st Century Literature* 41, no. 2. Available online at https://newprairiepress.org/cgi/viewcontent.cgi?referer=https://www.google.com/&httpsredir=1&article=1928&context=sttcl

Parker, Stephen. (2014). *Bertolt Brecht: A Literary Life*. London: Bloomsbury.

Pohle, Fritz. (1994). "Otto Rühle in Mexiko." In Karl Kohut (ed.), *Alternative Lateinamerika, Das deutsche Exil in der Zeit des Nationalsozialismus*. Mühlen: Vervuert Verlag. Available online at publications.iai.spk-berlin.de/servlets/.../BIA_051_133_151.pdf

Puech, Jules. (1925). *La vie et l'oeuvre de Flora Tristan*. Paris: Librairie Marcel Rivière.

Rigaudias-Weiss, Hilde. (1936). *Les Enquêtes Ouvrières en France. Entre 1830 et 1848*. Paris: Les Presses Universitaires de France.

Rühle, Otto. (1925). *Der Autoritäre Mensch und die Revolution*, https://www.marxists.org/deutsch/archiv/ruehle/1925/10/autoritaere.htmi; translated by Marcel van der Linden, 2004, 37, from Rühle, 1975, 141.

Rühle, Otto. (1927). *Karl Marx: Leben und Werk*. Hellerau: Avalun.

Rühle, Otto. (1929). *Karl Marx: His Life and Work*, translated by Eden and Cedar Paul. New York: The Viking Press.

Rühle, Otto. (1930). *Illustrierte Kultur- und Sittengeschichte des Proletariats*. Berlin: Neuer Deutscher Verlag.

Rühle, Otto. (1939). *The Living Thoughts of Karl Marx*, presented by *Leon Trotzki*. Based on *Capital: A Critique of Political Economy*. Philadelphia: David McKai.

Rühle, Otto. (1975). *Zur Psychologie des proletarischen Kindes*. Frankfurt am Main: März.

Rühle-Gerstel, Alice. (1932). *Die Frau und der Kapitalismus*. Frankfurt am Main: Verlag Neue Kritik.

Rühle-Gerstel, Alice. (1979). *Kein Gedicht für Trotzki. Tagebuchaufzeichnungen aus Mexico*, edited by Stephen S. Kalmar. Frankfurt am Main: Neue Kritik.

Samelson, Franz. (1986). "Authoritarianism from Berlin to Berkeley: On Social Psychology and History." *Journal of Social Issues* 42, no. 1: 191–208.
Scholem, Gershom. (1977). *Von Berlin nach Jerusalem: Jugenderrinerungen*. Frankfurt: Suhrkamp.
Seifert, Konstantin. (2017). "Mediziner, 'Rassenschänder', Interbrigadist . . .?" *Leben under Werk des Hans Serelman (1898-1944)*. Dissertation, Friedrich-Schiller-Universität, Jena.
Serge, Victor. (1937). *Destiny of a Revolution*. London: Jarrolds.
Sewell, Rob. (1988). "The Crisis of 1923." In Germany: From Revolution to Counter-Revolution, https://www.marxists.org/subject/germany-1918-23/sewell/chapter5.htm
Smith, David Norman. (1998). "The Ambivalent Worker: Max Weber, Critical Theory, and the Antinomies of Authority." *Social Thought & Research* 20, no. 3: 35–83.
Smith, David Norman. (2017). "Theory and Class Consciousness." In Michael Thompson (ed.), *The Handbook of Critical Theory*, 369–424. London and New York: Palgrave Macmillan.
Smith, David Norman. (2019). "Standing Marx on His Head: Isaac Deutscher's Apology for Bolshevik Reaction." In preparation for *Logos*.
Smith, David Norman. (2020). "Capital Fetishism and the Authoritarian Personality." In Jeremiah Morelock (ed.), *How to Critique Authoritarian Populism*, edited by Jeremiah Morelock. New York and London: Routledge, forthcoming.
Szakolczai, Arpád. (2000). "Norbert Elias and Franz Borkenau." *Theory, Culture & Society* 17, no. 2: 45–69.
Tristan, Flora. (1983 [1843]). *The Workers' Union*, translated with an introduction by Beverly Livingston. Urbana: University of Illinois Press.
Ulmen, Gary L. (1978). *The Science of Society: Toward an Understanding of the Life and Work of Karl August Wittfogel*. The Hague, Paris and New York: Mouton.
Weber, Alfred. (1912). "Das Berufsschicksal der Industriearbeiter." *Archiv für Sozialwissenschaft und Sozialpolitik* 34: 377–405.
Weber, Alfred. (1913). "Die Bureaukratisierung und die gelbe Arbeiterbewegung." *Archiv für Sozialwissenschaft und Sozialpolitik* 37: 361–79.
Weber, Alfred, Heinrich Herkner, and Gustave Schmoller. (1910–12). *Untersuchungen über Auslese und Anpassung (Berufwahl und Berufsschicksal) der Arbeiter in den verschiedenen Zweigen der Grossindustrie*, vols. 1–3. Leipzig: Duncker & Humblot.
Weber, Max. (1946 [1919]). "Politics as a Vocation." In *Essays from Max Weber*, edited and translated by Hans Gerth and C. Wright Mills, 77–128. New York: Oxford University Press.
Weiß, Hilde. (1926). *Rationalisierung und Arbeiterklasse: Zur Rationalisierung der deutschen Industrie*. Berlin: Führer-Verlag.
Weiß, Hilde. (1927a). *Abbe und Ford: Pläne für die Errichtung sozialer Betriebe*. Dissertation, Universität im Frankfurt am Main.
Weiß, Hilde. (1927b). *Abbe und Ford: Kapitalistische Utopien*. Berlin: R. L. Prager Verlag.
Weiß, Hilde. (1936a). "Die 'Enquêtes Ouvrières' von Karl Marx." *Zeitschrift für Sozialforschung* 5: 76–98.
Weiß, Hilde. (1936b). "Materialien zum Verhältnis von Konjunktur und Familie. Bericht über ein Manuskript von 109 Seiten." In Max Horkheimer (ed.), *Studien über Autorität und Familie*, 579–81. Paris: Alcan.
Weiss, Hilda. (2006 [1939]). "My Life in Germany Before and After January [30, 1933]." In Detlef Garz (ed.), *Hilda Weiss—Soziologin, Sozialistin, Emigrantin*, 8–70. Hamburg:

Verlag Dr. Kovač. See also: Houghton Archive, Harvard University; Folder: bMS Ger 91 (240).
Weiss, Hilda. (1949). "Human Relations in Industry: From Ernst Abbe to Karl Mannheim." *The American Journal of Economics and Sociology* 8: 287–97.
Weiss, Hilda. (2006 [1949]). "Marginal Woman (Pages from a Diary)." In Detlef Garz (ed.), *Hilda Weiss—Soziologin, Sozialistin, Emigrantin*, 71–92. Hamburg: Verlag Dr. Kovač.
Weiss, Hilda P. (1958). "Industrial Relations, Manipulative or Democratic?" *The American Journal of Economics and Sociology* 18: 25–33.
Weiss, Hilda P. (1964). "Durkheim, Denmark, and Suicide: A Sociological Interpretation of Statistical Data." *Acta Sociologica* 7: 264–78.
Wiggershaus, Rolf. (1994). *The Frankfurt School: Its History, Theories and Political Significance*, translated by Michael Robertson. Cambridge: Polity Press.
Wittfogel, Karl A. (1922). *Die Wissenschaft der bürgerlichen Gesellschaft: eine Marxistische Untersuchung*. Berlin: Malik-Verlag.
Wittfogel, Karl A. (1929). "Geopolitik. Geographischer Materialismus und Marxismus." *Unter dem Banner des Marxismus*. Bd. 3, 1 (17–51), 4 (485–522), and 5 (698–735).
Wittfogel, Karl A. (1929 [2006]). "Geopolitics, Geographical Materialism and Marxism," translated by G. L. Ulmen. *Antipode* 17, no. 1 (May): 21–71.
Wittfogel, Karl A. (1932). "Hitler: Versuch eines sozialpsychologischen Porträts." *Die Rote Aufbau* 5, no. 24: 1126–34.
Yagi, Kiichiro. (2011). "Was *Sozialforschung* an Aesopian Term? Marxism as a Link between Japan and the West." In Heinz-Dieter Kurz, Tamotsu Nishizawa, and Keith Tribe (eds.), *The Dissemination of Economic Ideas*, 315–36. Cheltenham: Edward Elgar.
Zaleski, Eugene. (1971). *Planning for Economic Growth in the Soviet Union, 1918–1932*. Chapel Hill: University of North Carolina Press.
Zeiss-Lupe. (1924–1928). *Betriebzeitung d. communist. Betriebszelle im Zeiss- u. Schott-Werk*. 8 Zwanglos.

Chapter 8

ESCAPE FROM REFLEXIVITY: FROMM AND GIDDENS ON INDIVIDUALISM, ANXIETY, AND AUTHORITARIANISM

Charles Thorpe

Introduction

The social theories of Anthony Giddens and Erich Fromm have shared existential foundations in a conception of the human being as inherently contradictory by virtue of existing within, and separately from, nature.[1] Fromm and Giddens both regard this contradictory aspect of human existence as the source of a basic anxiety that pervades human life. Both indicate the attempt to escape from or repress this anxiety as the psychological source of attraction to nationalist movements and authoritarian leaders. In opposition to such authoritarian tendencies, both Fromm and Giddens advocate social transformation toward a higher form of individuality. Giddens's notion of reflexivity and Fromm's conception of positive freedom intersect as they point toward a form of social selfhood capable of free self-shaping. But what Giddens carries no further than a politics of lifestyle, without challenging the prevailing market dynamics of capitalism, Fromm connects to the structural question of the social control over economic forces. Genuine individual self-realization, for Fromm, requires democratic social and economic planning. This chapter argues that the current turn toward authoritarian nationalism, represented by the Trump presidency in the United States, demonstrates the limits that capitalist relations impose on reflexivity. The attraction to Trump as authoritarian leader is an escape from the intense anxiety to which the uncertainties of everyday life under late capitalism give rise.

Giddens connected his social theory with the political project of the "New Democrats" in the United States and New Labour in Britain, as offering a "Third Way" between socialism and neoliberalism. The Third Way sought to renew social democracy by shedding its redistributive and structurally transformative inheritances of socialism in favor of market-oriented policies and realizing values through individualized politics of lifestyle. The Third Way, in its basic acceptance of the market as unchallengeable, left individuals unprotected from the insecurities of globalized financial capitalism. By accepting the constraints of the market and by supporting and continuing America's wars in the Middle East, the Third Way created the social and psychological conditions for the authoritarian backlash against reflexivity, including against the politics of lifestyle which threaten demarcations of identity and destabilize ontological security.

Since the turn of the new millennium, the fabric of social life has been continuously assaulted by endless war, a state-of-emergency atmosphere, a culture of militarism and xenophobia, widening inequality, housing crisis and mass repossessions and evictions, massive job losses, and policies of social austerity.[2] As Robert Antonio notes, such policies of austerity frequently draw legitimacy from appeals to racism and xenophobia.[3] Anxiety arising from economic insecurity reinforces status anxiety from threats to established cultural identity, threats which include progressive developments such as the shift away from overt racism and toward sexual and cultural tolerance by younger generations, changes symbolized in the United States by the election of Barack Obama as the first African American president.[4] Anxiety about status and identity undermine reflexivity by impelling the assertion of boundaries around the self and around categories of ingroup identification in order to exclude those defined as other.[5] Failure to challenge the market mechanisms that produce economic turbulence and concomitant anxiety, or the concentrations of power that drive war, meant that the Third Way was unable to produce social conditions capable of underpinning reflexivity and positive movements toward racial and sexual equality and personal autonomy. Third Way complicity in sustaining capitalist relations paved the way for the vicious fascistic reaction that followed.

Fromm's diagnosis of the mass appeal of fascism, as the attempt to evade the anxiety that arises from the fragility of the modern self, provides a fundamental basis upon which to analyze the sociopsychological appeal of the revival of authoritarianism today. Fromm's notion of the "escape from freedom" is particularly significant for understanding the American "tyranny of negative freedom" through which, in the United States, authoritarian politics is legitimized not only by the appeal to individual freedom but also, unconsciously, by the psychological needs that competitive individualist "freedom" leaves chronically unmet.[6]

Chronic anxiety arises from America's culture of disposability, from the impersonal viciousness of the workplace to the social abandonment of the poor.[7] Anxiety is systemically produced by a society that has reduced itself to little more than the workings of the market, from which there is no shield. In a society of market "winners" and "losers," the self is deeply vulnerable. Individual failure in the competition to survive and accumulate can only be an indictment of the individuals themselves.[8] The threat of having nothing is the threat of being nothing. Fromm describes the fragility of the self when the purpose of life is reduced to *having*:

> *If I am what I have and if what I have is lost, who then am I?* Nobody but a defeated, deflated, pathetic testimony to a wrong way of living. Because I can lose what I have, I am necessarily constantly worried that I shall lose what I have. I am afraid of thieves, of economic changes, of revolutions, of sickness, of death, and I am afraid of love, of freedom, of growth, of change, of the unknown. . . . I

have become defensive, hard, suspicious, lonely, driven by the need to have more in order to be better protected.[9]

This possessive individualism in American culture produces intense currents of fear and anxiety that are manifested in fear of freedom and of societal and cultural change.

The political reaction that draws power from the anxieties of possessive individualism threatens to undermine the positive potentialities that are also contained within individualism as a cultural and psychological force against traditional and religious prohibitions and historically and culturally rooted stigmas and inequalities.[10] Among these progressive developments that have generated backlash, there has been, in the United States and other Western societies, a marked decline in sexual prohibition and greater freedom of individuals to shape their identities and selves, as opposed to succumbing to mass conformity to taken-for-granted norms. Trends such as the lifting of societal prohibitions against, and normalization of, sexual relationships outside marriage, homosexuality, and nonbinary gender identities are accompanied by greater equality in relationships between men and women as women have entered the workplace in large numbers. In addition, there is, in general, far less racism present in everyday life than fifty years ago, in what are increasingly ethnically diverse societies, and now there are frameworks of antidiscrimination legislation that give legal force to these progressive societal changes. Further, there exists today a plethora of new social movements mobilizing around ethical and quality of life issues from LGBTQ communities, to patients' rights, and a broad range of health and environmental concerns.[11] These trends carry the potentiality for a new kind of individual.

Lauren Langman and George Lundskow suggest that such shifts in social identity, interpersonal relationships, and values reflect the emergence within late modernity of a flexible, fluid form of selfhood, which Robert Jay Lifton has called "the Protean self." While in some ways adapted to neoliberalism, this Protean selfhood also has the potential to undermine authoritarian rigidities and give rise to new forms of egalitarian politics.[12] Anthony Giddens has pointed similarly to such transformations of self and identity, bound up with the rise of new social movements, as evidence of a shift from the mass organization and accompanying forms of automatic conformity that characterized *simple modernization* to a new dimension of *reflexivity* that pervades late modern social life and is carried and expressed by "life-political" movements. Finn Bowring suggests that Fromm may be regarded as a herald of this new politics: the "modern politics of self-actualisation described by Giddens . . . [was] prefigured in Fromm's humanism."[13]

In order to understand contemporary authoritarianism, it is necessary to account for how it comes about in the context of, and in reaction against, the transformations of self identified by Giddens and Fromm, and the new forms of politics that constitute late modern reflexivity. This chapter seeks to build a theoretical understanding of contemporary authoritarianism through establishing a comparison and dialogue between the social-theoretical frameworks of Fromm and Giddens. Both Fromm and Giddens are concerned with the dilemma of the modern individual, set free from traditional authorities but cast adrift from traditional anchors of selfhood. Both are concerned with the question of whether this individual can achieve a higher form of freedom, self-realization, and social selfhood: "positive freedom" for Fromm, "reflexivity" for Giddens. The interconnectedness of these ideas is made evident by Giddens's linking of life politics with the notion of positive freedom. In *The Consequences of Modernity*, he writes:

> *Emancipatory politics* needs to be linked with *life politics*, or a *politics of self-actualisation*. . . . Life politics refers to radical engagements which seek to further the possibility of a fulfilling and satisfying life for all, and in respect of which there are no "others." This is a version of the old distinction between "freedom from" and "freedom to."[14]

Both Fromm and Giddens regard failure to achieve this higher form of freedom and selfhood as underpinning the appeal of nationalism and authoritarian forms of collectivism. The attraction of authoritarianism arises from the escape from freedom, but under contemporary conditions of late modernity this takes the form of an escape from reflexivity.

Fromm on Negative Freedom and Existential Anxiety

Fromm's humanism takes as its starting point a conception of the unique species characteristics of Homo sapiens as a being that is simultaneously part of nature and beyond nature. The human being is "an anomaly, the freak of the universe. . . . He is set apart while being a part."[15] Humans are biological organisms that evolved within, and depend upon, the broader world of physical and biological nature. And, yet, we also experience ourselves, as conscious agents with subjectivity and free will, as separate from the broader world. Through technology (from tool use to complex technological systems), sociality, language, and the cognitive capacity for reflective reasoning, humans constitute themselves and experience themselves as active self-conscious agents. Rather than being adapted to a specific ecological niche, human beings are able to adapt the natural world to their species needs. In comparison with other animals, human behavior is under-determined by instinct, leaving human beings with the freedom, but also the burden, of deciding how to live. The striving for purpose and meaning derives from the fact that the human being is inherently dichotomous and in disequilibrium and therefore is driven to try to overcome "the contradiction in his existence."[16]

Separateness from the greater world of being is the fundamental problem that characterizes the human condition as a species and that faces every human individual. This separateness is a condition of *freedom from* instinctual determination or from immediate determination by physical and biological nature. The condition of *negative freedom* is definitive of humanity. And yet, it is a condition that cannot be endured. According to Fromm, negative freedom presents humanity with the *task* of moving beyond or transcending this condition. The necessary movement for humanity is from negative to positive freedom and from separateness to a higher form of union. Failure to accomplish this movement toward positive freedom leads to the attempt to escape from freedom, the attraction to authoritarianism, sadism, masochism, and death.[17] The movement from negative to positive freedom is necessary for the growth and development of human individuals and for overcoming the destructive tendencies within civilization.[18]

What is true for the human species is also true for the individual, who emerges from within the mother and only gradually separates from the mother after birth to become an autonomous individual.[19] Negative freedom is an accomplishment of the development of the human being, both as species and as individual. But, the corollary of this accomplishment is anxiety. Whereas fear has an object so that one is afraid *of something*, anxiety is vague and potentially all-encompassing. Rollo May, in a discussion influenced by, and to a large extent compatible with, Fromm's thought, defines anxiety as

> the apprehension cued off by a threat to some value that the individual holds essential to his existence as a personality. The threat may be to physical life (the threat of death), or to some psychological existence (the loss of freedom, meaninglessness). Or the threat may be to some other value which one identifies with one's existence: (patriotism, the love of another person, "success," etc.).[20]

In other words, anxiety is objectless because it is the experience of threat to the entire sense of self or, as May puts it, to the "security pattern" of the self. May writes that anxiety "is 'cosmic' in that it invades us totally."[21] Anxiety concerns the very existence of the self as a distinct entity.[22] Precisely because anxiety operates at this fundamental level of the relationship between being and nonbeing, it is not possible to parse it as being "economic" or "religious," "sexual," or "racial" or some other compartmentalizing sociological category. In anxiety, we should expect all these dimensions of social identity and sources of security of the self to be implicated and compounded together. Anxiety, in this sense, is Kierkegaard's concept of *angst*, often translated as *dread*. Fromm thought that Kierkegaard had defined what would become the characteristic experience of life in the twentieth century: "The helpless individual torn and tormented by doubts, overwhelmed by the feeling of aloneness and insignificance."[23]

The anxiety of existing as a separate entity in a chaotic world, vulnerable before the forces of nature and faced with one's own mortality, poses the existential problem at the heart of the human condition. Fromm writes, "Any person who becomes aware, even for a moment, of the fundamental, essential aloneness of himself as an individual, must feel insecure."[24] Fromm's psychoanalysis was concerned, at its root, with how human individuals manage the problem of separateness. Are they able to find and foster new attachments, to positively transcend their individuality, to grow and develop as *social* individuals, or do they fall back into regressive solutions to anxiety, in seeking to escape from individuality into forms of masochism, sadism, destructiveness, and symbiotic submerging of self in collectivities that substitute for mother? The problem of the development of the human individual is necessarily bound up with the problem of whether society is constituted in such a way as to facilitate human growth and the development of human capacities or whether social structures hinder and retard this development and instead promote regressive solutions, for example, through rigid traditionalism or crushing authoritarianism.

Separateness is intrinsically related to knowledge of mortality. Fromm writes, "Gifted with self-awareness and reason, man is aware of himself as a being separate from nature and from others; he is aware of his powerlessness, of his ignorance; he is aware of his end: death."[25] While Fromm tended to emphasize the problem of separateness in itself, the psychological importance of the problem of death is entailed by his analysis. Fromm was a major influence on Ernest Becker's understanding of the fundamental role played by the "denial of death" in human action and society.[26] For Becker, the problem of death is interwoven with the problem of meaning. What human beings fear most, he says, "is not so much extinction, but extinction *with insignificance*."[27] Thinking about meaning and death in relation to one another shows the interconnectedness of the material and psychological-cultural aspects of human existence. While death is inevitable, how present it is in life and how quickly it comes for the individual depends on material economic well-being. Society mediates the relationship of the individual to death, through both its economy and its cultural system of meaning.[28]

It is in sociality that the human being finds protection from death, in both the material-biological and psychological-existential sense. The ability of human beings to meet their biological needs depends on the economic life of the broader social grouping in which they live. In a very material sense, society protects the individual from death and in this way provides a real, material solution to the terror of death. Of course, this is not absolute protection. But social life is itself a form of life after death, in the sense that the social group outlives the individual, and so identification with the group allows the individual to participate in its immortality. Society's self-representations, in religion and other cultural forms, provide protection against chaos, in the form of what Peter Berger calls the "sacred canopy." In an analysis which fits closely with that of Fromm, Berger argues that, unlike other animals, "man is curiously 'unfinished' at birth." Instinctual under-determination means that human beings have no natural "man-world." Instead the human being must construct a world. Berger argues that the purpose of the activity of culture construction "is to provide the firm structures for human life that are lacking biologically." Religion "externalizes" the social order into the wider cosmos and in so doing reflexively legitimizes, maintains, and reinforces that order.[29] Religion situates the individual within a human, natural, and cosmic order and provides the individual with a cognitive framework and set of social practices (e.g., rituals) that provide immediate answers to existential dilemmas.

Modernity is the breakdown of preexisting solutions to the existential problem of separateness. Modernity severs individuals from traditional bonds (attachments and restraints). The rise of market-based, capitalist society radically individualizes. It creates a new kind of individual, pursuing their self-interest in competition with others and conscious of being alone before the forces of necessity, not now so much nature in its immediacy but the "necessary" and seemingly mechanical dynamics of the market.

In *Escape from Freedom*, Fromm argues that the European Renaissance and the Reformation were the key moments of cultural transformation in the process of the social and psychological creation of the modern individual.[30] Fromm's historical account draws on Max Weber's *The Protestant Ethic and the Spirit of Capitalism*.[31] In both Weber and Fromm, there is a portrait of the powerful psychological motivation of the attempt to escape from or assuage anxiety, and the construction of social character as a defense against anxiety.[32] Just as Weber presents compulsive and bureaucratically regimented work as becoming generalized, through his metaphor of the "iron cage," and treats the early capitalist entrepreneur as the carrier of a rationalistic mode of life that becomes generalized across modern capitalist societies, so Fromm also suggests that the precariousness of existence as an individual severed from all traditional ties is a form of life that is generalized across modern societies.

Even though entrepreneurial capitalism gave way to the bureaucratic monopoly capitalism of the twentieth century, anxiety-driven compulsiveness continued to characterize social life and social character.[33] But in the bureaucratic society, what David Riesman called the "other-directed" individual, or what Fromm called "the marketing character," is more radically estranged than the "inner-directed" entrepreneur.[34] Bureaucratic society undermines the very possibility of autonomous selfhood. Fromm writes that "if the modern age has been rightly called the age of anxiety, it is primarily because of this anxiety engendered by the lack of self."[35] Bureaucratic advanced capitalism demands what Fromm called "automaton conformity." The bureaucratic society constitutes a vast, impersonal, anonymous authority, "the great It," toward which the atomized individual feels insignificant, fearful, inferior, and submissive.[36] Their lack of an inner core of self and of transcendent ideals renders the modern mass individual particularly vulnerable to feeling lost in a meaningless world and susceptible to the attraction of authoritarianism as an escape from this anxiety.[37]

Giddens on Modernity and Ontological Insecurity

Fromm's argument that modernity unleashes existential anxiety formerly contained by tradition and religious belief finds significant echo in the sociological theory of Anthony Giddens. Existential and humanist themes play a significant role in Giddens's sociology of modernity, thus making his work a fruitful addition to, and interlocutor with, Fromm's work. Giddens does not cite Fromm, except for a passing dismissive comment endorsing Herbert Marcuse's characterization of Fromm as a "revisionist."[38] Nevertheless, in his critique of economistic Marxism, Giddens draws on Lewis Mumford and Victor Frankl to advance a conception of the human being as primarily a meaning-making animal.³⁹ This pulls his theorizing very close to that of Fromm.

The deep resonance of Giddens's social theory with that of Fromm arises with Giddens's identification of the "existential contradiction." He writes, "Human life is contradictory in the sense that the human being, as *Dasein*, originates and disappears into the world of Being, the world of nature, yet as a conscious, reflective agent is the negation of the inorganic."⁴⁰ Giddens's influence here is Heidegger, as indicated by the use of the concept of *Dasein*.⁴¹ But the argument has a strong affinity, substantively, with Fromm's conception of the human being as "the freak of the universe."⁴² Giddens argues that it is "society itself" which mediates this "contradictory character of human existence, for only in and through membership of a society does the human being acquire 'second nature.'"⁴³ In societies "which remain closely involved with the modalities and rhythms of nature in day-to-day life" the contradiction is mediated by "religion, magic and myth."⁴⁴ In modern capitalist society the existential contradiction comes to be "suppressed."⁴⁵

Giddens's account of how existential contradiction is suppressed in modernity draws from Norbert Elias's studies of the internal pacification of modern societies, Foucault's studies of incarceration, and Philippe Aries's study of the contrast between the medieval familiarity with death and the modern medicalized exclusion of death from everyday life.⁴⁶ Giddens synthesizes these transformations under the concept of *sequestration*. The process of sequestration is the precondition for the very possibility of what we mean by "everyday life," the ordinary, repetitive, banal day-to-day, week-to-week, that excludes the extraordinary. Giddens emphasizes that, in traditional societies, "religion, magic and myth" are "chronically interpolated within" daily life.⁴⁷ What is modern is a profane daily life that is totally separate from experiences such as birth and death for which the sacred served to give meaning. Modern urban life operates with cultural and technological "second nature," and the experience of life is removed from direct dependency on, and interaction with, nature. Instead of hunting for meat, one buys it wrapped in plastic in the supermarket. The experience of acquiring meat becomes routine, predictable, unremarkable, and entirely without risk. The violence of factory farming and slaughter is kept out of sight, in specialized locations, backstage from everyday life. The modes of living that grew in capitalist, bourgeois urban life kept birth, death, illness, and madness out of sight and defined as apart from everyday life. At the same time, especially through medicalization, these experiences have become disenchanted and shorn of sacred significance. Hence, Giddens writes, everyday life is "smoothed of those interruptions that once provided the very marrow of the experience of temporality in the relations between human beings and nature."⁴⁸

By its very constitution, modern urban everyday life suppresses the existential contradiction and the anxiety that arises from it. However, Giddens also observes that this exclusion and suppression does not actually *solve* the problem of the anxiety that arises from the existential contradiction. He writes, "In respect of feelings of ontological security, the members of modern societies are particularly vulnerable to generalized anxiety. This may become intense either when, as individuals, they have to confront existential dilemmas ordinarily suppressed by sequestration, or when, on a larger scale, routines of social life are for some reason substantially disrupted."[49]

Giddens's concept of ontological security is derived from the radical psychiatrist R. D. Laing, who contrasted it with the state of mind of the schizophrenic.[50] Ontological security is confidence in one's existence and in that of the world as one experiences it. Giddens observes that everyday life depends on ontological security, but also through its routines generates this security (e.g., the ability to think that tomorrow will be another day much like today). Internal pacification (the sequestration of violence from everyday life) creates ontological security by allowing the individual to feel secure in the inviolability of their body and person, as well as reducing fear of untimely death and excluding the presence of mortality from the flow of life. In a post-traditional, disenchanted modern life, the sacred retreats to be replaced by routine orderliness. He writes, "Routinisation of social relations is the mode in which . . . potentially corrosive effects of anxiety are contained."[51]

In modernity, ontological security comes to rest on "abstract systems" of technology and science.[52] Anxiety is assuaged by the control of nature, through the technological devices and systems of machines and expertise that organize nature so as to be a predictable and passive object of human action.[53] The control of nature as a passive object and the suppression of existential dilemmas in social life are both reflected in, and reinforced by, "positivistic thought," which undermines the very language through which ethical dilemmas may be conceptualized.[54] As a result, Giddens writes, "Existential questions become institutionally repressed."[55]

Prefiguring Giddens's critique of positivism as productive of existential crisis, Max Weber writes in his 1917 lecture "Science as a Vocation" that science is "meaningless" because it can provide no answer to the question—"What shall we do and how shall we live?"[56] Giddens extrapolates from this to the rationalized modes of thought and technological dependency characteristic of modern life. The very success of modernity's abstract systems delegitimizes the traditional answers found in culture and religion. The need for ontological security comes to rest instead on these abstract systems of technology and organization (devices, infrastructure, brands, corporations, authoritative pronouncements of science). The smooth functioning of these systems suspends existential dilemmas. But this also leaves a dearth of answers when the individual is faced with some event that breaches everyday life and anxiety re-intrudes. Busily whizzing about in modernity's efficient systems, one can avoid looking at the existential contradiction. But, like a cartoon character furiously running in mid-air, as soon as one looks down, one plummets. Modernity offers nothing to cover the abyss. As modernity abolishes or erodes tradition and routinizes daily life, it evacuates life of meaning.[57] This meaninglessness is the source of what Giddens refers to as the "fragility of ontological security in the wasteland of everyday life."[58] When routine is traumatically disrupted, it leaves the individual vulnerable to the realization that the world has no rhyme or reason and that there is no security.

So long as modernity's machinery operated automatically, participation in the frenetic activity of modern living could be a kind of active avoidance of anxiety. But this machinery, in its very automaticity, produces instability, crisis, and risks that raise existential dilemmas to conscious awareness. The science that is trusted as an abstract system, part of the background architecture of everyday life, becomes the source of dread in the form of the atomic bomb and the threat of nuclear annihilation. The atomic bomb, the concentrated form of the external violence that accompanies internal pacification, the culmination of modern science's project of harnessing and controlling nature at the most basic level, was also the overarching fear that gave the lie to the security of everyday life.[59] Giddens emphasizes the contrast: "This unique conjunction of the banal and the apocalyptic, this is the world that capitalism has fashioned."[60]

The creation and use of the atomic bomb was the first major crisis of simple modernization and impetus toward reflexive modernization.[61] But the growth of awareness of environmental pollution and destruction, and especially the overarching problem of climate change, has upset the boundaries between human agency and nature which the instrumental relationship to nature of simple modernization both erected and assumed. Simple modernization's success in transforming nature creates a new hybridity of nature and society which is, in many ways, more unstable and threatening than the premodern dangers arising from uncontrolled nature. This new hybrid social nature, as in global warming, overwhelms the protections afforded by scientific prediction and technological control.[62] The existential contradiction rears up again, therefore, in the form of dangers that arise within "second nature," that is, from the intersection of society and nature.

These new risks open up the ethical dimension of reflexivity as a return of the question "how shall we live?" excluded by the rationalized systems that draw legitimacy from science.[63] Reflexive modernization represents the crisis of modernity's abstract systems faced with their inability to manage the "irrational," unruly consequences of their rationalization of the world. New social movements emerged to challenge these systems, through evaluating the qualitative consequences of modernity's impetus toward quantitative growth. These life-political movements subject economic, scientific, engineering, and medical rationalities to the question "how should we live?"

Life politics, Giddens argues, "pose with particular force the questions we must face when 'progress' has become sharply double-edged . . . and when there are ethical dilemmas that mechanisms of constant economic growth either cause us to put to one side or make us repress."[64] These concern not only the environmental issues that arise as blowback from simple modernization but also questions of identity for which traditional answers can no longer be taken for granted. Questions of identity are intimately bound up with the problem of how one should live and reflect the way in which this question more and more faces the individual as a matter of choice from a vast array of available cultural repertoires.

Behind this individualization of choice and pluralism of cultural options is globalization. Giddens emphasizes that globalization permeates everyday life.

It is not an "'out there' phenomenon . . . [but an] 'in here' matter, which affects, or rather is dialectically related to, even the most intimate aspects of our lives."[65] Globalization widens the scope for new, intentional choices by individuals in their personal relations and new definitions of self and patterns of social relations. This openness and potential for transformation is articulated and carried forward by life-political movements. These movements press for democratization of institutions at a subnation-state level and a supranational level. Giddens writes that "the intensifying of globalization empties out local contexts of action, demanding and stimulating the growth of institutional reflexivity."[66] Reflexive modernization reawakens existential dilemmas, but potentially overcomes the problem of meaninglessness by subjecting modes of living to reflexive life-political evaluation and deliberate transformation.[67]

For Giddens, then, the existential problems of the modern individual do not necessarily lead to nihilism or Fromm's escape from freedom. Rather, these existential problems, reawakened by the failure of simple modernization and by the ever more individualizing and fragmenting tendencies of globalization, begin to find creative expression in life-political movements and accompanying transformations of the self. For example, sexuality is "opened up and made accessible to the development of varying life-styles."[68] In contrast with the fragility of modern selfhood which required the suppression of existential dilemmas, the reflexive selfhood that is expressed in life politics is more resilient, capable of finding creative and productive answers to the problem of meaning in everyday life, and engaging in new forms of sociality that are deliberative, democratic, and cosmopolitan.[69]

Giddens thought that peace movements, a form of life politics, could become "much more convergent" with the interests of states in an era of post-militarist globalization.[70] After the end of the Cold War, he envisaged an "emergent post-military order" in which "most states no longer have any incentive to wage offensive war."[71] The decline of militarism would be an aspect, Giddens thought, of a new order that was cosmopolitan and reflexive from top to bottom. This vision of the post-Cold War era strongly informed his advocacy of the "Third Way" political program for harnessing these positive potentialities of globalization and individualization and giving institutional political articulation to the democratizing aspirations of life politics.[72]

The development of reflexivity solved, for Giddens, the problem of the fragility of the self in modernity. It represented a "third way" beyond isolated individualism and its opposed tendency, the search for security in nationalism. Giddens's writings on reflexive modernization and the Third Way mapped a search for a politics that escaped the dilemma of individualism versus collectivism. This dilemma took the form of neoliberal market ideology versus socialism but also that of the individual narcissism of consumerism versus the group narcissism of nationalism. Reflexivity was an alternative to the search for meaning in the collectivist symbols of nationalism. The pull of nationalism was, for Giddens, the greatest danger of modernity, intrinsically bound up with the threat of a third world war.

Giddens certainly recognized the potential for nationalist backlash. He wrote in his 2007 update of the Third Way, *Over to You, Mr Brown*, that "identity is closely related to security, since so many of the anxieties that affect both individuals and groups come from feelings of dislocation." But he thought that life politics would itself enable people to adapt themselves to the insecurities inherent in capitalist globalization and multiculturalism. The new risks "demand citizen involvement and many presume lifestyle change."[73] Giddens has called his perspective "utopian realism."[74] However, neither Giddens nor New Labour was able to reconcile this "utopian" conception of the transformation of selfhood with the reality of the radical undermining of security by the capitalist forces to which the Third Way insisted they must adapt.[75] The Third Way language of active and self-responsible citizenship (a language that Giddens notes that New Labour "inherited from the New Democrats") could be regarded as merely ideological cover for the abandonment of the population to the market.[76] In that case, the Third Way itself paved the way for a reactionary backlash. This was entirely predictable based on Giddens's own theorizing of the existential need for ontological security.

Peter Kolarz has argued that Giddens's Third Way thinking assumed the existence of the reflexive late modern self that Giddens had theorized as emerging in and through life politics. Kolarz points out that the Third Way also assumed the market as unquestionable and unchangeable. But these two assumptions were in inherent contradiction because capitalism creates obstacles to the participatory democratic realization of life politics.[77] Neoliberals argue that the dynamics of the market are themselves democratic, but that is belied by the immense inequality the market produces and the impossibility of real choice without publicly funded common goods. The potential for realizing dialogic democracy, and through this the reflexive self, is fundamentally constrained by the relations of private property.[78] Kolarz writes that "global capitalism and market forces are a significant source of structural constraint on the emergence of the late modern self."[79]

The market relations of global capitalism become a fetter on the full development of the reflexivity to which globalization itself gives rise. Vast inequalities of wealth, technological, cultural, political, and intellectual resources exist that constrain the ability of people to access globalization both in terms of any economic benefit and in terms of being able to participate in a globalized culture. The very ability to realize a global culture runs into the contradiction between global economy and the nation-state. This contradiction itself derives from the fundamental capitalist contradiction between socialized production and private appropriation. Workers are joined in a globally cooperative chain of production. But the dynamics of capital and the social relations of capitalism are competitive, both in market competition and in military hostility between states. Giddens's prediction that the end of the Cold War would lead to a post-militarist world order followed from his view of war as a dynamic independent of capitalism as an economic system.[80] This notion has proven to be deeply mistaken. The upsurge of imperialist war in the Middle East has been a major cause of the growth of authoritarianism and nationalism.[81] In an article published in 2012, sociologists William I. Robinson and Mario Barrera outlined a tendency toward fascism in the United States which was emerging as a response to the structural crisis of global capitalism, a key element of which they identified as the contradiction between global economy and nation-state and the dynamic of militarization that arose out of this. They also noted, citing Fromm's analysis of authoritarianism, that the US Christian evangelical right, militia-groups, the Tea Party, and the broader "psychopathology of white decline" indicate "the rise of fascist tendencies within US civil society and polity."[82]

Structural crisis destabilizes the ontological security of authoritarian petit-bourgeois layers in whom the psychological mechanisms for backlash are already in place. The turn to authoritarianism, led by ruling elites as a response to crisis, has its ready foot-soldiers. The insecurity and anxiety produced by economic crisis stirs up authoritarian nationalism as the sociopsychological corollary of the crisis and, through this, provides the active human agents of political backlash. In this way, the economic dynamics of globalization undercut the potential for the emergence of reflexivity both in individual selves and in the polity.

Globalization, Nationalism, and the Failure of the Third Way

Modernity's routinized everyday life is a fragile basis for ontological security. In these circumstances, Giddens argues, "feelings of communality of language, 'belongingness' in a natural community, etc. tend to form one strand contributing to the maintenance of ontological security." When routine is disrupted through "radical social disruption, mobilization for war etc." the breach of ontological security "threatens the stability of the ego through the upsurge of repressed anxieties founded upon primitive object-cathexes." As a result, "regressive forms of object-identification tend to come to the fore." There is a close relationship between nationalism and the regressive search for security under the all-powerful charismatic leader. The effects are profound when routines of modern everyday life are disrupted, since capitalist modernity is itself already a disruption of more communal ways of being and is inherently unstable. The lack of foundations for ontological security means that such disruptions can produce an infantile reaction in the desire to find security in the quasi-parental figure of the leader. Giddens writes that "regressive object-identification with a leadership figure is connected psychologically with increased 'suggestibility' and emotional volatility."[83] By associating themselves with the symbols of national belonging, populist leaders may become the focus of mass identification spurred by the attempt to escape from ontological insecurity.

However, *invented* national identity is itself fragile and this is especially true in an age of globalization.[84] "It isn't surprising, therefore," Giddens observes, "that in a post-traditional age nationalism stands close to aggressive fundamentalisms, embraced by neo-fascist groups as well as by other sorts of movements or collectivities."[85] Fundamentalism is the form that tradition takes "against a background of the prevalence of radical doubt." Rather than a stable source of ontological security, it is reckless: "Fundamentalism may be understood as an assertion of formulaic truth without regard to consequences."[86] The aggressiveness of fundamentalism arises from its real inability to solve existential dilemmas. Nationalism is constantly insecure in an age of globalization because of the structural contradiction between the nation-state and global economy.[87] Nationalist fundamentalism is a defensive counterreaction against globalization and its demands for reflexivity and cosmopolitanism.

Nationalism is closely linked to male violence against women as a backlash against the demands and pressures for the democratization of intimacy that are carried in the aspirations of women.[88] Nationalism, fundamentalism, and aggressive masculinity are linked as defensive reactions against reflexivity. But the optimism of Giddens's Third Way politics was guided by the belief that this defensive reaction would be overcome by the powerful tendencies borne by the currents of globalization toward reflexivity and dialogic democracy.

In the wake of the "Brexit" referendum vote for withdrawal of the United Kingdom from the European Union, driven by anti-immigrant nationalist sentiment, and in the midst of the Trump presidency in the United States, it seems clear that the reaction against democratic reflexivity is in the ascendant. The Third Way as a form of political strategy and governance failed as an attempt to combine social democratic aspirations with a "realistic" acceptance of the "free market," representing instead, a capitulation to market individualism. In *Why the Third Way Failed*, Bill Jordan argues that this failure arose from the Third Way "allying itself with the growing dominance of financial intermediaries over all other economic agents." He goes on to say that "in trying to develop the cult of self-improvement and personal realization in the mainstream with 'cognitive capitalism' and the financial sectors as its economic bulwarks, the Third Way approach lacked the means to give recognition to those large sections of the population which had neither the work roles nor the material assets through which that order was accessible."[89] Progressive hopes associated with New Labour foundered on the rocks of the Iraq war, which undermined multiculturalism and democracy, and the 2008 economic crisis which shattered economic well-being and ontological security.

In the United States, the "New Democrats," associated with the Clinton presidency, slashed social welfare and axed regulations so as to unleash financial speculation. They presided over the intensification of neoliberal insecurity in the culture.[90] Psychoanalytic anthropologist Howard F. Stein writes:

> The 1990's have long been called the decade of corporate mergers, buyouts, and takeovers ... "Hostile takeovers" and mergers wreak havoc with the experience and expression of group boundaries, aggression, identity-all of which are core issues in hypernationalist panics.[91]

The explosion of hypernationalism after 9/11 must be understood in relation to the dislocations of American society in the preceding neoliberal decades.[92]

Stein observes that "from the point of view of the unconscious, the September 11 attack ended the search for a reliable enemy upon which to externalize, and which could contain, repudiated American 'badness.'" The attacks and the military reaction enabled the creation of a group-narcissistic, and essentially fictitious, unity of a deeply fissured and fragmented American society. Stein writes that "the 'War Against Terrorism,' with its promise to be long-waged, was as much a solution to the problem of chronic, diffuse anxiety as it was a problem to those who also—and consciously—sought solid, safe borders."[93] The growth of militarism has bolstered the culture of violence in American society, awakened deep psychological currents of anxiety and aggression, and legitimized the deep erosion of democratic institutions and democratic culture by authoritarian forms of rule. The rise of militarism has far-reaching implications for the possibility of reflexivity in a society.

To the extent that the Obama presidency was a continuation of the Third Way, it must be judged on the record of the bank bailout which exacerbated inequality in American society and on its continuation of the state-of-emergency form of government legitimized by the "war on terror," for example, in drone assassinations and the bombing of Libya.[94] In 2016, Hillary Clinton, representing what the Third Way had become, was widely regarded as aloof and unconcerned with working people, a view confirmed by the release on the internet of transcripts of her paid, private speeches to Wall Street bankers. The vote for Trump must be seen as the expression of deep currents of a traumatized society.[95] Robinson and Barrera write that "the Obama project weakened the popular and Left response from below to the crisis, which opened a space for the rightwing response to the crisis—for a twenty-first century fascism—to become insurgent. Obama's administration appears in this way as a Weimar republic."[96]

Trump won the Republican primary by articulating the economic distress of working-class and lower middle-class Republicans without a college degree and giving particularly aggressive expression to the compensatory status identity of "white" and "male." Rory McVeigh and Kevin Estep state that Trump's "rhetoric appealed intuitively to those whose economic standing had fallen victim to globalization" and that his "appeal was rooted at the intersection of economics and what his supporters thought about gender, religion, and race."[97] According to McVeigh and Estep, "the Trump insurgency . . . largely played out within party politics" and the Republican primaries were its most important battles. Sociologists Shannon Monnat and David L. Brown argue that the trends in the general election "signify a story that is more about Clinton underperformance than Trump overperformance."[98] Hillary Clinton lost the general election by failing, or refusing, to articulate the economic grievances and anxieties of working-class Democrats.[99] Trump benefited from the combination of rising xenophobic nationalism stirred up by the ongoing wars in the Middle East and from the economic insecurity wrought by decades of neoliberal globalization and brought to a head by the 2008 financial crisis and ensuing recession. The migration crisis, caused by these wars and by the social and economic chaos created by neoliberalism and American imperialism in central America, provided targets for the more sadistic and authoritarian expressions of nationalism.[100] Trump promised to restore ontological security by reestablishing boundaries around identity categories of gender, race, and the nation. It is highly significant that his signature policy is the building of a wall.[101] He promises order through the exclusion and repression of those identified as other.

Trump presents himself as a figure in whom his followers can place their trust, allowing them to relinquish the burden of individual responsibility.[102] Arlie Hochschild describes witnessing, in the midst of the collective effervescence of a Trump rally "a middle-aged man, arms uplifted, as if in rapture, saying to those around him and no one in particular, 'To be in the *presence* of *such a* man!'"[103] "In Trump We Trust," reads a homemade roadside sign in rural southeast San Diego county about 10 miles from the US-Mexico border (see Figure 8.1).[104] It echoes the US national motto (since the Eisenhower years) "In God We Trust," which appears on the dollar bill. What the road sign expresses is an idea of the leader, Trump, as the foundation of order and security.

Trump's aggressive ignorance is appealing to those who desire escape from ambivalence. For example, climate change caused by human action simply does not exist. A potentially overwhelming source of ontological insecurity is erased by will. In this sense, the appeal of Trump is captured by Ernest Becker's statement that "the masses look to the leaders to give them just the untruth that they need."[105] Becker explains Freud's theory of how followers willingly gave up their judgment in following the leader: "They simply became dependent children again, blindly following the inner voice of their parents, which now came to them under the hypnotic spell of the leader. They abandoned their egos to his, identified with his power, tried to function with him as an ideal."[106] This concept of the handing over of the ego to the authoritarian leader is precisely that articulated by Giddens in his explanation of nationalist charismatic leadership as "regressive identification," and helps in understanding Trump's followers.

Trump is a simultaneously authoritarian and permissive father. He both allows and commands his followers to give vent to their rage. He goads them into violence at his rallies. Trump models, permits, and challenges his followers to reflect back an aggressive masculinity and compulsive sexuality. In October 2018, a man who groped a woman on an airline flight told arresting officers that "the president of the United States says it's OK to grab women by their private parts."[107] In this way, Trump embodies what Slavoj Žižek calls the "obscene superego."[108]

Trump by turns aggravates and soothes his followers. He lulls them to sleep with his sing-song-style hypnotic repetition of catchphrases that are at once empty platitudes but also for his followers laden with massive emotional projections of hatred, fear, awe, and status-reinforcing pride. The soothing, paternalistic tone in which he tells his followers not to worry, and to have faith in him turns the next second into incitement of violence against the outsiders.

The Trump phenomenon may be seen as a refusal of reflexivity. This is clear in the case of the natural environment. As well as denying anthropogenic climate change, Trump is pressing ahead with the Keystone oil pipeline and drilling in the Arctic and scrapping environmental regulations. The extractive orientation, promoting mining and drilling whatever the environmental cost, represents a reassertion of simple modernization, an orientation to nature as a resource to be exploited.[109] Nuclear fear is suppressed by the assertion of military-technological-

Figure 8.1 An expression of allegiance to Trump in rural southeast San Diego County, California. Photo Credit: Toby Thorpe.

phallic dominance, as in Trump's remark that his "Nuclear Button . . . is a much bigger and more powerful one" than that of North Korean leader Kim Jong-Un.[110] This assertion of aggressive masculinity meshes with Trump's sexual politics, for example, hostility to women's reproductive rights. The paranoid-schizoid demonization and exclusion of Muslims and Latin American immigrants rejects difference and cosmopolitanism. Despite the incongruity in a nation of immigrants such as the United States, Trump seeks to construct a sense of primordial ethno-cultural nationhood.[111]

The refusal of reflexivity that Trump embodies has important implications for evaluating the extent to which reflexive modernization is compatible with constraints of the dominant institutions and relations of power in capitalist society. The upsurge of anti-reflexivity expressed in the Trump phenomenon is an expression of a deeper, structural blockage of reflexivity. In the following, final section of this chapter, I will argue that reflexive modernization cannot be realized without the institutional and political articulation of reflexivity in socialist democratic planning.

Conclusion: Reflexive Modernization without Reflexivity

Reflexivity is structurally resisted by the dominance of the market over economic relations and of the nation-state over political participation, deliberation, and decision-making. The contradiction between global economy and the nation-state manifests itself in the failure of regulation both of the global environmental risks produced by capitalist production and of the economic risks produced by the global market. The nation-state remains, as Giddens called it, the "crucible of power," but the nation-state is structurally unable to control the dynamics of the global economy that spatially transcend national institutions and risks that escape the time-scales of policymaking.[112] Giddens writes:

> The issue is not only that . . . the nation-state has become too small to solve global problems and too large to deal with local ones; the intricate connections between changes in global and local life start to attack the very integrity of the state.[113]

The very survival of humanity is endangered by the failure to reach global agreement on regulating carbon emissions, and the consequently unchecked dynamic of climate change, as well as in the once again growing danger of world war driven by interstate competition between hegemonic and rising economic powers.

The contradiction between the nation-state and global economy is not merely an "external" problem of relations between nation-states; it also means the dominance of global economic forces over everyday life. The forces of modern production and organization confront individuals as out-of-control, alien forces, producing feelings of helplessness and anxiety. The experience of the conditions of life as being forces outside the individual's control ramifies through the self and relationships, undermining the possibility of any kind of reflexive development of relations between self and other.[114] Global economic turbulence is interiorized in anxiety (and this is not just "economic anxiety"), creating susceptibility to authoritarian forces offering escape from this anxiety.

The reflexive monitoring of risk is a psychologically difficult task under conditions of economic insecurity. Ronald Inglehart argues that the rise of "post-materialist" values that he has traced in advanced industrial societies rests upon the existential security that the postwar economy and welfare state provided.[115] He writes that "a substantial body of evidence confirms that existential security is conducive to open-mindedness, social tolerance, and trust, secularization and acceptance of diverse lifestyles, identities, and values."[116] It is no accident that "traditional values remain most widespread among the older generation, less-educated white men, and people living in rural communities—all declining sectors of the population." Inglehart thinks that the cultural shift toward tolerance and post-materialist values is likely to endure beyond the immediate backlash epitomized by the Trump phenomenon.[117] However, his research shows that the effects of economic conditions on social values are carried forward via generations. Therefore, the shattering of relatively generalized material prosperity and security, the loss of good jobs, the undermining of welfare, is likely to have long-term ramifications in undermining the formation of people who are secure enough from anxiety to carry reflexivity. How much have post-materialist values been extended on credit?

Late modernity remains under the sway of the automatic forces of modernity's economic juggernaut, even as this juggernaut radically disrupts and disorganizes social life (e.g., through economic dislocation and through war) so that there is *no possibility for automatic conformity* to its demands. It is extremely disorientating for those who do not have the resources to be reflexive agents, but are left with very little structure to which to conform as all economic and social ties are more and more insecure. Evangelical religion, the propaganda of Fox News, and Trump's intolerant simplifications seem to provide reassuringly solid ground. Now it is not that the cultural terrain is moving out from under their feet and that they are "strangers in their own land," but that *others* are strangers in *their* land.[118] The lack of institutionalization of reflexivity in fora for dialogic democracy and democratic control blocks and distorts the reflexive self-development of the individual, producing fear, anger, and resentment that seek outlet in the simplistic and anti-reflexive messages of the demagogic leader.[119]

Instead of producing security, capitalism today produces insecurity. Insecurity today is not due to level of development of the productive forces. Rather, it is the result of the social relations of capitalism. Inglehart observes, "Insecurity today results from growing inequality." He is wrong, however, to treat this as a "political question" and to contrast that with the rise of fascism in the 1930s which was a product he says of "objective scarcity."[120] Rather, in both cases, insecurity is the result of the contradiction between socialized production and private appropriation, which means that production is not for the purpose of satisfying human need but is ruled by the market which produces both inequality and economic crisis. The market means that production is not regulated for the common good but instead is dysregulated by speculative private interests. The metabolic relationship between human beings and the rest of nature is so dysregulated by capitalism that climate change threatens to return objective scarcity despite the high level of development of the productive forces.[121] The insecurity that gives rise to authoritarian backlash is a product of the underlying contradiction between the forces and relations of production.

In his 2009 book on climate change, Giddens goes some way toward recognizing the dysfunction of the market in calling for a "return to planning" in response to environmental problems.[122] But what he proposes as "planning" is technocratic rather than open to life politics. This lack of reflexivity in his conception of what he calls "planning" is perhaps surprising, given his social theory, but it follows from his subordination of planning to the overall dominance of the principle of the market.[123] Fromm's conception of "humanistic planning" may be understood as a program for the institutional articulation of life politics, bringing the life-political question "how should we live?" to bear directly in spheres of decision-making in which existentially rooted moral questions were previously subordinated to imperatives of technological efficiency and economic growth.[124] But this realization of life politics through planning is only possible because planning also provides for economic security.

Fromm was clear that the free self-development of the individual required security in the material conditions of life, "that no one shall be allowed to starve, that society is responsible for all its members, that no one shall be frightened into submission and lose his human pride through fear of unemployment and starvation." He stated plainly that "the irrational and planless character of society must be replaced by a planned economy that represents the planned and concerted effort of society as such."[125] It is not only that via the market resources are, as Inglehart puts it, "increasingly misallocated from the standpoint of maximizing human well-being," although that is certainly true. It is also that the purposeless anarchy of the market, in other words the alienation of economic activity from human well-being, results in a system that is both in crisis and producing crisis in every dimension of human activity and existence. But also, as Fromm argues, this purposelessness runs through individual life and psychology. The self-realization of individuals requires purposeful activity and in a complexly interdependent modern society that can only be achieved through participatory democratic planning.

Fromm writes, "Only in a planned economy in which the whole nation has rationally mastered the economic and social forces can the individual share responsibility and use creative intelligence in his work."[126] That was written in Fromm's 1941 work *Escape from Freedom*. It needs to be revised in only one way: to shift the conceptualization of planning from the nation to the globe, to meet the challenge and the great emancipatory potential of truly globalized production and a finely interconnected global human society. "Workers of all countries unite." You have nothing to lose but your anxiety, which is truly a chain.

Notes

1 I am grateful to Roddey Reid for his helpful comments on an earlier draft.
2 Reid, *Confronting Political Intimidation*, 20–30. See also Giroux, "War on Terror: The Militarising of Public Space and Culture in the United States."

3 Antonio, "Reactionary Tribalism Redux," 204.
4 Langman and Lundskow, *God, Guns, Gold and Glory*, 241–48; Norris and Inglehart, *Cultural Backlash*, 87–212, 453–56; Thorpe, *Necroculture*, 230; Parker and Barreto, *Change They Can't Believe In*; Hochschild, *Strangers in their Own Land*, esp. 135–51.
5 Stanley, *How Fascism Works*, 88–89; Antonio, "Reactionary Tribalism Redux," 202–3.
6 Thorpe, *Necroculture*, 205–59.
7 Stein, *Beneath the Crust*, 37–42; Giroux, *American Nightmare*, 189–215; Reid, *Confronting Political Intimidation*, 31–44.
8 Langman and Lundskow, *God, Guns, Gold and Glory*, 121.
9 Fromm, *To Have or to Be*, 89. Emphasis in original.
10 Langman, "Right Ressentiment as Reaction."
11 McVeigh and Estep, *The Politics of Losing*, 226; Langman and Lundskow, *God, Guns, Gold and Glory*, 256–68; Norris and Inglehart, *Cultural Backlash*; Inglehart, *Modernization and Postmodernization*.
12 Lauren Langman and George Lundskow, "Social Character, Social Change, and the Social Future," this volume. See also Langman and Lundskow, *God, Guns, Gold and Glory*, 263.
13 Bowring, "Negative and Positive Freedom: Lessons from, and to, Sociology," 165.
14 Giddens, *The Consequences of Modernity*, 156 (emphasis in original); Bowring, "Negative and Positive Freedom," 164–65.
15 Fromm, *The Anatomy of Human Destructiveness*, 225. See also Fromm, *Sane Society*, 23–24; Fromm, *The Heart of Man*, 116–17.
16 Fromm, *Man for Himself*, 29; Fromm, *The Anatomy of Human Destructiveness*, 226.
17 Fromm, *Escape from Freedom*, 23–36, 135–204; Fromm, *The Anatomy of Human Destructiveness*, 225–26, 230–67; Fromm, *The Heart of Man*, 117–23; Fromm, *Man for Himself*, 28–34.
18 Fromm, *Escape from Freedom*, 259–70; Kieran Durkin, *The Radical Humanism of Erich Fromm*, 77–83.
19 Fromm, *The Anatomy of Human Destructiveness*, 232; Fromm, *The Heart of Man*, 95–113; Fromm, *Sane Society*, 38–48; Fromm, *The Crisis of Psychoanalysis: Essays on Freud, Marx, and Social Psychology*; Cf. Chodorow, *The Reproduction of Mothering*; McLaughlin, "How to Become a Forgotten Intellectual," 244.
20 May, *The Meaning of Anxiety*, 205–06.
21 Ibid., 207.
22 Ibid., 208.
23 Fromm, *Escape from Freedom*, 132.
24 Fromm, *The Pathology of Normalcy*, 46.
25 Fromm, *Anatomy of Human Destructiveness*, 225. See also Fromm, *Sane Society*, 23–24; Fromm, *The Heart of Man*, 116; Fromm, *Man for Himself*, 30.
26 Becker, *The Denial of Death*, 134; Hardie-Bick, "Necessary Illusions," 855–56.
27 Becker, *Escape from Evil*, 4; emphasis in original; Hardie-Bick, "Necessary Illusions," 856.
28 Cf. Salzman, "Globalization, Culture, and Anxiety." I am grateful to Lauren Langman for bringing Terror Management Theory to my attention.
29 Berger, *The Sacred Canopy*, 3, 6.
30 Fromm, *Escape from Freedom*, 36.
31 Ibid., 51.
32 Ibid., 294. Cf. see Shafir, "The Incongruity between Destiny and Merit."
33 Fromm, *Man for Himself*, 63.

34 David Riesman with Glazer and Denney, *The Lonely Crowd*; Fromm, *Man for Himself*, 49–60; McLaughlin, "Critical Theory Meets America"; Durkin, *Radical Humanism of Erich Fromm*, 85.
35 Fromm, *Sane Society*, 204.
36 Ibid., 205.
37 Ibid., 206.
38 Giddens, *The Transformation of Intimacy*, 164.
39 Giddens, *Contemporary Critique*, 156.
40 Ibid., 236.
41 Ibid., 3, 30–35. See also Giddens, *Central Problems in Social Theory*, 161.
42 May asserted that Fromm's *Man for Himself* was "derivative from Heidegger": May, *Meaning of Anxiety*, 199.
43 Giddens, *Contemporary Critique*, 236.
44 Ibid.
45 Ibid., 238.
46 Giddens, *The Nation-State and Violence*, 194–95.
47 Giddens, *Contemporary Critique*, 236.
48 Ibid., 173.
49 Giddens, *Nation-State and Violence*, 196.
50 Scott and Thorpe, "The Sociological Imagination of R. D. Laing."
51 Giddens, *Central Problems in Social Theory*, 128.
52 Giddens, *Consequences of Modernity*, 79–87.
53 Giddens, *Modernity and Self-Identity*, 135–37.
54 Ibid., 155.
55 Ibid., 164. See also Thorpe and Jacobson, "Life Politics, Nature, and the State."
56 Weber, "Science as a Vocation," 143.
57 Giddens, *Contemporary Critique*, 11.
58 Ibid., 13.
59 Cordle, *States of Suspense*.
60 Giddens, *Contemporary Critique*, 252.
61 Cf. Welsh, *Mobilising Modernity*, esp. 17–33; Ulrich Beck in Beck, Giddens, and Lash, *Reflexive Modernization*, 180.
62 Giddens, *Modernity and Self-Identity*, 137.
63 Cf. Langman and Lundskow, "Erich Fromm and Contemporary American Politics," 16.
64 Giddens, *Beyond Left and Right*, 92.
65 Giddens in Beck, Giddens, and Lash, *Reflexive Modernization*, 95.
66 Ibid., 192.
67 Giddens, "Risk, Trust, Reflexivity," 192–94.
68 Giddens, *Transformation of Intimacy*, 2, 15, 58.
69 Giddens, *Beyond Left and Right*, 131.
70 Ibid., 234–35.
71 Ibid., 235.
72 Giddens, *The Third Way: The Renewal of Social Democracy*.
73 Giddens, *Over to You Mr Brown*, 59–60.
74 Giddens, *Consequences of Modernity*, 154–55; Giddens, *Beyond Left and Right*, 249–50.
75 Kolarz,. *Giddens and Politics beyond the Third Way*, 119–51.
76 Giddens, *Over to You Mr Brown*, 59; Clarke, "New Labour's Citizens," 447–63, esp. 453.

77 Monbiot, "Dare to Declare the System Dead—Before It Takes Us down with It."
78 Doppelt, "What Sort of Ethics Does Technology Require?"
79 Kolarz, *Giddens and Politics*, 126–42, quoting 129.
80 Giddens, *The Nation-State and Violence*.
81 Saccarelli and Varadarajan, *Imperialism Past and Present*; Robinson and Barrera, "Global Capitalism and Twenty-First Century Fascism."
82 Robinson and Barrera, "Global Capitalism and Twenty-First Century Fascisms," 11–12, quoting 12.
83 Giddens, *Contemporary Critique*, 195.
84 Giddens in Beck, Giddens, and Lash, *Reflexive Modernization*, 93.
85 Giddens, *Contemporary Critique*, 132.
86 Giddens in Beck, Giddens, and Lash, *Reflexive Modernization*, 100.
87 Giddens, *Contemporary Critique*, 197–198.
88 Giddens, *Beyond Left and Right*, 239.
89 Jordan, *Why the Third Way Failed*, 192–93.
90 Selfa, *The Democrats*, 63–119; Pearson, *The Roots of Defeat*.
91 Stein, *Beneath the Crust*, 62.
92 Reid, *Confronting Political Intimidation*, 17–44.
93 Stein, *Beneath the Crust*, 7. See also Clarke and Hoggett, "Empire of Fear." Cf. Shafir and Schairer, "The War on Terror as Political Moral Panic."
94 Pearson, *Roots of Defeat*, 195–219; Jutel, "Barack Obama, the New Spirit of Capitalism, and the Populist Resistance"; Savage, *Power Wars: Inside Obama's Post-9/11 Presidency*.
95 Singer, "Trump and the American Collective Psyche"; Chris Hedges, *America: The Farewell Tour*.
96 Robinson and Barrera, "Global Capitalism and Twenty-First Century Fascism."
97 McVeigh and Estep, *The Politics of Losing*, 67–147, 155–71, quoting 95, 107. See especially p. 121 on crucial differences between Trump's primary and general election voters.
98 McVeigh and Estep, *The Politics of Losing*, 210; Monnat and Brown, "More than a Rural Revolt: Landscapes of Despair and the 2016 Presidential Election," 228.
99 Moody, "Who Put Donald Trump in the White House?," 53–59.
100 On authoritarian and sadistic attitudes as the distinguishing feature of Trump voters, see David Smith and Eric Hanley, "The Anger Games: Who Voted for Donald Trump in the 2016 Election, and Why?" While Smith and Hanley argue that such attitudes are more important than demographic economic factors in distinguishing Trump voters in the 2016 general election, I think that such attitudinal data needs to be interpreted alongside and in the context of the kind of demographic explanation put forward by Monnat and Brown and the historical, economic, and cultural analysis of McVeigh and Estep. It is also important to note, in thinking about economic causes of anxiety, that anxiety is subjective and is not the same thing as economic hardship. For reasons why the middle class may be particularly anxious precisely because they have something to lose, see Thorpe, *Necroculture*, 225–27. On middle-class anxiety, see also Ehreinreich, *The Fear of Falling: The Inner Life of the Middle Class*. On lower-middle-class authoritarianism, see Fromm, *Escape from Freedom*, 96, 182–83, 206–19; Lundskow, "Authoritarianism and Destructiveness in the Tea Party Movement." See also Svend Ranulf's classic discussion of lower-middle-class resentment and punitiveness in his *Moral Indignation and Middle Class Psychology*. On the complex relationship between economic grievances, generational change, and

cultural reaction, based mainly on European data, see Norris and Inglehart, *Cultural Backlash*, 132–67, 454.
101 Yang, "The Trump Wall."
102 On the desire to give up responsibility, see Slater, *The Pursuit of Loneliness*, 24, 29.
103 Hochschild, *Strangers in Their Own Land*, 224; emphasis in original.
104 It is the title of a book by right-wing political commentator Coulter, *In Trump We Trust*.
105 Becker, *The Denial of Death*, 133.
106 Ibid., 132.
107 KHOU.com staff, "Man Arrested for Abusive Sexual Contact on a Plane: Trump 'Says It's OK to Grab' Women."
108 Žižek, *Metastases of Enjoyment*, 55.
109 Cf. McCright and Dunlap, "Anti-Reflexivity."
110 BBC News, "Trump to Kim: My Nuclear Button Is 'Bigger and More Powerful.'" Cf. Cohn, "Sex and Death in the Rational World of Defense Intellectuals."
111 Yang, "Trumpism: A Disfigured Americanism."
112 Giddens, *Contemporary Critique*, 147, 189; Adam, *Timescapes of Modernity*.
113 Giddens in Beck, Giddens, and Lash, *Reflexive Modernization*, 192.
114 For example, Fromm argues that alienated work relations create "defects in the system 'man,' both individually and socially": "Humanistic Planning," 85.
115 Inglehart, *Modernization and Postmodernization*, 33.
116 Norris and Inglehart, *Cultural Backlash*, 89.
117 Ibid., 449–50, 454–56.
118 Hochschild, *Strangers in their Own Land*.
119 Langman, "Donald Trump: Morbid Symptom of the Interregnum," 137; Langman, "Cycles of Contention"; Langman, "Right Ressentiment as Reaction."
120 Norris and Inglehart, *Cultural Backlash*, 464.
121 Foster, Clark, and York, *The Ecological Rift: Capitalism's War on the Earth*.
122 Giddens, *The Politics of Climate Change*, 96.
123 Thorpe and Jacobson, "Life Politics, Nature, and the State," 113–14.
124 Fromm, "Humanistic Planning."
125 Fromm, *Escape from Freedom*, 270.
126 Ibid., 271.

References

Adam, Barbara. (1998). *Timescapes of Modernity: The Environment and Invisible Hazards*. London: Routledge.

Antonio, Robert J. (2019). "Reactionary Tribalism Redux: Right-Wing Populism and De-Democratization." *The Sociological Quarterly* 60, no. 2: 201–9.

BBC News. (2018). "Trump to Kim: My Nuclear Button Is 'Bigger and More Powerful.'" *BBC News*, January 3, https://www.bbc.com/news/world-asia-42549687.

Beck, Ulrich, Anthony Giddens, and Scott Lash. (1994). *Reflexive Modernization: Politics, Tradition and Aesthetics in the Modern Social Order*. Stanford: Stanford University Press.

Becker, Ernest. (1975). *Escape from Evil*. New York: The Free Press.

Becker, Ernest. (1997). *The Denial of Death*. New York: Free Press Paperbacks.

Berger, Peter L. (1967). *The Sacred Canopy: Elements of a Sociological Theory of Religion.* New York: Anchor.

Bowring, Finn. (2015). "Negative and Positive Freedom: Lessons from, and to, Sociology." *Sociology* 49, no. 1: 156–71.

Chodorow, Nancy. (1978). *The Reproduction of Mothering: Psychoanalysis and the Sociology of Gender.* Berkeley: University of California Press.

Clarke, John. (2005). "New Labour's Citizens: Activated, Empowered, Responsibilized, Abandoned?" *Critical Social Policy* 25, no. 4: 447–63.

Clarke, Simon, and Paul Hoggett. (2004). "Empire of Fear: The American Political Psyche and the Culture of Paranoia." *Psychodynamic Practice* 10, no. 1: 89–106.

Cohn, Carol. (1987). "Sex and Death in the Rational World of Defense Intellectuals." *Signs* 12, no. 4: 687–718.

Cordle, Daniel. (2008). *States of Suspense: The Nuclear Age, Postmodernism and United States Fiction and Prose.* Manchester: Manchester University Press.

Coulter, Ann. (2016). *In Trump We Trust: E Pluribus Awesome!* New York: Sentinel Books.

Doppelt, Gerald. (2001). "What Sort of Ethics Does Technology Require?" *The Journal of Ethics* 5, no. 2: 155–75.

Durkin, Kieran. (2014). *The Radical Humanism of Erich Fromm.* New York: Palgrave Macmillan.

Ehrenreich, Barbara. (1989). *The Fear of Falling: The Inner Life of the Middle Class.* New York: Pantheon Books.

Foster, John Bellamy, Brett Clark, and Richard York. (2011). *The Ecological Rift: Capitalism's War on the Earth.* New York: Monthly Review Press.

Fromm, Erich. (1955). *The Sane Society.* New York: Holt, Rinehart and Winston.

Fromm, Erich. (1964). *The Heart of Man: Its Genius for Good and Evil.* New York: Harper & Row.

Fromm, Erich. (1969). *Escape from Freedom.* New York: Henry Holt and Co.

Fromm, Erich. (1970a). *The Crisis of Psychoanalysis: Essays on Freud, Marx, and Social Psychology.* New York: Henry Holt and Co.

Fromm, Erich. (1970b). "Humanistic Planning." In Erich Fromm, *The Crisis of Psychoanalysis: Essays on Freud, Marx, and Social Psychology,* 78–88. New York: Henry Holt and Co.

Fromm, Erich. (1973). *The Anatomy of Human Destructiveness.* New York: Holt, Rinehart and Winston.

Fromm, Erich. (2003). *Man for Himself: An Inquiry into the Psychology of Ethics.* London: Routledge.

Fromm, Erich. (2010a). *To Have or to Be?* London: Continuum.

Fromm, Erich. (2010b). *The Pathology of Normalcy.* New York: American Mental Health Foundation.

Giddens, Anthony. (1979). *Central Problems in Social Theory: Action, Structure and Contradiction in Social Analysis.* Berkeley: University of California Press.

Giddens, Anthony. (1981). *A Contemporary Critique of Historical Materialism. Vol. 1: Power, Property and the State.* London: Macmillan.

Giddens, Anthony. (1985). *The Nation-State and Violence. Volume Two of a Contemporary Critique of Historical Materialism.* Cambridge: Polity Press.

Giddens, Anthony. (1990). *The Consequences of Modernity.* Stanford: Stanford University Press.

Giddens, Anthony. (1991). *Modernity and Self-Identity: Self and Society in the Late Modern Age.* Stanford: Stanford University Press.

Giddens, Anthony. (1992). *The Transformation of Intimacy: Sexuality, Love & Eroticism in Modern Societies*. Stanford: Stanford University Press.
Giddens, Anthony. (1994). *Beyond Left and Right: The Future of Radical Politics*. Stanford: Stanford University Press.
Giddens, Anthony. (1998). *The Third Way: The Renewal of Social Democracy*. Cambridge: Polity Press.
Giddens, Anthony. (2007). *Over to You, Mr Brown: How Labour Can Win Again*. Cambridge: Polity Press.
Giddens, Anthony. (2009). *The Politics of Climate Change*. Cambridge: Polity Press.
Giroux, Henry A. (2004). "War on Terror: The Militarising of Public Space and Culture in the United States." *Third Text* 18, no. 4: 211–21.
Giroux, Henry A. (2018). *American Nightmare: Facing the Challenge of Fascism*. San Francisco: City Lights Books.
Hardie-Bick, James. (2015). "Necessary Illusions: Life, Death and the Construction of Meaning." *Oñati Socio-legal Series* 5, no. 3: 850–61.
Harvey, David. (1990). *The Condition of Postmodernity: An Enquiry into the Origins of Cultural Change*. Oxford: Blackwell.
Hedges, Chris. (2018). *America: The Farewell Tour*. New York: Simon and Schuster.
Hochschild, Arlie Russell. (2016). *Strangers in Their Own Land: Anger and Mourning on the American Right*. New York: The New Press.
Jordan, Bill. (2010). *Why the Third Way Failed: Economics, Morality and the Origins of the "Big Society."* London: Policy Press.
Jutel, Olivier. (2016). "Barack Obama, the New Spirit of Capitalism, and the Populist Resistance." *International Journal of Žižek Studies* 6, no. 3: 1–19.
KHOU.com staff. (2018). "Man Arrested for Abusive Sexual Contact on a Plane: Trump 'Says It's OK to Grab' Women." *USA Today* (October 23, 2018), https://www.usatoday.com/story/travel/flights/2018/10/23/accused-groping-southwest-flight-trump-women-private-parts/1736728002/
Klein, Naomi. (2008). *The Shock Doctrine: The Rise of Disaster Capitalism*. New York: Picador.
Kolarz, Peter. (2018). *Giddens and Politics beyond the Third Way: Utopian Realism in the Late Modern Age*. Houndmills, Basingstoke: Palgrave Macmillan.
Langman, Lauren. (2012). "Cycles of Contention: The Rise and Fall of the Tea Party." *Critical Sociology* 38, no. 4: 469–94.
Langman, Lauren. (2018a). "Right Ressentiment as Reaction: Whither Dignity?" Presentation at the International Sociological Association, World Congress of Sociology, Toronto, July 20, 2018.
Langman, Lauren. (2018b). "Donald Trump: Morbid Symptom of the Interregnum: Trump as Trope." *Monitoring of Public Opinion: Economic and Social Changes* 5: 124–46.
Langman, Lauren, and George Lundskow. (2016). *God, Guns, Gold and Glory: American Character and Its Discontents*. Boston: Brill.
Langman, Lauren, and George Lundskow. (2018). "Erich Fromm and Contemporary American Politics." *Free Associations* 73: 7–22.
Lundskow, George. (2012). "Authoritarianism and Destructiveness in the Tea Party Movement." *Critical Sociology* 38, no. 4: 529–47.
May, Rollo. (1977). *The Meaning of Anxiety*. New York: W. W. Norton and Co.
McLaughlin, Neil. (1998). "How to Become a Forgotten Intellectual: Intellectual Movements and the Rise and Fall of Erich Fromm." *Sociological Forum* 13, no. 2: 215–46.

McLaughlin, Neil. (2001). "Critical Theory Meets America: Riesman, Fromm, and the Lonely Crowd." *The American Sociologist* 32, no. 1: 5–26.

McCright, Aaron M., and Riley E. Dunlap. (2010). "Anti-Reflexivity: The American Conservative Movement's Success in Undermining Climate Science and Policy." *Theory, Culture and Society* 27, nos. 2–3: 100–33.

McVeigh, Rory, and Kevin Estep. (2019). *The Politics of Losing: Trump, the Klan, and the Mainstreaming of Resentment.* New York: Columbia University Press.

Monbiot, George. (2019). "Dare to Declare the System Dead—Before It Takes Us down with It." *The Guardian* (Journal) (Thursday, April 25, 2019): 1–2.

Monnat, Shannon M., and David L. Brown. (2017). "More than a Rural Revolt: Landscapes of Despair and the 2016 Presidential Election." *Journal of Rural Studies* 55: 227–36.

Moody, Kim. (2017). "Who Put Donald Trump in the White House?" In Lance Selfa (ed.), *US Politics in an Age of Uncertainty: Essays on a New Reality*, 45–59. Chicago: Haymarket Books.

Norris, Pippa, and Ronald Inglehart. (2019). *Cultural Backlash: Trump, Brexit, and Authoritarian Populism.* Cambridge: Cambridge University Press.

Parker, Christopher S., and Matt A. Barreto. (2013). *Change They Can't Believe In: The Tea Party and Reactionary Politics in America.* Princeton, NJ: Princeton University Press.

Pearson, Monte L. (2019). *The Roots of Defeat: The Clintons, Obama, and the Decline of the Democrats.* Maitland, FL: MCP Books.

Ranulf, Sven. (1964). *Moral Indignation and Middle Class Psychology.* New York: Schocken Books.

Reid, Roddey. (2017). *Confronting Political Intimidation and Public Bullying: A Citizen's Handbook for the Trump Era and Beyond.* San Bernadino, CA: Amazon Direct Publishing.

Riesman, David, with Nathan Glazer and Reuel Denney. (1961). *The Lonely Crowd: A Study of the Changing American Character.* New Haven: Yale University Press.

Robinson, William I., and Mario Barrera. "Global Capitalism and Twenty-First Century Fascism: A US Case Study." *Race & Class* 53, no. 3: 4–29.

Saccarelli, Emanuele, and Latha Varadarajan. (2015). *Imperialism Past and Present.* New York: Oxford University Press.

Salzman, Michael B. (2001). "Globalization, Culture, and Anxiety: Perspectives and Predictions from Terror Management Theory." *Journal of Social Distress and the Homeless* 10, no. 4 (October): 337–52.

Savage, Charlie. (2015). *Power Wars: Inside Obama's Post-9/11 Presidency.* New York: Little, Brown and Co.

Scott, Susie, and Charles Thorpe. (2006). "The Sociological Imagination of R. D. Laing." *Sociological Theory* 24, no. 4: 331–52.

Selfa, Lance. (2008). *The Democrats: A Critical History.* Chicago: Haymarket Books.

Shafir, Gershon. (1985). "The Incongruity between Destiny and Merit: Max Weber on Meaningful Existence and Modernity." *The British Journal of Sociology* 36, no. 4: 516–30.

Shafir, Gershon, and Cynthia E. Schairer. (2016). "The War on Terror as Political Moral Panic." In Gershon Shafir, Everard Meade, and William J. Aceves (eds.), *Lessons and Legacies of the War on Terror: From Moral Panic to Permanent War*, 9–46. London: Routledge.

Singer, Thomas. (2017). "Trump and the American Collective Psyche." In Brandy Lee (ed.), *The Dangerous Case of Donald Trump: 27 Psychiatrists and Mental Health Experts Assess a President.* New York: St. Martin's Press.

Slater, Philip. (1990). *The Pursuit of Loneliness: American Culture at the Breaking Point*. Boston: Beacon Press.
Stanley, Jason. (2018). *How Fascism Works: The Politics of Us and Them*. New York: Random House.
Stein, Howard F. (2004). *Beneath the Crust of Culture: Psychoanalytic Anthropology and the Cultural Unconscious in American Life*. Amsterdam: Rodopi.
Thorpe, Charles. (2016). *Necroculture*. New York: Palgrave Macmillan.
Thorpe, Charles, and Brynna Jacobson. (2013). "Life Politics, Nature and the State: Giddens' Sociological Theory and *The Politics of Climate Change*." *The British Journal of Sociology* 64, no. 1: 99–122.
Weber, Max. (1958). "Science as a Vocation." In H. H. Gerth and C. Wright Mills (eds.), *From Max Weber: Essays in Sociology*, 129–56. New York: Oxford University Press.
Welsh, Ian. (2000). *Mobilising Modernity: The Nuclear Moment*. London: Routledge.
Yang, Mimi. (2017). "The Trump Wall: A Cultural Wall and a Cultural War." *Lateral* 6, no. 2, http://csalateral.org/issue/6-2/trump-wall-cultural-war-yang/
Yang, Mimi. (2018). "Trumpism: A Disfigured Americanism." *Palgrave Communications* 4, no. 117: 1–13.
Žižek, Slavoj. (2006). *Metastases of Enjoyment*. London: Verso.

Chapter 9

SOCIAL CHARACTER, SOCIAL CHANGE, AND THE SOCIAL FUTURE

Lauren Langman and George Lundskow

Introduction

One of the most important contributions Erich Fromm made to the Frankfurt School tradition of critical theory was the notion of "social character": a notion that wove together Marx's critique of alienation, capitalism, and historical materialism, Freud's psychodynamics, and Weber's concerns with affective and value-oriented actions typical of religion in general that informed his specific concerns with Protestantism. For Fromm, these antecedents led to a dynamic conception of character based on socially shaped needs or desires, for human relationships (love, hate, and sadomasochism) or acquisition (receiving, taking away, saving, gathering, producing) that are specifically socially fostered and expressed, rather than biological drives as in Freudian theory.[1] For Fromm, social character referred to the most frequent pattern typical in a particular society at a particular moment in its history, and also the dominant characteristic but not necessarily the most common. Nevertheless, a large enough group of socially well-placed people embodied this social character that made them "best adapted" to the political economy and which thus reinforced their hold on economic, political, social, and cultural leadership of a particular society. Fromm also stipulated that "adaptation" to an existing society did not necessarily benefit the majority of people or even the stable functioning of that society, and more often than not, societies based on hierarchical domination fostered various types of nonproductive social characters whose "pathological normality" thwarted their capacity to love and find creative self-fulfillment.[2]

For Fromm, the underlying characterological structure was largely shaped by the material conditions of the age which in turn shaped the social relationships and values of that society, including the widely shared experiences of childhood, child development, and adult participation in work, family, friendship, and social groupings. Social character thus included the patterning of one's ego (e.g., self-conceptions and identity); internalized means of social control (fear of punishment, guilt, shame); psychological defenses in reaction to oppressive or unfulfilling social conditions which Fromm saw as "mechanisms of escape";

and the interactional patterns to avoid unpleasant experiences such as isolation, feelings of powerlessness, and empty conformity.[3] For Fromm, social character—and particularly its authoritarian, sadomasochistic expressions—was the primary factor disposing an "elective affinity" for the embrace of Nazism, and the subsequent conformism of the postwar consumer society.

Fromm's notion of social character differs significantly with three of Freud's fundamental assumptions. First, he foundationally rejects biologically based drives as motivating human behavior and sees them instead as socially based.[4] Second, he rejects Freud's ahistorical notion of character derived from an alleged universal primal horde in which sons murder their father to attain his power and sexual access to women, but which also produces guilt which they must repress in order to achieve a more orderly and stable form of social relations, which Freud calls civilization. In contrast, Fromm saw social character as not only historically constituted but malleable and changing as historical conditions change. Third, unlike the more classical Freudian notion in which character is pretty much established at about age five (more or less the time of the Oedipal resolution), Fromm argues that changing material, political-economic, and/or cultural factors foster "dynamic change" (change in character/motivation) potentially over an entire lifetime. In short, character always depends on social conditions and never becomes completely fixed in the individual. In a larger historical perspective, social character also changes dynamically, such that the "receptive" character typical of feudalism was transformed into the "hoarding and/or exploitative character" which was better adapted to the social realities and demands of the new market economy.[5] As modern consumer capitalism arose, the "marketing personality" displaced the hoarding character because it better fit the demands of a bureaucratically administered society of mass consumption. Scholars such as Stewart Ewen[6] and Herbert Marcuse[7] further unfolded the ways in which capitalist consumerism fostered particular forms of "social character" by creating artificial needs independent of biological need or practical use, which enfolded the individual in a world of consumer commodities rather than of social relations to people. This negated possible critique of the commodity system, which appears normal and natural, and thus constitutes invisible domination as a one-dimensional society that precludes the awareness of or desire for alternatives.

Today, we argue that the current form of neoliberal capitalism is dominated by immaterial production—the proliferation of service-based jobs, often temporary "gig" jobs, financialization, and the digital economy is now located within a de-nationalized global marketplace. Consistent with the concept of one-dimensional society, current neoliberal capitalism valorizes ownership of material goods over living social relationships—what Fromm calls *having* over *being*[8]—exalts self-aggrandizement (narcissism) over community (love), and masks domination as freedom. At the same time, the changing nature of contemporary capitalism, much like its earlier iterations, has fostered a degree of isolation, powerlessness, and meaninglessness that has engendered authoritarianism, intolerance, aggression, and indeed destructiveness, as seen in the proliferation of various reactionary mobilizations described later.

Despite what might be considered the technological advances of contemporary capitalism, the system nevertheless experiences episodic economic, political, and cultural crises of legitimacy which often provoke various authoritarian and reactionary social mobilizations in response. At the same time, movements of progressive, humanistic, productive social character also arise, marked by fluidity, openness, empathy, and genuine freedom to live with real autonomy (and not just freedom from overt oppression). These progressive movements emphasize inclusion and fully participatory democracy. The future of society thus depends on the outcome of reactionary movements and authoritarian character in conflict with progressive movements and life-loving character.

Capitalism and Crisis

Building from Marx, Fromm argues that capitalism inherently produces alienation because the production of commodities objectifies people as mere sources of labor power, which the employer expropriates as surplus value. In turn, this leads to growing inequality between capitalists and workers, such that a handful of men now own half of the world's wealth.[9] Moreover, between fostering nonproductive, truncated forms of character and fashioning a hegemonic ideology by fusing nationalism and consumerism, various psycho-cultural forces effectively reproduce structural domination and unproductive types of social character that sustain "insane societies" in which "pathological normality" legitimates the interests of the ruling classes.[10] Structural domination and truncated expressions of social character produce a vast amount of pain, suffering, and misery for masses who gain little economically (in many cases barely survive) and live in "quiet desperation." Periods of crisis draw these unsatisfying and dysfunctional social relations to the surface and open the established order to anger and resentment, which diminishes loyalty and assent.[11] But such crises also create spaces of hope and episodic "great refusals" in which progressive social movements seek social change or advocate for alternative systems.

Antonio Gramsci called this the "interregnum," when the old values died and the new values were emergent—a transitional period of "morbid symptoms."[12] We currently live in a period of morbid symptoms, such as intensifying economic inequality; growing precariat classes facing intermittent, poorly paid jobs rather than careers; opioid addictions, and environmental despoliation. All together, these symptoms give rise to the contemporary legitimation crises of capital and to new right-wing and left-wing mobilizations. On the one hand, those with a submissive, authoritarian, and resentful attitude are especially susceptible to "strongman" leadership that claims to restore an alleged glorious past, and in the process, will deploy aggression and violence against so-called undesirables and the undeserving, which excites authoritarian followers who exalt overt displays of power and revel in aggression against people who cannot defend themselves, such as impoverished immigrants and ethnic minorities. As the crisis worsens, and aggression increases, a culture and social character of destructive nihilism also increases correspondingly[13]—a desperate effort to preserve the "pure" communities, values, and authoritarian social characters of yesterday. This intensifies the many "morbid symptoms" of today, such as the various authoritarian, right-wing ethno-religious nationalisms, racism, xenophobia, homophobia, and misogyny that all too often move from hatred and *ressentiment* toward Others—people whose mere existence feels like an inherent threat—to unleash characterological destructiveness that seeks to obliterate the "undesirables" from existence. This yearning for a mythological yesterday—when everyone allegedly looked the same, lived the same lifestyle and by the same values—becomes an ideological rallying-cry for many right-wing movements today in the form of Brexit (England), the National Front (France), Alternative für Deutschland (Germany), 5 Star (Italy), Law and Justice (Poland), BJP (India), Justice and Development (Turkey), and the great enabler who legitimates ethno-fascism worldwide—Donald Trump.

Nevertheless, expressions of right-wing authoritarianism for Fromm are neither basic tendencies of "human nature" nor frenzied irrational mobs as Freud suggested, but rather characterological-based social reactions to particular circumstances that frustrated basic human desires for relatedness, self-fulfillment, and transcendence.[14] Just as crises invoke reactionary authoritarian movements, so they also invoke progressive forms of social character and behavior premised on inclusion and universal dignity—relationships that a "sane society" might provide. As crises produce conflicts between forward- and backward-looking movements, we can see the dialectical nature of social change and the social-psychosocial basis for what Rosa Luxemburg saw as the historical battle between socialism and barbarism.[15]

Character and Social Change

Society changes both gradually and during crisis periods that accelerate the pace of change. Sometimes governments and institutions retain their old names with relatively moderate updates, such as the transformation of The Holy Roman Empire into the German Confederation and then to the modern Empire.[16] Leaders and territories changed, but the essential institutions and culture remained intact. Sometimes an overtly revolutionary period dismantles the old regime entirely and creates a fundamentally new government, such as the French Revolution in 1789, or the fall of the Qing dynasty in 1912, or of the Romanov dynasty in 1917. The more moderate social changes generally do not create the dynamic characterological changes that define a new social character throughout society because they do not significantly alter the dominant political economy and/or culture. To the extent that social change occurs more quickly and crisis periods call more of the established order into question, crumbling old systems and emerging new forms often dispose people to isolation, feelings of powerlessness, and anomie (meaninglessness) that in turn dispose people to "mechanisms of escape," especially authoritarian domination-subordination (sadomasochism), conformity, and destructiveness. While these mechanisms may enable people to cope with changing social conditions, they remain "unproductive" forms of character marked by truncated and distorted human possibility.[17] Fromm said little about the specific factors disposing dynamic character change within the individual (which depend on both sociohistorical factors and individual experiences), nor did he catalog generationally based changes regarding the specific varieties or distributions of social character.

However, Fromm and Maccoby[18] do describe the process of change, a process of "social selection" analogous to Darwin's theory of natural selection in which, at any given time, there are a variety of "types," the most typical being the dominant social character, but at the same time, other, less frequent character types may be present. For Darwin, these were genotypes, and for Fromm and Maccoby, *social character types*—each of which occupies an ecological niche. When social conditions change, previously infrequent, perhaps "marginal" character types better adapted to the particular social changes, typically become ascendant. In both natural and Frommian social selection, the best adapted type thrives, which is not necessarily the smartest, strongest, or fastest. This distinguishes *natural* Darwinism and Frommian adaptation on one side, from *social* Darwinism on the other, which argues something very different: that the best and brightest in an absolute sense prosper. In the case of animal species (perhaps facing climate change or an invasion of predators), some are more likely to be better suited to adapt to these changes. Green lizards living in forests better survive lizard-eating birds than their brown cousins, who would have greater survivability on beaches where they blend into the sand more effectively. Green versus brown scales are not better in an absolute sense, but only in the context of environmental conditions. A similar process takes place with social changes in the case of humans. In the late feudal era, some more "independent," "risk-taking" peasants were able to quickly embrace the more individualistic emerging market economy, while more cautious, passive/dependent peasants were more likely to become workers in the "satanic mills" of emerging industrial production. According to Fromm's study in Mexico,[19] many of the *campesinos* (peasants), raised under conditions of domination in the hacienda system, had a submissive, passive, fatalistic personality prone to violence or alcoholism. But some of the villagers, the more "productive exploitative-narcissists" that had not lived on the haciendas and were therefore able to adapt to and embrace the changing capitalistic market economy, not only gained more wealth but also transformed the villages to better adapt to the expanding market economy.

Robert Levine's[20] elaboration of social selection theory argues that the dominant social character type is the one that is best adapted to the particular cultural or socioeconomic environment. But given the distributions of character types, the social character of the society may be less adaptive to changing circumstances (social, political, or technological) and at such times those less frequent types may be more adaptive, and more likely to intentionally socialize their young in ways that instill the qualities that made them better adapted to new circumstances. Consider, for example, scientific talent. In a poor, peasant society where higher education tends to be rare, very few peasants are likely to become doctors, engineers, or scientists, but with economic progress and expansion of educational opportunities, often in advanced countries, many who may have otherwise spent their lives tending cattle, toiling in fields or rice paddies can access unrealized cognitive/motivational qualities that enable them to more readily change and adapt to changing political-economic circumstances. Over time, that type becomes more acceptable, and successful variants become more numerous. Consequently, social norms, attitudes, and a more adaptive social character that may have been present but infrequently found in the group become more typical. When a previously rare character structure enables better adaptation to a new historical context—for example, "computer geeks" are better adapted to the recent rise of high-tech and instantaneous communication—people with the new character structure are likely to increase in number, acquire more social prestige, and receive greater monetary compensation.

This kind of characterological change and ascendance is neither automatic nor linear, but involves social-psychological levels or subsystems.[21] These subsystems begin as micro-interactions, especially face-to-face interactions in early childhood, which have a considerable impact on the development of social character. As the person develops, he or she moves into "meso-systems," organizations such as schools and churches where interactions take place on a wider scale. He or she is further exposed to the "exo-system," namely the larger society which is often mediated rather than directly experienced. Further, individuals live within a macro-system, the organization of cultural values, customs, and laws that shape social interactions and cultural comprehension. The "chrono-system" describes the grandest level, the flow of both individual and social time. The important point is that the changing social-historical situation, especially changing economic, cultural, and political factors that precipitate legitimation crises we previously discussed, impacts all five ecological subsystems in which characters develop and are articulated. Thus, larger social-historical events, processes, and changes are ultimately mediated through these different social contexts to foster dynamic changes of the individual that collectively result in historical-generational character changes, leading to social characters better adapted to the new social realities. As we mentioned, as feudal societies were first impacted by the rising market society, the small minority disposed to hoarding became more socially successful than the receptive characters. But in time, as they were likely to have an elective affinity with Protestantism, in part due to authoritarianism serving as an escape from isolation and powerlessness, as well as legitimating values acting to intentionally foster a character type that would eventually become the more typical social character. As will be argued, the same process of characterological change is taking place before our eyes. While rooted in the conditions of the 1960s, the new character type is becoming more evident today.

History and Social Character

Given what has been said, it is clear that the changing political economy is a central factor shaping the social relations and ideologies of an era that leads to the shifting of social character types from one to another. In Fromm's analysis of the sequential changes in character that were observed in the empirical study of the Mexican village, it was evident that the mix of character types was shifting, and that the more passive-accepting types were less likely to adapt to the rising commercialism of the day. In many ways, this was in microcosm, a glimpse of the historical changes in social character. More recent theory and research has suggested a number of other factors that have historically impacted the nature of early socialization, later socialization, and dynamic character change. One simple example concerns the change in household architecture, as people moved from huts with dirt floors to homes with wood or even tile floors, and often carpets, sometimes quite costly ones: this shift increased concern with toilet training, becoming a factor in instilling the anal compulsive qualities more conducive to petty bourgeois capitalism, including authoritarianism and asceticism. Similarly, with the "discovery of childhood," children came to have separate toys, outfits, games, and even their own rooms—again an ecological context fostering individualism.[22] As populations drifted out of small village life (*Gemeinschaft*) into more impersonal towns and ultimately into the modern metropolis of an associational society (*Gessellschaft*), individualism, rationality, and the predominant value of money replaced the old social ties of extended family and traditions.

In his historical analysis of social character, Fromm suggested that during the feudal era, the receptive character passively accepted the social structure, its hierarchy, rules, and regulations all dictated by tradition. With the spread of the market economy, the hoarding character emerged from a paid bourgeois class of artisans, merchants, and peasant landholders who socialized through negotiated business relationships rather than through more-or-less fixed traditional obligations. This negotiated relationship required diligent and rational work choices and commitment, because, unlike traditional relations which circumscribed the entire life course, the market promises no particular social outcomes—only the opportunity to earn more wealth or status than a person received at birth. Spiritually sanctioned as a "calling" coupled with an acquisitive and ascetic moral code, tireless work enabled greater success in the emerging market society. Yet along with this "economic success" came a great deal of anxiety over social status closely intertwined with Protestant "salvation anxiety" that in turn prompted even more compulsive work. Eventually, the rapid technological advances in chemistry and metallurgy enabled industrial capitalism and the emergence of large bureaucratic organizations increasingly part of consumer society—aided and abetted by the growth of advertising.[23] At this point, Fromm argues, the marketing character emerges, a development by which one's personality becomes a commodity, no different than any other commodity for sale, as a means to build and express an identity: "I shop, therefore I am." Far from an opportunity to broaden one's sense of self, the consumerist society requires a person to choose among the personality types offered for sale, such as intellectual, hipster, punk, goth, metalhead, serious professional, vegetarian, conservative, liberal, and whatever happens to be trendy. While free to choose among the parameters of socially recognizable types, the individual, in effect, conforms to Marcuse's one-dimensional society.[24]

On the basis of his historical analysis, Fromm suggested four basic character types in order of rise to dominance: receptive, hoarding, exploitative, and the marketing.[25] Each in their own way represented a different form of alienation, as a thwarting of self-realization coupled with uncritical submission to a system of domination that disposed what Fromm considered "unproductive" forms of social character. Moreover, many such characters were prone to authoritarianism, anger, hatred of the Other, or a destructiveness based on what he called *necrophilia*, the love of death and destruction as the symptom of thwarted and distorted selfhood. Fromm nevertheless insisted on a fundamentally optimistic view of human nature, because otherwise the cause would be hopeless. He saw the possibility of a "productive character" that would emerge along with an economic system that transcended capitalism, based on a fundamentally different kind of political economy and different values. This character would promote freedom, equality, democracy, and dignity[26] as a state of being in which alienation and domination become morally unacceptable social conditions that must be alleviated like any other social problem.[27]

The Coming of Liquid Selfhood

The growing postwar economy and broader prosperity enabled the progressive and countercultural movements of the 1960s, through rapid expansion of higher education, improved recreational time, and a higher standard of living. The rise of one-dimensional society sat side by side with resistance to racial, gender, and sexual/cultural repression grew, as progressive childrearing through Benjamin Spock specifically disdained authoritarian forms of socialization and began to create a new character type that started to take the values of caring and sharing seriously. In the political realm, the civil rights movement, itself the legacy of a century-old struggle against racism for equality and inclusion, heightened challenges to white male domination—a struggle not yet finished. Further, the sexual revolution undermined the sexual repression that was quite "normal" for Freud and promoted women as economic actors beyond domestic labor, roles already evident in the early 1940s, when vast numbers of women flocked to the "arsenals of democracy" to build the weapons used to defeat fascism. Within a generation, with the rise of feminism, there were definite changes in the values and identities of many women, especially the educated women who joined consciousness raising groups to critique patriarchy and empower women. Whatever might be said about the limits of second-wave feminism, more and more women pursued higher education and careers. These cultural movements initiated major changes in the nature of subjectivity and knowing, which white men had long monopolized, and opened the door for multiple perspectives from the differing experiences of women and people of color.

While consumer selfhood, characterized by the "marketing character," became ascendant after the Second World War, today the consumer self, at a time of shrinking economic prospects and growing debt, is no longer an adaptive or functional character type, especially for younger cohorts facing economic stagnation and career uncertainty, gig jobs, and burdensome student debts. Instead of joining the proletariat or the ranks of professionals, many of today's youth will join the precariat, who have neither the potential for solidarity like the old working class nor the autonomy, job security, or earning power of the old professional classes. In this fourth industrial revolution, automation increasingly replaces human labor, leading to vastly increasing rates of profit and poverty at the same time.[28] Almost all human employment will become independent contracting and temporary, or easily relocated to the lowest-wage locations whenever desired—trends that are already common.[29] At the same time, we can now note a new, emerging and growing form of social character, especially among younger cohorts, especially among later Gen X, Millennials, and Gen Z. From what has been said, three major political-economic and cultural factors have led to a radical transformation of the social context, fostering a new character type that is disposed to refusals of the older, more authoritarian society and that bears a new, inclusive, democratic, humanistic, and multidimensional society, that is, a sane society where the productive character might flourish as Fromm envisioned. Between advanced technologies of communication and the general liberalization of social values, the social character structure of our times is still in process and a new type is emergent, seen most often in college students and younger, and/or minority and other marginalized groups such as gay and transgender people. The central theme of this emerging character is that the seemingly rational, individualistic, singular person with a fixed and stable core of selfhood that was socialized by caretakers, schools, churches, and media is now inadequate if not obsolete in the face of present conditions.

It is hard to provide a singular term that captures the nature and qualities of the emerging form of typical subjectivity that tends to be more flexible and variable, indeed multiple and often contradictory depending on context. In 1977, Louis Zurcher[30] argued for the coming of the "mutable self," as changes in college students' self-definitions moved from notions of fixity and stability (the self as object, as a stable entity) to a self as flexible and open to change, and often as a process often of self-creation. Such a mutable self was flexible and adaptive to the emerging world of rapid change and growing uncertainty. Others, often influenced by postmodern critiques of grand narratives, argued that contemporary selfhood is decentered, lacks a stable core, and is without fixed identities and consistent self-presentations. Indeed, there was a shift from enduring essential qualities to inscriptions of identity, expressed not in enduring self-conceptions but through episodic performances. For Gergen (1977), the late modern, "saturated self" has gone through a dissolution into a variety of roles and identities articulated in a variety of different settings. He also argues that the traditional Western ideas of a stable, enduring, individualized, indivisible court to selfhood were no longer relevant. Instead, the "saturated self" of late modernity was a collage of multiple, often contradictory self-conceptions and presentations—a phenomenon heightened by the fact that many aspects of selfhood may exist largely on computers, social media, and other intangible locations. The bank officer may trade his or her daytime Armani suit for studded black leather and reveal his or her tattoo ink while playing an electric guitar in a heavy metal band while stoned. As Gergen describes it,

> This syndrome may be termed multiphrenia, generally referring to the splitting of the individual into a multiplicity of self-investments. As one's potentials are expanded by the technologies, so one increasingly employs the technologies for self-expression; yet, as the technologies are further utilized, so do they add to the repertoire of potentials. It would be a mistake to view this multiphrenic condition as a form of illness, for it is often suffused with a sense of expansiveness and adventure. . . . So multiphrenia is the name for the condition of having many possible selves and self-representations that conflict. So, basically, everyone has multiphrenia to some degree, some just have more of it. If it becomes too overwhelming, that is when people have mental breakdowns and succumb to it. I think the day of not distinguishing multiphrenia from "normal living" has come.[31]

Gergen clearly questions even the possibility of the coherent, unified self, of rationality, individualism, and psychological stability. This view has important implications for political practice/democratization.

Whereas Gergen sees fragmentation, chaos, and schizophrenia as the new normal, Robert Lifton argues that as people become more fluid and many sided, they would in fact be more likely to manage better in an age of uncertainty and restlessness. Lifton called this notion of self the "Protean self," after Proteus, the Greek sea god who took many shapes and forms. The essential quality of this Protean self is change, flexibility, discontinuity, and inconsistency.[32] So in a time of fragmentation and trauma, Lifton remains optimistic because Proteanism can awaken our species belonging, our species self: we can assert our organic relationship to each other and to nature. Amid increasing cultural diversity, common precariat insecurity, and dissatisfaction with the old order, these changes signal the rise of a new order to which the Protean self can more readily adapt and thus more actively shape, in contrast to older character forms that cling ever more tightly to a social order that is already gone. In this context, we are now at the end of the stable, solid, industrial world of late modernity based on heavy industries, and in an era of "liquid modernity,"[33] a more flexible, postindustrial, digitally based immaterial production within a globalized world of rapid flows information and social media. Of course, vast industrial production still provides the material goods of modern life, but value, profits, and political influence have shifted to the information industries, investment banking, private equity, and information services,[34] including businesses like Uber which own very little but organize extensive networks of independent contractors. There are ever fewer certainties given the rapid changes and fluidity in institutions, lifestyles, and—what becomes most salient—emerging forms of subjectivity. The contemporary individual must be more flexible, be able to engage in short-term relationships, and be adaptable to changing circumstances, relationships, and understandings of his or her own selfhood. The constantly changing constructions of selfhood and identities, and the variability of performances to fit changing contexts, have replaced notions of a seamless, coherent lifespan as a linear process with a clear identity and consistent narrative that has been established in early life which then endures. Instead, liquid selfhood/identity is recursively constructed and reconstructed, much like one's appearance, which is readily transformed through fashion, cosmetics, fitness, exercise, or plastic surgery—all this to enhance the visible self and its marketability in a competitive, changing, global world. For Bauman, consumption and selfhood are closely intertwined. (This has been called "shopping mall selfhood," once again: "I shop, therefore I am.")

Is the flexible, multiple self capable of effecting social transformation and working toward a "sane society"? The various theorists of subjectivity who have studied and theorized the forms of selfhood in character have noted the changes in institutions, technologies, and social life and see flexibility as an adaptation to these changes, but not necessarily as an agent of change. On the one hand, the nature of contemporary selfhood—mutable, flexible, liquid, or Protean—would seem ideally suited for the neoliberal contemporary world without strong certainties, loyalties, or enduring social bonds to identity that grant and recognize meaningful collective identities like the churches of old, or like hereditary descent or long-respected traditions. Commitment becomes an issue. Although unlikely to embrace dogmatic ideologies or submit to antiquated customs of heteronormativity, sexual abstinence until marriage, or other prejudicial relics of oppression, the liquid self similarly does not readily commit to consistent frames of reference and action. Yet, the younger generations embrace social justice and would readily trade higher pay for a more meaningful and secure livelihood,[35] and while hopes and attitudes do not make a social movement, they are a definite precondition. In fact, the earliest social-psychological studies from the Second World War era found that children have great difficulty and emotional conflict about taking on the hates and prejudices of their parents and other adults. Since then, surveys have found certain distinct features of the Millennial generation: they want to "make a difference" or have a purpose; be able to balance work with the rest of life; seek fun and variety; they are likely to question authority or refuse to respond to authority without "good reason"; they are likely to have an extreme sense of loyalty to family, friends, and self.[36] Especially noticeable is the embrace of a variety of "post-materialist" values that echo Fromm's distinction between being and having, seeking creative forms of self-fulfillment rather than extrinsic rewards. They are not adverse to commitment, but it needs to be meaningful commitment.

So, we assert that, as oppressive ideologies, hateful prejudices, and coercive normative controls weaken, the default human orientation emerges, which, as Fromm argued, is life-loving, socially committed, sharing, and egalitarian. This does not conclude history, however. Far from it. The old order and its corporations, militaries, systems of profit and oppression, and extreme concentrations of wealth will not just throw in the towel and go quietly into the garbage can of history. Neither will the people who identify with power and privilege—though they own little of it themselves—simply acquiesce as new values and lifestyles arise, not when their status and superior sense of self relies on the continued hegemony of political and cultural systems that privilege some people over and against others. Even if the demise of global capitalism and the old values is inevitable, that in no way guarantees that a more progressive social order will take its place. In the United States, for example, we contend that Donald Trump could easily win reelection and hold the Senate on his coattails, maybe even regain the House for the Republicans if the Democrats nominate a representative of the old order or a flimsy candidate with no substance. They are unlikely to inspire the Millennial and other progressive voters who want the "real deal" and not a smiling pretender like Beto O'Rourke, or an outdated relic like Joe Biden. Ironically, the oldest candidate is Bernie Sanders, who embodies many of the values and priorities that Millennials and younger want. Elizabeth Warren comes close, but does not clearly embrace socialism. Given their longing for authenticity and meaningful commitment, younger voters will not hold their nose and vote for the lesser of two evils; they will not vote at all. To get their vote and ongoing support and action between elections, the candidates need to genuinely stand up for progressive ideals. So, we are living through the strongest challenge yet to white male ethnonationalism and neoliberal capitalism—all of which has willing soldiers of its own.

Reactionary Reactions

Whatever else neoliberal globalization may provide, as a capitalist system, it cannot provide meaning and dignity.[37] Since meaning and dignity top the list for young people today, careers engaged in various kinds of alienated labor cannot provide what they most want in life. Unless their character changes radically, they will foment social change, although we can't predict the pace and magnitude at this time. The crises of neoliberal capital have clearly impacted the subjectivities of younger, more flexible cohorts who have joined the "great refusals" (Arab Spring/Indignados/Occupy Wall Street, and more recently, support for Bernie Sanders, Black Lives Matter, and, surprisingly, openness to socialism among most Millennials and Gen Z). It has also impacted the subjectivities of older, prejudiced, and authoritarian people. As Fromm noted, the characterological/normative changes that follow upon the political-economic tend to take generations, as the typical social character of one period wanes and the new, ascendant one replaces it. At such times of transition, Fromm argues, we typically note two patterns among those less able to adapt to the changing political-economic circumstances. For many it becomes a time of despair, depression, and often various forms of self-destruction. This was evident as the Mexican village adapted to the commercial economy and the less adaptive peasants, (those raised under the more authoritarian *hacienda* systems) turned to alcoholism or other forms of dysfunction. Today we see a similar pattern among older, working-class whites living in poor, economically stagnant communities in the form of opioid addiction and suicide. Retreatism and escapism in its ultimate form of suicide speaks to the hopelessness that many feel as sociocultural changes challenge and even threaten the legitimacy of one's very self, especially evoking not just "status anxiety," but, indeed, "existential anxiety"—leading one to fear for the very existence of oneself. Yet not all choose escapism. Given that Donald Trump has held a 42 percent approval rating for a year and a half, and which shows no signs of weakening as of November 1, 2019,[38] we see clearly that many will fight that social change that feels so threatening to "privileged" racial, ethic, gender, or religious identities seen as stable.

What do they fear, specifically? While that privilege is typically "invisible," when it becomes challenged, such challenges to one's very self become highly visible and are generally marked by intense emotional reactions. These changes, which as previously noted, have led to fears of "racial extinction," that today generate fear among white nationalists who imagine a "white genocide" or a "great replacement" and the white race will cease to exist. These fears are well grounded—not in the sense that white individuals or the white "race" may become extinct, but in the sense that demographic and cultural change suggest the erosion, if not end, of white supremacy and the various aspects of social life dependent on the "unquestioned" power and status of whiteness that provides certain groups social and personal gratifications. Intermarriage will likely change the physical complexion of the population somewhat darker, but of course when white people willingly reproduce with people of color, this does not constitute genocide. Far from genocide, the social change that white supremacists find so threatening is in the realm of the mind as white racial status eventually confers no automatic benefit. The real issue is white extinction anxiety, white displacement anxiety, white minority anxiety, all understood scientifically as a sense of futurelessness,[39] and conceptualized as backlash when white people act on those feelings,[40] which manifests as hostile attitudes toward nonwhites and calls for punitive action against allegedly undeserving and parasitical people of color,[41,42] especially nonwhite immigrants[43] and which relates today to the broader cultural changes we have been talking about. For example, the normalization of gay identity and the legal recognition of gay marriage intersects with changes in racial and gender attitudes and foments a generalized displacement anxiety for those who identify with the old standards.[44] The more things that change, the more broadly that change undermines white male ethnonationalist cultural dominance and weakens the sense of self for people attached to that cultural standard.

Who are the people who feel displacement/extinction anxiety most strongly? Contrary to popular perception that such people are low income, low educational attainment, rural white people, the truth is substantially different. Most research on this question centers on the 2016 US presidential election and specifically, who supported Donald Trump, given his overtly ethnocentric and misogynist campaign. Demographic variables, including income, age, and education, do not predict displacement anxiety. His supporters are not only working-class people anxious about their place in the economy.[45] Trump supporters have above-average incomes, above-average educational attainment, and a self-reported sense of financial security. In contrast to the stereotype, racism/ethnocentrism against Latinx immigrants, Muslims, and Black people overwhelmingly predicts Trump support.[46,47,48,49,50,51] As the empirical evidence clearly shows, Trump supporters are racist and ethnocentrist, far more than anything else. This actually makes sense in the American context, given that Americans, from all ethnicities and orientations, perceive the world in terms of many social variables, but almost never in terms of class consciousness.[52,53,54] Even for those with a strong sense of economic inequality or "haves" versus "have-nots," Americans are highly unlikely to evidence any sense of economic class.[55,56,57] Most commonly, Americans equate race with class,[58,59] which further reinforces Trump's appeal as a racist who will protect white hegemony more generally, presumably in economics as well although his entire economic policy seems to be to impose tariffs, a strategy the world generally abandoned after the First World War. Whether Americans have ever identified by class is open to debate,[60] but we cannot engage that here. Suffice to say that they don't in the present. We argue instead that Americans identify by race, gender, and power—whether on the right these things serve the interests of a white male elite and those who emotionally identify with them, or whether on the left they serve a multicultural and multi-gender diversity. We regard the various reactionary, authoritarian movements as desperate attempts to halt, and in some cases reverse (such as eliminating abortion rights and same-sex marriage) the social changes giving rise to more democratic and even productive social character.

Toward a Sane Society

For Fromm, modern capitalist societies create a "pathological normality" typically sustained by mindless conformity at best, and authoritarianism at worst, especially when it fueled hate, aggression, and morphed into a necrophilic deployment of death and destruction. In any case, capitalism fostered unproductive forms of social character and monstrous, truncated forms of selfhood that thwarted not only the capacity for empathy and genuinely loving social relationships but one's entire mode of life. Insofar as capitalism unleashed unprecedented technologies of production that could enable a world of plenty for all, Fromm envisioned the possibility of a sane society. In addition to material needs, Fromm's humanistic perspective emphasizes the equally vital need for a healthy inner life and the importance of human connection and individual spontaneity. From the changing nature of selfhood we have described, freer, more spontaneous, inclusive, critical of authority, "post-materialist" selves seek harmony with nature, a more flexible character as we have described. Just as the authoritarian church and dynastic monarchs mobilized and crushed the democratic movements of 1848, all the king's horses and all the king's men could not stop democratization. Fromm's notion of a sane society is not inevitable, but it is absolutely necessary for the human species to overcome mass poverty, social injustice, resource depletion, pollution, the global heat trap, endless wars, and widespread dissatisfaction and all that follows from that, such as anxiety and depression. That would of course initially require the radical transformation or abolition of capitalism, but that discussion must be left for another time and place.

Fromm's vision of the sane society, the culmination of his many writings on social character, destructiveness, love, and religion, rests upon his fundamental view of human nature and religious-humanistic-moral concept of humanity as an end in itself, as opposed to the means of providing the "surplus value" that enables the accumulation of monetary wealth and establishes the power of the capitalist class. Instead, Fromm believed life should aim at unleashing people's creative powers, living in a society based on democracy and freedom, truth and justice, with dignity for all. He felt that human beings had several basic social-psychological needs no less vital than physical needs, including relatedness, transcendence, rootedness, identity, and a frame of orientation, all of which capitalism systematically frustrates.

Like Fromm, we contend that people should work together cooperatively and enhance the self and the Other, which over time will eliminate the Other—those whom we perceive as fundamentally different and as a threat to or negation of our own identity. While we don't expect, nor desire, that the world will become monolithic, we do envision mutual respect and dignity. Freed from domination by a ruling class, or from the worship of the accumulation of goods that celebrates the "having" of things rather than "being," loneliness and isolation will disappear, undone by moral imperatives to help anyone in need and to connect to each other through mutual love, comradeship, and solidarity rather than through money or contractual and legal obligations. People must transcend nature through creation rather than destruction, to live sustainably within natural limits. Rather than mindless conformity, we envision everyone gaining a meaningful identity as a sense of self through the articulation and expression of one's own creativity and agency rather than through the standards of "desirability" that extol the private accumulation of wealth as well as notions of "desirable" selfhood purveyed by mass media and advertising. Solidarity and mutual recognition of death as a motivation to live life to the fullest will supersede punitive, authoritarian gods, judgmental cultural norms, and authoritarian cultures committed to ruling elites.

In a sane society:[61]

1. No one is a means to another's ends, but always an end in oneself.
2. No one uses another person in ways that limit that person's own development.
3. Acting according to one's conscience is morally correct and necessary.
4. Opportunism and lack of principles is morally wrong and condemned rather than rewarded.
5. Relationships to others in the social sphere and the private sphere follow the same principles of compassion and mutual respect.
6. All economic and political activities encourage the growth of the people.
7. Each person is an active and responsible participant in the life of society, as well as master of their own life.
8. People should develop and cherish reason and passion in equal measure and seek harmonious balance.
9. People have a chance to express their inner needs in collective art, rituals, and celebrations.
10. Qualities like greed, exploitativeness, possessiveness, and narcissism are considered pathological and socially disruptive.

How then do we get from here to there? This is the most difficult aspect of our argument, and we offer no specific programs or agendas that can easily speak to the realization of a sane society. To be sure, such a society needs to be envisioned before it can be realized, and notwithstanding the reactionary mobilizations previously discussed, the impending ecological catastrophe now facing us, and the general indifference on the part of a majority, we indeed see hopeful signs. The movements of the early 2000s, the Arab Spring, Mass public demonstrations in Greece and Spain, Occupy Wall Street, and many other such movements rejected authoritarian governments, challenged the power of global capital, or both.[62] Ironically, the election of Donald Trump has also mobilized a broad opposition, and exerted considerable pressure on the Democratic Party leadership to take a far more progressive stance than their big money corporate donors would like, or will likely support. Bernie Sanders proved in 2016, and is proving again (along with Elizabeth Warren), that a campaign can generate more than enough money relying only on small donors. Simultaneously, we see the sustained power of the #MeToo movement, and victories such as the self-described socialist Alexandra Ocasio-Cortez (AOC) over an entrenched Democratic Party boss (Joe Crowley), whose Twitter following in four months reached 4 million,[63] far surpassing the leader of the Democratic Party, Nancy Pelosi at 2.47 million.[64]—quite an accomplishment for a previously unknown and only twenty-nine-year-old Latina, but very much in line with what we have been saying about changing social character. Whatever else might be said of the current cohorts of youth—between the various oppressions they face, the contradictions of contemporary capitalism, as well as the various post-materialist values they embrace—there is ever more critique of capitalism: its inequality, its exploitation, its alienation. To be sure, this combination of self-awareness and openness to the critique of capitalism, moving beyond its hegemonic ideologies, its one-dimensional thought, and the intolerance of the reactionary expressions late capitalism has brought, will show itself to be the first step toward a sane society.

Conclusion

As Marx suggested, changing economic systems and changing class dynamics foster changes in cultural values and political structures, which Fromm noted result in psychosocial changes in social character. Today, the traditional values, identities, and lifestyles associated with late industrial capitalism and its marketing character have been reconfigured if not discarded by many people, especially younger generations, more typically with the kinds of malleable, flexible social characters previously described. But many more dominant authoritarian types would seek to arrest, if not reverse the social and cultural changes that challenge their established identities values and lifestyles. Otherwise said, the world in which we live today is in a period of transition, an interregnum, between the past and the present, and we have presented a 10-point outline for an alternative future. As the old order dies, the symptoms of its morbidity are clearly evident in the explosion of various right-wing political agendas, support for dictators, authoritarian populisms, and reactionary ethno-religious nationalisms that would not simply thwart social change, marked by steady progress toward tolerance, inclusion, and equality, but seek to restore a "lost society" that exists more as a fantastical reconstruction rather than an actual historical reality. The morbid symptoms of transition include reactionary nationalisms, authoritarian populisms, and indeed a creeping fascism evident in a variety of expressions of racism, anti-Semitism, ethnocentrism, Islamophobia, including an upsurge of violence from bullying in schools to mass shootings and bombings, as attempts to stop or reverse the waning of the old order. Perhaps the most blatant signifier of this trend has been the support for Donald Trump. The promises of neoliberal capitalism, especially the promise that the rising tide would raise all ships, have failed, much as did the dictatorial communism of the twentieth century.

The contemporary world, dominated by neoliberal capitalist globalization, is crisis prone and cannot possibly solve its problems of inequality, income stagnation and poverty, alienated labor that provides no gratifications to exploited workers, and perhaps the most serious issue of our times, little addressed and often denied, the fossil fuel industry fostering global warming and the in turn more violent and frequently destructive weather patterns, along with the despoliation of land and water, portending the possible extinction of the human race. If the global heat trap receives little news coverage, soil loss, habitat loss, desertification, and pollution receive even less. Herbicides, pesticides, biocides, industrial waste pollute the land, water, and the air, with ever rising rates of allergies, asthma, organ disease, and cancer. But there is another vision: the characterological changes that we have suggested, largely typical of the young, are surely likely to become more frequent and indeed the dominant social character type in the next generation or two. If this more productive character is ascendant, it can provide the psychosocial basis of what Fromm called a "sane society." Thus, facing careers that depend on alienated labor yet with less material rewards and facing massive student debts as well as a poor job market of short-term contracts, people increasingly withdraw their loyalty and support and with fluid characters, they can more easily embrace alternative visions of political economy. The crises of neoliberal capital have clearly impacted the subjectivities of younger, more flexible cohorts who have joined the "great refusals" (Arab Spring/Indigandos/Occupy Wall Street). In the United States, support for progressive politicians, Black Lives Matter, and the fact that among Millennials, 61 percent of liberals support socialism, and even 25 percent of conservatives. Overall, 49 percent favor socialism and 49 percent favor capitalism.[65] This testifies to a level of social change beyond an incremental passage of one year to the next. Unfortunately, fluid and Protean selves, specifically because they lack an essential personality base, could also turn toward new manifestations of fascism, such as the alt-right, incel (involuntarily celibate) misogyny, and other hate-directed orientations. Or, lacking any particular commitments, they might simply avoid all of it and adapt to whatever emerges. Modern technologies of production and distribution can potentially avoid pollution and environmental degradation, and yet provide all humanity with the material necessities of life (though not perhaps with the material aspects of abundance); freedom; spontaneity; universal self-fulfillment within democratic, egalitarian, and loving communities; and frames of devotion celebrating humanity and nature. By itself, modern technology offers only the potential for such a society. To complete the transition, we also need a vision and universally accepted recognition of humanity based on mutual respect, dignity, and cooperation as indicated in our ten-point outline and then brought to life by the creativity and compassion of millions of people worldwide thinking globally and acting locally. This would be a sane society.

Notes

1 Funk, "Erich Fromm's Concept of Social Character."
2 Fromm, *The Sane Society*.
3 Fromm, *Escape from Freedom*.
4 Fromm, *Man for Himself*.
5 Fromm, *The Sane Society*.
6 Ewen, *Captains of Consciousness*.
7 Marcuse, *One-Dimensional Man*.
8 Fromm, *To Have or to Be?*
9 Langman and Smith, *Inequality in the 21st Century*.
10 Fromm, *The Sane Society*.
11 Bonanno, *The Legitimation Crisis of Neoliberalism*.
12 Adamson, *Hegemony and Revolution*.
13 Fromm, *The Anatomy of Human Destructiveness*.
14 Fromm, *Man for Himself*.
15 Luxemburg, *Socialism or Barbarism—Selected Writings*.
16 Showalter, *The Wars of German Unification*.
17 Fromm, *Man for Himself*.
18 Fromm and Maccoby, *Social Character in a Mexican Village*.
19 Ibid.
20 Levine, *Culture, Behavior, and Personality*.
21 Bronfenbrenner, *Making Human Beings Human*.
22 Aries, *Centuries of Childhood*.
23 Ewen, *Captains of Consciousness*.
24 Marcuse, *One-Dimensional Man*.
25 Fromm, *The Sane Society*.
26 Fromm, *The Anatomy of Human Destructiveness*.
27 Fromm, *To Have or to Be?*
28 Johannessen, *The Workplace of the Future*.
29 Herod, *Labor*.
30 Zurcher, *The Mutable Self*.
31 Gergen. *The Saturated Self*, 73–74.
32 Lifton, *The Protean Self*.
33 Bauman and Raud, *Practices of Selfhood*.
34 Clausing, *Open*.
35 Hancock, *Solidarity Politics for Millennials*.
36 Englehart, "Changing Values among Western Publics from 1970 to 2006."

37 Langman, "Political Economy and the Normative."
38 FiveThirtyEight.com: https://projects.fivethirtyeight.com/trump-approval-ratings/?ex_cid=rrpromo
39 Nociforo, "The Invasion of Reality (Or of Negotiation)."
40 Walsh, "White Backlash, the 'Taxpaying' Public, and Educational Citizenship."
41 Aaronson, and Sullivan, "The Decline of Job Security in the 1990s."
42 Butler, Nyhan, Montgomery, and Torres, "Revisiting White Backlash."
43 Abrajano and Hajnal, *White Backlash*.
44 Cavalcante, "Anxious Displacements."
45 Manza, "Working Class Hero?"
46 Smith and Hanley, "The Anger Games."
47 Young, Ziemer, and Jackson, "Explaining Trump's Popular Support."
48 Major, Blodorn, and Blascovich, "The Threat of Increasing Diversity."
49 Fisher, "Definitely Not Moralistic."
50 Banks, *Anger and Racial Politics*.
51 Pettigrew, "Social Psychological Perspectives on Trump Supporters."
52 Newman, Johnston, and Lown, "False Consciousness or Class Awareness?"
53 Welburn and Pittman, "Stop 'Blaming the Man.'"
54 Walsh, "Putting Inequality in Its Place."
55 Solt, Hu, Hudson, Song, and Yu, "Economic Inequality and Class Consciousness."
56 Durant and Sparrow, "Race and Class Consciousness among Lower- and Middle-Class Blacks."
57 Payne, "The Construction of Class Consciousness."
58 Brueggemann, "Class, Race, and Symbolic Community."
59 Brannon, Markus, and Taylor, "'Two souls, Two Thoughts,' Two Self-schemas."
60 Fantasia, *Cultures of Solidarity*.
61 Adapted from Victor Daniels's website http://web.sonoma.edu/users/d/daniels/frommnotes.html (Accessed September 30, 2018).
62 Langman and Benski, "Global Justice Movements."
63 https://twitter.com/aoc
64 https://twitter.com/SpeakerPelosi
65 https://www.chicagotribune.com/news/opinion/chapman/ct-perspec-chapman-young-socialism-capitalism-20180520-story.html

References

Aaronson, Daniel, and Daniel G. Sullivan. (1998). "The Decline of Job Security in the 1990s: Displacement, Anxiety, and Their Effect on Wage Growth." *Economic Perspectives* 22, no. 1: 17–27.

Abrajano, Marisa, and Zoltan L. Hajnal. (2015). *White Backlash: Immigration, Race, and American Politics*. Princeton, NJ: Princeton University Press.

Adamson, Walter. (2014 [1980]). *Hegemony and Revolution: Antonio Gramsci's Political and Cultural Theory*. Brattleboro, VT: Echo Point Books.

Aries, Philippe. (1962). *Centuries of Childhood: A Social History of Family Life*. New York, NY: Random House.

Banks, Antoine J. (2014). *Anger and Racial Politics The Emotional Foundation of Racial Attitudes in America*. New York, NY: Cambridge University Press.

Bauman, Zygmunt, and Rein Raud. (2015). *Practices of Selfhood*. Cambridge, MA: Polity Press.
Bonanno, Alessandro. (2017). *The Legitimation Crisis of Neoliberalism: The State, Will-Formation, and Resistance*. New York, NY: Palgrave Macmillan.
Brannon, Tiffany N., Hazel Rose Markus, and Valerie Jones Taylor. (2015). "'Two Souls, Two Thoughts,' Two Self-Schemas: Double Consciousness Can Have Positive Academic Consequences For African Americans." *Journal of Personality and Social Psychology* 108, no. 4: 586–601.
Bronfenbrenner, Urie. (2005). *Making Human Beings Human: Bioecological Perspectives on Human Development*. Thousand Oaks, CA: Sage Publications.
Brueggemann, John. (1995). "Class, Race, and Symbolic Community." *Critical Sociology* 21, no. 3: 71–88.
Butler, Ryden Butler, Brendan Nyhan, Jacob M. Montgomery, and Michelle Torres. (2018). "Revisiting White Backlash: Does Race Affect Death Penalty Opinion?" *Research and Politics*, January–March 2018: 1–9.
Cavalcante, Andre. (2014). "Anxious Displacements: The Representation of Gay Parenting on Modern Family and the New Normal and the Management of Cultural Anxiety." *Television & New Media* 16, no. 5: 454–71.
Clausing, Kimberly. (2019). *Open: The Progressive Case for Free Trade, Immigration, and Global Capital*. Cambridge, MA: Harvard University Press.
Durant, Thomas J., and Kathleen H. Sparrow. (1997). "Race and Class Consciousness among Lower- and Middle-Class Blacks." *Journal of Black Studies* 27, no. 3: 334–51.
Englehart, Ronald. (2008). "Changing Values among Western Publics from 1970 to 2006." *West European Politics* 31, no. 1–2: 130–46.
Ewen, Stewart. (1976). *Captains of Consciousness: Advertising and the Social Roots of the Consumer Culture* New York, NY: McGraw-Hill.
Fantasia, Rick. (1989). *Cultures of Solidarity: Consciousness, Action, and Contemporary American Workers*. Berkeley and Los Angeles: University of California Press.
Fisher, Patrick I. (2016). "Definitely Not Moralistic: State Political Culture and Support for Donald Trump in the Race for the 2016 Republican Presidential Nomination." *Political Science & Politics* 49, no. 4: 743–47.
Fromm, Erich. (1992 [1941]). *Escape from Freedom*. New York, NY: Henry Holt.
Fromm, Erich. (1990 [1947]). *Man for Himself: An Inquiry into the Psychology of Ethics*. New York, NY: Henry Holt.
Fromm, Erich. (1990 [1955]). *The Sane Society*. New York, NY: Henry Holt.
Fromm, Erich. (1967). *The Anatomy of Human Destructiveness*. New York, NY: Henry Holt.
Fromm, Erich, and Michael Maccoby. (1970). *Social Character in a Mexican Village*. Englewood Cliffs, NJ: Prentice-Hall.
Funk, Rainer. (1998). "Erich Fromm's Concept of Social Character." *Social Thought & Research* 21, no. 1/2: 215–22.
Gergen, Kenneth J. (1991). *The Saturated Self: Dilemmas of Identity in Contemporary Life*. New York: Basic Books.
Goffman, Erving. (1956). *The Presentation of Self in Everyday Life*. Edinburgh: University of Edinburgh Press.
Hancock, Ange-Marie. (2011). *Solidarity Politics for Millennials: A Guide to Ending the Oppression Olympics (The Politics of Intersectionality)*. New York, NY: Palgrave Macmillan.
Herod, Andrew. (2018). *Labor*. Malden, MA: Polity Press.

Johannessen, Jon-Arild. (2019). *The Workplace of the Future: The Fourth Industrial Revolution, the Precariat and the Death of Hierarchies.* New York, NY: Routledge.

Lamas Andrew. (2017). *The Great Refusal: Herbert Marcuse and Contemporary Social Movements.* Philadelphia, PA: Temple University Press.

Langman, Lauren, and Dan Albanese (2016). "Political Economy and the Normative: Marx on Human Nature and the Quest for Dignity." In *Constructing Marxist Ethics: Critique, Normativity,* edited by Michael J. Thompson. Boston, MA: Brill: 59–85.

Langman, Lauren, and David Smith. (2017). *Inequality in the 21st Century: Marx, Piketty and Beyond.* Boston, MA: Brill.

Langman, Lauren, and Tova Benski. (2018). "Global Justice Movements: Past Present and Future." In *The Palgrave Handbook of Social Movements, Revolution, and Social Transformation,* edited by B. Berberoglu. New York: Palgrave McMillan.

Levine, Robert A. (1973). *Culture, Behavior, and Personality.* Chicago: Aldine Publishing Company.

Lifton, Robert J. (1993). *The Protean Self: Human Resilience in an Age of Fragmentation.* Chicago, IL: University of Chicago Press.

Luxemburg, Rosa. (2010). *Socialism or Barbarism—Selected Writings,* edited by Paul Le Blanc and Helen C. Scott. New York, NY: Pluto Press.

Major, Brenda. (2016). "The Threat of Increasing Diversity: Why Many White Americans Support Trump in the 2016 Presidential Election." *Group Processes & Intergroup Relations* 21, no. 6: 931–40.

Manza, Jeff. (2017). "Working Class Hero? Interrogating the Social Bases of the Rise of Donald Trump." *The Forum* 15, no. 1: 3–19.

Marcuse, Herbert. (1964). *One-Dimensional Man: Studies in the Ideology of Advanced Industrial Society.* Boston, MA: Beacon Press.

Miller, Clyde R. (1943). *What You Can Do to Promote Racial and Religious Understanding.* New York, NY: Robert Knopf and Sons.

Miller, Clyde R. (1946). *The Process of Persuasion.* New York, NY: Crown Publishers.

Newman, Benjamin J., Christopher D. Johnston, and Patrick L. Lown. (2014) "False Consciousness or Class Awareness? Local Income Inequality, Personal Economic Position, and Belief in American Meritocracy." *American Journal of Political Science* 59, no. 2: 326–40.

Nociforo, Nicola. (2017). "The Invasion of Reality (Or of Negotiation): The Psychoanalytic Ethic and Extinction Anxiety." *International Journal of Psychoanalysis* 98, no. 5: 1311–32.

Ogilvy, James A. (1977). *Many Dimensional Man: Decentering Self, Society, and the Sacred.* New York, NY: Oxford University Press.

Payne, Steven. (2018). "The Construction of Class Consciousness." *Dialectical Anthropology* 42, no. 1: 63–73.

Pettigrew, Thomas F. (2017). "Social Psychological Perspectives on Trump Supporters." *Journal of Social and Political Psychology* 5, no. 1: 107–16.

Showalter, Dennis. (2015). *The Wars of German Unification.* New York, NY: Bloomsbury.

Smith, David Norman, and Eric Hanley. (2018). "The Anger Games: Who Voted for Donald Trump in the 2016 Election, and Why?" *Critical Sociology* 44, no. 2: 195–212.

Solt, Frederick, Yue Hu, Kevan Hudson, Jungmin Song, and Dong "Erico" Yu. (2017). "Economic Inequality and Class Consciousness." *The Journal of Politics* 79, no. 3: 1079–83.

Walsh, Cammille. (2016). "White Backlash, the 'Taxpaying' Public, and Educational Citizenship." *Critical Sociology* 43, no. 2: 237–47.

Walsh, Katherine Cramer. (2012). "Putting Inequality in Its Place: Rural Consciousness and the Power of Perspective." *The American Political Science Review* 106, no. 3: 517–32.

Welburn, Jessica S., and Cassi L. Pittman. (2012). "Stop 'Blaming the Man': Perceptions of Inequality and Opportunities for Success in the Obama Era among Middle-Class African Americans." *Ethnic and Racial Studies* 35, no. 3: 523–40.

Young, Clifford, Katie Ziemer, and Chris Jackson. (2019). "Explaining Trump's Popular Support: Validation of a Nativism Index." *Social Science Quarterly* 100, no. 2: 412–18.

Zurcher, Louis. (1977). *The Mutable Self: A Self-Concept for Social Change*. Thousand Oaks, CA: Sage Publications.

CONCLUSION:
WHY ANTI-FASCISM NEEDS ERICH FROMM'S CRITICAL THEORY

Joan Braune

Here in the United States, it is not hard to see that something has shifted in the political and cultural landscape, a shift that reflects a global resurgence of right-wing nationalisms, including fascist and proto-fascist movements. Since my study over the past few years has been heavily focused on hate in the US American context, I will focus here on the United States as a kind of case study, but it is important to recognize the rise of similar movements around the globe, a phenomenon economist Mark Blyth has termed "global Trumpism."[1] At this moment, I would argue, the work of Erich Fromm is more essential and urgent than ever. Indeed, in the public discourse concerning recent events, one will occasionally hear Fromm's name or some of the terms with which he is associated. For example, some have informally diagnosed Donald Trump with a condition that Fromm called "malignant narcissism,"[2] while others have used Fromm's concept of "collective narcissism" to critique rising nationalist sentiments.[3] However, Fromm's work has not entered sufficiently into contemporary discourse concerning the resurgence of nationalism and fascism, and the left's strategy for confronting fascism, I would argue, is suffering as a result.

Fromm's work was in many ways a response to nationalism and fascism, an attempt to understand how the revolutionary sentiments of workers in Europe preceding the First World War had been stymied and channeled toward nationalism, and how the despair after that war was then mobilized into the apocalyptic, necrophilous fantasies of fascism. In his intellectual biography, *Beyond the Chains of Illusion: My Encounter with Marx and Freud*, Fromm tells us that a formative experience in his life was watching his adolescent classmates and teachers enthuse over the war, and encountering a couple of challenges to nationalist sentiments from wise and caring adults who did not share the widespread lust for violence. A formative intellectual question of his youth, as that war unfolded, became, "How is it possible?" How could people be apparently inspired by humanistic ideals of universal brotherhood one day, and turn on their neighbors the next? After he was forced into exile in the United States with the rise of the Nazis, Fromm continued to be troubled by this question in a new context. How could people profess to support, for example, a national founding idea that "all men are created equal," yet sustain a system of militarism, racism, economic exploitation, and bureaucratic authoritarianism? What made it possible to continue to sustain such inherently contradictory practices and professions of belief?

Americans in the United States are troubled by similar questions today: How is it possible? How is Trumpism possible? How are the violent activities of white nationalist and "Western Chauvinist" organizations now becoming a conventional part of the political landscape? How have we moved from a standard capitalist and imperialist state—in itself deeply violent and oppressive, but presenting a cleaner image to the world—to a state and society increasingly driven by aggressively nostalgic and destructive fascist ideologues, nakedly hateful and openly bigoted?

When Erich Fromm was first hired as a tenured member of the Institute for Social Research, shortly after Max Horkheimer took over as director, Fromm was tasked with synthesizing Marx and Freud. Fromm's first major study for the Institute was an empirical study of the German working class, which contributed to the development of the Institute's later work on the authoritarian personality. Based on a series of lengthy "interpretive questionnaires," Fromm found that roughly 10 percent of 1930s German workers were "authoritarian," roughly 15 percent were "democratic"/humanistic, and 75 percent were between the two extremes on the spectrum.[4] The authoritarians, Fromm predicted, would support the Nazis, while the humanists would oppose them. However, the humanistic 15 percent might prove unable to defeat the authoritarian 10 percent, if the 75 percent in the middle were psychologically ill-equipped to assert their opposition to fascism. A recent study in the United States relying on the simpler "Feldman test" concluded that 19 percent of white US Americans are likely authoritarian.[5] Although the different methods make it difficult to compare the outcomes of Fromm's study of Weimar Germany with contemporary US society, the statistic is troubling when one considers the wide degree of public compliance, partly a stunned silence stemming from something like traumatic shock, which can be found in the US American public. It is still largely possible to engage in dissent without facing repression, but griping on the internet seems to be the preferred method of opposition to rising fascist forces. It is not enough to be self-righteous or angry, however; something has shifted. To understand this stunned silence and unsettling compliance, and to understand how a minority of people are being mobilized into enthusiastic embrace of destructive ideological forces, we must examine the "social character" of Americans today, as Fromm sought to do in his study of the German workers. People are not passive playthings of history, for Fromm, but neither are they unaffected by their political-economic and cultural environment. Particular societal structures, especially economic systems, can encourage, mold, and create particular kinds of individuals and can reward particular character traits. If people are fleeing the burdens of life by retreating into authoritarian submission and attaching their sense of self to a leader or ideology, Fromm realized, then there are political and social conditions at play that go beyond any blithe generalizations about human nature in the abstract.

Following his empirical study of authoritarian and humanistic tendencies in the working class in Weimar Germany, Fromm's next major contribution to the study of fascism was his best-selling 1941 book, *Escape from Freedom*. There Fromm argued that fascism emerges partly from a desire to flee the burdens of freedom. In tearing down the old feudal structures, capitalism paved the way for certain political freedoms but also gave birth to an abyss of meaning that today people are frantically seeking to fill. Fromm writes, "The structure of modern society affects man in two ways simultaneously: he becomes more independent, self-reliant, and critical, and he becomes more isolated, alone, and afraid."[6] The experience of freedom created by the modern world is incomplete, leaving the individual with many negative freedoms—for example, the *freedom from* the state's encroachment on freedom of speech or religion—but without a sense of "positive freedom," a sense of what freedom can be *for*. The modern world professes to provide "freedom of speech" and "freedom of religion," for example, but people have "not acquired the ability to think originally" and have "lost to a great extent the inner capacity to have faith in anything which is not provable by the methods of the natural sciences."[7] Unmoored, thrashing about in a void of meaning and lacking a frame of orientation to make sense of their world, people will grasp for stability where they can find it. For most, Fromm suggested, this may unfortunately be found in social conformity, in adopting the views of those around them and in turn the ideas promoted to them by the shapers of public opinion. Others may turn to nihilistic violence or sadistic exercise of power, seeking to impose or extract from others a sense of meaning and identity. Until contemporary society can move past the limitations of a merely negative conception of freedom, Fromm suggests, people will paradoxically seek to cede that freedom to authorities, in a flawed quest for a sense of stability, oneness, and "at home"-ness in the world.

In 1973, Fromm published *The Anatomy of Human Destructiveness*, a systematic study of the destructive and "necrophilous" impulses that drive fascism. Some of Fromm's earlier articulations of the theory of necrophilia can be found in an anti-war pamphlet written for the American Friends Service Committee, *War within Man: A Psychological Inquiry into the Roots of Destructiveness* (1963), and in his subsequent book, *The Heart of Man: Its Genius for Good and Evil* (1964). Fromm contrasted the healthy, "biophilic" character orientation, which was open to growth, change, and the future, with the unhealthy "necrophilic" character, which was characterized by sentimentality, dwelling upon the past, and an attempt to render the world static, fixed, predictable, and dead. The biophilic character orientation is forward-looking, open to the future, to life and growth, while the necrophilic character orientation is afraid of life and seeks to kill it, metaphorically or literally, to make it easier to control and to understand. Not reducible to sadism or aggression, necrophilia is characterized by "the passion to destroy life and the attraction to all that is dead, decaying, and purely mechanical."[8] It is fascinated by all the manifestations of dead, accumulated waste, including wealth ("dead labor," in Marx's terms), feces, dirt, and corpses.

Necrophilous fascination was seen recently (July 17, 2017) in Fox News television host Tucker Carlson's lurid and racist depiction of Roma immigrants in a Pennsylvania town. The new Roma inhabitants, according to Carlson, had "little regard for the law or public decency." "Citizens say they defecate in public . . . leave trash everywhere." Carlson proceeded to insistently quiz his Roma show guest about public defecation, growing increasingly voyeuristic in his line of questioning, although Carlson also offered unconvincingly, "I'm not anti-Roma, but I am pro-American citizen."

Consider, similarly, Jean Raspail's racist novel *Camp of the Saints*, which has been influential on the far-right and has been approvingly referenced by former chief strategist to Trump and international far-right wheeler-dealer, Steve Bannon. Raspail depicts immigrants of color—people from the places that Donald Trump has called "shithole countries"—as an inhuman, unstoppable ocean tide of waste and corpses. The antagonist of the novel is an Indian refugee whom Raspail names "the turd-eater," and though Raspail intends to mock him, Raspail's own unconscious belief about humanity is revealed in his depictions: that is, that humanity is, by and large, waste and shit. Throughout the book, we meet humanity as a shapeless mass of stinking, lusting, turd-eating, corpse-discarding sludge. The book opens with thousands of bodies being burned on the banks of France, as refugees die attempting to reach its shore, the bodies too numerous to make burial possible. Later, we encounter a scene of ships so teeming with subhuman hordes stampeding onto them that many are killed in the process, thrown off casually into the sea. The book ends with a global race war that is clearly Raspail's own fantasy for the future.

If necrophilous impulses are growing or gaining a platform, and large portions of the populace are retreating and "escaping from freedom," how is the left to respond? Can Fromm's theories help us to forge a successful strategy for combating fascism and hate and building a humanistic future beyond capitalist alienation? Yes, and in order to make effective use of Fromm's critical theory in our time, we must understand the divergent approaches to overcoming fascism that are at play at present. What is lacking in current approaches reveals the need for critical theory, and especially for Fromm's enduring contribution, in developing a left strategy for our time.

Of the cottage industry of new books seeking to explain the neofascist "alt-right" and related fascist movements to the US American public, hardly any make explicit use of any member of the Frankfurt School, or of psychoanalysis. From Yale University philosopher Jason Stanley's treatise *How Fascism Works*,[9] to the work of journalists like Vegas Tenold,[10] to the work of esteemed political scientists like Cas Mudde,[11] to the work of those studying "radicalization" of extremists like Michael Kimmel,[12] with a smattering of exceptions,[13] hardly a writer can be found whose important recent works on current manifestations of fascism engages deeply with the Frankfurt School.

It seems strange that so little engagement with Fromm, or even critical theory generally, is occurring among many of the leading experts seeking to explain the resurgence of fascism and the far-right. After all, we have the Frankfurt School to thank for much of the theoretical impetus of contemporary studies of authoritarianism. (The far-right, ironically enough, remembers this better than the left and continues to spin out anti-Semitic conspiracy theories about the Frankfurt School's role in propagating "Cultural Marxism.") The Frankfurt School's extensive research on fascism, on the authoritarian personality, on anti-Semitism, and on mechanisms of social control and revolt bridged the analytical divide between the individual and society. Fromm's work rested at the very heart of the Frankfurt School's attempt to integrate Marx's philosophy and political economy with a deeper understanding of human individuals and society, transcending the determinism and mechanism of orthodox Marxism. It is a project that remains essential today.

We need critical theory, and Fromm specifically, because combating fascism requires a return to the philosophical (existential) problem of the relationship between the individual and society. At the opening of *Escape from Freedom*, Fromm makes clear that fascism emerges both as a response to economic conditions (crises of capitalism) and as a manifestation of deeply human, even spiritual perhaps, struggles for meaning and belonging in the face of alienation and loneliness. Neglecting either of these dimensions hampers work against fascism both theoretically and practically. "If we want to fight Fascism we must understand it.... In addition to the problem of the economic and social conditions which have given rise to Fascism, there is a human problem which needs to be understood," he writes. Fromm establishes his intent to "analyze those dynamic factors in the character structure of modern man, which made him want to give up freedom."[14]

Fromm's work on social character integrated an understanding of the way that human beings are formed by their environments with a strong commitment to human agency. With relation to individual free will, Fromm was what he called an "alternativist."[15] The alternativist does not believe that one is simply free or simply determined, but rather that certain choices in individual human lives lead to greater or lesser degrees of ability to be a free subject, an agent in the world. How one acts at certain crucial junctures can determine one's future capacity for agency—and the same goes for whole societies faced with fundamental choices. The function of the "prophet"—among whom Fromm includes Karl Marx, Rosa Luxemburg, Gustav Landauer, and others—is not to predict the future but to present people with "alternatives," and to show people the likely impact of choosing in one direction or the other. Rosa Luxemburg was acting prophetically when she called on the workers to make their choice for "socialism or barbarism." Writer Naomi Klein has posed a similar choice today, calling on us to choose between capitalism and survival, between capitalism and the climate, in her book *This Changes Everything: Capitalism vs. The Climate*. The prophet does not know if people will choose socialism or barbarism, survival or destruction (ecological, militaristic, fascistic), life or death. But the prophet knows that a crucial juncture has been reached, and he or she turns people to confront reality, posing the uncomfortable question of which choice they will make.

Viewing individuals in isolation from their social context—or viewing societies independent of the agency of the individuals that compose them—produces strategic limitations in work against fascism. Fascism is not solely the product of individual psychological "radicalization" factors, nor simply the faceless expression of capitalism in crisis. However, approaches seem to break down into those two categories. There are those who seek to understand fascism chiefly as a crime problem or psychological problem, to be fixed through law enforcement or social work interventions, and there are those who see fascism chiefly as a genocidal social movement seeking power, "not to be debated but to be smashed" by a countermovement aimed at its defeat. The first, individualized view does little to engage with traditions of critical theory or psychoanalysis, relying on data and interventions relatively uninterested in broader societal structures. The second view, emphasizing fascism as a social movement, tends to be more ambitious in its pursuit of social change but tends to dismiss questions of love and hate, destructiveness, necrophilia, and so on, as so much milquetoast liberalism or centrism.

The first approach, focusing on fascism as a problem of individuals resulting from various "radicalization factors," involves specialists in disengagement and deradicalization, often collaborating with law enforcement, seeking to disengage individuals from hate groups, while eliding broader social structures. This approach insufficiently accounts for the degree to which fascism is a social movement seeking power, not simply a collection of alienated individuals seeking to heal the wounds of life traumas. In fact, unlike the racist skinheads of the 1980s who often serve as the model target for this approach, today's young fascists in the United States are often taking a calculated risk that could yield them worldly success: a cushy job at an anti-immigration think tank, a position as an aid to a Congressman from Iowa, a profitable YouTube channel. Viewing them as marginal or criminal is a mistake, as is assuming they are depressed rather than exhilarated with their increased life possibilities.

Furthermore, the individualized approach to fighting fascism often capitalizes on what I call the "compassion narrative," a common rhetorical trope which elevates the role of love in social transformation but relies on an over-individualized, insufficiently structural analysis. In particular, many stories have been circulating in print, online media, and public lectures, about how unexpected acts of compassion, especially from members of marginalized groups, played a role in reforming fascists and white supremacists and leading them to leave their ideology behind. Although these stories can inspire hope, they can also encourage misconceptions among the public. For example, the compassion narrative easily moves into victim-blaming, suggesting that it is the duty of marginalized, oppressed, or victimized groups or individuals to reach out to those who wish them harm, putting themselves at even greater risk. Instead of being a project of collective liberation for all who are marginalized or oppressed, the individualized "deradicalization" approach can even unintentionally put those who are already facing racism or other prejudice into the service of outreach and inclusion, burdening them further.

Nevertheless, the stories of those who have left hate behind have something to teach us. When they speak of the ways in which a misguided search for identity and belonging led them to the far-right, and the ways that compassion and love helped them find their way out, former fascists are providing insights that are not irrelevant to left movements and should not be easily ignored. Understanding the relationship between society and the individual, a task for which Erich Fromm's critical theory equips us, requires accounting for love, theoretically and practically.

Fromm knew that love was more than a naive slogan (like the protest chant, "Love trumps hate!"). Properly understood, love is revolutionary and certainly not naive. (Fromm's book *The Art of Loving* is a contribution to Marxist philosophy, by the way, not a mere a self-help guide. And Rev. Dr. Martin Luther King, Jr. even credited Fromm with helping him to develop the "love ethic" that was central to King's philosophy.)

Although fascism is a dangerous social movement seeking power, not a product simply of individuals stymied in their search for belonging, love remains relevant to the struggle against fascism. Dismissing interest in the nature and causes of love and hate, in the individual's alienation and quest for meaning, leaves something to be desired, both theoretically and practically. At the most basic, practical level, the reduction of individuals to faceless social forces, to be smashed without being understood, needlessly alienates potential allies, making it more difficult to find ongoing allies in faith communities, for example, for whom concepts such as love and hate, and human dignity, can be paramount.

More crucially, dismissing questions of love and hate may suggest that love, or empathy, does not have a role to play in our understanding of the far-right. There are some truths that can be grasped only through love. Fromm speaks of a deep human need to know the other, to uncover the "secret" of what it means to be human. In fact, it is this profound failure to know the other through love that drives sadistic and necrophilic escapes from freedom. "Complete rational knowledge is possible only of *things*," Fromm writes. "*Man is not a thing*; he cannot be dissected without being destroyed, he cannot be manipulated without being harmed."[16] The way to uncover the "secret" is not through scientific knowledge but through love. Those who are unable to love can easily turn to the pursuit of power:

> The ultimate degree of this attempt to know lies in the extreme form of sadism, in the desire to make a human being suffer, to torture him, to force him to betray his "secret" in his suffering, or eventually to destroy him. In the craving to penetrate man's secret lies an essential motivation for the depth and intensity of cruelty and destructiveness.[17]

In Fromm's view, we are all caught in a tangled web of attempting to know.

Careful empathetic study of the far-right can have uses in assisting counter-recruitment and building class solidarity. Not everyone involved in fascist-adjacent militia-type movements, for example, is a hardened ideologue, and some leftist groups like Redneck Revolt have made inroads in right-wing rural movements. A grandmother at the Bundy family's right-wing occupation of the Oregon Malheur Wildlife Refuge told writer James Pogue that she got involved in the Bundy ranchers' movement because right-wing militia members in her hometown were building a playground for kids and fighting wildfires. If activists on the left are not involved in projects of direct aid in a spirit of solidarity, and are not building up structures of dual power, some people may turn to the far-right for structures of aid and support.[18] The "prepper" who has a hidden stockpile of canned food, guns, and gold, because he or she senses that things may soon come crashing down, is not wholly wrong in the sneaking suspicion that crisis may be coming and that if it does, there is no prepared social safety net or community support.

To be clear, the left need not, and should not attempt, to become experts at deprogramming fascists. In fact, a biophilic love of humanity requires drawing good protective boundaries to protect oneself from fascist violence as well as defending the vulnerable. Solidarity and community safety must never be sacrificed in the pursuit of winning over enemies. However, the left does need to strive to understand what is driving people to join far-right movements and at times needs to interact with people at the fringes who are at risk of being recruited to these movements.

Our social analysis must be able to account for authoritarian impulses, feelings of humiliation and despair, and passions for control, destruction, and revenge, as well as feelings of love, empathy, compassion, and desires for transcendence, solidarity, and creativity. This goes beyond immediate needs of counter-recruitment or strategy. It goes to the heart of building within the present, the society we expect to see tomorrow, or to at least begin the project of theorizing (always open to expansion, questioning, and correction) our understanding of the humanistic, socialist future.

According to Fromm, the true revolutionary is biophilic, motivated by a love of life. It is easy, he suggests, to confuse "rebels" with revolutionaries. The "rebel" will defy authority or majority opinion, but is still deeply authoritarian.[19] The rebel defies authority out of resentment of the powerful because the rebel desires power for him or herself. At a time when the far-right present themselves as populists, "edgelords," defenders of "free speech," trolls, and "truth-tellers," it is important to remember the difference between rebels and revolutionaries. The rebel can easily appear as a revolutionary—the rebel may appear revolutionary as he or she is engaged in tearing down "PC culture," staring down the silencing forces of deplatforming. But the ultimate test of one's revolutionary commitment lies in one's love of human beings and of life, a commitment to which fascist and far-right rebellion is antithetical.

The Need for Radical Hope

Finally, one more crucial concept which we must take from Erich Fromm is his radical hope or "prophetic messianism." While confronting the challenges posed by capitalism, militarism, nationalism, fascism, racism, and other forms of bigotry, and ecological devastation, we cannot lose sight of our ultimate aim—socialism, the humanistic society, human flourishing—and radical hope for its attainment.

Fromm's humanistic prophetic messianism was driven by a "horizontal longing,"[20] oriented toward a future that would be the product of collective human activity. Fromm's radical, messianic hope avoided both determinism and voluntarism. Prophetic messianism was not passive waiting, resignation, and the whittling down of dreams to fit the strictures of capitalism. It also avoided accelerationist dreams of "bringing it all crashing down" through dramatic acts of disruption or symbolic heroism. Revolutionary change requires enough people having the psychic readiness to begin to carry it out: making democracy real in communities and workplaces, and making art, education, and spirituality expressions of human need and flourishing, not dead ideological burdens (idols). The prophet, as stated earlier, can bring people's options to their attention.

Radical, prophetic-messianic hope resonates with Antonio Gramsci's famous quip about "pessimism of the intellect and optimism of the will." While the phrase does not perfectly encapsulate Fromm's messianism, it captures prophetic messianism's commitment to both realism and hopeful action. Hope is not an abandonment of reality—it takes fully into account the risks of failure. However, going beyond Gramsci's quip, Fromm's prophetic-messianic hope not only is a commitment to action but unveils seeds of potential in the present that remain invisible to the cynic or the detached observer. Just as there are some truths of the other that can only be uncovered by love, there are some truths about the future that can only be uncovered by hope. Like Georg Lukács, we see that "the standpoint of totality"[21] requires both theoretical and practical commitment; from within the standpoint of revolutionary transformation, we achieve both understanding and community.

Attending to the sources of alienation and constructing a humanistic movement against fascism can be a function of what Fromm calls "the common struggle against idolatry": the formation of new communities, identities, and social movements around the shared project of embracing "living ideas" and unfolding traditions, not dead concepts and idols. This common struggle unites humanists of all stripes in a united front in defense of reason and compassion: "Those who participate [in the common struggle against idolatry] must be able to talk from their heart and to the heart. They must not fear to displease anybody, and must consider that reducing hate and arrogance within themselves must be one of their daily efforts."[22] This broad coalitional struggle does not mean that we must compromise our dreams for a humanistic socialism or give up the longer haul of revolutionary transformation, however. Even within the present, projects of "humanistic planning" can be undertaken, as we begin to construct and envision a postcapitalist future.

Fromm's propensity to dialogue, interdisciplinarity, and prophetic critique and engagement with various traditions (Marxism, psychoanalysis, and Judaism, among others) made him difficult to classify during his life and has made his legacy complex. Philosophers, psychoanalysts, social scientists, and socialist activists can all lay claim to parts of his legacy. Furthermore, he was also for a long time written out of crucial histories of the disciplinary studies in which he was engaged, especially in the canonical texts on the history of the Frankfurt School, as Kieran Durkin notes in his introduction to this book. Despite or perhaps because of Fromm's interdisciplinary complexity, he remains crucially relevant today, as we struggle again with the questions: "How are nationalism and fascism possible?" and "How can an alternative future be constructed?" "Anti-fascism," in the broadest possible sense of that term, needs Erich Fromm's critical theory more now than ever.

Notes

1. Blyth, "Global Trumpism."
2. Gartner, *Rocket Man*, 29. The debate occurred largely in response to the organizing of psychologist John Gartner, who heads up the organization Duty to Warn, composed of mental health professionals who believe they have a duty to break standard ethics protocol in order to make public warnings and diagnoses of Donald Trump.
3. Langman and Lundskow, *God, Guns, Gold, and Glory*, xxi.
4. Fromm, "The Revolutionary Character," 123.
5. Taub, "The Rise of American Authoritarianism."
6. Fromm, *Escape from Freedom*, 124.
7. Ibid., 125.
8. Fromm, *The Anatomy of Human Destructiveness*, 27.
9. Stanley, *How Fascism Works*.
10. Tenold, *Everything You Love Will Burn*.
11. Mudde, *The Far Right in America*.
12. Kimmel, *Healing from Hate*.
13. Some very limited use of the Frankfurt School is made in a couple of the best recent books on fascism: Shane Burley's *Fascism Today: What It Is and How to End It*; Ross's *Against the Fascist Creep*. I also know from a discussion with him that David Neiwert, whose research on the history of white supremacy in the Northwest is invaluable, has been influenced by the work of the Frankfurt School and takes Erich Fromm's important book *Escape from Freedom* seriously.
14. Fromm, *Escape from Freedom*, 20.
15. Fromm, *The Heart of Man*, 119; "Application of Humanistic Psychoanalysis," 243.
16. Fromm, "On the Limitations and Dangers of Psychology," 159; emphasis in original.
17. Ibid., 161; emphasis in original.
18. James Pogue, *Chosen Country*, 102.
19. Fromm, "The Revolutionary Character."
20. Fromm, *You Shall Be As Gods*, 133.
21. Lukacs, *History and Class Consciousness* passim—chiefly the essay "What is Orthodox Marxism?"
22. Fromm, *On Being Human*, 99.

References

Blyth, Mark. (2016, November 15). "Global Trumpism: Why Trump's Victory Was 30 Years in the Making and Why It Won't Stop Here." *Foreign Affairs*. Retrieved from https://www.foreignaffairs.com/articles/2016-11-15/global-trumpism

Burley, Shane. (2017). *Fascism Today: What It Is and How to End It*. Chico: AK Press.

Fromm, Erich. (1964). *The Heart of Man: Its Genius for Good and Evil*. New York: Harper & Row.

Fromm, Erich. (1965). "The Application of Humanist Psychoanalysis to Marx's Theory." *Socialist Humanism: An International Symposium*, Garden City, NY.

Fromm, Erich. (1966). *You Shall Be As Gods: A Radical Interpretation of the Old Testament and Its Tradition*. New York: Holt, Rinehart, and Winston.

Fromm, Erich. (1969). *Escape from Freedom*. New York: Avon Books.

Fromm, Erich. (1973). *The Anatomy of Human Destructiveness*. Greenwich: Fawcett Publications.
Fromm, Erich. (1994). *On Being Human*. New York: Continuum Publishing Company.
Fromm, Erich. (2004a). "On the Limitations and Dangers of Psychology." In Erich Fromm (ed.), *The Dogma of Christ*. 157–65. New York: Routledge Classics.
Fromm, Erich. (2004b). "The Revolutionary Character." In Erich Fromm (ed.), *The Dogma of Christ*, 122–39. New York: Routledge Classics.
Gartner, John, and Steven Buser, eds. (2018). *Rocket Man: Nuclear Madness and the Mind of Donald Trump*. Asheville: Chiron.
Kimmel, Michael. (2018). *Healing from Hate: How Young Men Get Into—And Out Of—Violent Extremism*. Oakland: University of California Press.
Langman, Lauren, and George Lundskow. (2016). *God, Guns, Gold, and Glory: American Character and Its Discontents*. Chicago: Haymarket.
Lukács, George. (1971). *History and Class Consciousness: Studies in Marxist Dialectics*, translated by R. Livingstone. Cambridge, MA: MIT Press.
Mudde, Cas. (2017). *The Far Right in America*. London: Routledge.
Pogue, James. (2018). *Chosen Country: A Rebellion in the West*. New York: Henry Holt and Company.
Raspail, Jean. (1994). *The Camp of the Saints*. Petoskey: Social Contract Press.
Ross, Alexander Reid. (2017). *Against the Fascist Creep*. Chico: AK Press.
Stanley, Jason. (2018). *How Fascism Works: The Politics of Us and Them*. New York: Random House.
Taub, A. (2016, March 1). "The Rise of American Authoritarianism." *Vox*. Retrieved from http://www.vox.com/2016/3/1/11127424/trump-authoritarianism
Tenold, Vegas. (2018). *Everything You Love Will Burn: Inside the Rebirth of White Nationalism in America*. New York: Nation Books.

CONTRIBUTORS

Joan Braune teaches Philosophy at Gonzaga University and holds a PhD in Philosophy from the University of Kentucky. She is the author of *Erich Fromm's Revolutionary Hope: Prophetic Messianism as a Critical Theory of the Future*, along with numerous articles on critical theory, humanistic Marxism, and resistance to fascism. She serves on the Council of Experts for the Gonzaga Institute for Hate Studies.

Lynn S. Chancer is Professor of Sociology at Hunter College and the Graduate Center of the City University of New York. She is the author of numerous books and articles including *Sadomasochism in Everyday Life: Dynamics of Power and Powerlessness* (1992); *High Profile Crimes: When Legal Cases Become Social Causes* (2005); and, most recently, *After the Rise and Stall of American Feminism: Taking Back a Revolution* (2019). With John Andrews, she coedited the volume *The Unhappy Marriage of Sociology and Psychoanalysis* (2014).

Kieran Durkin is Marie Skłodowska-Curie Global Fellow at University of York and Visiting Scholar at University of California Santa Barbara, where he is conducting the first dedicated study of the Humanist Marxist tradition. He is author of *The Radical Humanism of Erich Fromm* (2014) which was shortlisted for the British Sociological Association's Philip Abrams Memorial Award in 2015, and coeditor of *Raya Dunayevskaya's Intersectional Marxism: Race, Gender, and the Dialectics of Revolution* (forthcoming).

Roger Foster teaches philosophy at the Borough of Manhattan Community College of the City University of New York. He is the author of *Adorno: The Recovery of Experience* (2008) and *Adorno and Philosophical Modernism: The Inside of Things* (2016). He has also written numerous articles on the tradition of critical social theory.

Lauren Langman is a professor of sociology at Loyola University of Chicago. He received his PhD from the University of Chicago. He has long worked in the tradition of the Frankfurt School of Critical Theory, especially nationalism and reactionary movements, relationships between culture, identity, and politics/political movements. He is the past president of Alienation Research and Theory, Research Committee 36, of the International Sociological Association as well as past president of the Marxist section of the American Sociological Association, where he recently received the Lifetime Achievement Award. Recent publications deal with globalization, alienation, global justice movements, the Tea Party, the body, nationalism, and national character. His most recent publications include *Trauma Promise and Millennium: The Evolution of Alienation*, with Devorah Kalekin, *Alienation and Carnivalization* with Jerome Braun, and a special issue of *Current Sociology* on Arab Spring, the Indignados and Occupy. His latest books are *God, Guns, Gold and Glory: American Character and Its Discontents* (with George Lundskow) and *Inequality in the 21st C: Marx, Piketty and beyond* (with David Alan Smith). He is on several editorial boards, including *Critical Sociology* and *Current Perspectives in Social Theory*.

Michael Löwy is a French-Brazilian social scientist and Emeritus Research Director at the Centre National de la Recherche Scientifique (CNRS), Paris. He is the author of *Fire Alarm: Reading Walter Benjamin's "On the Concept of History"* (2005).

George Lundskow received his PhD in Sociology from the University of Kansas in 1999. Since then, George has published numerous articles, chapters, and a few books on the social-psychology of right-wing populism, religion, and American social character. In general, George studies the intersection of political-economic and cultural forces that legitimate popular acceptance of economic exploitation, cultural-identity oppression, militarism, and destruction, and at the same time, the competing forces that promise a more fulfilling and broadly prosperous future.

Michael Maccoby is a globally recognized expert on leadership. His most recent books are *The Leaders We Need: And What Makes Us Follow*, *Strategic Intelligence*, and *Transforming Health Care Leadership*. He is coediting a book on The Trump Phenomenon in Context that describes Donald Trump's personality, how it determines his behavior and policy, and what is needed to repair the damage he has caused. Jointly (with Mauricio Cortina) he teaches a seminar on Erich Fromm's approach to psychoanalysis at the Washington School of Psychiatry where he was given a Lifetime Achievement Award. And he is the strategic consultant of Nuestros Pequenos Hermanos (our Little Brothers and Sisters) with homes for children, schools, clinics, hospitals, and community centers in nine countries in Latin America and Haiti.

Neil McLaughlin teaches sociological theory at the McMaster University, and writes about the sociology of ideas/knowledge and Erich Fromm's social psychology. He has published about Noam Chomsky, David Riesman, Edward Said, George Orwell, as well as Canadian sociology, the sociology of public sociology and the public intellectual in Canada. He is presently studying the spread of conspiracy theories against George Soros and the political consequences of private higher education in the United States along with a number of collaborative projects in the sociology of knowledge. He is also completing a book about Erich Fromm's public sociology.

David Norman Smith received an AB in Economics at the University of California-Berkeley and a PhD in Sociology at the University of Wisconsin-Madison. Since 1990 he has taught sociology at the University of Kansas in Lawrence, where, in 2012–16, he also served as Department Chair. Smith's writings include *Marx's Capital Illustrated* (2014, with art by Phil Evans), which has appeared in ten languages; *George Orwell Illustrated* (2018, with art by Mike Mosher); and articles in journals including *Sociological Theory, The American Psychologist, Rethinking Marxism, Antisemitism Studies,* and *Research in Political Economy.* Smith's recent articles include "Authoritarianism Reimagined: The Riddle of Trump's Base" (*Sociological Quarterly*, 2019); "The Anger Games: Who Voted for Donald Trump in the 2016 Election, and Why?" (*Critical Sociology*, 2018, with Eric Hanley); "Sharing, Not Selling: Marx Against Value" (*Continental Thought & Theory*, 2017); "Theory and Class Consciousness" (*The Handbook of Critical Theory*, 2017); and "Capitalism's Future" in the volume of the same name (2016). For Yale University Press, he is editing *Marx's World: Global Society and Capital Accumulation in Marx's Late Manuscripts* (forthcoming). The National Association of Social Workers (Kansas chapter) named Smith the Public Citizen of the Year in 2004 in recognition of his efforts on behalf of the campaign that won the passage of a living wage ordinance in Lawrence the previous year.

Michael J. Thompson is Professor of Political Theory in the Department of Political Science at William Paterson University. His recent books include *The Domestication of Critical Theory, The Specter of Babel: A Reconstruction of Political Judgment,* and the forthcoming *Twilight of the Self: Cybernetic Society and the Eclipse of Autonomy.*

Charles Thorpe studied philosophy, politics, and economics at Oxford University and sociology and science studies at the University of California, San Diego (UCSD). He has lectured in sociology at Cardiff University and Science and Technology Studies at University College London. He is today Professor of Sociology and a member of the Science Studies Program at UCSD. He is the author of *Oppenheimer: The Tragic Intellect* and *Necroculture* and coeditor of the *Routledge Handbook of the Political Economy of Science.*

INDEX

Abbe, Ernst   142–4, 155 n.48, 156 n.67
Adler, Max   44, 149
Adorno, Theodor   5, 16 n.27, 76, 92 n.20, 111, 138, 152, 158 nn.104, 105
Althusser, Louis   122
Antonio, Robert   167, 186 nn.3, 5
Apel, Karl-Otto   11, 23
Arendt, Hannah   43, 44, 51 n.2
Aries, Philippe   173, 211 n.22
Aristotle   27, 40 n.9, 84

Baal Shem Tov, *see* Eliezer, Rabbi Isaac Ben
Bach, Fritz   150
Bachofen, Johann Jakob   102–4
Bannon, Steve   219
Barrera, Mario   177, 180, 188 nn.81, 82, 96
Bauer, Otto   44
Bauman, Zygmunt   204, 211 n.33
Becker, Ernest   171, 181, 186 nn.26, 27, 189 n.105
Benjamin, Jessica   16 n.22, 40 n.8, 41 n.15, 100, 105, 106 n.24
Benjamin, Walter   5, 12, 43, 45
Berger, Peter   60, 69 n.83, 171, 186 n.29
Bernfeld, Siegfried   2, 133
Bernstein, Eduard   14, 44, 134
Biden, Joe   205
Bismarck, Otto von   43, 57, 144
Bleichröder, Gerson, Barron von   43
Bloch, Ernst   12, 44, 45, 48
Blyth, Mark   216, 225 n.1
Boltanski, Luc   13, 87, 91 n.3, 92 n.54
Bonaparte, Napoléon   144
Bonss, Wolfgang   16 n.14, 154 n.24, 157 n.71
Borkenau, Franz   50, 133, 142, 152, 153 n.5, 156 n.62, 159 nn.108, 109
Bouglé, Céléstin   146, 157 n.81
Bourdieu, Pierre   103, 106 n.20, 108–25

Bowring, Finn   168, 186 n.13
Brandt, Heinz   135, 136, 138
Braune, Joan   15 n.1, 17 n.32, 17 n.43, 155 n.35
Brown, David L.   180, 188 nn.98, 100
Brown, Wendy   89, 93 n.59
Buber, Martin   45, 46, 48
Buddha   62
Bukharin, Nikolai   135, 154 n.19, 158 n.96
Buret, Eugène   147, 158 nn.87, 90
Butler, Judith   96, 100, 104, 212 n.42

Calvin, John   7, 79
Carlson, Tucker   218–19
Castel, Robert   88, 93 n.56
Chancer, Lynn   13, 16 n.22, 17 n.36, 106 nn.1, 6
Chiapello, Eve   13, 87, 91 n.3, 92 n.54
Chodorow, Nancy   16 n.22, 105, 106 n.25, 186 n.19
Clinton, Bill   179
Clinton, Hillary   180
Comte, Auguste   116
Confucius   53
Connell, Raewyn   101, 106 n.10

David, Anan Ben   47
Davies, William   87, 89, 92 nn.49, 51, 93 n.61
De Beauvoir, Simone   98, 100
Derrida, Jacques   96
Deutsch, Helene   99, 106 n.8
Dewey, John   150
Dostoevski, Fyodor   45
Durkheim, Émile   58, 68 n.32, 110, 111, 146
Durkin, Kieran   15 n.1, 16 n.4, 19, 23, 25, 26, 17 nn.30, 37, 40, 80, 92 n.21, 97, 106 n.4, 116, 125 n.8, 125 n.16, 154 n.24, 186 n.18, 187 n.34, 224

Index

Eckhart, Master (Meister) 62
Einstein, Albert 43, 156 n.63
Eisenstein, Zillah 103, 106 n.18
Elias, Norbert 173
Eliezer, Rabbi Isaac Ben (Baal Shem Tov) 47
Engels, Friedrich 3, 102, 115, 153 n.12
Estep, Kevin 180, 186 n.11, 188 n.97
Ewen, Stewart 195

Fanon, Frantz 123
Federn, Paul 133
Firestone, Shulamith 98, 101, 106 n.12
Fleming, Peter 87, 92, 94
Ford, Henry 142–3, 156 n.67
Forst, Rainer 11, 23
Foster, Roger 12, 13, 15, 17 nn.40, 44
Foucault, Michel 96, 106 n.9, 173
Frankl, Viktor 172
Fraser, Nancy 75, 91 n.1, 92 n.46
Freire, Paulo 123
Freud, Sigmund 4–6, 11, 14, 28, 43, 48, 50, 98, 104, 106 n.7, 108, 111, 115, 131, 133, 149, 151, 152, 153 nn.6, 7, 181, 194, 195, 197, 201, 217
Frölich, Paul 44
Funk, Rainer 5, 15 n.1, 16 n.24, 92 n.21, 105, 106 n.21, 119, 125 nn.6, 25, 147, 153, 157 n.85, 159, 211 n.1

Geiger, Abraham 47
Gergen, Kenneth 202, 203, 211 n.31
Giddens, Anthony 14, 15, 166, 168, 169, 172–9, 181, 183, 185, 186 n.14, 187 nn.38, 39, 43, 46, 47, 49, 51, 52, 53, 57, 60, 62, 64, 65, 67, 68, 69, 72, 73, 74, 76, 188 nn.80, 83, 84, 85, 86, 87, 88, 189 nn.112, 113, 122
Goethe, Johann Wolfgang von 44
Gramsci, Antonio 15, 196, 224
Groddeck, Georg 2
Gross, Neil 110, 125 n.7
Grünberg, Carl 135, 142, 144, 157 n.81

Habermas, Jürgen 11, 23, 37, 38, 76, 77
Hedges, Chris 57, 68 n.29, 188 n.95
Hegel, G. W. F. 23–4, 28, 29, 31, 36, 41 n.12, 78, 84, 100

Heidegger, Martin 135, 173, 187 n.42
Heine, Heinrich 43, 44
Hirsch, Raphael Samson 47
Hitler, Adolf 124, 131, 135, 144, 145, 146, 150
  Hitlerian 134
Hochschild, Arlie Russell 181, 186 n.4, 189 n.103, 189 n.118
Honneth, Axel 11, 23, 38, 76, 77, 90
Horkheimer, Max 1, 2, 3, 4, 5, 16 n.12, 16 n.20, 37, 48, 76, 78, 79, 80, 83, 91 n.15, 92 nn.19, 20, 39, 110, 111, 131, 138, 144, 146, 147, 148, 149, 152, 157 n.83, 159 n.107, 217
Horney, Karen 105, 106 n.22, 149, 150, 157 n.83
Huxley, Aldous 26

Inglehart, Ronald 15, 84, 92 n.43, 184, 185, 186 nn.4, 11, 189 nn.100, 115, 116, 120

Jesus (Christ) 49, 53, 54, 62, 63, 134, 148
Jong-Un, Kim 182
Jordan, Bill 179, 188 n.89

Kafka, Franz 43, 44
Kant, Immanuel, Kantian idealism 78
  Kantianism 23, 28, 29, 34
Kautsky, Karl 49, 134, 135, 154 n.21
Kavanaugh, Brett 58
Kayser, Rudolf 45
Kierkegaard, Soren 170
Kilmister, Lemmy 56
Kimmel, Michael 101, 219, 225 n.12
King Jr., Rev. Dr. Martin Luther 66, 222
Klein, Melanie 105, 106 n.23
Klein, Naomi 220
Kohn, Hans 45
Korsch, Karl 14, 137, 140, 141, 152, 154 n.26, 155 nn.37, 50

Lacan, Jacques 124
Laing, R. D. 174
Landauer, Gustav 12, 44, 45, 220
Landauer, Karl 2
Langman, Lauren 15, 15 n.1, 17 n.44, 52, 60, 68 n.1, 69 nn.39, 52
Laqueur, Walter 44, 51 n.4

Lazare, Bernard 43
Lenin, V. I. 143, 145, 152, 156 n.66
Levi, Paul 44
Levine, Robert 198, 211 n.20
Liebknecht, Karl 139, 149, 150
Lifton, Robert Jay 168, 203, 211 n.32
Lowenthal, Leo 16 n.20, 45, 137, 154 n.32, 156 n.62
Lowy, Michael 7, 12, 17 n.32, 137
Lozovsky, Solomon 142
Lukács, Georg 2, 12, 14, 43–5, 134–5, 140, 152, 154 nn.19, 21, 156 nn.63, 66, 70, 159, 224, 225 n.21
Lundskow, George 12, 15, 15 n.1, 17 nn.44, 46, 52, 68 n.1, 69 nn.39, 51, 52, 168, 186 nn.4, 8, 11, 12, 63, 188 n.100, 194, 225 n.3, 228
Luther, Martin 7, 79, 144
Luxemburg, Rosa 44, 134, 139, 140, 141, 149, 150, 153 n.12, 197, 211 n.15, 220

Maccoby, Michael 13–15, 17 n.47, 92 n.47, 108, 109, 111–14, 117, 119, 121, 123–4, 125 nn.10, 12, 13, 19, 20, 23, 198, 211 n.18
McLaren, Brian 62, 69 n.43
McLaughlin, Neil 13, 14, 15 n.1, 16 nn.3, 19, 17 n.47, 91 n.6, 125 nn.5, 22, 158 n.104, 186 n.19, 187 n.34
McVeigh, Rory 180, 186 n.11, 188 nn.97, 98, 100
Mann, Michael 124, 126 n.45
Mann, Thomas 44, 96
Marcuse, Herbert 16 n.27, 76, 119, 172, 195, 200, 211 nn.7, 24
Marx, Karl 3, 11, 17 n.38, 23, 24, 25, 26, 27, 28, 29, 31, 32, 33, 36, 40 nn.5, 10, 41 nn.16, 17, 18, 43, 48, 50, 51 n.11, 64, 66, 83, 84, 108, 110, 111, 115, 116, 122, 131, 132, 133, 134, 135, 138, 142, 144, 146, 147, 148, 149, 153, 153 nn.8, 12, 158 nn.87, 90, 194, 196, 209, 217, 218, 220
Maslow, Abraham 81, 92 n.28
Maslow, Arkadij 137, 154 n.26
May, Rollo 170, 186 n.20, 187 n.42
Mead, Margaret 117–18
Mehring, Franz 150

Mendelssohn, Moses 47
Meng, Heinrich 2
Meyer, Edward 49
Millett, Kate 101, 106 n.11
Mills, C. Wright 57
Mirowski, Philip 87, 92 n.53
Monat, Shannon 180
Mudde, Cas 219, 225 n.11
Mumford, Lewis 172
Munzenberg, Willi 142, 150, 156 n.62
Murtola, Anne-Marie 87, 92 n.50

Nanak 53
Nathan, Otto 144, 156–7 nn.70
Newton, Huey 12, 64–8, 69 nn.57, 58, 59, 61, 65, 66

Obama, Barack 167, 180, 188 n.94
Ocasio-Cortez, Alexandria 209
O'Rourke, Beto 205

Paine, Thomas 62–3, 69 n.47
Pascoe, C. J. 101, 106 n.10
Pelosi, Nancy 209, 212 n.64
Petigny, Alan 81, 92 nn.30, 32
Pfattheicher, Stefan 64, 69 n.56
Piketty, Thomas 83, 92 n.38, 228
Plato 64
Pogue, James 222, 225 n.18
Polanyi, Karl 75
Prothero, Stephen 61, 69 n.41

Rabinkow, Rabbi Salman Baruch 46
Rahman, K. Sabeel 91, 93 n.65
Ramadan, Tariq 62, 69 n.44
Raspail, Jean 219
Rathenau, Walther 43, 139–41, 143, 155 n.46
Reich, Wilhelm 2, 48, 158 n.103
Reichmann, Frieda 2, 48
Reik, Theodor 50, 133, 153 n.7
Rieff, Philip 82, 92 n.31
Riesman, David 118, 172, 187 n.34, 228
Rivera, Diego 150
Robinson, William I. 177, 180, 188 nn.81, 82, 96
Rosenzweig, Franz 46
Rothschild, Mayer 43
Rousseau, Jean-Jacques 28–9, 40 n.12

Rühle, Otto 14, 149–53, 158 nn.98, 99, 100, 102, 103
Rühle-Gerstel, Alice 149–50
Ryazanov, David 144, 156 n.70

Saint-Simon, Henri de 116
Sanders, Bernie 15, 205, 209
Sartre, Jean-Paul 113
Schindler, Simon 64, 69 n.56
Scholem, Gershom 45, 48, 50, 51 n.12, 136–8, 154 nn.24, 25
Schwartz, Lola 117–18
Schwartz, Theodore 117–18
Seale, Bobby 64, 66
Serge, Victor 132, 153 n.2
Simmel, Georg 110, 111
Singer, Paul 44
Smith, David 14, 16 n.14, 68 n.8, 153 n.3, 158 n.94, 188 n.100, 212 n.46
Sombart, Werner 46–7, 141
Somers, Margaret 88, 93 n.57
Sperber, Manès 12, 45
Spock, Benjamin 201
Stalin, Josef 14, 50, 113, 122, 124, 131–2, 135–7, 140, 148, 150, 151, 153 n.2, 157 nn.74, 86
Stanley, Jason 186 n.5, 219, 225 n.9
Stein, Howard F. 179–80, 186 n.7, 188 nn.91, 93
Steinmetz, George 121, 123, 125 n.32, 126 nn.35, 36, 42
Swartz, David 108, 111, 120, 122, 125 nn.2, 9, 17, 27, 29, 126 n.38

Tenold, Vegas 219
Thompson, Michael 11–12, 17 nn.40, 47, 84, 91 n.9, 92 n.42
Thorpe, Charles 14, 15, 15 n.1, 17 n.44, 55, 68 n.26, 186 nn.4, 6, 187 nn.50, 55, 188 n.100, 189 n.123

Traverso, Enzo 43, 44, 51 n.3
Tristan, Flora 147, 158 n.91
Troeltsch, Ernst 49
Trotsky, Leon 14, 51 n.13, 132, 137, 138, 150–2, 154 n.27, 157 n.86
Trump, Donald 12, 52, 56, 58, 108, 125, 166, 179–84, 188 n.100, 197, 205–7, 209, 210, 216, 217, 219, 225 n.2

Ulbricht, Walter 136

Voltaire 113

Warhol, Andy 56
Warren, Donald 86, 92 n.48
Wasson, Fr. William 117
Weber, Alfred 46, 110
Weber, Max 12, 44, 46, 47, 48, 49, 110, 111, 131, 135, 153 n.1, 172, 174
Weiss, Fritz 150, 156 nn.63, 64
Weiss, Hilde 4, 14, 16 n.14, 137–48, 152, 154 n.29, 155 nn.37, 38, 40, 41, 46–50, 52, 54, 56, 156 nn.60, 63, 65–70, 157 nn.71, 73, 75, 79–86, 158 nn.88–93
Wellmer, Abrecht 77, 91 n.8
Welzel 84, 92 n.43
Wittfogel, Karl 14, 135, 136, 137, 140, 141, 142, 152, 154 nn.19, 20, 21, 23, 50, 156 nn.60, 61, 63, 64, 157 n.83, 158 n.106, 159 n.107
Wittfogel, Rose 135

X, Malcolm 67

Zedong, Mao 66, 124
Zizek, Slavoj 181, 189 n.108
Zola, Émile 113
Zurcher, Louis 202, 211 n.30
Zweig, Stefan 43

www.ingramcontent.com/pod-product-compliance
Lightning Source LLC
Chambersburg PA
CBHW052035300426
44117CB00012B/1838